THE G8–G20 RELATIONSHIP IN GLOBAL GOVERNANCE

GLOBAL GOVERNANCE

Series editor: John J. Kirton, University of Toronto, Canada

Global governance is growing rapidly to meet the compounding challenges brought by a globalized twenty-first-century world. Many issues once dealt with largely at the local, national or regional level are now going global, in the economic, social and political-security domains. In response, new and renewed intergovernmental institutions are arising and adapting, multilevel governance is expanding, and sub-national actors play a greater role, and create complex combinations and private-partnerships to this end.

This series focuses on the new dynamics of global governance in the twenty-first century by:

- Addressing the changes in the structure, operation and impact of individual inter-governmental institutions, above all their innovative responses to the growing global challenges they confront.
- Exploring how they affect, are affected by and relate to non-state actors of global relevance and reach.
- Examining the processes of co-operation, competition and convergence among international institutions and the many global governance gaps where global challenges such as terrorism, transnational crime and energy do not confront powerful international institutions devoted to their control.
- Dealing with how global institutions govern the links among key issues such as climate change and health.

In all cases, it focuses on the central questions of how global governance institutions and processes generate the effective, legitimate, accountable results required to govern today's interconnected, complex, uncertain, crisis-ridden world.

Forthcoming titles in the series:

Local Politics, Global Impacts
Steps to a Multi-disciplinary Analysis of Scales
Edited by Olivier Charnoz, Virginie Diaz Pedregal and Alan L. Kolata

Shaping a New Global Development Consensus
The G20 Contribution and the UN Post-2015 Framework
Edited by Dries Lesage, Peter Debaere and Jan Wouters

Hegemony, Passive Revolution and Globalisation
The G7/8 System
Leonardo Ramos

The G8–G20 Relationship in Global Governance

Edited by

MARINA LARIONOVA
National Research University Higher School of Economics, Moscow, Russia

JOHN J. KIRTON
University of Toronto, Canada

ASHGATE

© Marina Larionova and John J. Kirton 2015

All rights reserved. No part of this publication may be reproduced, stored in a retrieval system or transmitted in any form or by any means, electronic, mechanical, photocopying, recording or otherwise without the prior permission of the publisher.

Marina Larionova and John J. Kirton have asserted their right under the Copyright, Designs and Patents Act, 1988, to be identified as the editors of this work.

Published by
Ashgate Publishing Limited
Wey Court East
Union Road
Farnham
Surrey, GU9 7PT
England

Ashgate Publishing Company
110 Cherry Street
Suite 3-1
Burlington, VT 05401-3818
USA

www.ashgate.com

British Library Cataloguing in Publication Data
A catalogue record for this book is available from the British Library.

Library of Congress Cataloging-in-Publication Data
The G8-G20 relationship in global governance / [edited by] Marina Larionova and John J Kirton.
    pages cm. -- (Global governance)
  Includes bibliographical references and index.
  ISBN 978-1-4094-3918-9 (hardback) -- ISBN 978-1-4094-3919-6 (ebook) -- ISBN 978-1-4724-0203-5 (epub) 1. Group of Eight (Organization) 2. Group of Twenty. 3. International economic relations. 4. International organization. 5. Economic policy--International cooperation. 6. Economic assistance. I. Larionova, Marina, editor. II. Kirton, John J., editor.
  HF1359.G4 2015
  337--dc23
                                                                                              2015004259

ISBN 9781409439189 (hbk)
ISBN 9781409439196 (ebk – PDF)
ISBN 9781472402035 (ebk – ePUB)

Printed in the United Kingdom by Henry Ling Limited,
at the Dorset Press, Dorchester, DT1 1HD

Contents

List of Figures	*vii*
List of Tables and Appendices	*ix*
Notes on Contributors	*xi*
Preface	*xiii*
Acknowledgements	*xv*
List of Abbreviations and Acronyms	*xvii*

PART I INTRODUCTION

1   Introduction   3
John J. Kirton and Marina V. Larionova

PART II ARCHITECTURE

2   Changing Global Governance for a Transformed World   15
John J. Kirton

3   The G7/8 and G20: Parallel Paths to Pragmatic Partnership   35
Dries Lesage

4   A World without G20 Summits   45
Martin Gilman

5   Global Risk Governance and G20, G8, and BRICS Capabilities   55
*Marina V. Larionova, Mark Rakhmangulov, Andrei Sakharov,
Andrey Shelepov, and Vitaly Nagornov*

PART III ACHIEVEMENTS

6   Assessing G7/8 and G20 Effectiveness in Global Governance   77
Marina V. Larionova, Mark Rakhmangulov, and Andrey Shelepov

7   Working Together for G8–G20 Partnership:
The Muskoka-Toronto Twin Summits of 2010   109
John J. Kirton

| 8 | G20: From Crisis Management to Policies for Growth
Zia Qureshi | 123 |
| 9 | B20–G20 Engagement: Achievements and Challenges
Marina V. Larionova, Mark Rakhmangulov, Andrei Sakharov,
and Andrey Shelepov | 143 |

PART IV ACCOUNTABILITY

10	The Muskoka Accountability Report: Assessing the Written Record *Ella Kokotsis*	183
11	G7/8 and G20 Accountability and Civil Society *Peter I. Hajnal*	201
12	Mapping G7/8 and G20 Accountability *Marina V. Larionova and Andrei Sakharov*	233
13	Advancing G8 and G20 Effectiveness through Improved Accountability Assessment *John J. Kirton*	241

PART V CONCLUSION

| 14 | Conclusion
John J. Kirton | 255 |

| *Bibliography* | *265* |
| *Index* | *281* |

List of Figures

5.1	Global risks map	58
5.2	G20 global risks map	60
5.3	G7/8 global risks map	62
5.4	BRICS global risks map	64
5.5	Map of G20, G7/8, and BRICS global risks and priorities	66
6.1	G8 and G20 global governance functions, 1998–2013	79
6.2	G8 and G20 deliberation, 1998–2013	80
6.3	G8 and G20 direction setting, 1998–2013	81
6.4	G8 and G20 decision making, 1998–2013	82
6.5	G8 and G20 delivery, 1998–2013	83
6.6	G8 and G20 development of global governance, 1998–2013	85
6.7	G8 and G20 mandates, 2008–13	86
6.8	G8 and G20 commitments, 1998–2013	87
6.9	G8 and G20 compliance, 1998–2012	87
6.10	G20 compliance, 2008–12	88
6.11	G20 priorities, 2008–13	89
6.12	G8 priorities, 2008–13	90
6.13	G8 and G20 priorities, 2008–13	91
6.14	G8 and G20 references to the economy, 1998–2013	92
6.15	G8 and G20 references to finance, 1998–2013	93
6.16	G8 and G20 references to trade, 1998–2013	94
6.17	G8 and G20 references to energy, 1998–2013	95
6.18	G8 and G20 references to the environment and climate change, 1998–2013	97
6.19	G8 and G20 references to development, 1998–2013	99
6.20	G8 and G20 references to political issues, 1998–2013	100
6.21	G8 and G20 references to security, 1998–2013	101
6.22	G8 and G20 references to international organizations, 1998–2013	103
6.23	Top 10 international organizations in G8 documents, 2008–13	104
6.24	Top 10 international organizations in G20 documents, 2008–13	105
8.1	Government debt relative to gross domestic product	125
8.2	Middle-income traps	127
8.3	Ease of doing business: Distance to frontier, 2005–12	128
8.4	Ease of doing business: Distance to frontier in component areas, 2012	129
8.5	Major constraints to business, as reported by firms	130
8.6	Infrastructure investment, global growth and balancing	131

8.7	Three-layered approach to job creation	133
8.8	Labour policies off the efficiency plateau in India	134
8.9	Rising protectionism	135
8.10	G20 trade measures, 2008–12	136
8.11	Increasing use of less transparent trade restrictions	137
8.12	Environmentally harmful subsidies	138
9.1	Recommendations on financial regulation	149
9.2	Recommendations on macroeconomic issues	152
9.3	Recommendations on food security	154
9.4	Recommendations on trade	155
9.5	Recommendations on investment	157
9.6	Recommendations on infrastructure	161
9.7	Recommendations on employment, human capital and social issues	162
9.8	Recommendations on green growth	165
9.9	Recommendations on ICT, technology, and innovation	167
9.10	Recommendations on energy	168
9.11	Recommendations on corruption	170
9.12	Recommendations on financing for development	172
9.13	Recommendations on global governance	174
12.1	Mapping G8 and G20 accountability reports	234

List of Tables and Appendices

Tables

9.1	B20 recommendations (by issue area and summit)	146
9.2	Recommendation scores (by summit)	147
9.3	Recommendation scores (by issue area)	147

Appendices

2.A	G20 members in plurilateral summit institutions	28
2.B	G8 summit performance, 1975–2013	29
2.C	G20 summit performance, 2008–13	32
2.D	BRICS performance, 2009–13	33
5.A	Assessments of global risk importance in G20, G8, and BRICS documents	69
5.B	Global risks: Descriptions and expert assessments, 2012	71
9.A	B20 task forces, 2010–13	178
9.B	2013 task force priorities by summit	179
10.A	G7/8 communiqué conclusions on development, 1975–2012	195
10.B	G7/8 development commitments, 1975–2013	196
10.C	G8 research group compliance, 2010–2012	197

Notes on Contributors

Martin Gilman is the director of the Centre for Advanced Studies at the National Research University Higher School of Economics in Moscow and a former assistant director of the International Monetary Fund's policy department responsible for official debt and financing issues.

Peter I. Hajnal is a research associate at Trinity College and the Munk School of Global Affairs at the University of Toronto.

John J. Kirton is the director of the G8 Research Group, co-director of the G20 Research Group and BRICS Research Group, a fellow of the Munk School of Global Affairs and Trinity College, and a professor of political science at the University of Toronto.

Ella Kokotsis is the director of accountability for the G8 and G20 Research Groups at the Munk School of Global Affairs and Trinity College at the University of Toronto.

Marina V. Larionova is the head of the International Organisations Research Institute and a professor in the Department of International Economic Organizations and European Integration in the Faculty of World Economy and International Affairs at the National Research University Higher School of Economics in Moscow, and the head of International Programmes at the National Training Foundation of the Russian Federation.

Dries Lesage is a professor of globalization and global governance at the Ghent Institute for International Studies at Ghent University.

Zia Qureshi is a senior advisor in the Office of Senior Vice President and Chief Economist of the World Bank.

Mark Rakhmangulov is the deputy director of the Global Governance Research Centre at the International Organisations Research Institute at the National Research University Higher School of Economics in Moscow.

Andrei Sakharov is a researcher at the Global Governance Research Centre at the International Organisations Research Institute at the National Research University Higher School of Economics in Moscow.

Andrey Shelepov is a researcher at the Global Governance Research Centre at the International Organisations Research Institute at the National Research University Higher School of Economics in Moscow.

Vitaly Nagornov is the director of the Research Centre for International Development Assistance is at the International Organisations Research Institute at the National Research University Higher School of Economics in Moscow.

Preface

This volume explores the performance of the Group of Seven (G7), Group of Eight (G8), and Group of 20 (G20) summits, their comparative strengths and limitations, the division of labour, and the relationship between them as it is emerging over the period of their coexistence, and how the future G7/8–G20 partnership can be improved to the benefit of both bodies, the well-being of their citizens, and the sustainable and balanced growth of the world economy as a whole.

It presents the results of a collaborative research program of the International Organisations Research Institute of the National Research University Higher School of Economics (HSE) and the G8 and G20 Research Groups at the University of Toronto. It thus combines the talents of two research teams that have worked together for many years on the analytic and empirical components essential to accomplish the task in this book. The first team, led by Marina V. Larionova at HSE in Moscow, includes her scholarly colleagues, researchers, and practitioners in Russia and beyond, in the person of Martin Gilman, director of HSE's Centre for Advanced Studies, and Zia Qureshi of the World Bank. The second team, led by John J. Kirton at the University of Toronto, includes his colleagues at Toronto and Dries Lesage from University of Ghent in Europe. This combination has facilitated the task of producing a cumulative, coherent work.

The initial drafts of some chapters on accountability by Kirton and Larionova were presented at a conference on global governance at Princeton University. The full set of HSE workshop papers, and initial drafts of many of the chapters in this volume, were published as a special edition of the *International Organisations Research Journal*, on the theme of 'G-x Summitry', in December 2010. These initial analyses were subsequently extensively developed and expanded to take full account of the subsequent summits of the G8 and G20 in 2011, 2012, 2013, the work of other international institutions, and new trends in summitry. New chapters were added to produce an integrated set.

Acknowledgements

In this project and the preparation of the volume, we are grateful to our sponsors and to many individuals at HSE, the G8 and G20 Research Groups, and Ashgate Publishing. At HSE we are grateful to the Russian Foundation for Humanities for financial support of the research project on supply-demand models in global governance, the results of which are presented in several chapters. We thank the participants and experts of the Business 20 (B20) who contributed to the consultations on assessing the effectiveness of G20–B20 engagement. And we acknowledge with great thanks the tireless and efficient work of Elizaveta Safonkina.

At the University of Toronto we express our gratitude, as always, to Madeline Koch, as well as to senior researchers Julia Kulik and Caroline Bracht. We are most grateful for the research produced by Aurora Hudson, Heather Keachie, Olga Milkina, Rebeca Ramirez, Jenilee Guebert, Zaria Shaw, and Sarah Cale.

At Ashgate we owe a great deal to the faith and the patience of Kirstin Howgate, Brenda Sharp, and their colleagues.

Above all, our greatest debt is to our students, for their continuing criticisms, insights and inspiration for our work and their dedicated, high-quality contribution to creating the data sets that sustain the empirical claims that we make.

Marina V. Larionova
John J. Kirton
June 2015

List of Abbreviations and Acronyms

APEC	Asia-Pacific Economic Cooperation
AUC	African Union Commission
AWG	Accountability Working Group
B20	Business 20
BASIC	Brazil, Australia, South Africa, Indonesia, and Canada
BEPS	base erosion and profit shifting
BRIC	Brazil, Russia, India, and China
BRICS	Brazil, Russia, India, China, and South Africa
C20	Civil 20
CCCE	Canadian Council of Chief Executives
CIVETS	Colombia, Indonesia, Vietnam, Egypt, Turkey, and South Africa
CSO	civil society organization
DAC	Development Assistance Committee of the Organisation for Economic Co-operation and Development
DATA	Data, AIDS, Debt, Africa
DWG	Development Working Group
EMDEs	emerging markets and developing economies
FIM	FIM-Forum for Democratic Global Governance
FSB	Financial Stability Board
G5	Group of Five (France, Germany, Japan, United States, United Kingdom, which met in 1974)
G5	Group of Five (Brazil, China, India, Mexico, and South Africa, which were invited to the G8 summits from 2005 to 2009)
G6	Group of Six (France, Germany, Italy, Japan, United States, United Kingdom)
G7	Group of Seven (Canada, France, Germany, Italy, Japan, the United Kingdom, the United States, and the European Union)
G8	Group of Eight (G7 plus Russia)
G20	Group of 20 (G8 plus Australia, Argentina, Brazil, China, India, Indonesia, Korea, Mexico, Saudi Arabia, South Africa, and Turkey)
G77	Group of 77
GDP	gross domestic product
GCAP	Global Call to Action against Poverty
HIC	high-income country
HIPC	heavily indebted poor country
HSE	National Research University Higher School of Economics
IAEA	International Atomic Energy Agency

IBSA	India, Brazil, and South Africa
ICC	International Chamber of Commerce
ICT	information and communication technologies
IEA	International Energy Agency
IEF	International Energy Forum
IFI	international financial institution
IMF	International Monetary Fund
IORI	International Organisations Research Institute at the National Research University Higher School of Economics
J8	Junior Eight
L20	Labour 20
LIC	low-income country
MAP	Mutual Assessment Process
MDB	multilateral development bank
MDG	Millennium Development Goal
MEF	Major Economies Forum on Energy Security and Climate Change
MIC	middle-income country
MYAP	Multi-Year Action Plan on Development
NATO	North Atlantic Treaty Organization
NCD	noncommunicable disease
NEPAD	New Partnership for Africa's Development
NGO	nongovernmental organization
NIE	newly industrializing economy
NPT	Nuclear Non-Proliferation Treaty
ODA	official development assistance
OECD	Organisation for Economic Co-operation and Development
P5	Permanent Five members of the United Nations Security Council
PPP	public-private partnership
PSI	plurilateral summit institution
SARS	severe acute respiratory syndrome
SDR	special drawing right
SME	small and medium-sized enterprise
UNCAC	United Nations Convention against Corruption
UNCTAD	United Nations Conference on Trade and Development
UNESCO	United Nations Educational, Scientific, and Cultural Organization
UNICEF	United Nations Children's Emergency Fund
UNIDO	United Nations Industrial Development Organization
UNFCCC	United Nations Framework Convention on Climate Change
UNSC	United Nations Security Council
WEF	World Economic Forum
WHO	World Health Organization
WTO	World Trade Organization
WWF	World Wildlife Fund

PART I
Introduction

Chapter 1
Introduction

John J. Kirton and Marina V. Larionova

The Challenge

The twenty-first century has brought a proliferation of pressing global problems that break out far more suddenly and surprisingly, spread more swiftly and extensively, and interact in more complex and uncertain ways than ever before. On the eve of the century there was a financial crisis in Asia that began in 1997 and consumed countries in the Americas, Europe, and the Middle East over the following years. The terrorist attacks on the United States on September 11, 2001, began a new era of global mega-terrorism, which quickly spread to many other countries and led to a war in Afghanistan that endured for over a decade. The collapse of the investment bank Lehman Brothers in New York on September 15, 2008, catalysed an American-turned-global financial crisis that immediately created the world's worst recession since the one in the 1930s that had brought such great destruction in its wake. This new recession was followed by a European financial crisis that erupted in 2010.

These new crises and their accompanying challenges have demanded and received a forceful, innovative, global governance response. The established Group of Seven (G7) major market democracies added Russia as a full member in 1998 to become the Group of Eight (G8) and reached out to embrace as participants the leading African countries in 2001, the emerging powers of China, Brazil, India, Mexico, and South Africa by 2005, and then Korea and Indonesia to address climate change by 2008. In November 2008, the Group of 20 (G20) systemically significant countries, formed in 1999 at the level of finance ministers and central bank governors, leapt to the leaders' level to become a vibrant summit club. And in 2008 another plurilateral summit institution (PSI), assembling the big emerging economies of Brazil, Russia, India, China, and, later, South Africa (BRICS), arrived on the scene.

If the great and growing demand for twenty-first century global governance gave new life to both the old G7/8 and the new G20 summits, it raised the key questions of the comparative performance and the evolving and desired relationship between the two. An initial answer came from the G20's third summit, held in Pittsburgh in September 2009, when the G20's leaders from the G8, BRICS, and other emerging countries indicated that the new G20 would govern global finance and economics, while the old G8 would continue with the development and security files. Yet this rough division of labour left unanswered the questions of what issues lay within each category and how the overlaps and interconnections would be addressed to create comprehensive, coherent, continuous global governance for a complex, uncertain but ultimately common world.

The Purpose

This volume takes up these questions. It explores the performance of the G7/8 and G20 summits, their comparative strengths and limitations, the division of labour emerging during their coexistence, their evolving relationships, their involvement with civil society and BRICS summitry beyond, and how the future G7/8–G20 relationship can be improved to the benefit of both and the global community as a whole.

This volume has five particular purposes. The first is to chart and compare, according to a common analytic framework, the G7/8 and G20 summits, especially during their half decade of coexistence from 2008 to 2013 (Baker 2006; Bayne 2005; Cooper and Thakur 2013; Dobson 2006; Hajnal 2007, 2014; Kirton 2013; Postel-Vinay 2011). This comparison embraces their creation, their core characteristics as PSIs, their performance along a comprehensive array of global governance dimensions, and the common and distinctive causes that determine why and how they work. This analysis is often guided by the concert equality model developed to account for G7/8 governance and the overlapping but distinctive systemic hub model developed for G20 governance (Kirton 2013).

The second purpose is to consider the connection between G8 and G20 summitry, as their relationship evolved over their first five years together. Here the central concern is with how close and how cooperative, convergent, or competitive the connection became and how capable both bodies were in combination to cope with the challenges of the contemporary world. This analysis is inspired and guided in general by the framework developed by the co-editors to explore the relationship between, on the one hand, the informal, plurilateral, soft law, summit-level G7/8 and G20 and, on the other, the formal, broadly multilateral, hard law, ministerially managed organizations of the Bretton Woods–United Nations system born in the 1940s to govern the world of that time (Ikenberry 2001, 2011; Kirton et al. 2010; Nye 2011).

The third purpose is to consider the performance and relationship of the G8 and G20 in the context of the other consequential new actors importantly involved in global governance in that five-year period. These include in particular an empowered civil society, led by the business community in the Business 20 (B20), and the new BRICS summit beyond, amid broader forces at work in the contemporary world (Cooper 2007; Hajnal 2002; Scholte 2011).

The fourth purpose is to assess the compliance and accountability of G7/8 and G20 members, both individually and collectively, as both are critical to the effectiveness and legitimacy of these institutions (Grant and Keohane 2005; Keohane 2002; Kokotsis 1999). Here several central questions arise. What compliance monitoring and accountability mechanisms were used for each group in that five-year period? Which ones worked best, given the distinctive character of each? How did each learn and borrow from the other? And how does this dynamic sustain each group's competitive and cooperative quest to provide the kind of global governance the world today needs?

The fifth purpose is to reach conclusions for strengthening the connection between the two groups. It seeks to identify, on the basis of this shared empirical and analytic foundation, how the G7/8–G20 relationship can realistically be improved to better meet the needs of those living in today's tightly wired world.

INTRODUCTION

This book thus offers the first systematic analysis of the evolving and potential performance of G7/8 and G20 summitry and the relationship between the two groups, in the context of civil society and the BRICS summit beyond and the broader changes in the twenty-first century world.

The Contributors

To fulfil these purposes, this book assembles the contributions of a broad range of leading experts. They come from the disciplines of political science and economics from Russia, Europe, and North America, from scholars, and from past and present practitioners representing national governments and international organizations.

Most importantly, this volume combines the talents of two research teams that have worked together for many years on the analytic and empirical components essential to accomplish the task taken up here. The first team, led by Marina V. Larionova at the National Research University Higher School of Economics in Moscow, includes her scholarly colleagues, researchers, and practitioners in Russia and beyond. The second team, led by John Kirton at the University of Toronto, includes his colleagues in Toronto and in Europe beyond. This combination has facilitated the task of producing a cumulative, coherent work.

The Arguments

The authors from these two teams have come together to address G7/8–G20 governance from several vantage points.

They begin in Part II with a focus on the architecture of the G7/8 and G20 and the comparative performance of the two groups.

In Chapter 2, 'Changing Global Governance for a Transformed World', John Kirton comparatively assesses G7/8, G20, and BRICS summitry, including the relationship among the three. First, he examines fundamental changes in the world system in the twenty-first century: shifting relative capabilities among rising and retreating powers; growing globalized connectivity, complexity, and uncertainty; and equal vulnerability for all to new non-state threats. Second, he explores their governance by the G8 from 1998 to 2013, through its outreach to rising powers from 2003 to 2009, to its work alongside the G20 and the BRICS since 2009. Third, he analyses the G20 at its first eight summits, from Washington DC in 2008 to St Petersburg in 2013. Fourth, he considers the BRICS through its first five scheduled summits from 2009 to 2013.

Kirton challenges the many who dismiss each or all of these new bodies as mere photo opportunities and talk shops, with a declining performance after their hopeful start, and ones where competitive sibling rivalry erodes the cooperation needed to meet today's global demands. He makes three central claims. First, each summit group performs a full range of global governance functions, from domestic political management, deliberation, and normative direction setting, through to decision making, delivery of these decisions, and the institutional development of global governance. Second, each group has a rising performance across most of these functions, long after the crisis or calculations that created it have passed and as each has become an increasingly cohesive club. Third, they offer mutual support to produce summit-level global governance several times a year, to counter and control the new vulnerabilities that all now confront.

In Chapter 3, 'The G7/8 and G20: Parallel Paths to Pragmatic Partnership', Dries Lesage presents a closer comparative analysis of the evolution of these two groups. He highlights the division of labour as the G20 moved from finance ministers' meetings to leaders' meetings. The proposed scenarios of future coexistence are based on the application of functional and pragmatic approaches and the idea of representing the interests of different countries through the mechanisms already being developed and applied during the deepening of the G7/8 and G20 agendas.

Lesage argues that there are several striking similarities between the G7/8 and G20 in their creation as a response to globalization and multipolarity, their character as informal, plurilateral institutions, their start as finance forums, the European initiative to elevate them to the leaders' level, and the expansion of their agenda. Moreover, the differences are less than they first appear to be. The likely relationship between the G7/8 and the G20 is thus a very complex, pragmatic one, rather than a rigid division of labour. Dividing labour was not the logic that led both bodies to arise and expand.

In Chapter 4, 'A World without G20 Summits', Martin Gilman assesses the efficiency and results of the first eight G20 summits. He evaluates their performance on their core economic functions of ensuring global financial stability and sustained economic growth and reducing imbalances between rising creditors and new debtors to this end. He suggests that G20 summits have outlived their usefulness in addressing the major economic issues today. He recommends that the G20 process be maintained at the ministerial level until more representative and effective mechanisms can be introduced into global economic governance or until a new crisis erupts.

In Chapter 5, 'Global Risks Governance and G20, G7/8, and BRICS Capabilities', Marina Larionova, Mark Rakhmangulov, Andrei Sakharov, Andrey Shelepov, and Vitaly Nagornov assert that global problems generate a demand for global governance that should be met by the available supply of international institutions. Members' priorities also shape the demand for collective action and confront the institutional capacity for forging consensus and making collective decisions. The country chairing an institution should align both types of demand with the capacity of that institution and the chair's own national priorities, interests, and capabilities. The chair should be guided by a comparative assessment of the institution's effectiveness for dealing with specific global governance problems. This was particularly relevant for Russia, which chaired the G20 in 2013, was scheduled to host the G8 in 2014, and would chair the BRICS in 2015. The authors thus present a comparative assessment of the capabilities of the G20, the G7/8, and the BRICS and their missions' relevance to surmounting the key global governance challenges of the forthcoming decade.

They argue that each institution should address the risks and challenges most relevant to its missions and capabilities, with the G20 focusing on economic risks, the G7/8 on geopolitical and technological ones, and the BRICS on innovative long-term societal ones.

INTRODUCTION

This division of labour will maximize the three institutions' contribution to overcoming failures in global governance. However, such systemic risks as severe income disparity, unforeseen negative consequences of regulation, the prolonged neglect of infrastructure, and the extreme volatility in energy and agriculture prices demand cooperation and coordination among all three. A proper balance between an appropriate division of labour and cooperation will enhance their capacity to manage global risks.

Part III turns to the achievements of the G7/8 and G20, as assessed from the perspective of scholars and practitioners alike. Here the focus shifts from a comparative analysis of the two groups to their connection and to the contribution of civil society's business community within.

In Chapter 6, 'Assessing G7/8 and G20 Effectiveness in Global Governance', Marina Larionova, Mark Rakhmangulov, and Andrey Shelepov assess the G7/8 and G20 within a common functional framework. They compare the two groups across several criteria for performance: global governance functions, accountability and compliance, contribution to the global governance agenda, and engagement with other international institutions. They seek to build a quantified data base that permits an assessment of the effectiveness of these two groups and informs forecasts of their future roles.

The authors argue that claims of G20 inefficiency and the demise of the G7/8 are overstated. They share global governance functions. The G20 has a proven performance in setting directions, making decisions, and developing global governance, while the G7/8 continues to be a concert for leaders' deliberation and the good delivery of its commitments. The G20 has substantially improved its delivery, too. Both groups have built accountability mechanisms. Their relationship is cooperative rather than competitive. While there is no clear division of labour on global governance functions or on policy areas, each group has a distinctive core agenda and they cooperate on certain priorities. Such cooperation should be consolidated. Both institutions contribute to enhancing multilateralism through intense engagement with international institutions on a wide range of issues.

In Chapter 7, 'Working Together for G8–G20 Partnership: The Muskoka-Toronto Twin Summits of 2010', John Kirton examines from a scholarly perspective how and why Canada's twin 2010 summits worked well separately and together, and how the future G7/8–G20 partnership can be improved to the benefit of both in the years ahead. Kirton compares the performance of the Muskoka G8 and Toronto G20 summits, identifies their synergistic convergence, and explores the causes of the successes and shortcomings of each alone and both together. He does so by applying the closely related but distinct concert equality model of G7/8 governance and the systemic club model of G20 governance as analytic guides. On the basis of this analysis, he suggests ways for strengthening G7/8–G20 partnership.

Kirton argues, first, that crisis alone is not enough to generate G7/8, G20, or combined success, as there was no crisis on a similar subject to generate Muskoka's successes on maternal, newborn, and child health and on accountability. Rather, there was a smart, responsible civil society with expertise and capacity and a smart, strategic host willing to use its prerogative of chair and work well with multilateral organizations, most directly the G20 with the International Monetary Fund (IMF) in the domain of finance. Second, both groups need to work together at the same time and throughout the year. Third, both need to work together, on the same things if need be. Fourth, both need to work together on the same things for as long and as often as needed – either once a year as is the G7/8 norm, twice a year as was the initial G20 norm, or more often should the global demand arise. Fifth, even two Gs working well together is not enough to meet the great and growing demands for global governance in today's intensely globalized world. Thus, each should work more closely with at least the major multilateral organizations and supportive civil society in several ways.

In Chapter 8, 'G20: From Crisis Management to Policies for Growth', Zia Qureshi examines some key elements of the G20 agenda for strong, sustainable, and balanced growth. He looks in turn at restoring fiscal sustainability, avoiding middle-income traps, investing for growth, improving the investment climate, investing in infrastructure, addressing the jobs challenge, advancing trade reform, and promoting green growth.

Qureshi argues that G20 policy actions since the start of the global financial crisis have emphasized short-term crisis management. Economic stabilization has been necessary but is not sufficient to restore robust economic growth. It must be accompanied by structural reforms and investments that boost productivity as well as bolster the longer-term sustainability of growth. In the future, this deeper, long-term agenda should receive more attention from the G20.

In Chapter 9, 'G20-B20 Engagement: Achievements and Challenges', Marina Larionova, Mark Rakhmangulov, Andrei Sakharov, and Andrey Shelepov review the progress of G20–B20 interaction to identify achievements and challenges, since the start of the B20 at the G20 Toronto Summit in 2010 through to its fifth installment at St Petersburg in 2013. They do so on the grounds that the extensive investment in the dialogue by both business and governments in G20 members deserves an independent, rigorous analysis of what has been achieved and what lessons can be learned.

The authors conclude that the B20 has transformed itself from an ad hoc meeting inspired by G20 governments into a reliable stakeholder in the G20-led process of generating strong, sustainable, and balanced growth. The B20 has been more successful in getting its recommendations heard when they relate to the G20's core agenda. Those on other issues have little chance of getting the leaders' attention. Under the Russian presidency in 2013, the B20 advanced B20–G20 engagement, consolidated its contribution to G20 decision making and direction setting, and made substantive progress toward establishing the B20 as a global governance actor. However, the B20 still needs to ensure its own transparency, efficiency, legitimacy, and accountability, by developing a mid-term strategy, communicating it clearly to stakeholders including international organizations and small and medium-sized enterprises, and agreeing on a mid-term engagement regime with the G20. It also needs to become more representative, share with the G20 responsibility for delivery of the commitments, and account for its own actions in a transparent, coherent, and unbiased way. Forthcoming G20 chairs can consolidate the B20's status as a recognized global governance actor, in line with the B20's own ambitious goals, by acting in this way.

Part IV addresses the accountability of the G7/8 and G20 alike. It examines the compliance of members with their summit commitments, the compliance mechanisms used by each group, their impact, and how each has learned and borrowed from the other to improve their effectiveness and legitimacy.

INTRODUCTION

In Chapter 10, 'The Muskoka Accountability Report: Assessing the Written Record', Ella Kokotsis assesses compliance with G8 summit commitments and the importance of the first full and comprehensive G8 accountability report that was released for Muskoka. Kokotsis focuses on how the 2010 'Muskoka Accountability Report' came to be, and how the report fared in its delivery, its strengths, and its limitations. She offers recommendations for future G7/8 accountability reporting.

Kokotsis argues that the 'Muskoka Accountability Report' was a landmark event that moved from an earlier focus on inputs to a concern with outcomes. It showed that at Muskoka G8 leaders knew that leadership and accountability begin with keeping promises, that regular, clear, transparent reporting is important in this process, and that the need for an ongoing accountability working group is essential to stay on track. The impact of the report is seen in the G7/8's increasing compliance scores across most development-related commitments and a general rise in overall compliance over the mid term. The report further inspired similar accountability assessments by other Gx forums, most notably the G20 in 2013. However, the G7/8 effort should be strengthened through the use of more measureable objectives, better baseline data, on-the-ground monitoring, and support from nongovernmental organizations (NGOs), foundations, civil society, and private sector associations. Moreover, the G7/8's many working groups should engage in such monitoring with a consistent methodology and civil society support.

In Chapter 11, 'G7/8 and G20 Accountability and Civil Society', Peter I. Hajnal examines the role and impact of civil society in increasing the accountability of the G7/8 and G20, with particular emphasis on the twin Canadian G8 and G20 summits and the Korean G20 summit in 2010. He clarifies the key concepts of civil and uncivil society, and accountability, and then discusses for what and to whom the G7/8 and the G20, as global governance institutions, are accountable. He next examines the kinds of civil society organizations that play a role in the G7/8 and G20, and considers the motivations for, and range of, civil society interaction with them. Finally, he analyzes how and to what extent civil society engagement has had an impact on accountability.

Hajnal argues that the G7/8 and G20 have increasingly recognized the crucial role of accountability in gauging progress and building legitimacy. The G20's Mutual Assessment Process, conducted through a series of IMF reports (with other intergovernmental organizations also playing a role) has an important accountability dimension. Civil society groups have tracked the groups' performance, using a variety of methods. These methods all contribute to enhancing accountability by exposing strengths and weaknesses. But much remains to be done, especially in correction or redress and democratic accountability. Solutions lie in continuous and substantive consultations between civil society organizations and G7/8–G20 officials independent monitoring by civil society organizations, the publication of policy papers, and alternative summits to some extent, as well as the involvement of parliamentarians and well-prepared civil society expertise relevant to the summit priorities.

In Chapter 12, 'Mapping G7/8 and G20 Accountability', Marina Larionova and Andrei Sakharov examine a flow of accountability reports made public in the G8 and G20 process from 2008 to 2013 – a total of 206 for both institutions. They explore how these reports addressed the four accountability components of transparency, consultation, evaluation, and correction, by reviewing for the first three. These are, respectively, the provision of the evidence base and data presented for each of the members, recommendations provided by the reports' authors to promote consultation, and scorings or ratings to give clear signals of the evaluation results. Larionova and Sakharov then consider the role of academics and NGOs in the accountability process.

Larionova and Sakharov argue that G7/8–G20 accountability is not sufficiently developed to allow performance to be assessed according to the fourfold framework developed by Jan Aart Scholte (2011). However, the two groups conduct accountability in a similar but dispersed way, using a multitude of formats. Their indirect accountability procedures and the absence of clear connections among commitment, results monitoring, and further decision making decrease the effectiveness of their monitoring. The technocratic nature of the accountability reports makes them inscrutable to the public. The reports of academic institutions and NGOs tend to lack recommendations. International organizations do not provide their evidence base, data by member, or recommendations. The G20 and G7/8 reports would benefit from greater transparency and better data provision. The quality, not the quantity, of assessments should be addressed. In this effort, academics should build on their strengths in terms of information and analytic quality, while NGOs could harness their advocacy and lobbying capabilities, and both should develop recommendations. Academics and NGOs can help build the needed pluralistic accountability system through a network of epistemic groups aspiring to become independent monitoring agents.

In Chapter 13, 'Advancing G7/8 and G20 Effectiveness through Improved Accountability Assessment', John Kirton asks how, and how well, has effectiveness been conceptualized, operationalized, and assessed. How can it be improved through accountability processes from all, and for all, with the greatest stake?

Kirton offers four arguments in response. First, the effectiveness of international institutions has largely been conceptualized and operationalized as first-order implementation by the member governments with their public, written commitments over the short term or their achievement of authorized expenditures and conditions in specific programs and projects. Second, there is a need to extend effectiveness assessments from actors' conformity in their public commitments to assess the causal links, from compliance with decisional commitments to that with direction setting and principled consensus, from implementation to its impact on outcomes and results, from linear calculations to synergistic co-benefits in sequential or simultaneous form, and from the actions of individual institutions to their interaction as it affects effectiveness overall. Third, better measurements of consensus, commitment, and compliance are required, and are better concepts about the institution's overall 'mission accomplished', 'human lives improved', and 'problem solved'. Fourth, it requires better mechanisms, by expanding multilateral organizations' mandates, mobilizing members' legislatures and auditors general, establishing an independent accountability institute, foundation, and network, and creating a multi-stakeholder compliance consortium for all the assessors to share, compare, improve, and be accountable to their peers for what they do.

Part V presents the conclusions of the authors on the central issues that define the purposes of this book. In Chapter 14, 'Conclusions', John Kirton synthesizes the consensus about the G7/8–G20 relationship, its impact, and how it can be improved. He

INTRODUCTION

summarizes the agreement and continuing debate among the authors and offers evidence-based recommendations, built on an empirical and analytic foundation, about how G7/8 and G20 performance, their relationship, their association with other actors, and their accountability can be improved and strengthened for the global good.

References

Baker, Andrew (2006). *The Group of Seven: Finance Ministries, Central Banks, and Global Financial Governance*. London: Routledge.

Bayne, Nicholas (2005). *Staying Together: The G8 Summit Confronts the 21st Century*. Aldershot: Ashgate.

Cooper, Andrew F. (2007). *Celebrity Diplomacy*. Boulder: Paradigm Publishers.

Cooper, Andrew F. and Ramesh Thakur (2013). *Group of Twenty (G20)*. London: Routledge.

Dobson, Hugo (2006). *Group of 7/8*. London: Routledge.

Grant, Ruth W. and Robert O. Keohane (2005). 'Accountability and Abuses of Power in World Politics'. *American Political Science Review* 99(1): 29–43. doi: 10.1017.S0003055405051476.

Hajnal, Peter I., ed. (2002). *Civil Society in the Information Age*. Aldershot: Ashgate.

Hajnal, Peter I. (2007). *The G8 System and the G20: Evolution, Role, and Documentation*. Aldershot: Ashgate.

Hajnal, Peter I. (2014). *The G20: Evolution, Interrelationships, Documentation*. Farnham: Ashgate.

Ikenberry, G. John (2001). *After Victory: Institutions, Strategic Restraint, and the Rebuilding of Order after Major Wars*. Princeton: Princeton University Press.

Ikenberry, G. John (2011). *Liberal Leviathan: The Origins, Crisis, and Transformation of the American World Order*. Princeton: Princeton University Press.

Keohane, Robert O. (2002). 'Global Governance and Democratic Accountability'. Chapter prepared for a volume to be edited by David Held and Mathias Koenig-Archibugi from the Miliband Lectures, London School of Economics, Durham NC. Available at: http://unpan1.un.org/intradoc/groups/public/documents/apcity/unpan034133.pdf (December 2014).

Kirton, John J. (2013). *G20 Governance for a Globalized World*. Farnham: Ashgate.

Kirton, John J., Marina V. Larionova and Paolo Savona, eds (2010). *Making Global Economic Governance Effective: Hard and Soft Law Institutions in a Crowded World*. Farnham: Ashgate.

Kokotsis, Eleanore (1999). *Keeping International Commitments: Compliance, Credibility, and the G7, 1988–1995*. New York: Garland.

Nye, Joseph S. (2011). *The Future of Power*. New York: PublicAffairs.

Postel-Vinay, Karoline (2011). *Le G20, laboratoire d'un monde émergent*. Paris: Les Presses de Sciences Po.

Scholte, Jan Aart, ed. (2011). *Building Global Democracy? Civil Society and Accountable Global Governance*. Cambridge: Cambridge University Press.

PART II
Architecture

Chapter 2
Changing Global Governance for a Transformed World

John J. Kirton

Introduction

Central Challenges

In September 2013, immediately after the Group of 20 (G20) summit in St Petersburg hosted by Russia, Syria's government agreed to the key G20 leaders' request to voluntarily eliminate its major asset – chemical weapons – for deterrence and defence against its major enemy – Israel. All G20 members and Syria now agreed that a government should not use chemical weapons against its own civilians, and also that such deadly weapons had been and would be used by non-state actors – terrorists of global reach – for their own open-ended ends. That threat had been rendered more real more than a decade earlier, when al Qaeda terrorists from Afghanistan had hit the World Trade Center and Pentagon in the heart of the world's greatest power, the United States.

In October 2013, the world faced the danger that the US government itself would default on its debt and create a global financial crisis larger than that catalysed five years before with the default of American investment bank Lehman Brothers on September 15, 2008. That American-turned-global financial crisis had reawakened memories of the Asian-turned-global financial crisis that started in Thailand in the summer of 1997 and spread over a few years to engulf many major countries around the world, including, for a moment, the mighty United States itself.

These events vividly showed how the twenty-first century world has changed. New powers have emerged, global connectivity has come, complexity and uncertainty have compounded, and all countries and peoples have become more equally vulnerable to proliferating non-state threats. These changes have overwhelmed the major multilateral organizations – led by the United Nations, the International Monetary Fund (IMF), and the World Bank – that had been created by the victors of World War II in the 1940s to govern the slow-moving, geographically separated, state-centric world of that time (Ikenberry 2001; Kirton et al. 2010). There thus has now arisen a new generation of global governance institutions, designed in an inclusive, integrated, informal, and flexible form, to cope with today's tightly wired world.

This future was foreseen by the leaders of the Group of Seven (G7) major market democracies at their summit in Toronto in June 1988. They identified a new generation of emerging powers, a new phenomenon they called 'globalization', with intensifying global economic interdependence at its core, and the need for a new kind of international institution in response. They declared:

> Certain newly industrializing economies (NIEs) in the Asia-Pacific region have become increasingly important in world trade. Although these economies differ in many important respects, they are all characterized by dynamic, export-led growth which has allowed them to treble their share of world trade ... With increased economic importance come greater international responsibilities and a strong mutual interest in improved constructive dialogue and cooperative efforts in the near term between the industrialized countries and the Asian NIEs, as well as the other outward-oriented countries in the region. The dialogue and cooperative efforts could center on such policy areas as macroeconomic, currency, structural and trade to achieve the international adjustment necessary for sustained, balanced growth of the world economy. We encourage the development of informal processes which would facilitate multilateral discussions of issues of mutual concern and foster the necessary cooperation (G7 1988).

New Governance Response

This vision inspired the creation of the Asia-Pacific Economic Cooperation (APEC) forum in 1989 and then the Group of 20 (G20) finance ministers and central bank governors of systemically significant states in 1999, the latter formed in response to the Asian-turned-global financial crisis that erupted in 1997. The G20 added a leader-level summit in November 2008 to cope with the much greater American-turned-global financial crisis that had just exploded. The G7, which had become the Group of Eight (G8) with the admission of Russia in 1998, and the G20 summits were soon joined by a summit for the big emerging countries, with the birth in 2009 of the BRICS of Brazil, Russia, India, China, and, later, South Africa.

This trilogy of the G8, G20 and BRICS has much in common in the basic design of these twenty-first century global governance institutions. Their membership is deliberately restricted according to their distinctive mission, as compact clubs of collectively predominant ranking powers that constitute a small minority of the 200 or so countries in the world. They include today's ranking powers as full, equal members. They govern globally, both in their geographically spread membership and in their comprehensive agendas, which cover economic, social, and security issues alike. They meet once or twice a year at the leaders' level to cope with the connections among issues and the uncertainties and complexities of new threats, just as the national leaders do back at home alone. And they are devoid of the legal charters, fixed locations, and international bureaucrats that can confine the fast, flexible, creative, and coherent global governance needed in today's world.

In their institutional evolution, each has expanded to embrace permanent new entrants, unlike the Permanent Five members of the UN Security Council (UNSC) from 1945. They have increasingly and vigorously gone beyond government to include components from many civil society communities, notably business, labour, nongovernmental organizations (NGOs), youth, young entrepreneurs, academics, think tanks, and faith-based groups.

Together, they feature an overlapping membership, unlike the fixed blocs of the former East-West or North-South global divides (see Appendix 2-A). All operate according to flexible winning coalitions of individual countries that combine across old categories, rather than rely on UN-like rigid caucuses ill-suited to representing their members' interests in the complex, uncertain challenges at hand.

Central Argument

Many observers dismiss each or all of these new bodies as mere photo opportunities and talk shops, with a declining performance after a hopeful start, and as bodies where competitive sibling rivalry erodes the cooperation required to meet growing global demands. But the evidence tells a different tale, in three central ways. First, each body performs a full range of global governance functions, from domestic political management, deliberation, and normative direction setting, through to decision making, delivery of these decisions, and the institutional development of global governance inside and out. Second, the performance of each is rising across most of these functions, coming long after the crisis or calculations that created the body have passed and as a changing world has made them increasingly cohesive clubs. Third, as a group they offer mutual support to produce summit-level global governance several times a year, to counter and control the new vulnerabilities that all their members and others now confront.

To develop these arguments, this chapter proceeds in four stages. It first examines the fundamental changes in the world system in the twenty-first century: shifting relative capabilities among rising and retreating powers, globalized connectivity, complexity and uncertainty, and equal vulnerability for all to new non-state threats. Second, it explores the governance of those challenges by the G8 since 1998, through its outreach to rising powers from 2003 to 2009 to its work alongside the G20 since 2008 and the BRICS since 2009. Third, it analyses the G20 at its first eight summits, from Washington in November 2008 to St Petersburg in September 2013. Fourth, it considers the BRICS through its five summits from 2009 to 2013.

Twenty-First Century Changes in the Global System

Today's international system has experienced four fundamental changes that have transformed it from the territorially and temporally separated, static, slow-moving, state-centric system dominated by sovereign countries from the Treaties of Westphalia in 1648 through to the end of the war-drenched twentieth-century world (Ruggie 1993; Ikenberry 2001). They are changes in the relative capability among countries, the connectivity among countries and their citizens brought by post-Cold War globalization, the ensuing complexity and uncertainty about common enemies, and the vulnerability arising for all from new, non-state threats.

Capability: Diffusion and Convergence from Rising and Retreating Powers

The first change is in capability among countries. Since the beginning of the twenty-first century, the relative capabilities of countries have changed, in a particular way. There is no post-Cold War, sole, remaining US superpower, and no single rival or replacement. Rather, there is a diffusion arising from a relative decline in most established G7 powers and a relative rise in a broad range of those in the BRICS, in the other emerging members of the G20, and now in new sets such as the mid-sized rapidly growing CIVETS of Colombia, Indonesia, Vietnam, Egypt, Turkey, and South Africa, the resource-rich BASIC of Brazil, Australia, South Africa, Indonesia, and Canada, or the African region itself. Nor is this rise and decline reliable, as all countries plummeted downward in 2009 and the BRICS and 'fragile five' are doing so again in 2013 and 2014, even if China has dropped less. The overall result is a general diffusion of relative capability to create a new set of top-tier powers with an overlapping convergence in the ranking of countries within. Gone are the days when the G7 members all reliably stood at the top and the BRICS all behind in the next tier, and Australia, Korea, Mexico, Indonesia, Turkey, Saudi Arabia, and Argentina in a third rung below. A new top tier containing 20 relatively equal powers is what the status ordering of the international system is now (cf. Ikenberry 2011). Never before have so many powers been clustered so closely together at such a large top tier.

Connectivity: The Globalized, Tightly Wired World

The second change is in connectivity among countries and their citizens. Post-Cold War openness in so many countries and the revolution in information and communications technologies (ICT) and cyberspace have brought the death of distance and delay to the ever increasing many who are now connected to a tightly wired world, in which global contagion has become common. Also intensely interwoven are the issues that have spread from the local to the global level to affect all, such as the connection between climate change and human health and the link between water and health, and the way that financial regulation can influence social policy through the stability and sustainability of how pension plans invest (Kirton et al. 2014). Connectivity also creates empowered civil society organizations and individuals, from the NGOs that credibly confirmed the chemical weapons attack on August 18, 2013, in Syria to the revelations of Edward Snowden and WikiLeaks.

Complexity and Uncertainty: Common Unknown Enemies

The third change is complexity and uncertainty, and the resulting collective quest to comprehend common enemies and to calculate and change a country's interests and even identity in response. Intense interconnectivity instantly propels global 'bads' along unpredictable pathways, leaving little time to calculate how one will be affected and how best to respond. In this global complex adaptive system, the resulting uncertainties increasingly place all countries in a common cause to identify causal pathways and processes, their own impacts and interests, and the best ways to mount the collective response required to control these now global threats. A retreat from the benefits of globalization back toward the simplicity of a static Westphalian or autarkic North Korean-like solution is seldom the dominant response. And the slow-moving, siloed, multilateral organizations from the 1940s, with their built-in bureaucratic procedures and linear logic, are increasingly unable to cope and are thus set aside.

Vulnerability: The Primacy of Equal, Non-State Threats for All

The fourth change is the vulnerability of even the most powerful countries and their citizens to non-state threats that cause indiscriminate death and destruction, as they flow through penetrated borders that states can no longer protect. Such non-state threats come in three major forms. The first is from humans, such as terrorists intending harm to selected targets, as in the United States on September 11 and the Boston bombing in 2013, or hackers mounting cyber attacks. The second is from non-human living things, such as civet cats, bats, chickens, or swine, which intend no harm to anyone but cause deadly diseases such as severe acute respiratory syndrome (SARS) in 2003, avian influenza in the mid 2000s, and swine influenza in 2009 (Kirton and Guebert 2010). The third is from non-living things, such as climate change, causing unintended, untargeted, cumulative, complex potential death and destruction to all, as was seen in 2005 when Hurricane Katrina destroyed New Orleans and in 2012 when Superstorm Sandy ravaged the US northeast coast. The catastrophic collapse of financial systems and markets in the United States in the autumn of 2008 flowed from the first type of threat, namely humans not intending to cause anyone harm, while the embedded computer programs that cause automatic trading and the 'flash crash' brought the third type – non-living agents – into the mix.

The ultimate new non-state threat is climate change (High-Level Panel of Eminent Persons on the Post-2015 Development Agenda 2013). The established great powers that have most of their major cities and capital located on ocean coasts – such as the United States and Japan – are likely to suffer first and most fully from sudden oceanic extreme weather events and from cumulative sea-level rise. But most big emerging powers are also very vulnerable and have less capacity to respond. And given the uncertainties and complexities about climate change, it could conceivably end all human life on the planet for all time.

The G7/8 Established Democratic Major Powers, 1975, 1998

The Creation of the G7/8

These new threats in their initial form spurred the creation of the annual summit of G7 major market democracies in 1975 (Putnam and Bayne 1984, 1987). With the arrival of post-Cold War globalization, a democratizing Russia was added as a full member in 1998 (Hodges et al. 1999). The G7/8 is a club defined by capability and democracy, along with the political, economic, and social openness and like-mindedness that democracy brings. Its foundational distinctive mission is to protect within its members and promote globally the values of open democracy, individual liberty, and social advance.

G7/8 Successes

The G7/8 summit has often successfully governed the new non-state vulnerabilities since its start. It staved off the bankruptcy of New York City in 1975, stopped 'skyjacking' after 1978, controlled climate change since 1979, combatted terrorists using chemical weapons of mass destruction since 1995, fostered the birth of the convention prohibiting chemical weapons and its implementing organization, and addressed SARS in 2003. Its continuing club for G7 finance ministers and central bankers, often without Russia, was the first responder to the 2008 global financial crisis, flooding the world with liquidity that October to prevent a complete financial system collapse (Savona et al. 2011).

G7/8 Performance

The G7/8's rising performance rising performance can be seen across all six dimensions of its governance (see Appendix 2.B). Its domestic political management had a sustained spike since 2005. Its public deliberation shot up in 2004, with only brief if big dips in 2010 and 2012. Its direction setting for its core democratic mission soared in 2005. Its decision making did so in 2002, with brief dips in 2010 and 2012. Its delivery of these decisions has been consistently high since 2003. And its institutionalized development of global governance for itself soared after 1999, with a drop to zero again in 2013. This comprehensive regular rise has been challenged only briefly, selectively, and in an unsustained fashion since 2010.

G7/8 Expansion

This rising performance coincides well with the G7/8's decade-long expansion in membership and participation. This expansion started with the addition of Russia as a full summit member in 1998. It continued with invitations to heads of selected international organizations and countries in 2001, became regularized with the ongoing invitations to the leaders of the 'Group of Five' (G5) or 'Outreach Five' of Brazil, China, India, Mexico, and South Africa from 2005 to 2009, expanded to the 17 leaders of the Major Economies Forum on Energy Security and Climate Change in 2008, and culminated when 40 leaders gathered on the last day of the G8 L'Aquila Summit to discuss food security in 2009.

From 2010 to 2013, only a changing, smaller set of smaller countries was invited to participate. But the G8 still often performed well on many dimensions at its four summits from 2010 to 2013, notably at the two European-hosted summits (France in 2011 and the United Kingdom in 2013), rather than the two North American–hosted ones (Canada in 2010, the United States in 2012).

G8 Achievements

Yet each of these four summits had its standout, signature achievements: 2010 on the Muskoka Initiative on Maternal, Newborn, and Child Health (the two of the eight UN Millennium Development Goals that were furthest behind from their fast-approaching

2015 due date); 2011 on the G8-led, UNSC-approved, NATO-delivered military intervention to stop the civil war and slaughter of civilians in Libya, and the Deauville Partnership to reconstruct a reforming North Africa and Middle East during the 'Arab spring'; and 2012 on the New Alliance for Food Security and Nutrition and the military, political, and economic transition in Afghanistan where the al Qaeda terrorist network had been largely destroyed.

The 2013 G8 Lough Erne Summit

This strong performance is seen in the diplomatic dynamics and results at the 2013 summit, hosted by British Prime Minister David Cameron and held in Lough Erne, Northern Ireland, on June 17–18. From the start of British planning nine months earlier, the summit focused on the economic and development themes of trade, tax, and transparency (Kirton and Koch 2013b). As it approached, increasing attention was accorded to a fourth 'T' of terrorism, and to the mounting civil war and use of chemical weapons in Syria. Different cleavages and coalitions among the members arose on each of these issues, with France being most reluctant on trade, the United States on tax, Canada on transparency, Japan on terrorism, and, above all, Russia on Syria. In the end, however, all members came together to produce substantial advances.

On trade, the summit saw the announcement of the opening of negotiations for a full free trade, investment, and economic cooperation deal between the European Union and the United States, the two largest marketplaces in the world. It strongly endorsed the speedy conclusion of a similar deal between the EU and Canada, leading to an agreement on October 18, 2013, that was big in its own right and a model and catalyst for the much larger EU–US one. On tax, summit leaders agreed that automatic information exchanges would be the new global standard. Their decisions prompted new adherents to the multilateral convention on tax, and saw many British dependencies and some others join the new regime. On terrorism, the leaders agreed that ransoms would no longer be paid. On Syria, despite fears of a G7-versus-Russia division, all agreed to advance the Geneva peace process, under which a transitional government would have full executive authority and Syrian president Bashir Assad would thus go.

G8 Support for Sibling Summits

These achievements were outward-looking, G20-supportive, and BRICS-compatible ones. They showed that the G8 was governing not just for itself but also inclusively for the global good. The leaders' communiqués provided explicit support for the G20. On trade, the summit endorsed the Doha Development Agenda of the World Trade Organization, the Trans-Pacific Partnership, and other inclusive initiatives. On tax it gave a major boost to the work of the G20 and the Organisation for Economic Co-operation and Development (OECD). On terrorism, it supported all those countries whose citizens had just been killed by terrorists in Algeria and Mali and were being assaulted in Somalia and elsewhere, and would be in Kenya soon after the summit was held. And the step toward a negotiated settlement in Syria, which would contain the use of chemical weapons, was in the interests of many countries in the region and the world.

The G20 Systemically Significant States, 2008

The Creation of the G20

The broader G20 summit, composed equally of established and emerging, systemically significant, top-tier powers, was created in response to one new threat in its twenty-first century form – the vulnerability activating and intensifying shock of the great global financial crisis exploding in the autumn of 2008 (Cooper and Thakur 2013; Kirton 2013; Postel-Vinay 2011). The choice to respond by upgrading the existing G20 finance forum to the leaders' level reflected the G20's successful performance in response to two earlier events – the Asian-turned-global financial crisis in 1997–99 and the terrorist attack on the United States on September 11, 2001. The G20 is a club defined by both the capability and connectivity of its members, to provide crisis response, crisis prevention, and global steering for a complex, uncertain world. The centrality of connectivity as a criterion is reflected in both of its foundational distinctive missions – to provide global financial stability and to make globalization work for the benefit of all.

G20 Successes

The finance G20 successfully prevented a global financial crisis from 1999 to 2008 and then helped its once stricken Asian members avoid the financial system collapse that the mighty Anglo-Americans suffered when the 2008 crisis came. Its work on controlling terrorist finance since 2001 remains effective. At the summit level, the G20 stopped the great global financial crisis from 2008 to 2009, prevented the new European sovereign debt crisis from going global from 2010 to 2013, and, during the same period, governed a substantively broadening, domestically deepening, increasingly global long-term agenda.

G20 Performance

This increasing summit performance through two clear stages is seen across all six dimensions of governance (see Appendix 2.C). In domestic political management it regained its leaders' perfect attendance record and saw an increase in the number of compliments to its members in its communiqués after 2011. In deliberation its public conclusions rose rather steadily, with a sharp spike in 2013 in both the number of documents issued and their overall words. In direction setting, references to democracy and liberty – the core principles of the G7/8 – also rose and became robust. In decision making, the number of commitments grew regularly, and reached 281 in 2013. In delivery, members' overall compliance with these collective commitments started strong, dropped, but then rose to the initially strong level, similar to that of the G7/8. In its development of global governance, the G20's declared support for, or leadership of, its internal and outside international institutions rose too.

G20 Expansion

This performance accompanies the expansion of the leaders participating in G20 summits. The G20's full membership has remained fixed since 1999 at 19 countries and the EU, along with the IMF and World Bank. Since the start, its summit hosts have also invited about five outside countries as participants, increasingly institutionalized to reflect major geographic regions, and an expanding array of multilateral organizations from the UN galaxy and the OECD.

G20 Achievements

Each G20 summit has had its memorable achievements. Washington in November 2008 created the summit and its pioneering in work on financial stability, system repair, and reform. London in April 2009 affirmed massive fiscal and monetary policy stimulus and mobilized $1.1 trillion in new money, including $250 billion for an innovative Chinese initiative to vastly expand the IMF's special drawing rights (SDRs). Pittsburgh in September 2009 made the G20 its members' proclaimed, permanent, premier forum for their international economic cooperation and created the Framework for Strong, Sustainable, and Balanced Growth and its Mutual Assessment Process. Toronto in June 2010 agreed on fiscal consolidation for advanced economy members to help contain the erupting euro crisis in its initial instalment from Greece. Seoul in November 2010, the first summit hosted by a non-G8 member, by an Asian member, and by an emerging country, brought the historic deals on Basel III bank standards and the shift of shares of voice and vote at the IMF from the declining established states to the rising emerging ones. Cannes in November 2011 contained the latest instalment of the euro crisis arising in Greece again and elsewhere. Los Cabos in June 2012 brought the euro crisis under control, in part by having almost all established members and all emerging ones raise a new 'firewall' fund of close to $0.5 trillion to rescue stricken countries through the IMF.

The 2013 G20 St Petersburg Summit

The St Petersburg Summit on September 5–6, 2013, saw a more striking, surprising, and comprehensive advance (Kirton and Koch 2013a). Its standout success in incubating the agreement to eliminate chemical weapons from Syria, impressive in its own right, turned the G20 into a clear political-security club, in part through the G20 foreign ministers who had come to St Petersburg to help. On its broad, built-in agenda, St Petersburg made many small advances on several fronts, catalysed the next steps on tax fairness regarding base erosion and profit shifting, and launched an innovative work program on financing for investment, with a central place for infrastructure and small and medium-sized enterprises (SMEs).

G20 Support for Sibling Summits

This G20 governance has largely supported the interests of the G7/8 and the BRICS members within. The BRICS members have seen the G20 agree to their central objective of IMF voice and vote reform, and their desire to shift toward SDRs as a composite global currency. They have used the G20 summits as a nest to hold their now routine BRICS summits each year. The G7/8 has seen the G20 broadly affirm its principles of democracy and liberty, emphasize democratic polities in the composition of the group, and forward the tax agenda that the G8 Lough Erne Summit had as a central advance.

The BRICS Big Emerging Powers, 2009

The Creation of the BRICS

The great global financial crisis of autumn 2008 also crystallized the creation of the BRICS summit in the summer of 2009 (Kirton and Larionova 2012). The four leaders had met during the 2008 G8 summit in Hokkaido, Japan (Kremlin 2008). But the summit gained significance once the full impact of the crisis had hit the big but less globally connected BRICS countries and it was clear that the G8, G20, and major multilateral institutions were not fully able to protect the BRICS and the full global economy on their own. The BRICS as a group was based on both capability (countries that were big and growing) and power-proportionate equality, based on relative capability, that was not adequately reflected in the multilateral organizations from the 1940s, the G8 plus the G5, and even an early G20 summit preoccupied with other things. The BRIC summit's distinctive foundational mission, as declared in its first communiqué, was 'strengthening collaboration within the BRIC' (South Africa not yet being a member) supporting the G20 summit in the face of financial crisis, and, less clearly, supporting the common interests of emerging countries in their economic development (BRIC 2009).

BRICS Successes

BRICS summits addressed a wide array of new security issues, including not only finance but also energy, terrorism, climate change, health, and ICT (Kirton et al. 2014). Each summit has shaped the evolving institution in clear ways. The first stand-alone BRIC summit took place at Yekaterinburg, Russia, in 2009, where energy was given centre stage. At Brasilia in 2010 leaders agreed to admit South Africa, which attended at Sanya in China in 2011. Delhi in 2012 began the process of creating a BRICS development bank, which was announced in Fortaleza in Brazil in 2014.

BRICS Performance

The first five BRICS summits produced a solid, strengthening performance in many ways (see Appendix 2.D). In domestic political management, the leaders' perfect attendance record beat the G7/8 and G20 summits, and communiqué compliments soon regularly appeared. BRICS public deliberation increased. Its decision making was stable and substantial, if lower than that of the G7/8 or G20 at a similar stage. In delivery, its compliance record was the same as that of the G7 summit during its first 14 years, but well below that of the G8 and G20 in recent years. Its development of global governance, both inside and outside, grew, but remained much below that of the G20.

BRICS Expansion

This pattern of performance has coincided with an expansion of BRICS participation. It arrived first with the admission of South Africa at the third summit. Then came extensive outreach to African leaders invited to Durban in 2013. The summit has also steadily developed a wide array of civil society communities to enrich its work.

The 2013 BRICS Durban Summit

At Durban in 2013, the BRICS Development Bank was launched in principle (Larionova and Kirton 2013). Durban emphasized both the agenda and the inclusion of the countries and continent surrounding the host for the first time. This gave Africa and development a major place in the BRICS's attention and advances.

BRICS Support for Sibling Summits

On balance the BRICS broadly supports the work of the G20 and even the G7/8. On issues such as terrorism, all three bodies share a singular resolve and approach. The BRICS supports the G20 as part of its distinctive foundational mission and frequently expresses support for the G20 explicitly in BRICS communiqués. The G20 summit is the nest where informal BRICS summits take place.

Conclusion

In conclusion, this analysis shows that changing country capabilities, increasing connectivity, and resulting complexity and uncertainty are making all countries more equally vulnerable to new, deadly, destructive non-state threats. As a result issues such as global financial crises, terrorism, climate change, and transnational tax transfers are moving to the central global stage. In response, the global plurilateral summit institutions of the G7/8, the G20, and the BRICS have arisen and expanded to offer robust and rising global governance across an increasingly broad range of issues, in ever more domestically intrusive ways. Most G20 countries are also members of the BRICS or the G7/8. Russia was the connector as a member of all three and was scheduled to host them in sequence: the G20 in 2013, G8 in

2014, and the BRICS in 2015.[1] Thus, despite different distinctive missions, membership, and historical paths, these twenty-first century triplets are working in mutually supportive ways to supply badly needed global governance, at the collective comprehensive, integrated leaders' level, on a face-to-face basis, four times a year.

References

BRIC (2009). 'Joint Statement of the BRIC Countries' Leaders'. Yekaterinburg, June 16. http://www.brics.utoronto.ca/docs/090616-leaders.html (March 2014).

Cooper, Andrew F. and Ramesh Thakur (2013). *Group of Twenty (G20)*. London: Routledge.

G7 (1988). 'Toronto Economic Summit Economic Declaration'. Toronto, June 21. http://www.g8.utoronto.ca/summit/1988toronto/communique.html (March 2014).

High-Level Panel of Eminent Persons on the Post-2015 Development Agenda (2013). 'A New Global Partnership: Eradicate Poverty and Transform Economies through Sustainable Development'. United Nations, New York. http://www.post2015hlp.org/wp-content/uploads/2013/05/UN-Report.pdf (March 2014).

Hodges, Michael R., John J. Kirton and Joseph P. Daniels, eds (1999). *The G8's Role in the New Millennium*. Aldershot: Ashgate.

Ikenberry, G. John (2001). *After Victory: Institutions, Strategic Restraint, and the Rebuilding of Order after Major Wars*. Princeton: Princeton University Press.

Ikenberry, G. John (2011). *Liberal Leviathan: The Origins, Crisis, and Transformation of the American World Order*. Princeton: Princeton University Press.

Kirton, John J. (2013). *G20 Governance for a Globalized World*. Farnham: Ashgate.

Kirton, John J. and Jenilee Guebert (2010). 'North American Health Governance: Shocks, Summitry, and Societal Support'. *Revista Norteamericana* 5(1): 221–44. http://www.scielo.org.mx/scielo.php?script=sci_arttext&pid=S1870-35502010000100008 (July 2012).

Kirton, John J. and Madeline Koch, eds (2013a). *Russia's G20 Summit: St. Petersburg 2013*. London: Newsdesk. http://www.g8.utoronto.ca/newsdesk/stpetersburg (March 2014).

Kirton, John J. and Madeline Koch, eds (2013b). *The UK Summit: The G8 at Lough Erne 2013*. London: Newsdesk. http://www.g8.utoronto.ca/newsdesk/lougherne (March 2014).

Kirton, John J., Julia Kulik and Caroline Bracht (2014). 'The Political Process in Global Health and Nutrition Governance: The G8's 2010 Muskoka Initiative on Maternal, Child, and Newborn Health'. *Annals of the New York Academy of Sciences* 40: 1–15. doi: 10.1111/nyas.12494.

Kirton, John J. and Marina V. Larionova, eds (2012). *BRICS: The 2012 New Delhi Summit*. London: Newsdesk. http://www.brics.utoronto.ca/newsdesk/delhi (March 2014).

Kirton, John J., Marina V. Larionova and Paolo Savona, eds (2010). *Making Global Economic Governance Effective: Hard and Soft Law Institutions in a Crowded World*. Farnham: Ashgate.

---

1   However, as a result of Russia's actions in Ukraine in March 2014, the G7 leaders suspended their preparations in the Russian-hosted G8 summit and decided to meet on their own in Brussels on June 4–5, as originally scheduled.

Kremlin (2008). 'BRIC Leaders Meet'. Moscow, July 9. http://www.brics.utoronto.ca/docs/080709-leaders.html (November 2014).

Larionova, Marina V. and John J. Kirton (2013). 'Prospects for the BRICS Summit'. In *Invest in South Africa 2013*, Barry Davies, ed. London: Newsdesk, p. 113. http://www.brics.utoronto.ca/newsdesk/durban (March 2014).

Postel-Vinay, Karoline (2011). *Le G20, laboratoire d'un monde émergent*. Paris: Les Presses de Sciences Po.

Putnam, Robert and Nicholas Bayne (1984). *Hanging Together: Co-operation and Conflict in the Seven-Power Summit*. 1st ed. Cambridge MA: Harvard University Press.

Putnam, Robert and Nicholas Bayne (1987). *Hanging Together: Co-operation and Conflict in the Seven-Power Summit*. 2nd ed. London: Sage Publications.

Ruggie, John G. (1993). 'Territoriality and Beyond: Problematizing Modernity in International Relations'. *International Organization* 47(1): 139–74.

Savona, Paolo, John J. Kirton and Chiara Oldani, eds (2011). *Global Financial Crisis: Global Impact and Solutions*. Farnham: Ashgate.

Appendix 2.A: G20 members in plurilateral summit institutions

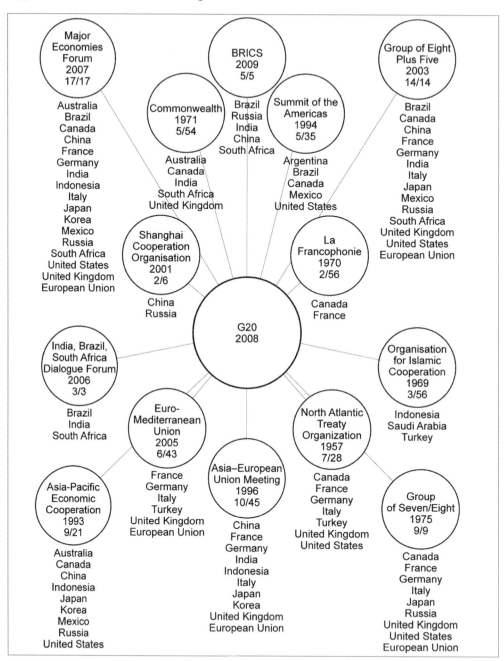

Note: Date indicates year of first summit. First number indicates the number of G20 members in the plurilateral summit institution (listed); second number indicates total members in the plurilateral summit institution.

Source: Based on John J. Kirton (2013, 470).

Appendix 2.B: G8 summit performance, 1975–2013

Summit	Grade	Domestic political management		Deliberation			Direction setting	Decision making	Delivery	Development of global governance		Participation	
		# compliments	Spread	# days	# docs	# words	# references to core values	# commitments	Compliance	# bodies created ministerial/official		Members	Guests (C/IO)
1975	A-	2	29%	3	1	1,129	5	14	0.57	0	1	6	0/0
1976	D	0	0%	2	1	1,624	0	7	0.09	0	0	7	0/0
1977	B-	1	13%	2	6	2,669	0	29	0.08	0	1	8	0/0
1978	A	1	13%	2	2	2,999	0	35	0.36	0	0	8	0/0
1979	B+	0	0%	2	2	2,102	0	34	0.82	1	2	8	0/0
1980	C+	0	0%	2	5	3,996	3	55	0.08	0	1	8	0/0
1981	C	1	13%	2	3	3,165	0	40	0.27	1	0	8	0/0
1982	C	0	0%	3	2	1,796	0	23	0.84	0	3	9	0/0
1983	B	0	0%	3	2	2,156	7	38	-0.11	0	0	8	0/0
1984	C-	1	13%	3	5	3,261	0	31	0.49	1	0	8	0/0
1985	E	4	50%	3	2	3,127	1	24	0.01	0	2	8	0/0
1986	B+	3	25%	3	4	3,582	1	39	0.58	1	1	9	0/0
1987	D	2	13%	3	7	5,064	0	53	0.93	0	2	9	0/0
1988	C-	3	25%	3	3	4,872	0	27	-0.48	0	0	8	0/0
1989	B+	3	38%	3	11	7,125	1	61	0.08	0	1	8	0/0
1990	D	3	38%	3	3	7,601	10	78	-0.14	0	3	8	0/0
1991	B-	1	13%	3	3	8,099	8	53	0.00	0	0	9	1/0
1992	D	1	13%	3	4	7,528	5	41	0.64	1	1	8	0/0
1993	C+	0	0%	3	2	3,398	2	29	0.75	0	2	8	1/0
1994	C	1	13%	3	2	4,123	5	53	1.00	1	0	8	1/0
1995	B+	3	25%	3	3	7,250	0	78	1.00	2	2	8	1/0
1996	B	1	13%	3	5	15,289	6	128	0.41	0	3	8	1/4
1997	C-	16	88%	3	4	12,994	6	145	0.13	1	3	9	1/0

Appendix 2.B: continued

Summit	Grade	Domestic political management		Deliberation			Direction setting	Decision making	Delivery	Development of global governance		Participation	
		# compliments	Spread	# days	# docs	# words	# references to core values	# commitments	Compliance	# bodies created ministerial/official		Members	Guests (C/IO)
1998	B+	0	0%	3	4	6,092	5	73	0.32	0	0	9	0/0
1999	B+	4	22%	3	4	10,019	4	46	0.38	1	5	9	0/0
2000	B	1	11%	3	5	13,596	6	105	0.81	0	4	9	4/3
2001	B	1	11%	3	7	6,214	3	58	0.55	1	2	9	0
2002	B+	0	0%	2	18	11,959	10	187	0.35	1	8	10	0
2003	C	0	0%	3	14	16,889	17	206	0.66	0	5	10	12/5
2004	C+	0	0%	3	16	38,517	11	245	0.54	0	15	10	12/0
2005	A-	8	67%	3	16	22,286	29	212	0.65	0	5	9	11/6
2006	N/A	6	44%	3	15	30,695	256	317	0.47	0	4	10	5/9
2007	N/A	12	100%	3	8	25,857	86	329	0.51	0	4	9	9/9
2008	B+	8	78%	3	6	16,842	33	296	0.48	1	4	9	15/6
2009	B	13	67%	3	10	31,167	62	254	0.53	2	9	10	28/10
2010	C	10	89%	2	2	7,161	32	44	0.46	0	1	10	9/0
2011	B+	14	67%	2	5	19,071	172	196	0.54	1	0	10	7/4
2012	B+	7	67%	2	2	3,640	42	81	0.60	0	1	10	4/1
2013	N/A	7	44%	2	4	13,494	71	214	N/A	0	0	10	6/1
Total	N/A	131	N/A	104	214	374,954	828	3,764	15.66	15	101	329	115/53
Average all	B-		44%	1.74	2.7	5.63	9,867	21.79	99	0.42	0.42	2.81	8.65	3.03/1.40
Average cycle 1	B-		47%	1.94	2.1	2.9	2,526	1.1	29	0.32	0.14	0.71	7.43	0/0
Average cycle 2	C-		46%	2.45	3	3.3	3,408	1.3	34	0.32	0.29	1.14	8.43	0/0

Summit	Grade	Domestic political management		Deliberation			Direction setting	Decision making	Delivery	Development of global governance		Participation	
		# compliments	Spread	# days	# docs	# words	# references to core values	# commitments	Compliance	# bodies created ministerial/official		Members	Guests (C/IO)
Average cycle 3	C+	33%	1.26	3	4	6,446	4.4	56	0.48	0.58	1.29	8.14	0.57/0
Average cycle 4	B	43%	2.04	2.9	6.7	10,880	5.7	106	0.42	0.58	3.57	9.00	0.86/1.00
Average cycle 5	B-	52%	0.88	2.9	10.88	23,677	65.75	237.88	0.52	0.37	5.87	8.75	12.63/5.63

Note: N/A = not available. Only documents issued at a summit in the leaders' name are included. Grades up to and including 2005 are given by Nicholas Bayne. Grades after 2006 are given by John Kirton and the G8 Research Group. Domestic Political Management: Compliments are references to G7/8 members in summit documents; spread is the percentage of members complimented. Deliberation refers to the duration of the summit and the documents collectively released in the leaders' name at the summit. Direction Setting: number of references to the G7/8's core values of democracy, social advance and individual liberty. Delivery: scores are measured on a scale from −1 (no compliance) to +1 (full compliance, or fulfilment of goal set out in commitment). Figures are cumulative scores based on compliance reports. Development of Global Governance: number of G7/8 institutions created at the ministerial and official levels at or by the summit or during the hosting year, at least in the form of having one meeting take place. Attendees: number of member leaders in attendance, including the European Union and European Commission. Guests: C = non-G7/8 members; IO= international organizations.

Appendix 2.C: G20 summit performance, 2008–13

Summit	Grade	Domestic political management			Deliberation			Direction setting			Decision making	Delivery	Development of global governance			
													Internal		External	
		Attendance	# compliments	% complimented	# days	# documents	# words	Democracy	Liberty	Total	# commitments	Compliance	# references	Spread	# references	Spread
2008 Washington	A-	100%	0	0%	2	2	3,567	10	2	12	95	0.53	0	4	40	11
2009 London	A	100%	1	5%	2	3	6,155	9	0	9	88	0.42	12	4	116	27
2009 Pittsburgh	A-	100%	0	0%	2	2	9,257	28	1	29	128	0.28	47	4	117	26
2010 Toronto	A-	90%	7	15%	2	5	11,078	11	1	12	61	0.28	71	4	171	27
2010 Seoul	B	95%	3	15%	2	5	15,776	18	4	22	153	0.50	99	4	237	31
2011 Cannes	B	95%	11	35%	2	3	14,107	22	0	22	282	0.54	59	4	251	29
2012 Los Cabos	A-	95%	6	15%	2	2	12,682	31	3	34	180	0.56	65	4	143	22
2013 St Petersburg	A	90%	15	55%	2	11	28,766	15	3	18	281	0.44	114	4	237	32
Total	N/A	N/A	43	N/A	16	33	101,388	144	14	158	1,268	N/A	467	32	1,312	205
Average	N/A	96%	5.38	18%	2	4.13	12,674	18	1.75	19.75	158.50	0.44	58.38	4	164	25.63

Note: N/A = not applicable. Only documents issued at a summit in the leaders' name are included. Domestic Political Management: participation by G20 members and at least one representative from the European Union and excludes invited countries; compliments are references to full members in summit documents. Deliberation: duration of the summit and the documents collectively released in the leaders' name at the summit. Direction Setting: number of statements of fact, causation, and rectitude relating directly to open democracy and individual liberty. Decision Making: number of commitments as identified by the G20 Research Group. Delivery: scores are measured on a scale from −1 (no compliance) to +1 (full compliance, or fulfilment of goal set out in commitment). Figures are cumulative scores based on compliance reports. Development of Global Governance: internal are references to G20 institutions in summit documents; external are references to institutions outside the G20. Spread indicates the number of different institutions mentioned.

Appendix 2.D: BRICS performance, 2009–13

	Domestic political management		Deliberation		Decision making	Delivery		Development of global governance	
	Attendance	Compliments	# words	# documents		Compliance	# commitments assessed	Internal	External
2009 Yekaterinburg	100%	0	1,844	2	16	1.00	1	2	13
2010 Brasilia	100%	1	2,436	1	46	0.13	5	16	34
2011 Sanya	100%	5	2,253	1	38	0.48	5	12	28
2012 Delhi	100%	2	4,415	2	32	0.28	5	32	43
2013 Durban	100%	3	4,789	2	43	0.48	5	26	51
Average	100%	2.2	3,157	1.6	35	0.47	4.2	18	34
Total		11	15,737	8	175	N/A	21	88	169

Note: Only documents issued at a summit in the leaders' name are included. Domestic Political Management: participation by BRICS members. Compliments are references to members in summit documents. Deliberation: documents issued in the leaders' name at the summit. Decision Making: number of commitments as identified by the BRICS Research Group. Delivery: scores are measured on a scale from -1 (no compliance) to $+1$ (full compliance, or fulfilment of goal set out in commitment). Figures are cumulative scores based on compliance reports. Development of Global Governance: internal are references to G20 institutions in summit documents; external are references to institutions outside the G20.

Chapter 3
The G7/8 and G20: Parallel Paths to Pragmatic Partnership

Dries Lesage

How does the development of the Group of 20 (G20) compare with that of the Group of Seven (G7) and Group of Eight (G8)? This exercise is informative for considering future scenarios for the G20. The central question is whether the G20 is likely to undergo an evolution as the G7/8 has done, given the conspicuous parallels in their respective development until now and in the international context in which this development has occurred. From this perspective, such an analysis will also contribute to current debates on the relationship and division of labour between the G7/8 and G20. The first section of this chapter thus compares the historical evolution of both groups. The second section examines major differences between the two bodies that could result in different pathways. The final section addresses the likelihood of alternative scenarios.

This analysis argues that there are several striking similarities between the G7/8 and G20 in their creation as a response to globalization and multipolarity, their character as informal plurilateral institutions, their start as finance ministers' forums, the European initiative to elevate them to the leaders' level, and the expansion of their agenda. Moreover, there are fewer differences than there first appear to be. The likely relationship between the G7/8 and G20 is thus likely to be a very complex, pragmatic one, rather than a rigid division of labour, for such a division was not the logic that led to the creation and expansion of either body.

Similarities between the G7/8 and G20

The similarities between the historical evolution of the G7/8 and of the G20 are too striking to be overlooked in a consideration of their respective futures, and the future of the upgraded G20 in particular. Given the parallels, the G20's emulation of the G7/8 trajectory may not be stoppable at all.

Both the G7/8 and G20 arose from a severe international financial and economic crisis (Hajnal 2007). The diplomatic format that became the G7 was born in the context of the crisis of the Bretton Woods regime, the first oil shock, and the subsequent economic slowdown in the mid 1970s. The group originated in a meeting of the finance ministers of the United States, Germany, United Kingdom, and France in 1973 – the so-called Library Group – to be joined in 1974 by Japan to form the Group of Five. The first Group of Six (G6) summit (which included Italy) took place in 1975 in Rambouillet, France. That group was joined in 1976 by Canada to form the G7, in 1977 by the European Community, and in 1998 by Russia to form the G8. The G7 has continued to meet without Russia on certain financial and economic matters. In March 2014, the G7 decided to meet at the summit level again without Russia, due to severe differences over Ukraine. The G20, similarly, was created in 1999 in response to the Asian financial crisis and its global ramifications. Between 1999 and 2008 it assembled as a meeting of finance ministers and central bank governors. Thus both the G7/8 and G20 originated from monetary turbulence and financial crisis as indicators of deepening complex interdependence, or globalization, and the increased demand for international cooperation that such globalization brought.

Both cases of creation occurred in a comparable geopolitical context as well. In the 1970s, there was a sense among western leaders that dealing with the economic crisis required high-level cooperation among the states that mattered most at that time. Leaders felt that the United States could no longer respond alone. In 1999, the G7/8 equally realized that it had now become too small, and that the new rising powers had to be brought on board. The creation of the G7/8 and G20 thus reflected an ongoing process of deepening multipolarity. Between 1973–75 and 1999, the circle of countries that, in the perception of world leaders, was needed to tackle the financial and economic crises had expanded.

By launching first the G7/8 and then the G20, leaders wanted to add a new layer of governance to the existing global institutional architecture, namely two flexible and informal mechanisms among the most powerful states for consulting, coordinating domestic policies, and giving the right impulses to official multilateral organizations. They deemed these new forums, with their very specific diplomatic methods, necessary to manage a world characterized by both risk-prone globalization and multipolarity.

In this respect, was the creation of the G7/8 and the G20 inevitable? Of course, the launch of each group required the voluntary agency of certain individuals, who could influence the exact composition and working methods of each one. But the two specific structural factors of globalization and multipolarity acted as highly permissive causes, ready to be picked up by entrepreneurial leaders. In this sense, even though the G7/8 and the G20 remain controversial in terms of legitimacy as both are self-appointed clubs trying to exert global leadership, they almost had to come into existence, whether one likes that or not.

Given the demand for international cooperation in these specific contexts of global monetary or financial crisis and growing multipolarity, both forums started at the level of finance ministers, to be elevated to leaders' level at a later stage. In the case of the G7, this happened quite quickly. For the G20, it took 10 years until the 2007–09 global financial crisis prompted it to convene for the first time at the level of heads of state and government in Washington DC in November 2008. At its third summit, in September 2009 in Pittsburgh, the G20 designated itself the premier forum for its members' international economic cooperation and decided to convene as an annual summit from 2011 onward.

The initiative to set up a process of G7 summitry came from French president Valéry Giscard d'Estaing and German chancellor Helmut Schmidt. Both were finance ministers at the time of the Library Group, and probably appreciated that process. The administration of US president Gerald Ford, who led a country traumatized by the Vietnam War and Watergate, understood the new international context and agreed to the idea of a summit.

The launch of the G20 at the leaders' level was equally a European initiative. French president Nicolas Sarkozy and British prime minister Gordon Brown went to see US president George W. Bush in the final months of his term and convinced him to convene a summit. The idea to have a G20 at leaders' level had been around for some time. A few years before the global financial crisis, Canadian prime minister Paul Martin was already campaigning for a 'Leaders' 20', based on his positive experiences with the G20 at the finance ministers' level. Together with his American counterpart Lawrence Summers, former finance minister Martin is generally seen as the founder of the G20 in 1999. Given the wide series of global challenges and global political gridlocks, a few years later he found it necessary to elevate the existing G20 process to the leaders' level and extend its agenda beyond the financial and economic realm. Thus (former) finance ministers and non-US actors played critical roles in moving forward the process of creating a major power group.

Since its inception, the G7/8 process has gradually expanded its agenda. Started as a financial-economic crisis committee, it now deals with issues such as security, development, energy, climate, and health. All this work is supported by an established practice of functional ministerial meetings, apart from the meetings of the G7 finance ministers. The actual contributions of the G7/8, often at a technocratic level far removed from the spotlight, are not fully appreciated by global media and public opinion. Agenda broadening is also the order of the day in G20 summitry. Although it can be argued that new issues have some connection with financial and economic cooperation, the G20 summit has added development, anticorruption, and marine environmental protection to its agenda. In addition to the ongoing G20 finance ministerial meetings, between 2008 and 2013 the group held four meetings of labour ministers, as well as two of agriculture ministers, one of development ministers who met jointly with the finance ministers, and even two of foreign ministers.[1] It is an open question to what extent the G20's agenda will expand in the same way as the G8's has done, which would almost automatically entail the necessity of more ministerial meetings.

Differences

At first glance, it seems that the G20 is set to undergo an evolution very similar to that of the G7/8 in the years ahead. Globalization and growing multipolarity, which fuelled the expansion of the G7/8, have grown in intensity. Thus the question is not whether the G20 will embark upon a more general global governance agenda and preparatory ministerial meetings, but when. At the onset of G20 summitry, many observers prematurely depicted the G20 as a kind of enlargement of the G8, with the latter soon due to disappear. Yet,

---

1   Since 2010, a few meetings of tourism ministers have taken place as well, but their configuration did not fully correspond with the G20, while the G20 chairs did not highlight it in their declarations.

substantial differences between both bodies prevent the G20 from simply copying the evolution of the G7/8.

The G7/8 is much more of a 'like-minded' group than the G20. From the start in 1975, the G6 underlined a common identity. As the leaders stated in their first communiqué:

> We came together because of shared beliefs and shared responsibilities. We are each responsible for the government of an open, democratic society, dedicated to individual liberty and social advancement. Our success will strengthen, indeed is essential to, democratic societies everywhere. We are each responsible for assuring the prosperity of a major industrial economy. The growth and stability of our economies will help the entire industrial world and developing countries to prosper. (G7 1975)

The G20 will be unable to agree on any similar text in the foreseeable future. It is much more heterogeneous economically, politically, and culturally than the G7/8. The larger number of members makes things even more difficult. The more unwieldy character of the G20 decreases the appetite among certain members to engage in broadening the agenda and proliferating G20 ministerials. It also leads to a more formal way of interaction, with more 'written speeches' during meetings, and less opportunity for interpersonal 'chemistry' among the leaders and their top aides.

Summitry through bodies such as the G7/8 and G20 is predominantly a western idea. For large developing countries such as China, India, Brazil, and South Africa, it is not self-evident why they should fully engage in these mechanisms. Being part of a future G20 as the apex body for global governance could alienate them from their partners in the Group of 77, the largest intergovernmental organization of developing countries in the United Nations. Moreover, these countries feel more comfortable in official multilateral environments such as the UN and World Trade Organization (WTO), where things tend to move slowly, and these countries can claim to be developing countries rather than rising powers with commensurate responsibilities. For the rising powers for which it is relevant, obtaining a permanent seat at the UN Security Council (UNSC) is a much more important goal than seeing the G20 develop into the central political steering committee for global governance. For the same reasons, the enthusiasm of emerging powers for the G8's 'outreach' processes remained mixed. They were reluctant to buy the predominantly western-driven agendas. As far as the G20 is concerned, its upgrade came after a global financial meltdown caused by mismanagement in the western financial sectors. The crisis also inflicted damage to the emerging world, but banking systems there continued to function well. Much recent G20 work is basically directed at the western countries.

For all these reasons, the G20 agenda is not likely to expand in a way analogous to the G7/8 in the near future. Yet these differences need to be put into perspective. The G7/8's common identity (liberal-democratic, pro-market) based on a long history among most members is a fact. But the G8 has already seen serious disagreement on a broad range of issues as well (e.g., the Iraq war, fiscal stimulus versus consolidation, climate change). Relations between Russia and western countries are often under strain because of conflicting security and economic interests, and different views on international and domestic political issues, as seen in the developments in 2014 that led to Russia's suspension from the G8. Russia's G8 membership in a way reduces the identity gap between the G8 and G20, since the G8 is no longer regarded as a 'western lobby' and has become more like a pluralist 'concert' – which is what the G20 is all about. In other words, the vitality of the G8 after Russia's accession was good news for the G20; the necessity to cooperate helps to overcome the difficulties that pluralism entails. However, if the exclusion of Russia from the G8 becomes definitive, divergence between the G8 and G20 profiles will grow.

At the same time, within the G20 there is a growing potential for political convergence due to the exigencies of globalization. Common interests can flow from a common identity with common values, but also from common threats and challenges in a world of advanced complex interdependence. There is, however, little automaticity in such a dynamic. Political elites must still acknowledge the causal linkages between global issues and concrete domestic problems, and regard stronger international engagement through the G20 as more beneficial to their national interests than isolationism or unilateralism. Structural factors in the background can only facilitate the mental realization that closer cooperation with other major powers is preferable. They can be counterbalanced by other considerations.

By elevating the group to an annual summit at the leaders' level, a crucial hurdle has already been cleared. Sceptics of the G20 process should not underestimate the importance of this decision. From now on, the leaders of 19 major economies plus the European Union (and the representatives of other well-established regional organizations) will gather each year to discuss a certain global (economic) governance agenda. In most cases the process will be propelled by an enthusiastic chair. In the same way as the G7/8, G20 leaders will be scrutinized by the global media and public opinion and, thanks to the periodicity of the meetings, will feel pressure to deliver and live up to their promises and to be held accountable. Notwithstanding the difficulties encountered by the G20, members – including the major powers – have endorsed its continuation. If those major powers really thought the G20 summit to be a threat to their national interests, they could have blocked it. Because of these indications, the G20 will further develop, although very gradually. It will not vanish within a few years. Indeed, the 2010 National Security Strategy of the United States (2010), in a remarkable way, recognized the prominence of the G20, even though actual enthusiasm in Washington about the process is now at a lower level than it was at the time of the relatively successful 2009 London Summit.

Moreover, agenda broadening within the G20 is already well under way. The extensive November 2010 'Seoul Development Consensus for Shared Growth' can no longer be considered as the work of a crisis committee. Although the Seoul development agenda received much less attention in the international media than the so-called currency war for which the Seoul Summit could not find a solution, it demonstrated that the G20 has gradually embarked on a broad, long-term agenda. Other cases include the G20's work on food security, fossil fuel subsidies, marine environment protection, and anticorruption. Those who want to restrict the G20 to a traditional financial/economic agenda already seem to plead in vain.

A complicating factor for the future of the G20 is the persistence of the G7/8. The G7/8 did not have such a competitor during its own evolution. It is likely to survive the upgrade of the G20 to a leaders' summit, at least for some years. At its summit in Muskoka in June 2010, the G8 found a new life. By limiting the number of invitees, it returned to basics: an informal gathering of a small group of like-minded leaders. By focusing on the Millennium Development Goals (MDGs) with regard to mothers and children and thus endorsing an ongoing UN process through the Muskoka Initiative on Maternal, Newborn, and Child Health, the G8 (2010a) tried to enhance its legitimacy. The presentation of the 'Muskoka Accountability Report' on development promises served a similar goal (G8 2010b). Apart from the announced agenda and the communiqué, leaders also discussed pressing issues such as UNSC reform. Notwithstanding legitimate criticisms about the broken promises, the insufficient amounts of new money pledged, and the all too positive tone of the accountability report, Muskoka demonstrated the usefulness of having world leaders gathering periodically, even in the restricted G8 configuration. Officials also kept stressing the value of having a like-minded group that can make substantive decisions and statements on delicate political issues. Illustrative of this back-to-basics idea was the set-up of the 2012 G8 summit chaired by US president Barack Obama at Camp David in May 2012. Again, no leaders of emerging powers were invited, in contrast to the period from 2005 to 2010. In the woods of Camp David, far away from crowds and cameras, G8 leaders dealt with intricate security issues, partly in preparation of the North Atlantic Treaty Organization's summit in Chicago scheduled the following day. Going back to the 'fireside chat' among a small group of like-minded leaders is exactly how British prime minister David Cameron (2012) conceived the 2013 summit at Lough Erne in Northern Ireland.

Plausible Scenarios for the G7/8–G20 Relationship

The expected coexistence of G7/8 and G20 in the years ahead gives rise to a lively debate on a division of labour between the two, which is of course likely to affect their respective futures. Many observers and practitioners prefer a strict functional division of labour, and also believe this outcome is the most likely. Consistent with the Pittsburgh decision, they contend the G20 will continue to focus on the financial and economic realm. The G7/8 will deal with political issues, such as security and human rights. This approach would radically change the identity of the G7/8, and block a future evolution of the G20 analogous to the G7/8's development between 1975 and 2010.

What are the prospects for this functional division of labour scenario, with the G20 addressing financial and economic issues, and the G7/8 political ones? In this case, the G20 would continue to be run mostly by the finance ministries, while foreign affairs and other functional ministries would play a larger role in the G7/8 – with leaders coordinating the two. One problem with this distinction is that it is hard to define the boundaries between the two realms. For example, on development in 2010, the G8 Muskoka Summit put forward a few MDGs as a top priority, and a few months later the G20 Seoul Summit ambitiously launched a new approach to development cooperation. According to the division-of-labour school, this should be seen as an anomaly that is soon to disappear. Development as such should move to one of the two groups. If development is basically an economic issue, then the G20 should adopt it and the G7/8 lose it. Energy is equally hard to categorize. It is hard to argue that energy is non-economic. But if it moves to the

G20, the finance ministers will increasingly have to share their show with the ministers of foreign affairs, energy, environment, and probably others, since energy is a multidimensional and strategic issue par excellence. With energy a key issue on the G20 agenda, it would become difficult to treat the G20 as an exclusively financial/economic forum. Is climate change an economic or a political issue? Some argue that climate finance is for the G20, while the rest of the matter belongs to the G7/8, given the opposition from big emerging economies to thoroughly discuss climate in the G20 parallel to UN climate negotiations. If this pattern persists, climate is a matter for the G7/8 (and, of course, the UN).

Another problem is the rejection of duplication, which is inherent to the functional division-of-labour approach. Suppose that preparedness to discuss climate in the G20 increases. One could use the G7/8 for coordinating climate-friendly domestic policies among its members – perhaps regarding relatively stronger emissions reduction targets – while the G20 fosters mutual understanding among old and emerging industrialized countries, to boost international technological collaboration and, in the end, to break political gridlocks. This would not be an example of undesirable duplication with both the G7/8 and G20 working on climate change. Both groupings can add value to the same issue area, by dealing with it from their specific perspectives. A variant of this is that the G7/8 and G20 do apply a kind of division of labour within an issue area, such as development. At a more operational level, among other things, the G7/8 could focus on health while the G20 addresses infrastructure.

The fundamental problem with work divided along functional lines is that the two bodies' respective identities have nothing to do with a functional division of labour. The G7/8 is a small group of more or less like-minded countries. Due to the recent rise of non-western powers, it can no longer claim to be a leading group for global governance. To some extent it could do so during the Cold War for the western world, and shortly afterwards for the entire world, but now it has definitely lost its position of 'group hegemony' (Bailin 2005). It tried to maintain this role through its outreach process toward China, India, Brazil, Mexico, and South Africa, in particular from 2005 to 2009. But this approach no longer has much of a future since the advent of the G20, in which the emerging powers have more chances to enjoy genuine co-ownership of the process. The G7/8 has not become irrelevant, but must redefine its role. In a more modest way, it can continue to give impulses to global governance and existing multilateralism. Perhaps more than in the past, it can lobby for certain views and values as well. But it will be rather a caucus similar to the BRICS grouping of Brazil, Russia, India, China, and South Africa, or the IBSA grouping of India, Brazil, and South Africa, than an apex body for global governance. In contrast, the G20, as an emerging global concert, possesses more potential to play a coordinating role in global (economic) governance, provided that political standpoints can converge over time. Given these very distinctive identities, the notion of a functional division of labour makes little sense.

As a result, a much more pragmatic approach will be likely. In practice, this approach will be driven mainly by the leaders themselves. They will decide case by case which forum will deal with which topic. In certain cases, there will be a clear division of labour; in others, the G7/8 and G20 will address different aspects of the same issue area; and, in still others, there will be full duplication. The leaders are likely to apply more complex criteria to decision making than the simple distinction of economic versus political. These (probably) unwritten criteria will depend on the respective comparative advantage of the two groups. In some cases, the G7/8 will touch upon some of the same issues as the G20, just because the G7/8 wants to convey certain messages, or wants to be more ambitious and set an example with regard to the issues at hand. Who could stop the G7/8 leaders from discussing the state of the world economy during their summit, or from declaring that more action is needed to tackle harmful international tax competition and non-transparent tax havens? This financial issue featured as a priority during the United Kingdom's 2013 G8 presidency, for example (G8 2013).

Certain issues will move to the G20, where the countries that matter most on a particular issue are sitting at the same table, provided that G20 partners are willing to discuss that issue. In these cases, dealing with the issue at the G20 instead of the G7/8 is a matter of necessity with a view to success. This might explain a shift of the point of gravity for financial and economic matters from the G7/8 to the G20. Or if the G7/8 and G20 are to play a role in multilateral trade negotiations, in today's world it makes more sense for the G20 to lead. Yet in 2013 the G8 (2013) discussed bilateral trade deals as an alternative to the stalled WTO talks. More technical and less contentious issues – for example, in the realm of energy technology cooperation – can be sent relatively easily to the G20, which can be expected to contribute more to certain global public goods.

In the long term, such a shift might even include forms of cooperation in the security realm, where common understanding and willingness can bring the matter within a wider forum such as the G20. Such cases include maritime piracy or terrorism. It is logical, to the contrary, that more delicate and contentious issues, such as Iran's nuclear program or human rights abuses, are dealt with by the G7/8 or by ad hoc minilateral forums rather than the G20. However, shared outrage led G20 leaders to discuss the civil war in Syria at the first evening of the 2013 G20 summit in St Petersburg, notwithstanding their profound differences on the matter. This topic was neither on the official agenda nor mentioned in the communiqué, but it definitely left its mark on the summit (Parker et al. 2013). To many observers, such 'mission creep' was unthinkable in 2009.

From the most optimistic point of view, the coexistence between the G7/8 and G20 should not hamper each other's development. Moreover, their coexistence adds to institutional diversity in global governance, and thus may increase the likelihood of progress. If something does not work in one forum, states can try the other. This way, 'messy multilateralism' is not necessarily a bad thing. This idea counterbalances the assumed advantages of putting as much as possible under the G20 umbrella (e.g., economies of scale in diplomatic interaction; more opportunities to address linkages among issue areas and even reach package deals; the fostering of a common sense of global responsibility) with the risk that if the G20 as a whole gets into trouble for one reason or another, there are negative repercussions for several issues at the same time.

Based on this pragmatist dynamic, the G20 agenda is likely to expand incrementally, and do so beyond the traditional financial and economic spheres. An all too clear-cut functional division of labour is unlikely and undesirable. Admittedly, a fast and spectacular broadening of the agenda is not to be expected; the G20 is not being catapulted to the centre of global governance. Reluctance on the part of certain great powers, as well as some G7/8 middle powers (Canada, Japan, Italy) that remain very much attached to their smaller grouping, is too strong. However, some non-G8 middle powers such as Korea, Australia, and Turkey have already expressed enthusiasm about a more prominent role for the G20. In the years ahead, they could be the drivers behind the further development and deepening of the G20 process. Korea has already made a great contribution through its 2010 presidency. It will be interesting to see the legacy of Australia and Turkey as chairs in 2014 and 2015 respectively.

Conclusion: No Functional Division of Labour

There are striking parallels between the historical evolution of the G7/8 and the G20. Both are rooted in processes of intensifying globalization and intervulnerability as well as growing multipolarity. Informal groupings of major powers appeared to be a favourite answer to financial and economic crises and other global challenges. After becoming a leaders' summit, the G7/8 saw its agenda expand and its ministerial activity increase. The G20 seems set for a similar future trajectory. The question is whether this process is stoppable. The differences between the two groups (e.g., the differing degree of like-mindedness and size) will not necessarily block an evolution of the G20 along the historical lines of the G7/8's. Yet the coexistence of the G7/8 and G20, combined with the rather strict functional division of labour that many advocate (namely the belief that the G20 deals with financial/economic and the G8 with political issues), could disrupt such an analogous evolution. However, this outcome is less probable, since the distinct identities of the G7/8 and G20 have nothing to do with a functional division of labour. Leaders have little reason to adopt such an artificial assignment of roles. The more likely outcomes are therefore an increased but very incremental expansion of the G20's agenda, even beyond the financial and economic realms, an unexpectedly interesting future for the G7/8, and a very pragmatic but complex division of labour between the two.

References

Bailin, Alison (2005). *From Traditional to Group Hegemony: The G7, the Liberal Economic Order, and the Core-Periphery Gap.* Aldershot: Ashgate.

Cameron, David (2012). 'In Fight for Open World, G8 Still Matters'. *Globe and Mail*, November 20. http://www.theglobeandmail.com/report-on-business/economy/david-cameron-in-fight-for-open-world-g8-still-matters/article5508595/ (December 2014).

G7 (1975). 'Declaration of Rambouillet'. *Rambouillet*, November 17. http://www.g8.utoronto.ca/summit/1975rambouillet/communique.html (December 2014).

G8 (2010a). 'G8 Muskoka Declaration: Recovery and New Beginnings'. Huntsville, Canada, June 26. http://www.g8.utoronto.ca/summit/2010muskoka/communique.html (December 2014).

G8 (2010b). 'Muskoka Accountability Report'. June 20. http://www.g8.utoronto.ca/summit/2010muskoka/accountability (December 2014).

G8 (2013). 'Lough Erne Declaration'. Lough Erne, Northern Ireland, United Kingdom, June 18. http://www.g8.utoronto.ca/summit/2013lougherne/lough-erne-declaration.html (December 2014).

Hajnal, Peter I. (2007). *The G8 System and the G20: Evolution, Role, and Documentation.* Aldershot: Ashgate.

Parker, George, Charles Clover and Courtney Weaver (2013). 'G20 Leaders Split over Syria'. *Financial Times*, September 6. http://www.ft.com/intl/cms/s/0/5ba75aac-1619-11e3-a57d-00144feabdc0.html#axzz2zCeogh74 (December 2014).

United States (2010). 'The National Security Strategy'. Washington DC, May. http://www.whitehouse.gov/sites/default/files/rss_viewer/national_security_strategy.pdf (December 2014).

Chapter 4
A World without G20 Summits

Martin Gilman

G20 Summits Have Already Seen Their Best Days

International institutions and mechanisms do not have 'sunset' clauses. They are not usually mortal, unlike their creators.[1] Sometimes they lumber on irrespective of a changing global environment or they evolve into new institutional forms.[2] Thus, the informal meeting of the Group of Five finance ministers in the White House library in 1973 (also known as the Library Group) eventually became the Group of Seven (G7) and then the Group of Eight (G8), with various ministerial meetings and rotation of annual summit meetings since the first one at Rambouillet in 1975.

The Group of 20 (G20) was created in 1999 in response to the financial crises in the late 1990s, the growing influence of emerging market economies on the global economy, and their relatively modest formal role in the decision-making process, being excluded from the G7/8.[3] The main objective of convening consultations within the G20 at the ministerial level was to cope with the financial crisis at the time and to work toward a framework for preventing financial instability, while securing sustainable and balanced global growth and reforming the architecture of global governance.

Working closely with existing international institutions such as the International Monetary Fund (IMF), the Financial Stability Board (FSB), the World Trade Organization, and the World Bank, and relying largely upon their research and inputs, the G20 finance ministers and central bank governors seemed to promote some modest progress on a number of technical issues.

Meanwhile, the pace of the globalization of finance and the transmission mechanisms through trade and investment has continued to intertwine economies much faster than global growth. According to the Bank for International Settlements, before the financial crisis erupted in 2008, the sum of all trade surpluses and deficits had risen to above 6 per cent of global gross domestic product (GDP) (Cecchetti 2011). By comparison, in the mid

---

1 The League of Nations, the Southeast Asian Treaty Organization, the Warsaw Pact, and the Council for Mutual Economic Assistance are notable exceptions of organizations that did not survive in the last century.

2 The United Nations Industrial Development Organization (UNIDO) is a classic case of anomalous institutions that continue to exist, and Latin America Free Trade Agreement, the Western European Union, and General Agreement on Tariffs and Trade are examples of institutions that have adapted over time.

3 Of course, the G7 still continues nevertheless, because no one wants to take responsibility for ending it.

1980s when global GDP had reached half of that amount, the G7 was so worried by the implied trade imbalances that it adopted the Plaza and Louvre Accords for coordinated exchange rate action.

Financial globalization has been even more profound. International assets, defined as foreign holdings by a country's residents, rose from 50 per cent to 150 per cent of global GDP in the 15 years between 1995 and 2010 (Cecchetti 2011). In absolute dollar terms, the rise was even more dramatic: from $15 trillion to nearly $100 trillion.

This crescendo of globalization relied on financial intermediaries to fund the trading of all these flows across borders. And the ensuing crisis, which still lingered into 2014, showed how problems both on and off the intermediaries' balance sheets can have very large, real negative effects. Gross financial flows can stop suddenly, or even reverse. They can overwhelm weak or weakly regulated financial systems. And they can feed credit booms even in the absence of domestic credit growth. It is, in fact, gross inflows that a financial system needs to be able to absorb and intermediate, not the net flows. And the proliferation of debt-like instruments raises the possibilities of rollover risk, liquidity risk, counterparty risk, and currency mismatch, among other risks. There has been no clearer illustration of these effects than in late 2013 and early 2014 when market perceptions of tightening global liquidity conditions – attributed to the United States Federal Reserve Bank's timid steps to rein in the rate of growth of its balance sheet – provoked a large-scale exodus of capital from major emerging market economies and notably the so-called 'fragile five' consisting of Brazil, India, Indonesia, Turkey, and South Africa.

The Aftermath of 2008 Debt Crisis

The debt crisis, already brewing in 2007, burst with the unanticipated bankruptcy of Lehman Brothers on September 15, 2008. With panic in financial markets reaching a climax, the gathering of the leaders of the G20's large economies in Washington in November 2008 seemed to calm investor concerns, with the meeting itself as the catalyst. There is nothing like a real crisis to motivate politicians to move quickly and decisively. There was a sense of relief, at least in financial markets, that governments were seemingly determined to put a floor under collapsing asset prices.

Governments felt compelled to act quickly to implement coordinated fiscal policies and announce bold monetary policies. Had the global economy been left to its own devices in 2007–08, the consensus view is that it would have no doubt gone through an even more wrenching purging process. Unemployment would have spiked even higher, additional financial institutions would have failed, and larger market segments, nationally and internationally, would have become even more dysfunctional. No democratically elected government would have been able to remain passive when its electorate faces such a situation.

It was hoped that a collective will to continue the effort would be galvanized through summit meetings of the leaders. Once the G20 became a venue for meetings of heads of state and governments, it was transformed into the major mechanism for international economic cooperation to regulate financial markets and influence global economic policy.

Ironically, that first G20 summit in Washington and the second one in London in April 2009 may come to be viewed as the high points for this non-homogeneous grouping that has neither a formal structure nor any specific powers.

Since these much-hyped gatherings began amid high expectations in 2008, their added value seems to have declined. Meaningful results are increasingly unlikely. Even with global economic growth still teetering close to what Nouriel Roubini (2011) calls 'stall speed', there is no longer a panic to galvanize a consensus. Instead, a form of complacency predominates. To be sure, there have been plenty of elements that the G20 Research Group at the University of Toronto can certify as positive in its regular compliance reports.[4] Unfortunately, the really important policies affecting the global economy will hardly get a mention because the commitments made were minimal or so vague as to defy meaningful monitoring.

The G20 has succeeded in finding generally amorphous common denominators on issues as broad ranging as financial reform, global warming, and development aid; in the end, most of the major players pursue policies more closely aligned with their perceived national concerns rather than address longer-term issues in the common interest. And on the critical issue of global imbalances, each country goes its own way. The G20 has retained boiler-plate language on exchange rates at recent summits. It has called on countries to refrain from 'competitive devaluation', which the United States denies doing through its reliance on quantitative easing (G20 Finance Ministers and Central Bank Governors 2013). It has urged countries to move 'toward more market-determined exchange rate systems and exchange rate flexibility to reflect underlying fundamentals', which China claims it is already doing (G20 Finance Ministers and Central Bank Governors 2013). It has allowed tools 'to overcome sudden reversals of international capital flows', which refers to capital controls increasingly imposed in many emerging economies faced with unwanted speculative capital movements (G20 2010). In other words, each country can and does continue whatever it already was doing.

For instance, at the Seoul Summit in 2010, the assembled leaders promised to assess global imbalances by developing some nebulous-sounding future 'indicative guidelines' (G20 2010). There was nothing particularly new in the IMF's toolkit to square such a circle. In the end, all the G20 members could sign on to only anodyne communiqués as each of them insisted existing policies and exchange rate regimes already met the commitments.

As groups go, the G20, bringing together the top financial officials of most of the world's largest economies, has been a relative success in addressing some technical issues of common interest since 1999, while securing a broader mandate than feasible in the IMF's executive board still dominated by Europe and the United States. That said, the test for effectiveness of any multilateral grouping based upon voluntarism is understandably low. However, elevating it to the summit level has exposed just how divergent the interests of its various members are. Even though the summits only began in 2008, one can begin to wonder – after nine summits in six years – whether it had already seen its best days.

---

4   See the G20 Information Centre website at http://www.g20.utoronto.ca/analysis.

Taking Stock of Reality

This does not, of course, mean that the world economy will not be rebalanced just because the G20 does not ordain a solution. Unsustainable imbalances will eventually be adjusted by economic forces. In refraining from collective action, the world's leaders have chosen to let the world rebalance itself, without political steering, or to address the process at the national level only, with the inevitable result of making things harder for each other.[5] This is not collective leadership but a joint abdication of power.

To prove its usefulness, the G20 must do more than help advanced and emerging economic powers agree to disagree. However, in the absence of necessity, it just does not seem able to move the world toward a new order of international monetary arrangements, whether formal – like the gold standard that prevailed before World War I or the Bretton Woods system of fixed exchange rates that functioned from 1944 to 1971 – or informal – like the more recent so-called Bretton Woods II system where many emerging markets pegged (or managed) their exchange rates at levels relative to the dollar that implied large current account surpluses and the resulting reserve growth that financed large external deficits in the United States and to a lesser degree in Europe.[6]

At best, a globally coordinated support package, as in 2009, would promote an aggressive rebalancing of the global economy by ensuring that debts are written down by the private sector, banking systems are supported (but large banks are allowed to fail), and surplus countries stimulate consumption spending while deficit countries pursue credible medium-term deleveraging and macroeconomic tightening (Alpert et al. 2011).

Many, especially among public officials and private investment institutions, remain cautiously optimistic that policy makers will make appropriate decisions so that the world can get the crisis behind them and resume global growth in a more balanced manner. It is normal that they should believe that governments will do what is needed.

Despite pious public endorsements by attending G20 leaders, it is difficult to discern any real progress on the core issue then, as now, of currency wars and addressing global trade and payment imbalances. The assembled leaders have been generally unable to agree on the key issues at recent summits because there has been no consensus that the world is facing an impending and collective crisis; thus the sense of unity that had been present at the initial summits during the worst of the global financial crisis of 2008–09 has been absent.

But, as the late economist Hyman Minsky (1992) theorized, such stability will usually lead eventually to financial instability. This implies that, after such a long period of excess debt build-up, there are still some major adjustments globally that must take place before these massive global debt and payment imbalances are reversed.

What the world has been living through collectively since the nadir in early 2009 is not unique. More generally, there seems to be a historical tendency for economic crises

---

5   An illustrative example was the press release of the US Federal Reserve's (2014) Federal Open Market Committee on January 29, 2014, without a single reference to the recent financial problems in emerging market economies.

6   As a plausible basis for a new architecture, see Jack T. Boorman and André Icard (2011).

to follow a long period of growth and increasing globalization. For instance, an earlier seemingly irreversible phase of globalization a hundred years ago ended with World War I and the Bolshevik revolution. Many analysts and concerned citizens seem to appreciate that globalization is not inevitable and can be reversed. The world may be at another turning point now. Hopefully, history will not repeat itself.

The risk now is that the inevitable adjustment to global imbalances will not be gradual. Instead of a smooth rebalancing, there could be an abrupt contraction in global liquidity, a sharply rising risk premium, substantial deleveraging, and a sharp contraction in international trade and capital imbalances.

This should be a real concern because the capital flows of the relatively new creditor countries, combined with debt-financed flows from advanced economies, have become increasingly volatile, swinging between a search for yield in a world of a zero interest-rate policy and a search for safety as risk perceptions change. These flows, including Chinese, East Asian, Russian, and Gulf savings, exacerbate the initial imbalances, leading very likely to one of the largest misallocations of global capital in recent history. Thus, the export-led growth in the surplus countries feeds the debt-led growth in deficit countries. This symbiotic relationship, beyond normal parameters, is really an unhealthy co-dependency. It could lead to another financial disaster. Stopping it means adjusting; but how? Ensuring that imbalances in cross-border financial flows decline smoothly requires a combination of structural and price adjustments – in both deficit and surplus countries.

Replacing Photo Opportunities with More Substance

It could be that the G20 is just too diverse to do the job. Perhaps it will fall to the new global creditors to make common cause with traditional net savers such as Germany, Japan, and Switzerland to impose their conditions on the debtors of the world, similar to the pattern of earlier international monetary arrangements. Although the prolonged and disappointing economic growth since 2008 has created global tensions and a possible willingness to contemplate significant reform, it is unlikely to lead to reforms as radical as those reached in 1944 at Bretton Woods, New Hampshire. In addition, after World War II, the United States was the only major economic hegemon and could dictate the rules of the global economy. That system ended when this was no longer the case, and a rising Europe and Japan pursued different interests.

Even now, what most Europeans mean when they talk about changes to the international monetary system is at least in part expanding arrangements to tap the vast financial resources of these new creditors in support of the traditional policies applied through the IMF, which they still control, even after some symbolic concessions that were endorsed at the 2010 Seoul Summit.[7] However, they and the Americans would no doubt be reluctant to cede much real power over the use of the financial resources and other key decisions affecting global finance.

---

7   Those commitments have still not been implemented pending ratification of the US Congress, in view of protecting its blocking share.

It will be up to the new creditors to push to fashion a deal that brings China, Korea, Russia, and the other creditors into the heart of the multilateral system. Here there may be an echo of the first Bretton Woods system, for underneath the camouflage of a multilateral process there was a bargain to be reached. In 1944, Britain, the proud but indebted imperial power, needed American savings to underpin monetary stability in the post-war era; the quid pro quo was that the United States had the final say on the IMF's design and structure. Today the United States might be cast in Britain's role, and China, Russia, and other creditors could play the American one. Without greater recognition of a much more dominant role within the IMF for the new creditors, they could hold back in efforts to help re-capitalize western finance.

These new creditors do not yet share a common view of a new global financial order. Even if united, they would face considerable opposition from highly indebted but politically dominant western countries. Perhaps it is premature and the time is not yet right. But, so long as financial and economic power continues to migrate to the East and South, a time will come when the new creditors will see it as in their individual interests to make common cause either to reform existing institutions or to create new ones free of the dominance of the debtor countries. A new grouping of major creditors may be just a question of time. If the G20 is a step in the transition from the old power structures of the Euro-centric world of the twentieth century, it is no doubt premature to prescribe the destination.

The debate will continue on whether the world, or at least some major economies, will be stuck in a prolonged debt-deflation recession or rather a particularly severe but classic boom-bust recession from which recovery is painful but relatively automatic.

A Return to an Earlier Structure

What about the future of the G20 itself? The G20 can be seen as strengthening the role of emerging economies, such as the big ones of Brazil, Russia, India, China, and South Africa in the BRICS, and reforming international financial institutions, improving discipline and tightening oversight over national financial institutions and regulators, improving the quality of financial regulations in economies whose regulatory problems led to the crisis, and creating financial and organizational safety nets to prevent severe economic slumps in the future. The issue, however, is that none of these modest steps can really be attributed to summits. Whatever has been done in these areas is conceived and implemented through existing institutions, notably the IMF and the FSB.

In fact, elevating the G20 to the summit level has exposed the diverging interests of its various members. One can even begin to wonder – after the first five years of disappointed expectations with each passing summit – whether these much-hyped meetings and their attendant expectations should continue in the absence of a clearly perceived crisis. It may be well to argue that summiteers should sharpen the G20 agenda, avoid politicization, and frame issues in ways that prevent the formation of opposition along national lines (see Knaack and Katada 2013). Unfortunately, such reasonable suggestions are divorced from the political reality of 20-plus participants, each with its own list of priorities.

The critical issue now in the global economy is how to make consumer demand and business investment self-sustaining without unprecedented levels of central-bank-supported debt. Since a significant share of global consumption comes from the US, Europe and Japan, the stagnation in their demand will ultimately be very painful for the BRICS and the rest of the developing world. China, in particular, but many other Asian countries as well, had postponed the impact of contracting consumption by increasing domestic investment, in some cases very sharply, but higher current investment can be seen as postponed, higher, future consumption. So the deficit countries need to break their addiction to debt, and the surplus countries need to wean themselves away from their dependence on exports.

Ideally, the G20 would actively coordinate policies to ensure a gradual and more balanced adjustment to this evolving set of conditions. Yet because of the comprehensive and technical nature of the issues, this work is best done in existing institutions – such as the IMF – that are both more representative and more effective. It could be argued that the IMF board of governors, with its near universal representation at finance minister level, would be a more appropriate locus for such considerations.

The global economy does not need to be a zero-sum game. All countries would be better off if cooperation could prevail. Therein lies the difficulty as, in the absence of leadership or at least an immediate systemic threat, each country will focus on how to export its unemployment through relative depreciation (Fitoussi and Stiglitz 2011). Imposing hardship on countries on a sustained basis will become politically impossible because the 'gains' from the hardship are theoretical while the hardships will be immediate and real.

In the absence of significant reform in the governance of the IMF and World Bank, which still remain dominated by the US and Europe, it was a needed step to introduce more legitimacy into international economic policy coordination. Proposals for new governance structures like a global economic council are well meaning but simply unrealistic (see Vestergaard and Wade 2012). So the G20 should continue to be a signalling device for further adaptation.

In the meantime, the G20 format should be reconsidered before one leader after another starts finding convenient excuses to skip the event altogether.

The St Petersburg Summit on September 5–6, 2013, illustrates the point even if there were no major no-shows. It was eclipsed by the US threat of an unsanctioned attack on Syria. The agenda of the summit, a kind of wish list of all kinds of sensible initiatives that were meticulously shepherded into final drafts by earnest subcommittees of bureaucrats nominally headed by Russian representatives as the host country for the year, was rubber-stamped by preoccupied leaders. Vladimir Putin, as the host, tried hard to keep the focus on the formal agenda but to little avail.

It was not just Syria that distracted and divided the summiteers. On economic policy, supposedly its core focus, the G20 was completely overshadowed by the much more significant meeting on September 18 of the US Federal Reserve's Federal Open Market Committee, which had been expected to announce whether its policy of quantitative easing would be reduced.

The key question is whether a push on a few practical and worthwhile policies being developed by international institutions with their own more representative governance bodies necessitated a summit at all.

The St Petersburg Summit should have entailed a serious discussion about the extreme turmoil affecting the global economy that has subsequently embroiled major emerging market members. Problems affecting global stability and employment in the Eurozone and Japan have not been resolved.

Since the G20 summits in Seoul, Cannes, Los Cabos, St Petersburg, and now Brisbane, it is hard to claim that the modest achievements could not have been done as well or even more effectively by meetings at ministerial level. For instance, the real meat from the St Petersburg Summit was considered more attentively at the G20 finance ministers' meeting a month later in Washington.

Perhaps, until the time of the next global financial panic, it makes more sense to let leaders meet when it makes sense but to revert to the earlier model of regular G20 ministerial meetings to get the job done. Sadly the Australian Prime Minister, Tony Abbott, who took over the G20 presidency from Putin to host the Brisbane Summit in November 2014, took no real action to end these empty stage-managed photo opportunities. It seems unlikely that this will change before Turkey's Prime Minister Ahmet Davutoglu hosts the Antalya Summit in November 2015.

References

Alpert, Daniel, Robert Hockett and Nouriel Roubini (2011). 'The Way Forward: Moving from the Post-Bubble, Post-Bust Economy to Renewed Growth and Competitiveness'. New America Foundation, October. http://newamerica.net/sites/newamerica.net/files/policydocs/NAF--The_Way_Forward--Alpert_Hockett_Roubini.pdf (December 2014).

Boorman, Jack T. and André Icard (2011). 'Reform of the International Monetary System: A Cooperative Approach for the 21st Century'. In *Reform of the International Monetary System: The Palais Royal Initiative*, Jack T. Boorman and André Icard, eds. Thousand Oaks, CA: Sage Publications.

Cecchetti, Stephen G. (2011). 'Global Imbalances: Current Accounts and Financial Flows'. Remarks repared for the Myron Scholes Global Markets Forum, University of Chicago, September 27, Bank for International Settlements, Basel. http://www.bis.org/speeches/sp110928.pdf (December 2014).

Fitoussi, Jean-Paul and Joseph Stiglitz, eds (2011). *The G20 and Recovery and Beyond: An Agenda for Global Governance for the Twenty-First Century*. Paris: Paris Group. http://www.ofce.sciences-po.fr/pdf/documents/ebook2011.pdf (December 2014).

G20 (2010). 'The G20 Seoul Summit Leaders' Declaration'. Seoul, November 12. http://www.g20.utoronto.ca/2010/g20seoul.html (December 2014).

G20 Finance Ministers and Central Bank Governors (2013). 'Communiqué'. Moscow, July 20. http://www.g20.utoronto.ca/2013/2013–0720-finance.html (December 2014).

Knaack, Peter and Saori N. Katada (2013). 'Fault Lines and Issue Linkages at the G20: New Challenges for Global Economic Governance'. *Global Policy* 4(3): 236–46.

Minsky, Hyman (1992). 'The Financial Instability Hypothesis'. Working Paper No. 74, May, Levy Economics Institute of Bard College, Annandale-on-Hudson NY. http://www.levyinstitute.org/pubs/wp74.pdf (December 2014).

Roubini, Nouriel (2011). 'That Stalling Feeling'. Project Syndicate (Blog), 21 June. http://www.project-syndicate.org/commentary/that-stalling-feeling (December 2014).

United States Federal Reserve System (2014). 'Press Release'. Washington DC, January 29. http://www.federalreserve.gov/newsevents/press/monetary/20140129a.htm (December 2014).

Vestergaard, Jakob and Robert H. Wade (2012). 'Establishing a New Global Economic Council: Governance Reform at the G20, the IMF and the World Bank'. *Global Policy* 3(3): 257–69.

Chapter 5
Global Risk Governance and G20, G8, and BRICS Capabilities

Marina V. Larionova, Mark Rakhmangulov, Andrei Sakharov,
Andrey Shelepov, and Vitaly Nagornov[1]

Global governance challenges generate a demand for global governance from multilateral international institutions that cannot be met by the available supply. The national priorities of the member states of international institutions also shape the demand for collective action. The institutions' capacity for forging consensus and making collective decisions can be transformed into global governance supply. The country chairing an institution should align both types of demand (global risks and members' priorities) with the capacity of the institution and its national priorities, interests, and capabilities. The chair should also be guided by a comparative assessment of the effectiveness of international institutions in dealing with specific global problems.

This approach enables the chair to elaborate an innovative agenda on the basis of comparative analysis of the capabilities of plurilateral summit institutions (PSIs) such as the Group of Seven or Eight (G7/8), the Group of 20 (G20), and the BRICS (Brazil, Russia, India, China, and South Africa) to respond to forecasted global challenges. Without constraining the chair's flexibility, it provides an opportunity to extend cooperation among presidencies, such as the G20 troika of outgoing, current, and incoming presidencies. It also helps enhance coordination across the institutions. Thus for Russia, scheduled to chair the G20 in 2013, the G8 in 2014, and the BRICS in 2015, a sequence of the three presidencies presented a unique opportunity to influence global processes balancing external conditions and national priorities.

This chapter offers a forward-looking, demand-responsive approach to PSI agenda setting and action taking, rather than the prevailing approach of focusing on core subjects, seeing what is undelivered, and shrinking or sinking the rest. It argues that each institution's work should address the risks and challenges most relevant to its missions and capabilities. The G20 agenda should focus on managing economic risks. The G7/8 should prioritize geopolitical and technological risks. The BRICS summit's innovative long-term agenda should address societal risks. Such an approach will serve as a solid foundation for a division of labour that maximizes the three institutions' contribution to overcoming failures in

---

1 This chapter draws on the research project on 'Elaborating a Supply-Demand Model to Balance External Demand and National Priorities in the Presidency Proposals for Agenda in G20, G8, and BRICS', Project No. 12-03-00563, with financial support from RFH – Russian Foundation for Humanities.

global governance. However, systemic risks arise, such as severe income disparity, the unforeseen negative consequences of regulation, the prolonged neglect of infrastructure, and extreme volatility in energy and agriculture prices. These risks demand cooperation and coordination among the G7/8, the G20, and the BRICS. A proper balance between cooperation and the division of labour will enhance the institutions' capabilities of managing global risks.

Methodology

To identify global challenges, this chapter draws on the findings of the seventh and eighth editions of the Global Risks reports published by the World Economic Forum (WEF2011, 2012).[2] This annual risk analysis for the forthcoming decade, an initiative of the WEF's Risk Response Network since 2006, was used because, first, it identifies the most important global problems and their interconnections, and contributes to understanding the shared goals of the international community and the three institutions under examination here. Second, the 2011 and 2012 WEF reports identified economic inequality and global governance failures as the most pressing risks. Those risks 'both influence the evolution of many other global risks and inhibit [the] capacity to respond effectively to them' (WEF 2011, 6). Global risk management is hindered by a twenty-first century paradox: 'the conditions that make improved global governance so crucial – divergent interests, conflicting incentives and differing norms and values – are also the ones that make its realization so difficult, complex and messy' (WEF 2011, 6). The G20 was regarded as 'the most hopeful development in global governance', but it has not proven its effectiveness (WEF 2011, 6).

All five risk categories identified – economic, societal, geopolitical, technological, and environmental – are on the G20, G7/8, and BRICS agendas. Better comprehension of the priorities and capabilities of each institution thus helps formulate proposals that can enhance the effectiveness of their governance. Additionally, the results of the foresight analysis of global risks can be an objective basis for supporting the presidency's positions and proposals for the institution's agenda, in discussions with its partners.

This chapter assesses the capabilities of the G20, the G7/8, and the BRICS in managing future risks. It draws on the analysis of the official documents and decisions made at summits and in other institutional formats. The 25 risks with the greatest number of 'impact and likelihood' indicators were analysed (see Appendix 5.A). They include seven environmental, seven geopolitical, six economic, four societal, and one technological risk. The documents that were analyzed were the G20 documents issued from the first summit in 2008 until 2013, all G8 documents issued between 1998 (the year that Russia joined the institution as an equal member) and 2013, and the BRICS documents issued between the foreign affairs ministers' meeting in 2008 and the summit in 2013. For the G8, the importance of a risk in the past was thus considered, but the assessment was primarily

---

2   Global Risks 2012, Seventh Edition, prepared by the Risk Response Network, has been used with the permission of the World Economic Forum.

based on risks included on the agenda between 2009 and 2013, after the start of the global financial crisis that led to new forms of cooperation and altered the agendas of the multilateral institutions.

The importance of an issue was assessed on a scale of one (low importance) to three (high importance). Importance was assessed as high if it was not only deliberated in the institution's documents and leaders agreed on a direction, but also if the leaders made specific commitments or created relevant special forms of cooperation within the institution. If a risk and associated collective action were identified, and specific commitments were made without implementation mechanisms, its importance was assessed as medium (a score of two). A low level of importance was attributed to those risks that were mentioned but not addressed by the leaders through concrete decisions or mandates.

First the global risk categories most relevant to each institution's mission were identified. Then the risks were verified and adjusted according to their level of importance for the current agendas. The categories were thus supplemented by the risks with the highest importance for each institution. The comparison of categories for each institution made it possible to offer recommendations for the G20, G7/8, and BRICS agendas that aspire to enhance their governance capabilities.

Global Risks

Expert assessments of 50 global risks were carried out in 2012. The likelihood and potential impact of each risk were estimated on a five-point scale (see Appendix 5.B).

A centre of gravity, which is the risk with the greatest systemic importance, was identified for category, as follows:

- *chronic fiscal imbalances (economic)*, exacerbated by unmanageable inflation or deflation, recurring liquidity crises, prolonged infrastructure neglect, chronic labour market imbalances, and the mismanagement of population aging;
- *greenhouse gas emissions (environmental)*, exacerbated by irremediable pollution, failure of climate change adaptation, and persistent extreme weather;
- *global governance failure (geopolitical)*, positioned at the centre of the system, exacerbating other systemically important risks, and affected by all other risks, particularly pervasive entrenched corruption, critical fragile states, failure of diplomatic conflict resolution, backlash against globalization, and terrorism;
- *unsustainable population growth (societal)*, related to unmanaged migration, mismanaged urbanization, unsettled problems in critical fragile states, mismanagement of population aging, food shortage crises, and land- and waterway-use mismanagement; and
- *critical systems failure (technological)*, exacerbated by cyber attacks, massive incidents of data fraud or theft, massive digital misinformation, terrorism, and prolonged infrastructure neglect.

The main clusters of the global risk system, which include risks in several categories, are linked by the 'critical connectors' of severe income disparity, major systemic financial failure, unforeseen negative consequences of regulation, and extreme volatility in energy and agriculture prices. All critical connectors fall under the economic category. The

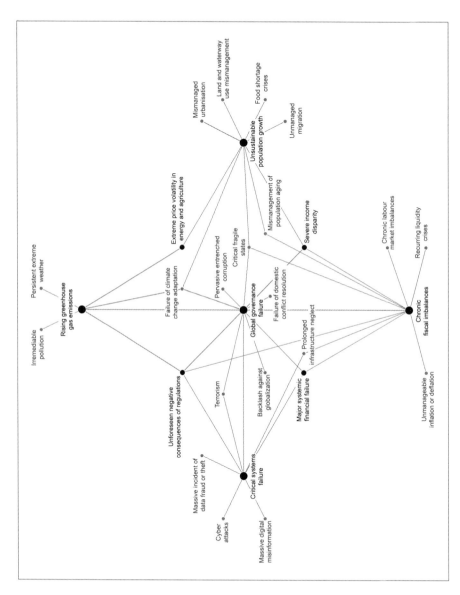

Figure 5.1 Global risks map

Note: Risks without strong connections are not shown.
Source: World Economic Forum (2012, 6).

interconnections within each category and among the risks from different categories are shown in Figure 5.1.

Global Risk Clusters in the Context of Each Institution

Global risk governance can be most effective if it is approached systemically. This means that the cooperation in the frameworks of the G20, the G7/8, and the BRICS should focus on each institution's relevant risk clusters. The central elements of each cluster are systemically important risks. The key risks connected with them, including the critically important ones, can belong to several clusters. Thus the risk of severe income disparity is a critical connector linking the economic, geopolitical, and societal clusters with chronic fiscal imbalances, global governance failure, and unsustainable population growth as the respective centres of gravity. Another example is the risk of a major systemic financial failure connecting the economic, geopolitical, and technological clusters, with critical systems failure as the centre of gravity in the latter. Extreme volatility in energy and agricultural prices is a critical connector linking the societal, geopolitical, and environmental clusters. The fourth critical connector – the risk of unforeseen negative consequences of regulation – links the technological, geopolitical, and environmental clusters. On such risks a decision is required regarding the institution's mode of cooperation, engagement, or division of labour. Such a systemic approach to risk clusters applies well to the G20 and G8 analysis, as illustrated below.

G20

The risk of chronic fiscal imbalances is the centre of gravity in the economic category. The chronic fiscal imbalances cluster contains all systemically important risks – critical connectors, as well as the risks of unmanageable inflation or deflation, recurring liquidity crises, prolonged infrastructure neglect, and chronic labour market imbalances (see Figure 5.2). All risks in this cluster belong to the economic category. The risk of global governance failure, which is at the core of the geopolitical risks category, is also included in the chronic imbalances cluster. Closely connected is the geopolitical risk of pervasive entrenched corruption, which is also included in the chronic fiscal imbalances cluster.

Economic risks have been a part of the G20 agenda since its start. G20 priorities include reforming the international monetary and financial system and finding new forms of financial sector regulation. While collective action aims at overcoming gaps in global governance, in strengthening existing regulations and creating new ones, the G20 pays insufficient attention to the risk of unforeseen negative consequences. In the run-up to the 2012 Los Cabos Summit, the Financial Stability Board ([FSB] 2012) presented a report to the G20 leaders on the potential unforeseen effects of regulatory reforms in emerging markets and developing economies. However, the Los Cabos documents did not contain any decisions on the recommendations and the matters discussed in the report. The declaration only mentioned the usefulness of further monitoring and a 'dialogue among the FSB, standard-setters, international financial institutions and national authorities of

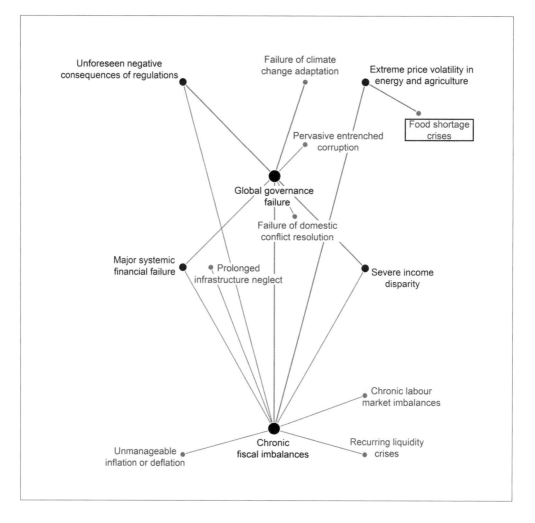

Figure 5.2 G20 global risks map
Note: The boxed risk has been added to the cluster, based on an analysis of G20 priorities and risk significance.
Source: Based on World Economic Forum (2012, 6).

EMDEs [emerging markets and developing economies], to address material unintended consequences as appropriate without prejudice to our commitment to implement the agreed reforms' (G20 2012). In St Petersburg in 2013, the leaders took a step further by inviting the FSB to monitor the impact of financial regulatory reforms on the supply of long-term investment financing (G20 2013b).

The systemic approach also requires the G20 to focus more on the issue of income disparity, which is not yet well established among its priorities. Income disparity was first raised during the French presidency in 2011 in the context of the 'social dimension of globalization' (G20 2011). However, no specific decisions followed. The issue was raised during the 2012 Mexican presidency in the context of stimulating employment.

At Los Cabos, the leaders recognized the importance of establishing at least minimal social protection floors in each country, but again made no commitments on this issue. The Global Partnership for Financial Inclusion, launched by the G20 at the 2010 Seoul Summit, approved the G20 Basic Set of Financial Inclusion Indicators in 2013, which can be considered a step toward reducing the income distribution gap. Yet here, too, no specific commitments were made.

In the St Petersburg declaration, the G20 leaders stated their resolve to promote inclusive growth, committed to increase efforts to support inclusive labour markets, and emphasized their determination to work together to achieve strong, sustainable, balanced, and inclusive growth (G20 2013b, 2013a). However, there is a need to strengthen G20 coordination and cooperation in reducing the income distribution gap both within and across countries, a need that was explicitly stated by the Civil 20 Task Force on Inequality (2013) in its proposals to combat economic inequality presented to the G20 during the Russian presidency.

Given the G20 priorities, the societal risk of food security has been added to the chronic fiscal imbalances cluster. This risk is linked to the critical connector, namely the economic risk of extreme volatility in energy and agriculture prices.

Therefore, the G20 core agenda, which focuses on overcoming economic risks, should be supplemented by cooperation that reduces the risk of growing income disparity. The unforeseen negative consequences of regulation merit the G20's unwavering attention, and efforts to overcome food shortage crises should be consolidated.

G8

The geopolitical risks cluster lies within the G7/8's focus (see Figure 5.3). It is based on the risk of global governance failure and encompasses four geopolitical risks: the failure of diplomatic conflict resolution, critical fragile states, terrorism, pervasive entrenched corruption, and one societal risk – the negative consequences of globalization. The cluster also includes three critical connectors from the economic category: income inequality, major systemic financial failure, and unforeseen negative consequences of regulation. Geopolitical and societal risks are among the G7/8's traditional priorities. Since the G20 leaders began meeting, the G20 has assumed the traditional G7/8 priority of fighting corruption. However, given that this risk is a major factor in overcoming global governance failure, it should also remain on the G7/8 agenda.

The interconnectedness between the geopolitical and the critically important economic risks suggests that the G7/8 should not abandon the economic agenda. At the 2012 Camp David Summit G8 leaders explicitly brought the economy back onto their agenda, devoting 29 per cent of their deliberations to the economy. This was a significant surge over previous years: 2.4 per cent in 2011, 0.34 per cent in 2010, 10.56 per cent in 2009, and 1.97 per cent in 2008. Their decisions mainly pertained to the areas of fiscal consolidation and structural reforms within members, aimed at facilitating economic recovery. At Lough Erne in 2013, G8 leaders expanded the economic agenda. They committed to taking action to restore confidence, encourage investment and job creation, support the recovery, and reduce global imbalances. They focused on facilitating trade, combatting tax evasion

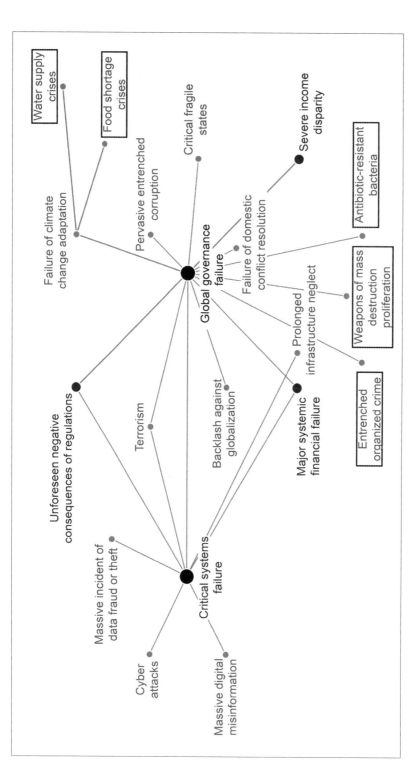

Figure 5.3 G7/8 global risks map

Note: The boxed risk has been added to the cluster, based on an analysis of G7/8 priorities and risk significance.
Source: Based on World Economic Forum (2012, 6).

and avoidance, raising global standards for transparency in the extractives industries, and increasing the supply of open government data across a number of key categories (G8 2013). However, they paid insufficient attention to the issues of income distribution, major systemic financial failure, and the unforeseen negative consequences of regulation.

Based on the analysis of G8 priorities, the geopolitical cluster was supplemented with the geopolitical risks of entrenched organized crime and the proliferation of weapons of mass destruction, the societal risks of water and food shortage, and the environmental risk of antibiotic-resistant bacteria.

While neither the G20 nor the G7/8 prioritize the risks of the unforeseen consequences of regulation and income disparity, it is evident that at least one of these institutions should take up these issues. There are two possible approaches. The first, given the division of labour between the G20 and the G7/8 in the areas where respective risk clusters belong, is to strengthen cooperation on overcoming these risks in the framework of the G20. G7/8 members would then focus their agenda on the geopolitical risks, while simultaneously working to resolve such issues as the income gap, major systemic financial failure, and the unforeseen consequences of regulation within the G20. These issues can also be prioritized on the G7/8 agenda when necessary.

The second approach is to include the issues of the unforeseen consequences of regulation and income disparity in the G7/8 agenda. The G7/8's overarching goal would thus be to overcome the risk of global governance failure, through the governance of geopolitical, societal, and economic risks.

The technological risks cluster can also contribute to a new G7/8 agenda. The critical systems failure risk is rapidly gaining prominence. After Japan's Fukushima disaster in March 2011, the G8 leaders called on the International Atomic Energy Agency to review existing standards and consider the development or upgrading of nuclear power plants and operating requirements in seismically hazardous or otherwise dangerous areas. This risk, however, relates to critically important systems in addition to nuclear security. Information systems security, for example, was addressed by the G8 at the 2011 Deauville Summit in the context of ensuring network and service security on the internet.

This cluster includes the technological risks of massive digital misinformation, cyber attacks, and massive incidents of data fraud or theft, the geopolitical risk of terrorism, and the economic risk of infrastructure neglect. It also includes two critically important economic risks: major systemic financial failure and the unforeseen negative consequences of regulation. The technological risks cluster is closely connected to the geopolitical risks cluster. Thus, these two interconnected clusters can form the G7/8's agenda priorities. The key political and security issues on the G7/8 agenda should therefore be complemented by cooperation aimed at reducing the risks of the technological cluster.

BRICS

The BRICS agenda encompasses all three risk clusters (see Figure 5.4). However, unlike the G7/8 and the G20, the BRICS agenda is significantly diffused across the clusters and the priority level of each risk on the agenda differs drastically.

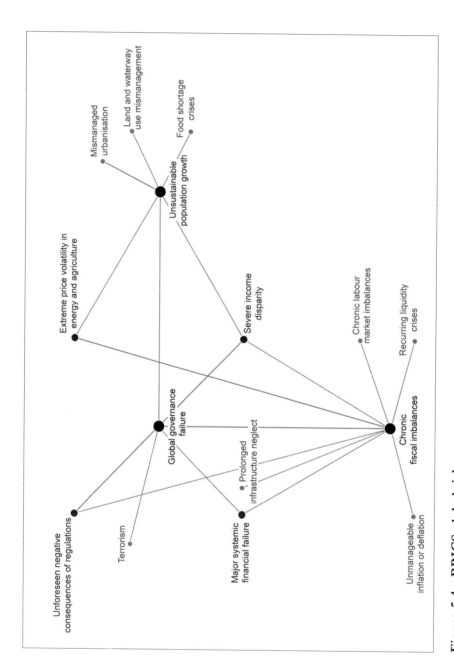

Figure 5.4 BRICS global risks map
Source: World Economic Forum (2012, 6).

The BRICS countries have strengthened their coordination on financial and economic issues in the post-crisis period. Thus their agenda focuses on the chronic fiscal imbalances risk at the centre of the economic category. The BRICS countries, which do not experience chronic fiscal imbalances but regard this risk as a global threat, coordinate their positions on this agenda. They and their fellow G20 members 'designated the G20 to be the premier forum for [their] international economic cooperation' (G20 2009). As a result, the task of governing the economic risks cluster is on the agenda of both the BRICS and the G20. For the BRICS, decisions are made within a highly restricted membership, which justifies the group's perception as a political forum for coordinating members' positions within the G20. This strategy is viable from the point of view of the BRICS members, but it can produce distrust of the forum among other countries, including other G20 members. The establishment of the BRICS as a global governance institution demands its own positive agenda, aimed at creating global public goods.

Given the analysis of global risks, the BRICS agenda should prioritize the governance of the societal risks cluster, with the unsustainable population growth risk as the centre of gravity. That cluster also includes the societal risk of food shortages and the environmental risks of uncontrolled urbanization and the mismanagement of land and waterway use. It is also connected with the two critically important economic risks of commodity price volatility and income disparity, which are already on the BRICS agenda. The dialogue on urbanization management started under India's presidency at the 2012 Delhi Summit and led to the launch of the BRICS Urbanization Forum. Land- and waterway-use management was touched upon at the first BRIC summit in Yekaterinburg in 2009, before South Africa became a member, in the context of discussions on the effects of changing agro-ecological conditions on food security. Both issues continue to be discussed by senior BRICS officials on the margins of relevant international forums related to sustainable development, the environment, and climate. The relevance of these risks increases in relation to the infrastructure development goals faced by the BRICS countries and other developing economies. The quality of the management of natural and land resources could become one criterion for infrastructure development projects selected by the BRICS Development Bank, given that its purpose is to raise 'resources for infrastructure and sustainable development projects in BRICS and other emerging economies and developing countries' (BRICS 2013).

Thus, without relinquishing its core cooperation priorities of improving global governance and coordination on governance of the chronic fiscal imbalances risks cluster, the BRICS can shape a long-term innovative agenda to control all the societal risks.

Conclusion: Proposals for the G20, G7/8, and BRICS Agendas

This analysis of the key global risks and the missions of the G20, G7/8, and BRICS, and the capabilities of those institutions to manage key challenges in global governance leads to several conclusions for their effectiveness.

First, each institution should direct its efforts to reducing the risks from the categories most relevant to its mission and capabilities. The G20 agenda should thus focus on

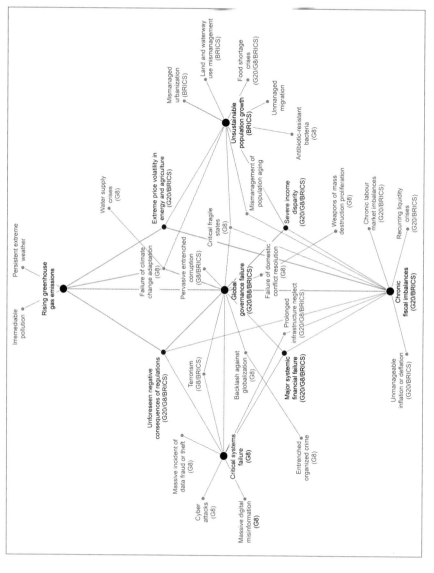

Figure 5.5 Map of G20, G7/8, and BRICS global risks and priorities

Note: Priorities are identified based on an analysis of the missions, capabilities, and agenda of each institutions and the authors' recommendations.

Source: Based on World Economic Forum (2012, 6).

managing economic risks; the G7/8 should prioritize geopolitical and technological risks; and the BRICS should develop a long-term agenda that addresses societal risks.

Second, the agenda of each institution should integrate the relevant risk categories that have been neglected or inadequately addressed; otherwise these risks and their categories will increase and be aggravated in the future.

Third, the G7/8 agenda should include technological risks, particularly critical systems failure. The agenda can be strengthened by supplementing the geopolitical priorities with economic centres of gravity such as major systemic financial failure and severe income disparity.

Fourth, the G20 economic agenda can be strengthened by including severe income disparity and the unforeseen negative consequences of regulation, and by increased attention to the societal risk of food shortage crises and economic risk of extreme price volatility in energy and agriculture.

Fifth, the BRICS agenda should focus on managing the societal risks of unsustainable population growth and food shortage crises and on the environmental risks of mismanaged urbanization and the mismanagement of land and waterway use.

Sixth, a category-based approach should be taken to provide a solid foundation for dividing the labour among these three summit institutions according to the different risk categories, in order to maximize each institution's contribution to overcoming global governance failures. Areas of cooperation, primarily on the most systemically important critical connectors, should be defined (see Figure 5.5). Several risks are already on the agenda of all three institutions, including global governance failure and major systemic financial failure. The economic risks of recurring liquidity crises, unmanageable inflation or deflation, chronic labour market imbalances, and extreme price volatility in energy and agriculture are already on the G20 and BRICS agendas; corruption is on the G7/8 and BRICS agendas; and the issue of food shortage crises is on both the G20 and G7/8 agendas.

Seventh, cooperation and coordination should be ensured among the G20, the G7/8, and the BRICS on the critical connectors of severe income disparity, the unforeseen negative consequences of regulation, and the prolonged neglect of infrastructure, which fall in both the economic and technological categories.

A proper balance between cooperation and the division of labour will enhance the capabilities of all three institutions in managing global risks.

References

BRICS (2013). 'BRICS and Africa: Partnership for Development, Integration, and Industralisation'. Durban, March 27. http://www.brics.utoronto.ca/docs/130327-state ment.html (December 2014).

Civil 20 Task Force on Inequality (2013). 'Civil 20 Proposals for Strong, Sustainable, Balanced and Inclusive Growth'. Civil 20, Moscow. http://www.g20.utoronto.ca/c20/ C20_proposals_2013_final.pdf (December 2014).

Financial Stability Board (2012). 'Identifying the Effects of Regulatory Reforms on Emerging Market and Developing Economies: A Review of Potential Unintended

Consequences'. Report to the G20 Finance Ministers and Central Bank Governors, June 19, Basel. http://www.financialstabilityboard.org/publications/r_120619e.pdf (December 2014).

G8 (2013). 'Lough Erne Declaration'. Lough Erne, Northern Ireland, United Kingdom, June 18. http://www.g8.utoronto.ca/summit/2013lougherne/lough-erne-declaration. html (December 2014).

G20 (2009). 'G20 Leaders Statement: The Pittsburgh Summit'. Pittsburgh, September 25. http://www.g20.utoronto.ca/2009/2009communique0925.html (December 2014).

G20 (2011). 'Communiqué: G20 Leaders Summit'. Cannes, November 4. http://www.g20. utoronto.ca/2011/2011-cannes-communique-111104-en.html (December 2014).

G20 (2012). 'G20 Leaders Declaration'. Los Cabos, June 19. http://www.g20.utoronto. ca/2012/2012-0619-loscabos.html (December 2014).

G20 (2013a). 'G20 5th Anniversary Vision Statement'. St Petersburg, September 6. http:// www.g20.utoronto.ca/2013/2013-0906-vision.html (December 2014).

G20 (2013b). 'G20 Leaders Declaration'. St Petersburg, September 6. http://www.g20. utoronto.ca/2013/2013-0906-declaration.html (December 2014).

World Economic Forum (2011). 'Global Risks 2011, Sixth Edition'. Davos. http://reports. weforum.org/global-risks-2011/ (December 2014).

World Economic Forum (2012). 'Global Risks 2012, Seventh Edition'. Davos. http:// reports.weforum.org/global-risks-2012/ (December 2014).

Appendix 5.A: Assessments of global risk importance in G20, G8, and BRICS documents

G20

Domain	Risk	Score
Economic	Chronic fiscal imbalances	3
Economic	Extreme volatility in energy and agriculture prices	3
Economic	Major systemic financial failure	3
Economic	Recurring liquidity crises	3
Economic	Chronic labour market imbalances	3
Geopolitical	Pervasive entrenched corruption	3
Geopolitical	Global governance failure	3
Societal	Food shortage crises	3
Environmental	Rising greenhouse gas emissions	2
Economic	Severe income disparity	1
Environmental	Failure of climate change adaptation	1
Environmental	Land- and waterway-use mismanagement	1
Environmental	Irremediable pollution	1
Geopolitical	Terrorism	1
Geopolitical	Critical fragile states	1
Geopolitical	Entrenched organized crime	1
Societal	Water supply crises	1
Societal	Mismanagement of population aging	1
Environmental	Antibiotic-resistant bacteria	0
Environmental	Mismanaged urbanization	0
Environmental	Persistent extreme weather	0
Geopolitical	Failure of diplomatic conflict resolution	0
Geopolitical	Proliferation of weapons of mass destruction	0
Societal	Rising religious fanaticism	0
Technological	Cyber attacks	0

G8

Domain	Risk	Score
Environmental	Antibiotic-resistant bacteria	3
Geopolitical	Terrorism	3
Geopolitical	Critical fragile states	3
Geopolitical	Global governance failure	3
Geopolitical	Failure of diplomatic conflict resolution	3
Geopolitical	Entrenched organized crime	3
Geopolitical	Proliferation of weapons of mass destruction	3
Societal	Water supply crises	3
Societal	Food shortage crises	3
Economic	Chronic fiscal imbalances	2
Economic	Severe income disparity	2

Domain	Risk	Score
Economic	Chronic labour market imbalances	2
Environmental	Rising greenhouse gas emissions	2
Environmental	Failure of climate change adaptation	2
Environmental	Persistent extreme weather	2
Environmental	Irremediable pollution	2
Societal	Mismanagement of population aging	2
Technological	Cyber attacks	2
Economic	Extreme volatility in energy and agriculture prices	1
Economic	Major systemic financial failure	1
Economic	Recurring liquidity crises	1
Environmental	Land- and waterway-use mismanagement	1
Geopolitical	Pervasive entrenched corruption	1
Societal	Rising religious fanaticism	1
Environmental	Mismanaged urbanization	0

BRICS

Domain	Risk	Score
Economic	Chronic fiscal imbalances	3
Economic	Severe income disparity	3
Geopolitical	Global governance failure	3
Societal	Food shortage crises	3
Economic	Extreme volatility in energy and agriculture prices	2
Economic	Major systemic financial failure	2
Economic	Chronic labour market imbalances	2
Environmental	Rising greenhouse gas emissions	2
Environmental	Antibiotic-resistant bacteria	2
Environmental	Mismanaged urbanization	2
Environmental	Irremediable pollution	2
Geopolitical	Terrorism	2
Geopolitical	Failure of diplomatic conflict resolution	2
Geopolitical	Proliferation of weapons of mass destruction	2
Economic	Recurring liquidity crises	1
Environmental	Failure of climate change adaptation	1
Environmental	Land- and waterway-use mismanagement	1
Societal	Water supply crises	1
Technological	Cyber attacks	1
Environmental	Persistent extreme weather	0
Geopolitical	Pervasive entrenched corruption	0
Geopolitical	Critical fragile states	0
Geopolitical	Entrenched organized crime	0
Societal	Mismanagement of population aging	0
Societal	Rising religious fanaticism	0

Appendix 5.B: Global risks: Descriptions and expert assessments, 2012

	Risk	Description	Impact	Likelihood	Sum
Economic					
1	Chronic fiscal imbalances	Failure to redress excessive government debt obligations	387	403	79
2	Severe income disparity	Widening gaps between the richest and poorest citizens	374	403	777
3	Extreme volatility in energy and agriculture prices	Severe price fluctuations make critical commodities unaffordable, slow growth, provoke public protest, and increase geopolitical tension	381	363	744
4	Major systemic financial failure	A financial institution or currency regime of systemic importance collapses with implications throughout the global financial system	408	314	722
5	Recurring liquidity crises	Recurring shortages of financial resources from banks and capital markets	362	349	711
6	Chronic labour market imbalances	A sustained high level of unemployment that is structural rather than cyclical, coinciding with a rising skills gap and high underemployment, especially among youth	336	341	677
7	Prolonged infrastructure neglect	Chronic failure to adequately invest in, upgrade, and secure infrastructure networks	326	332	658
8	Unmanageable inflation or deflation	Failure to redress extreme rise or fall in the value of money relative to prices and wages	345	282	627
9	Hard landing of an emerging economy	The abrupt slowdown of a critical emerging economy	312	307	619
10	Unforeseen negative consequences of regulations	Regulations that do not achieve the desired effect and instead negatively affect industry structures, capital flows, and market competition	277	304	581
Environmental					
11	Rising greenhouse gas emissions	Governments, businesses, and consumers fail to reduce greenhouse gas emissions and expand carbon sinks	362	388	75
12	Failure of climate change adaptation	Governments and business fail to enforce or enact effective measures to protect populations and transition businesses affected by climate change	36	361	721

	Risk	Description	Impact	Likelihood	Sum
13	Land- and waterway-use mismanagement	Deforestation, waterway diversion, mineral extraction, and other environment modifying projects with devastating impacts on ecosystems and associated industries	347	36	707
14	Antibiotic-resistant bacteria	Growing resistance of deadly bacteria to known antibiotics	348	352	7
15	Mismanaged urbanization	Poorly planned cities, urban sprawl, and associated infrastructure that amplify drivers of environmental degradation and cope ineffectively with rural exodus	325	364	689
16	Persistent extreme weather	Increasing damage linked to greater concentration of property in risk zones, urbanization, or increased frequency of extreme weather events	347	34	687
17	Irremediable pollution	Air, water, or land permanently contaminated to a degree that threatens ecosystems, social stability, health outcomes, and economic development	349	326	675
18	Species overexploitation	Threat of irreversible biodiversity loss through species extinction or ecosystem collapse	306	353	659
19	Unprecedented geophysical destruction	Geophysical disasters such as earthquakes and volcanic activity of unparalleled magnitude or unforeseen frequency that overwhelm existing precautions	339	286	625
20	Vulnerability to geomagnetic storms	Critical communication and navigation systems disabled by effects from colossal solar flares	294	275	569

Geopolitical

	Risk	Description	Impact	Likelihood	Sum
21	Terrorism	Individuals or a non-state group successfully inflict large-scale human or material damage	367	359	726
22	Pervasive entrenched corruption	The widespread and deep-rooted abuse of entrusted power for private gain	341	371	712
23	Critical fragile states	A weak state of high economic and geopolitical importance that faces strong likelihood of collapse	344	368	712
24	Global governance failure	Weak or inadequate global institutions, agreements, or networks, combined with competing national and political interests, impede attempts to cooperate on addressing global risks	372	333	705
25	Failure of diplomatic conflict resolution	The escalation of international disputes into armed conflicts	352	338	69

GLOBAL RISK GOVERNANCE AND G20, G8, AND BRICS CAPABILITIES

	Risk	**Description**	**Impact**	**Likelihood**	**Sum**
26	Entrenched organized crime	Highly organized, disciplined, and deep-rooted global networks, committing criminal offences	322	347	669
27	Proliferation of weapons of mass destruction	The availability of nuclear, chemical, biological, and radiological technologies and materials leads to crises	378	288	666
28	Widespread illicit trade	Unchecked spread of illegal trafficking of goods and people throughout the global economy	304	338	642
29	Unilateral resource nationalization	Unilateral moves by states to ban exports of key commodities, stockpile reserves, and expropriate natural resources	301	315	616
30	Militarization of space	Targeting of commercial, civil, and military space assets and related ground systems as core to defence strategy	29	265	555

Societal

31	Water supply crises	Decline in the quality and quantity of fresh water combined with increased competition among resource-intensive systems, such as food and energy production	399	379	778
32	Food shortage crises	Inadequate or unreliable access to appropriate quantities and quality of food and nutrition	393	358	751
33	Mismanagement of population aging	Failure to address both the rising costs and social challenges associated with population aging	336	343	679
34	Rising religious fanaticism	Uncompromising sectarian views that polarize societies and exacerbate regional tensions	351	328	679
35	Vulnerability to pandemics	Inadequate disease surveillance systems, failed international coordination, and the lack of vaccine production capacity	351	315	666
36	Unsustainable population growth	Population size and its rate of growth create intense and rising pressure on resources, public institutions, and social stability	355	304	659
37	Unmanaged migration	Mass migration driven by resource scarcity, environmental degradation, and lack of opportunity, security, or social stability	328	327	655
38	Rising rates of chronic disease	Increasing burden of illness and long-term costs of treatment threaten recent societal gains in life expectancy and quality	325	329	654

	Risk	Description	Impact	Likelihood	Sum
39	Backlash against globalization	Resistance to further increased cross-border mobility of labour, goods, and capital	31	314	624
40	Ineffective drug policies	Continued support for policies that do not abate illegal drug use but do embolden criminal organizations, stigmatize drug users and exhaust public resources	292	324	616

Technological

	Risk	Description	Impact	Likelihood	Sum
41	Cyber attacks	State-sponsored, state-affiliated, criminal, or terrorist cyber attacks	345	38	725
42	Massive incident of data fraud or theft	Criminal or wrongful exploitation of private data on an unprecedented scale	322	34	662
43	Critical systems failure	Single-point system vulnerabilities trigger cascading failure of critical information infrastructure and networks	368	294	662
44	Mineral resource supply vulnerability	Growing dependence of industries on minerals that are not widely sourced with long extraction-to-market time lag for new sources	323	327	65
45	Massive digital misinformation	Deliberately provocative, misleading, or incomplete information disseminates rapidly and extensively with dangerous consequences	314	319	633
46	Unintended consequences of climate change mitigation	Attempts at geo-engineering or renewable energy development result in new complex challenges	305	28	585
47	Unintended consequences of new life science technologies	Advances in genetics and synthetic biology produce unintended consequences or mishaps or are used as weapons	307	278	585
48	Failure of intellectual property regime	Ineffective intellectual property protections undermine research and development, innovation, and investment	274	303	577
49	Unintended consequences of nanotechnology	The manipulation of matter on an atomic or molecular level raises concerns on nanomaterial toxicity	291	267	558
50	Proliferation of orbital debris	Rapidly accumulating debris in high-traffic geocentric orbits jeopardizes critical satellite infrastructure	253	299	552

PART III
Achievements

Chapter 6

Assessing G7/8 and G20 Effectiveness in Global Governance

Marina V. Larionova, Mark Rakhmangulov, and Andrey Shelepov[1]

As the global community reflects on the contentious outcomes of the summits of the Group of 20 (G20) and looks to future presidencies to come up with ambitious agendas, the legitimacy and effectiveness of both the G20 and the Group of Seven (G7) and the Group of Eight (G8) are put to the test.

The G20's claim to serve as the premier forum for its members' international economic cooperation needs to be supported by its ability to show political leadership in steering the world to a new international order, deliver on its pledges, account for decisions made at its summits, and engage with a wide range of partners. The G20's early success in managing the global financial crisis does not predetermine its role as a global governance steering committee. Although it may have eclipsed the smaller group, assertions of the demise of the G7/8 are premature. Much qualitative analysis supports the sometimes contradictory perspectives on the future of G7/8 and G20 summitry.

This chapter attempts to put both institutions within the same assessment paradigm using a functional approach. This approach allows a comparison of the G7/8 and G20 across three groups of indicators: the performance of global governance functions, accountability, and compliance; contribution to the global governance agenda; and engagement with other international institutions.[2] It thus contributes to a quantifiable evidence base for assessing the effectiveness of these two institutions and informing the forecast of their future roles.

This analysis looks at the balance and dynamics of the main global governance functions of deliberation, direction setting, decision making, delivery, and the development of global governance as expressed in G7/8 and G20 documents, including summit declarations, ministerial statements, progress reports, and material issued by officials and working groups.[3] Contribution to the global governance agenda was assessed on the basis of comparative weights of the key issues in G8 and G20 documents, the dynamics of

---

1   This chapter draws on the research project on 'Elaborating a Supply-Demand Model to Balance External Demand and National Priorities in the Presidency Proposals for Agenda in G20, G8, and BRICS', Project No. 12-03-00563, with financial support from RFH – Russian Foundation for Humanities.

2   On the functions of global governance, see John J. Kirton (2006, 2013).

3   The database includes 243 documents: 154 issued by the G7/8 (55 issued by the leaders and 99 by ministers, working groups, or other bodies) and 89 issued by the G20 (45 issued by the leaders and 44 by ministers, working groups, or other bodies).

their agendas, and responsiveness to new challenges. Finally, the contribution of the two groups to effective multilateralism was assessed on the basis of the intensity and modes of engagement with other multilateral institutions on key priorities and values. The analysis covers the period from 2008, when the G20 leaders first began meeting, to 2013.[4]

Dynamics of Global Governance Functions

The analysis of the performance of global governance functions was conducted using absolute and relative data on the number of inclusions and characters (including spaces and punctuation marks) relating to a certain function in the text. Relative parameters were defined as the share of the function in the total of all functions and expressed in percentages. An inclusion was defined as a word or passage expressing a function.

The G20 has assumed and effectively shared with the G7/8 the global governance functions of deliberation, direction setting, and decision making. The G20 summits in Washington DC in November 2008 and London in April 2009 contributed significantly to the development of global governance (in terms of the international financial architecture). London set the trend for delivery, reinforced in Pittsburgh in September 2009 and consolidated in Toronto and Seoul in June and November 2010 respectively. The share of delivery in the G20 discourse dropped from 43 per cent in Seoul to 13 per cent in Cannes in 2011, before increasing to 28 per cent in Los Cabos in 2012, in a push for transparency and efficiency, and then peaking at 51 per cent at the 2013 St Petersburg Summit. Accountability has been extended from several core issues of the financial reform agenda to include most of the priorities. Thus, for the St Petersburg Summit the G20 accounted for progress in such policy areas as fiscal policy, monetary and exchange rate policies, structural reforms, financial sector reforms, job creation, development, and anticorruption.

Nevertheless, overall the G20 was still significantly less effective on delivery than the G8, with an average of 36 per cent compared to the G8's 54 per cent for the period under study.

The data on each function allow a comparison of G8 performance in the decade before the crisis and the emergence of the leaders-level G20 and afterward until 2013. It is also possible to compare the G8 and G20's relative emphasis on their respective functions and to assess where each of the summits stood against the institution's average for the period (see Figure 6.1).

As indicated in Figure 6.2, the financial crisis shocked both institutions into action. G8 deliberation dropped by more than a half, from an average of 42 per cent to 16 per cent. Even in the voluminous L'Aquila documents only 30 per cent of the text was devoted to deliberation, whereas the laconic Muskoka Summit pushed it down to 7 per cent, the lowest for the period studied. At Deauville and Camp David, deliberation increased to

---

4   It therefore covers the period from 1998, when Russia began participating in the G8 summit as a full member until 2013, before the G7 leaders started meeting again without Russia, in 2014.

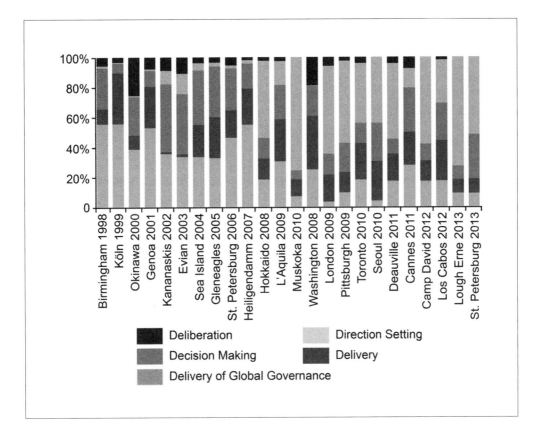

Figure 6.1 G8 and G20 global governance functions, 1998–2013

17 per cent each, still much lower than the pre-crisis average of 42 per cent, and declined to 9 per cent in Lough Erne, where the discourse was dominated by delivery (73 per cent).

At their first summit in Washington, G20 leaders needed to establish a shared language. A quarter of their declaration was devoted to deliberation, moving on to direction setting (36 per cent) and decision making (20 per cent). The leaders agreed on principles and an action plan for financial market reforms, and actions to reform the international financial institutions (IFIs) and reinforce cooperation, with the highest level of global governance development of 19 per cent in the G20 and in the G8 since 1998, except the 2000 Okinawa Summit. Deliberation in the G20 discourse dropped abruptly to 4 per cent in London, as the leaders focused on delivery. It rose slightly in Pittsburgh and even more in Toronto, reflecting the focus on the Framework for Strong, Sustainable, and Balanced Growth. In Seoul the leaders were able to move forward with the Seoul Action Plan, which contained comprehensive, cooperative, and country-specific policy actions, as well as the Multi-Year Action Plan on Development, building on Toronto. Deliberation on the future of global governance in Cannes brought the G20 a historic peak of 28 per cent. Deliberation declined to 17 per cent at Los Cabos, and further to 9 per cent at St Petersburg. These

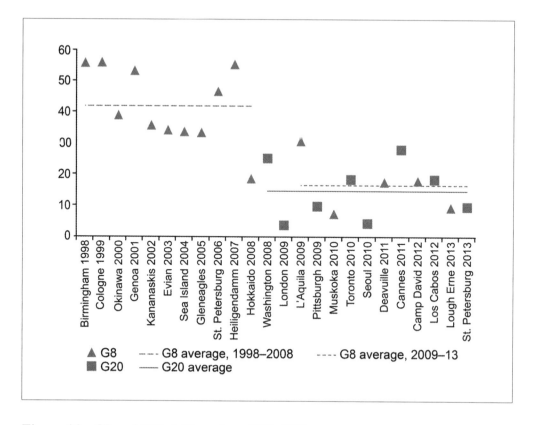

Figure 6.2 G8 and G20 deliberation, 1998–2013

trends clearly reflect the need for deliberation in search of shared responses to persistent and new challenges, and the role of deliberation in forging decisions.

On direction setting, G8 performance remained steady, dropping slightly from an average of 17 per cent from 1998 to 2008 to a 16 per cent average in the post-crisis period, mostly as a result of L'Aquila and Deauville. The G20's average performance was higher (see Figure 6.3). The G20 Toronto declaration set out a substantial number of mandates and preparatory work to be implemented by Seoul. Seoul took over, agreeing on the need for further work on macro-prudential policy frameworks and regulatory reform, and on strengthening regulation and supervision, improving market integrity and efficiency, fighting protectionism, and promoting trade and investment. The Seoul Development Consensus for Shared Growth outlined G20 development principles as a basis for decisions specified in the Multi-Year Action Plan on Development. At Cannes the G20 emphasized the social dimension of globalization, prioritizing employment and social inclusion. Los Cabos expanded G20 coordination on employment and social protection issues, recognizing the importance of nationally determined social protection floors. The leaders continued their dialogue on inclusive green growth in the context of development and economic goals.

ASSESSING G7/8 AND G20 EFFECTIVENESS IN GLOBAL GOVERNANCE

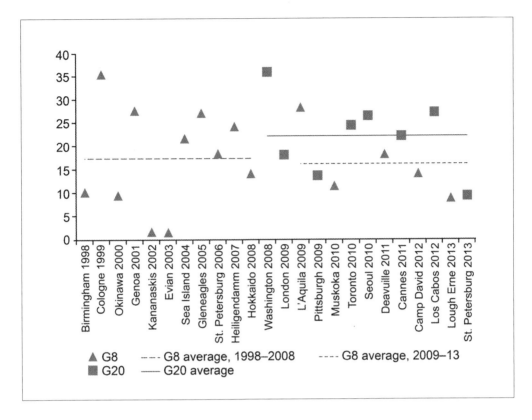

Figure 6.3 G8 and G20 direction setting, 1998–2013

At St Petersburg, direction setting dropped to 9 per cent, covering issues such as managing debt, financing investment, and addressing base erosion and profit shifting (BEPS). The St Petersburg Strategic Framework for the G20 Anti-Corruption Working Group and the principles on mutual legal assistance, combating solicitation, and enforcing foreign bribery offences aimed to strengthen the fight against corruption, while the St Petersburg Development Outlook framed a new approach to development, building on the Seoul Development Consensus.

Decision making in G8 documents declined after Kananaskis, when it reached almost 46 per cent (see Figure 6.4). The leaders agreed on actions to deliver on the promise of the Enhanced Heavily Indebted Poor Countries Initiative, support the objectives of Education for All and the New Partnership for Africa's Development (NEPAD), launch the new G8 Global Partnership against the Spread of Weapons and Materials of Mass Destruction, and promote greater security of land, sea, and air transport. The pre-crisis Heiligendamm and Hokkaido summits fell well below average to 17 per cent and 14 per cent respectively. Although decision making in the crisis-hit L'Aquila increased to almost 23 per cent, which is higher than the G20 average, it fell to 6 per cent in Muskoka, and increased only marginally subsequently in Deauville (10 per cent), Camp David

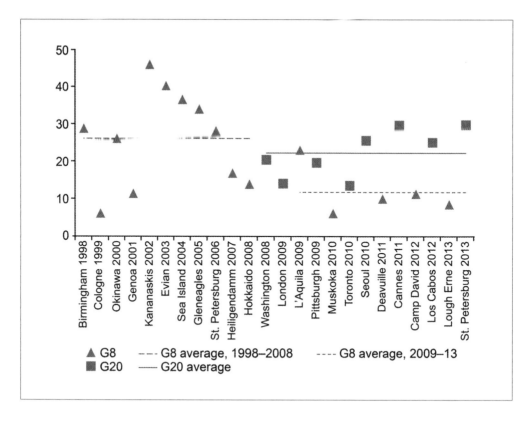

Figure 6.4 G8 and G20 decision making, 1998–2013

(11 per cent), and Lough Erne (8 per cent), remaining well below the G8 average of 26 per cent in the decade before the crisis.

However, this trend cannot be attributed solely to the decline in the G8's capacity to forge decisions. Enhanced attention to accountability and the expansion of the delivery function after 2002 were also factors (see Figure 6.5). Accountability was pronounced at Hokkaido and L'Aquila, culminating at Muskoka with a score of 75 per cent and the 'Muskoka Accountability Report', and remaining a priority at Deauville (51 per cent), Camp David (56 per cent), and Lough Erne (73 per cent). From L'Aquila to Lough Erne, the G8 mandated and submitted 14 reports. This new focus changed the balance of functions.

The delivery function, which emerged in 2002 and subsequently expanded in the G8, was present in the G20 after its second summit in London. G20 members resorted to two main mechanisms of accountability and performance enhancement: progress reports and compliance catalysts embedded in the summit declarations. The G20's preference was to mandate ministers or working groups to report on an agreed target by a specified forthcoming meeting. In 2009, the British presidency prepared four progress reports, delivered in March 2009, April 2009 on the eve of the London Summit, in the ministerial meetings in September, and, finally, in November. After that reporting on delivery became an established practice, expanding from the core financial reform issues to

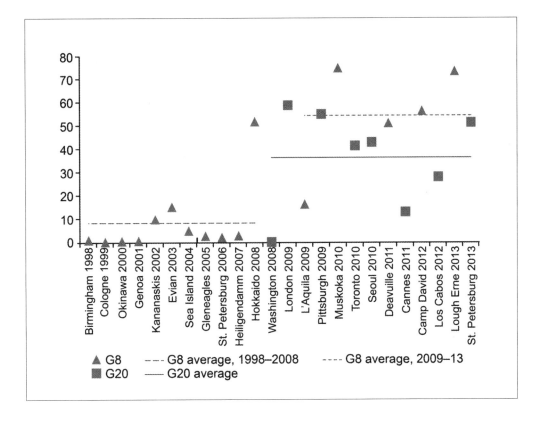

Figure 6.5 G8 and G20 delivery, 1998–2013

include development, agriculture, clean energy, and anticorruption, reflecting the G20's mission creep. The number of the reports prepared between the 2009 London Summit and the 2013 St Petersburg Summit totalled 25. In 16 of those reports, most data were presented in an aggregated form. However, after Los Cabos G20 members reported their progress on individual commitments to achieve strong, sustainable, and balanced growth (see G20 2013a, 2013b, 2013c, 2013d). The G20 thus subjected its performance to accountability mechanisms: accountability constitutes almost 36 per cent of the volume of G20 documents. However, it remained a highly sophisticated but low-key exercise. Nevertheless, there is clear evidence that the G20 as well as the G8 increasingly heeded the need for more accountability.

One measure of the contribution of both the G8 and G20 to the development of global governance is the share of their discourse devoted to that function. Another measure is their contribution to establishing new institutions and mechanisms of cooperation, and formulating new mandates to existing institutions, through decisions made at summits.

The G20 made crucial decisions on reforming financial markets and regulatory regimes, as well as IFI reform at its first leaders' meeting. At London the leaders established the Financial Stability Board (FSB), with a strengthened mandate, as a successor to the Financial

Stability Forum. The FSB includes all G20 countries, the members of the Financial Stability Forum, Spain, and the European Commission, as well as the Bank for International Settlements, the World Bank, the IMF, the Organisation for Economic Co-operation and Development (OECD), and several standard-setting bodies. At Pittsburgh the leaders launched the Framework for Strong, Sustainable, and Balanced Growth, and designated the G20 as the premier forum for their international economic cooperation. Moreover, they detailed the mechanisms for strengthening the international financial regulatory system in cooperation with international institutions, and committed to reforming the mandate, mission, and governance of the IMF and multilateral development banks (MDBs). At Toronto the leaders pledged to act together to achieve the commitments to reform the financial sector made at the Washington, London, and Pittsburgh summits and agreed on the next steps on financial sector reform, with regard to the MDBs, the World Bank, and the IMF. They set the Seoul Summit as their target date for delivery.

Seoul's achievements were numerous and diverse, including enhancing the framework's Mutual Assessment Process (MAP) by indicative guidelines composed of a range of indicators to facilitate the timely identification of large imbalances, shifting the IMF quota shares to dynamic emerging market and developing economies and to under-represented countries to more than 6 per cent, creating the precautionary credit line, and agreeing on the Seoul Development Consensus and the Multi-Year Action Plan on Development. At Cannes the discourse focused on the future of global governance and the G20's (2011) capability 'to build and sustain the political consensus needed to respond to challenges, remain efficient, transparent and accountable'. The leaders also committed to improving market information and transparency through new initiatives such as the Agricultural Market Information System and the Global Agricultural Geo-monitoring Initiative. The G20 Principles for Cooperation between the IMF and Regional Financing Arrangements and the G20 Action Plan to Support the Development of Local Currency Bond Markets were endorsed by G20 finance ministers and central bank governors. At Los Cabos G20 members agreed on the Accountability Assessment Framework. At St Petersburg, they endorsed the development of a new global tax standard as well as the principles of long-term investment financing by financial institutional investors. The Anti-Corruption Working Group was confirmed as a permanent body. The G20's contribution to global governance development remained at an average of about 5 per cent, whereas in the G8 documents it dropped from 7 per cent in the 1998–2008 pre-crisis period to 2 per cent (see Figure 6.6).

The data on mandates to other international institutions confirm that G20 took the lead on the development of global governance. Although the number of mandates ranged from 15 at Washington to 79 at St Petersburg, it increased steadily, and G20 leaders agreed to a total of 341 mandates (see Figure 6.7). Over the same period the G8 agreed to 91 mandates.

While the G8 and G20 summits coexisted, the G20 demonstrated a higher capacity for direction setting, decision making, and the development of global governance. The G8 remained a forum for the leaders' deliberation, where decision making is reinforced by the institution's accountability. However, there is a gap between broadly formulated decisions and concrete commitments, as well as between commitments and compliance

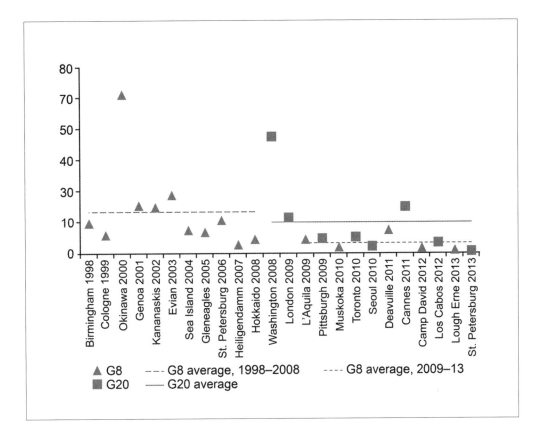

Figure 6.6 G8 and G20 development of global governance, 1998–2013

performance. On the number of commitments from 2008 to 2013, the G8 surpassed the G20, although after the global financial crisis and the advent of the G20 summit, the G8 made comparatively few commitments at Muskoka (see Figure 6.8). At subsequent summits, the number increased, but did not reach the pre-crisis level. The G20 made an increasing number of commitments, peaking at 282 at Cannes and remaining higher than average at the two subsequent summits.

The proof of effectiveness rests on compliance, and the compliance performance is a good indicator of the institutions' comparative strengths in that regard. The same methodology was used to assess the compliance performance of both the G20 and G8.[5] The findings, although mixed so far, indicate that compliance has been picking up (see Figure 6.9). Notwithstanding substantial differences in compliance scores by issue or individual commitments, G20 compliance increased from summit to summit between 2008 and 2012, reaching +0.56 on the Los Cabos commitments, much higher than +0.27 on the Toronto commitments, +0.24 on the Pittsburgh commitments, and +0.23 on the

---

5   A detailed description of the methodology can be found on the G8 Information Centre at http://www.g8.utoronto.ca/evaluations/index.html#method.

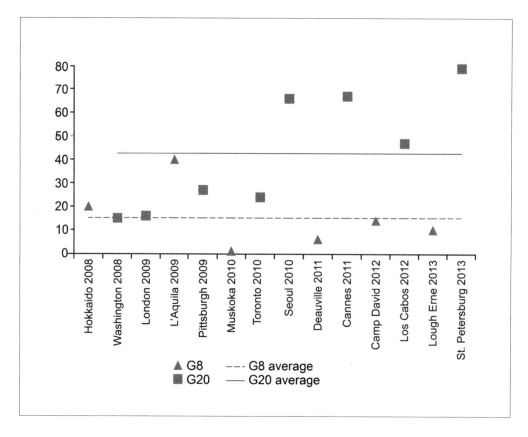

Figure 6.7   G8 and G20 mandates, 2008–13

London commitments. Compliance with the Los Cabos commitments surpassed the G8 average of +0.52. However, the G20's average of +0.42 still fell below the G8 average.

Within the G20, the G8 members' compliance on G20 commitments was also significantly and consistently higher than that of the other G20 members (see Figure 6.10). At Cannes and Los Cabos, however, Brazil, Russia, India, China, and South Africa (BRICS) performed higher than the G20 average and close to the G8 average. At +0.56 and +0.51 respectively, there was a sharp increase compared to the +0.07 performance for Toronto, +0.03 for Pittsburgh, and +0.04 for London.

Although the G20 enjoyed a positive compliance record, the G8 was more effective on the function of delivery. The G20 should continue its push for accountability and delivery, because noncompliance combined with high expectations will lead to diminished confidence, reputation, and legitimacy, and the G20 will be criticized for its inability to meet the increasing number of pledges made at summits – criticisms that are most familiar to the G8. Low compliance and inefficiency will mean that global rebalancing and economic growth will be left without 'political steering' (Gilman 2010, 122).

The evidence provides grounds for optimism. First, a rise in the G20's compliance performance suggests the institution can consolidate its effectiveness. Second, the G20's

ASSESSING G7/8 AND G20 EFFECTIVENESS IN GLOBAL GOVERNANCE

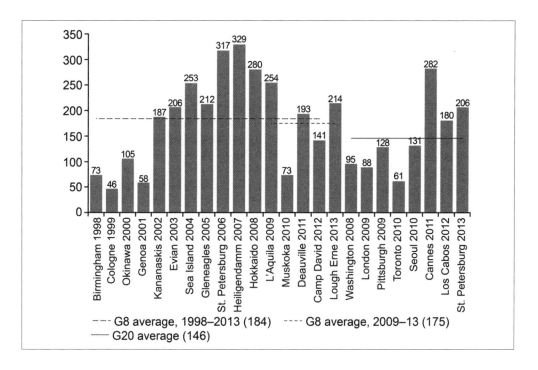

Figure 6.8 G8 and G20 commitments, 1998–2013

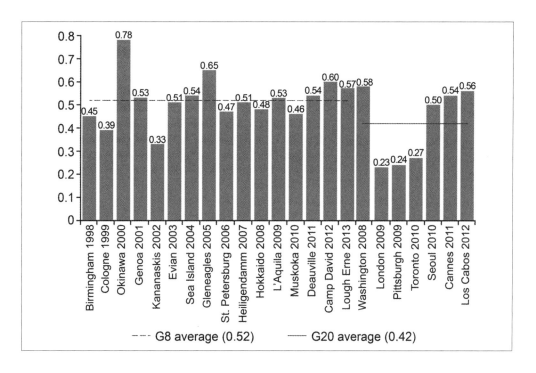

Figure 6.9 G8 and G20 compliance, 1998–2012

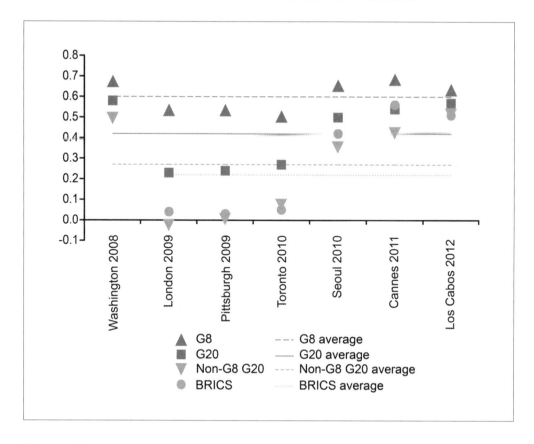

Figure 6.10 G20 compliance, 2008–12

accountability mechanism can be instrumental in enhancing compliance, credibility, and legitimacy. Third, the division of labour and coordination between the G7/8 and G20 allows their agendas to be leaner and more focused, and their commitments more deliverable, and thus enhances their contributions to the global public good and to the benefit of their citizens.

Global Governance Agenda: Cooperative or Competitive?

An analysis of the global governance priorities of the G8 and G20 has been carried out on 12 broad issues present on both institutions' agendas. In the content analysis, a text unit could be earmarked as implementing only one priority. The comparison was made using the absolute and relative data on the number of characters (including spaces and punctuation) denoting a certain priority in G8 and G20 documents. Relative parameters were defined as the share of each priority in the total number of characters in all documents and expressed in percentages.

At Pittsburgh the leaders designated the G20 as the key forum for their economic cooperation. A valid argument can be made in favour of a lean and focused debate enabling better decision making in a broad group of peers. However, once the G20 meetings were upgraded to the leaders' level, the new forum's capabilities for governance were not likely to be restricted to a pre-set list of financial, economic, and trade issues. In fact, at their first meeting in Washington the leaders reaffirmed the importance of the Millennium Development Goals (MDGs) and commitments on official development assistance (ODA), and urged both developed and emerging economies to undertake commitments consistent with their capacities and roles in the global economy (G20 2008). They also indicated their intention to address other critical challenges such as energy security, climate change, food security, the rule of law, and the fights against terrorism, poverty, and disease (G20 2008). Thus, the G20 agenda was set for growth.

Since Washington, the G20 has expanded its agenda on the economy and remained focused on finance; however, much less attention has been devoted to trade (see Figure 6.11). Climate change, anticorruption, and development have been integrated into the list of issues for coordination. At Seoul, in addition to financial safety nets and IFI reform, Korean initiatives included development as one of the key priorities, which is clearly an important issue for the G20 as its nine middle-income members account for

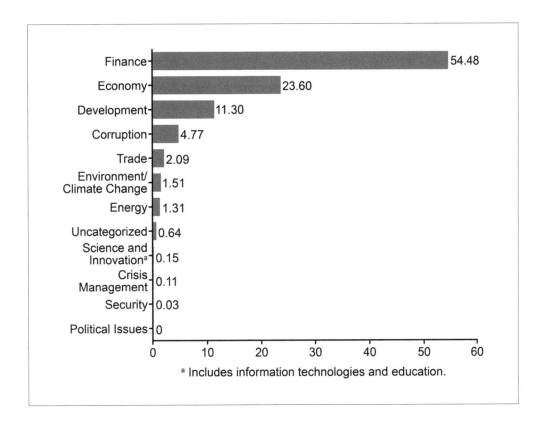

Figure 6.11 G20 priorities, 2008–13

58 per cent of the world's poor (Qureshi 2010). Cannes prioritized growth and jobs, and at Los Cabos the leaders reiterated their resolve to generate labour market opportunities, mobility, and jobs. St Petersburg issued an anniversary statement that emphasized the need to work for strong, sustainable, balanced, and inclusive growth, for the first time explicitly putting the people's well-being at the heart of the G20 growth agenda.

The G8 agenda began contracting in 2008 (see Figure 6.12). The Muskoka Summit was trimmed to include development, political and security issues, climate change, and trade. The prevailing view was that the G8 should focus more on the security, political, and development agendas, whereas the G20 should concentrate on the global economy and financial regulation. At Deauville, development, political, and security issues dominated the agenda with a share of 61 per cent, 20 per cent, and 9 per cent respectively. However, G8 leaders were determined to ensure that macroeconomic policies promote sound economic growth, together with employment and social policies, aiming at reducing unemployment and enabling a quick re-entry into the labour market. At Camp David and Lough Erne, global economy and trade opened the leaders' declaration and communiqué respectively.

There is thus no clear division of labour between the G8 and G20, either in terms of policy spheres or global governance functions (see Figure 6.13). A clear division would reduce the flexibility and responsiveness of the summits, and the opportunities of the

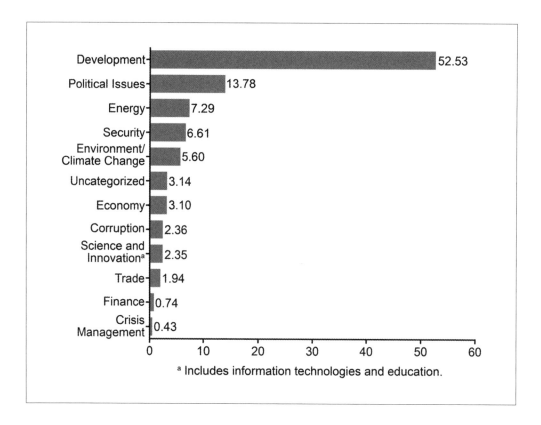

Figure 6.12 G8 priorities, 2008–13

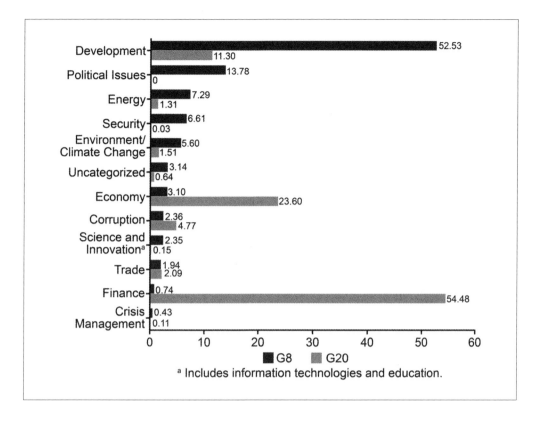

Figure 6.13 G8 and G20 priorities, 2008–13

leaders working on different topics in "variable G-eometry" in a complementary fashion. At the same time, there is a risk of mission creep and an ever broadening agenda at the expense of focus and of the capacity to forge consensus and deliver, especially in the broad and diverse G20.

As Figure 6.14 shows, between 1998 and 2008 the economy was a top priority for the G8, which began as an economic summit; the economy constituted an average of 11 per cent of the agenda over that decade. There were no significant fluctuations except for a spike in 1999 when the leaders met for their 25th economic summit to agree on how to get the global economy back on track for sustained growth after the Asian financial crisis. At Heiligendamm in 2007 the leaders sought agreement on a roadmap for adjusting global imbalances (G8 2007). Could the crisis have been mitigated, had they been more successful and had the incoming chair made economy and finance the key topics of its summit? That is a rhetorical question now.

Once the global financial crisis hit, the G8 ceded economic issues to the G20, which consistently expanded the economic agenda. At L'Aquila the G8 leaders reaffirmed commitments undertaken a few months earlier at the G20 London Summit and spelled out 'steps to return the global economy to a strong, stable and sustainable growth path, including continuing to provide macroeconomic stimulus consistent with price stability and

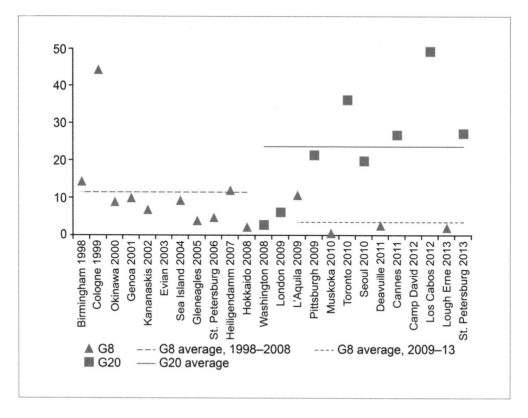

Figure 6.14 G8 and G20 references to the economy, 1998–2013
Note: The figures representing the main priorities in the G8/G20 agendas are presented on different scales, as the shares differ substantially.

medium-term fiscal sustainability, and addressing liquidity and capital needs of banks and taking all necessary actions to ensure the soundness of systemically important institutions' (G8 2009). However, the economy constituted only about 10 per cent of the L'Aquila documents. At Muskoka the following year, when the Canadian presidency divided the labour clearly between the G8 and G20, a mere 0.34 per cent of the leaders' discourse was devoted to the economic agenda. At Deauville the G8 confirmed its commitment to the ongoing processes in the G20, particularly on reforming the financial sector, mitigating commodity price volatility, strengthening the international monetary system, and assessing the causes of persistently large external imbalances, as well as on the full range of policies to foster strong, sustainable, and balanced growth under the MAP. G8 leaders devoted their attention equally between the economy on the one hand and, on the other, innovation and knowledge (2 per cent each) as sources of growth.

The number of references to economic priorities in the G8 documents remained low at 1.5 per cent and 1.8 per cent in Camp David and Lough Erne respectively. At the same time, the G20 consistently expanded its attention to economic issues. From a mere 3 per cent at Washington, the number of references to the economy in G20 documents peaked at 49 per cent at Los Cabos. Despite some decline at St Petersburg, at 27 per cent it scored still higher than finance for a second summit in a row, including all the traditional issues such as fiscal imbalances and structural reforms.

On finance, the trend in the G20 was the reverse (see Figure 6.15). Although financial regulation and reform dominated the G20 discourse, with an average 55 per cent, it gradually but substantially declined, from 88 per cent at Washington and London to 21 per cent at St Petersburg. This trend reflects the integration of other priorities into the G20's work, as well as progress made on financial regulation and the delegation of authority to other institutions.

The G8 still included finance on its agenda, but the number of references fell from the average of 10 per cent in the 1998–2008 period to a meagre 0.8 per cent after the crisis.

Trade was an unloved baby in the G8 discourse before the financial crisis, taking up only 3 per cent of the leaders' attention. With the advent of a new parent – the G20 – G8 attention fell even lower to 1.2 per cent (see Figure 6.16). Leaders repeatedly confirmed their commitments to keep markets open and free and to reject protectionism of any kind, as well as to conclude the Doha round of trade negotiations at the World Trade Organization

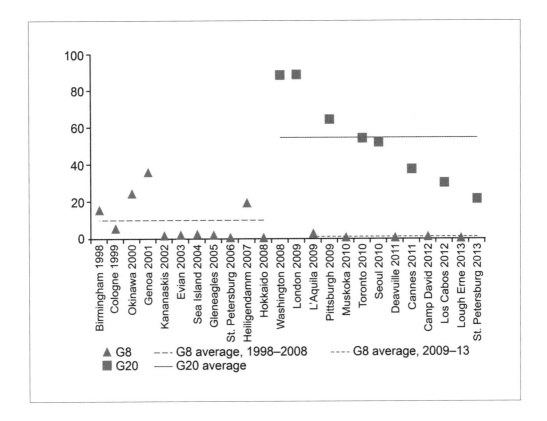

Figure 6.15 G8 and G20 references to finance, 1998–2013

Note: The figures representing the main priorities in the G8/G20 agendas are presented on different scales, as the shares differ substantially.

(WTO), but they always found it hard to comply. At −0.78, compliance with their L'Aquila trade commitment proved to be the lowest among all the commitments assessed. Average compliance with Muskoka's antiprotectionist commitments rose to +0.22, but was still twice below the overall average for the summit. The Deauville and the Camp David compliance reports, however, indicated an improvement in compliance with trade-related commitments with scores of +0.67 and +0.56 respectively. The G20, with 2.08 per cent of its discourse devoted to trade issues, kept reiterating its Washington Summit commitment to reject protectionism and to refrain from raising new barriers to investment and trade in goods and services, imposing new export restrictions, implementing measures to stimulate exports that do not comply with the WTO; the G20 also pledged to conclude the Doha Development Agenda. But G20 members, too, found it hard to comply. Compliance scores remained significantly below average for Toronto (+0.15), Seoul (−0.05), Cannes (+0.25), and Los Cabos (+0.25).

Energy was not omnipresent on the G8 agenda (see Figure 6.17). Birmingham in 1998 promoted cooperation on energy matters with the objective of ensuring reliable, economic, safe, and environmentally sound energy supplies to meet the projected increase in demand.

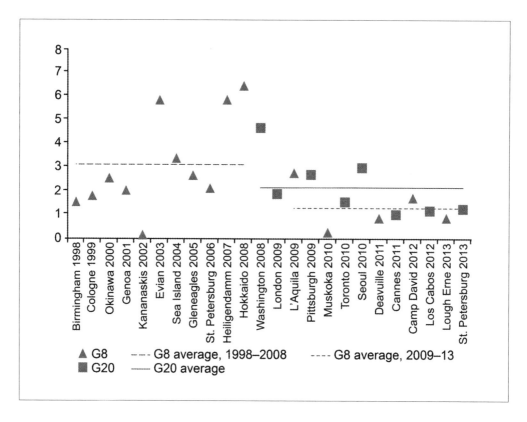

Figure 6.16 G8 and G20 references to trade, 1998–2013

Note: The figures representing the main priorities in the G8/G20 agendas are presented on different scales, as the shares differ substantially.

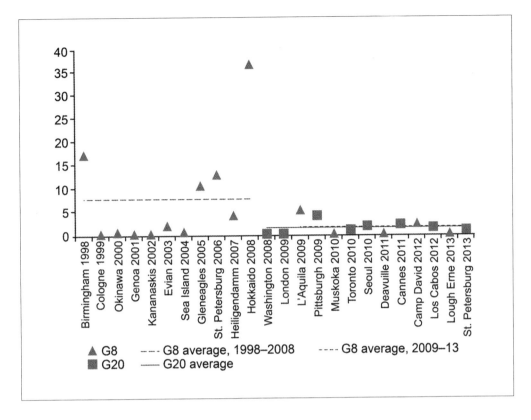

Figure 6.17 G8 and G20 references to energy, 1998–2013

Note: The figures representing the main priorities in the G8/G20 agendas are presented on different scales, as the shares differ substantially.

The leaders committed to encourage the development of energy markets and reaffirmed the commitment made at the 1996 Moscow Nuclear Safety and Security Summit on the safe operation of nuclear power plants and the achievement of high safety standards worldwide. In 2005 the Gleneagles Plan of Action: Climate Change, Clean Energy, and Sustainable Development focused on managing the impact of energy generation on climate change. At St Petersburg G8 leaders adopted the comprehensive Plan of Action for Global Energy Security. In 2008 and 2009 the G8 reaffirmed its commitment to the 2006 St Petersburg global energy security principles and implementation of its action plan.

At Muskoka energy issues were dealt with in relation to the role of nuclear energy in addressing climate change and energy security concerns, and the potential of bioenergy for sustainable development, climate change mitigation, and energy security. The Fukushima disaster in Japan in March 2011 underlined the vital importance of nuclear safety, and at Deauville the leaders confirmed that it should be a top priority on the G8 agenda. At Camp David the G8 leaders recognized the essential role of universal access to environmentally safe, sustainable, secure, and affordable sources of energy for economic growth and environmental protection. Expressing concerns about oil price volatility, the G8 issued a special declaration, in which it committed to take appropriate actions to ensure full and timely supply of the international oil markets. At Lough Erne the leaders reiterated their commitment to the Action Plan on Nuclear Safety produced by the International Atomic Energy Agency (IAEA). Thus much of the G8's energy agenda was interconnected with environmental protection both before and after the G20 stepped onto the field.

The G20 first brought energy on its agenda in Pittsburgh. Emphasizing that access to diverse, reliable, affordable, and clean energy is critical for sustainable growth, the leaders committed to increase energy market transparency and market stability, and strengthen the producer-consumer dialogue to improve understanding of market fundamentals, including supply and demand trends and price volatility. This implied improving the regulatory oversight of energy markets and enhancing energy efficiency, including through rationalizing and phasing out inefficient fossil fuel subsidies that encourage wasteful consumption over the medium term. The G20 leaders reconfirmed their commitment on fossil fuel subsidies at subsequent summits. Thus, although the scope of energy issues on the G8 and G20 agendas were different, both shared a concern with energy security and the environment. After the financial crisis, energy's share of the G8's agenda dropped from 8 per cent to 1.4 per cent, but remained higher than the average of 1.3 per cent for the G20.

On the environment, from 1998 to 2008 in the G8, the average number of references (7.3 per cent) is slightly lower than the average for energy (7.6 per cent) (see Figure 6.18). In the post-crisis years its share remained higher than that of energy (3 per cent compared to 1 per cent). At L'Aquila the leaders reconfirmed their commitment to ensure proper regulatory and other frameworks to move toward low-carbon and resource-efficient growth. At Muskoka, following the 1999 United Nations Copenhagen climate conference, the G8 (2010) reiterated its 'willingness to share with all countries the goal of achieving at least a 50% reduction of global emissions by 2050', and expressed a desire for a 'comprehensive, ambitious, fair, effective, binding, post-2012 agreement involving all countries, and including the respective responsibilities of all major economies to reduce greenhouse gas emissions'. At Deauville, the G8 (2011b) reiterated that commitment, 'recognising that this implies that global emissions need to peak as soon as possible and decline thereafter'. At Camp David the G8 supported the efforts to reduce emissions and acknowledged the need for increased mitigation in the period leading up to 2020, pledging to limit the increase in global temperature below 2° Celsius above pre-industrial levels. At Lough Erne the leaders committed to take environmental action through several international forums, such as the Major Economies Forum (MEF) on Energy Security and Climate Change, the International Civil Aviation Organization, the International Maritime Organization, and the Climate and Clean Air Coalition.

G20 leaders first raised the issue of the environment at London, committing to address the threat of irreversible climate change, based on the principle of common but differentiated responsibilities, and to reach an agreement later that year at Copenhagen in December 2009. They underscored their resolve to take strong action to address the threat of dangerous climate change, and reiterated commitments to the objectives, provisions, and principles of the United Nations Framework Convention on Climate Change (UNFCCC) and the principles endorsed by the leaders at the MEF gathering in L'Aquila.

ASSESSING G7/8 AND G20 EFFECTIVENESS IN GLOBAL GOVERNANCE

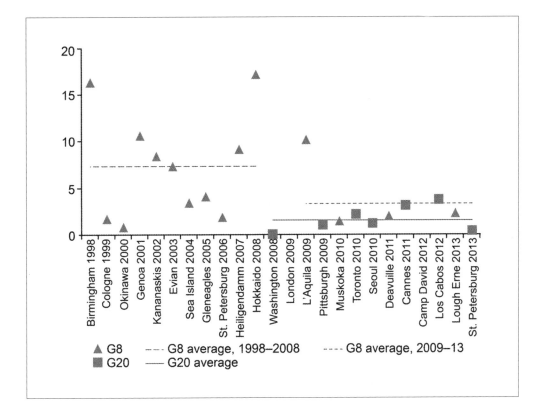

Figure 6.18 G8 and G20 references to the environment and climate change, 1998–2013
Note: The figures representing the main priorities in the G8/G20 agendas are presented on different scales, as the shares differ substantially.

At Toronto the G20 introduced a new theme of marine environment protection, with a view to preventing accidents related to offshore exploration and development and dealing with the consequences of such accidents. Later that year at Seoul, the leaders confirmed yet again the commitment to the UNFCCC and pledged to stimulate investment in clean energy technology, energy and resource efficiency, green transportation, and green cities by mobilizing finance, establishing clear and consistent standards, developing long-term energy policies, supporting education, enterprise and research and development, and cross-border collaboration and coordination of national legislative approaches.

At Cannes the leaders agreed to work toward operationalizing the Green Climate Fund and reaffirmed the role of the private sector in supporting climate-related investments, calling on the MDBs to develop appropriate innovative financial instruments. At Los Cabos they reiterated their commitment to fight climate change and pledged to pursue the full implementation of the outcomes of the 2010 Cancun and 2011 Durban climate change conferences. This commitment was repeated at St Petersburg, as was the commitment on the Green Climate Fund. However, on average the environment constituted a very low share of G20 discourse (1 per cent), substantially lower than the G8 average for the same period (3 per cent).

Development was a key issue on the G8 agenda throughout the 1998–2008 decade, with an average of almost a quarter of the discourse (23 per cent). After the global financial crisis, G8 leaders renewed their commitment to development, reiterating the importance of fulfilling the pledges to increase aid made at Gleneagles, Heiligendamm, and Hokkaido, thus increasing the number of references at L'Aquila to 42 per cent, and up to 62 per cent at Muskoka, 61 per cent at Deauville, and 68 per cent at Lough Erne (Camp David was an exception at 37 per cent) (see Figure 6.19).

While development was not prominent in the G20 discourse until Seoul, where it reached 19 per cent, it was present in the G20 documents after the Washington pledge to continue to fight against poverty. At London, the G20 explicitly recommitted to meeting the MDGs and to achieving respective ODA pledges, including commitments on aid for trade, debt relief, and the Gleneagles commitments, especially to sub-Saharan Africa. Leaders also agreed to make resources available for social protection for the poorest countries, including through voluntary bilateral contributions to the World Bank's Vulnerability Framework, the Infrastructure Crisis Facility, and the Rapid Social Response Fund. Pittsburgh and Toronto built on the development agenda, establishing the Development Working Group with a mandate to elaborate a development agenda and multi-year action plans consistent with the G20's focus on promoting economic growth and resilience, to be adopted at Seoul. The Seoul Development Consensus for Shared Growth and the Action Plan were adopted as planned.

By Cannes the Development Working Group issued its first report on the implementation of the Seoul Development Consensus, which was supported by the leaders. At Los Cabos the G20 focused on three specific policy areas on the development agenda: food security, infrastructure development, and inclusive green growth. At St Petersburg the leaders approved the St. Petersburg Development Outlook, stipulating concrete actions in the five priority areas of food security, financial inclusion, infrastructure, human resources development, and domestic resource mobilization. References to development in the St Petersburg documents amounted to 18 per cent, a sharp increase over 10 per cent for Los Cabos, but still significantly less than 27 per cent at Cannes. Thus, while the average share of the development issues on the G20 agenda remained substantially lower than that of the G8, it reinforced the G20's focus on economic growth, and on engaging with developing countries and removing the obstacles to growth.

Political and security issues remained in the G8 domain, although for both priorities the 2008–13 average was a bit lower than that for 1998–2008. From 2008 to 2013, 16 per cent of the G8 discourse was devoted to the political agenda, compared to 18 per cent for the earlier period (see Figure 6.20). Issues included nuclear nonproliferation, cooperation for Iran's compliance with UN Security Council (UNSC) resolutions, and North Korea's abandoning all nuclear weapons and existing nuclear and ballistic missile programs. G8 leaders condemned North Korea's attack on South Korea's *Cheonan* in March 2010, and demanded it refrain from any further hostilities. Neither the call on North Korea nor the expression of a strong commitment to cooperate closely on regional peace and security

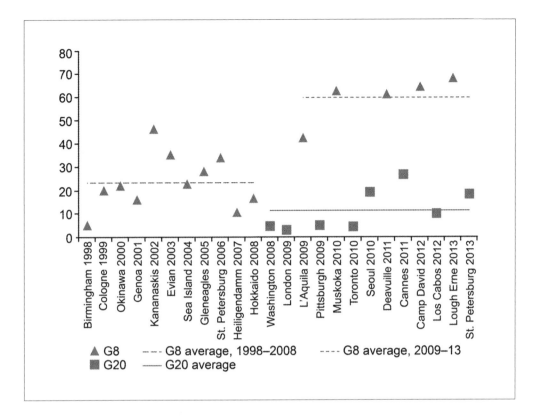

Figure 6.19 G8 and G20 references to development, 1998–2013
Note: The figures representing the main priorities in the G8/G20 agendas are presented on different scales, as the shares differ substantially.

prevented North Korea from launching an artillery attack on the South Korean island of Yeonpyeong in November 2010. Nevertheless, this failure does not mean that the G7/8 should not persevere in efforts to restore peace and stability to the region.

Based on regular reporting on progress of the Global Partnership against the Spread of Weapons and Materials of Mass Destruction, at Muskoka the G8 leaders began to consider possible future developments beyond 2012, focusing on nuclear and radiological security, biosecurity, scientist engagement, and the implementation of UNSC Resolution 1540, as well as the potential participation of new countries in the initiative. The political agenda, as ever, included support to UN peacekeeping operations and African-led peace support operations.

Pakistan, Afghanistan, and Palestine and Israel remained at the centre of the G8's attention. The G8 remained responsive to emergencies threatening security, such as the ethnic conflicts in the Kyrgyz Republic, the longstanding conflict in Sudan, and the aftermath of the earthquake in Haiti.

At Deauville G8 decisions included strong support to the changes in the Middle East and North Africa along with the traditional issues of the Israeli-Palestinian conflict,

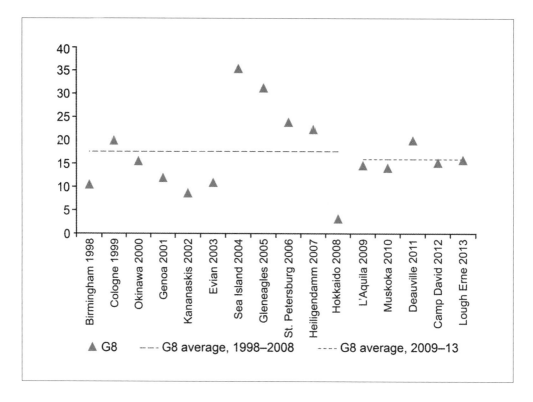

Figure 6.20 G8 and G20 references to political issues, 1998–2013
Note: The figures representing the main priorities in the G8/G20 agendas are presented on different scales, as the shares differ substantially.

nonproliferation, North Korea, reconciliation and reintegration processes, and support for the UN mission in Afghanistan. The leaders launched the Deauville Partnership aimed at 'improving governance, transparency, accountability and citizens' participation in economic life; increasing social and economic inclusion …; modernising their economies, supporting the private sector … to aid job creation, and developing human capital and skills; [and] fostering regional and global integration to reap the benefits of globalisation' (G8 2011a).

Camp David called on the Syrian government and all parties to 'immediately and fully adhere to commitments to implement the six-point plan of UN and Arab League Joint Special Envoy (JSE) Kofi Annan, including immediately ceasing all violence so as to enable a Syrian-led, inclusive political transition leading to a democratic, plural political system' (G8 2012). The conflict dominated the foreign policy discourse the following year at Lough Erne. G8 leaders endorsed the decision to hold talks on implementing the Geneva Communiqué of June 30, 2012, which set out several key steps, principles, and guidelines for a Syrian-led transition.

Closely connected to the political agenda, security issues constituted 6 per cent of the discussions at L'Aquila, and about 9 per cent at Muskoka and Deauville, but decreased subsequently to 3 per cent at Lough Erne (see Figure 6.21). Cooperation on fighting transnational organized crime and piracy and collaboration on antiterrorism within international initiatives, through the Roma/Lyon Group and the Counter-Terrorism Action Group, remained at the core of the G8 security agenda. At Muskoka the G8 committed to three interrelated initiatives to strengthen civilian security systems. Civilian reinforcements for stabilization, peace building, and the rule of law help build capacity to recruit, deploy, and sustain civilian experts from developing countries and emerging donors to increase deployable civilian capacities to reinforce state institutions. The initiative on maritime security provides for cooperation on capacity building in areas such as maritime governance, patrol aviation, coast guards, fisheries enforcement, and maritime intelligence sharing, as well as legislative, judicial, prosecutorial, and correctional assistance. Through their international police peace operations, G8 members committed to mentoring, training, and, where appropriate, equipping police, including new formed police units for duty on United Nations and African Union peace operations.

At Deauville, the G8 security agenda included support for the Biological and Toxin Weapons Convention, the fight against illicit drug trafficking, international negotiations

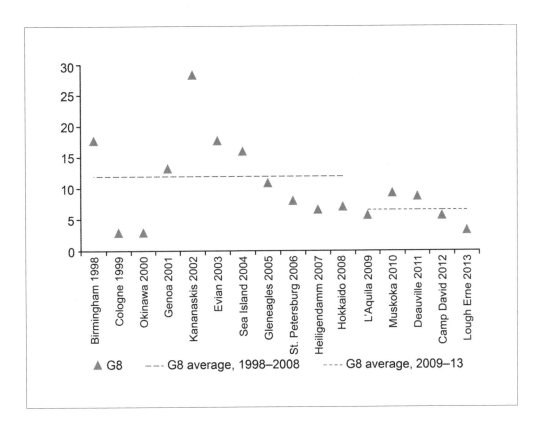

Figure 6.21 G8 and G20 references to security, 1998–2013

on a fissile material cut-off treaty, the use of nuclear energy for peaceful purposes, and the completion and expansion of the Global Partnership.

At Camp David the G8 leaders focused on countering transnational organized crime and terrorism through enhancing national capacities in governance, education, and criminal justice systems and curbing illicit trafficking in arms; they also confirmed the UN's central role in this process. They continued to work on increasing nuclear safety and security in line with their Deauville commitments. Lough Erne expanded the antiterrorist agenda by supporting stabilization in northern Africa and the Sahel region, in particular in Mali and Somalia, which had been affected by terrorist activities, and by reducing the vulnerability of multinational companies and addressing the drivers of instability such as poverty and socioeconomic disparities. On nuclear safety, the leaders supported the IAEA's work on improving the effectiveness of the Convention on Nuclear Safety and confirmed their full support to the IAEA's action plan. To help curb illicit financial activities in Africa, at Lough Erne G8 leaders agreed to launch the Sub-Saharan Africa Public-Private Sector Dialogue, involving governments and financial institutions from G8 members and eastern and southern Africa.

There is no clear division of labour between the G7/8 and G20 and it should not be pre-determined. Both institutions will continue to focus on their core agenda issues. However, they also can cooperate on certain priorities if need be. Tackling BEPS is a good example of such cooperation, whereas development is an issue on which the two agendas, if built on the comparative advantages of the G7/8 and the G20, can yield productive complementarity.

Engagement with Other International Institutions

For the assessment of the G8 and G20 engagement with other international institutions, references to international organizations were identified in all the documents in the data base. These produced a list of 186 international institutions. The analysis used two parameters: the number of references made to institutions in the period and the intensity, expressed as the correlation between the number of references to institutions to the number of characters (including spaces and punctuation) in the documents as follows:

$$D_1 = M_1/S_1,$$

where D_1 is intensity of references to international organizations in a certain year (period), M_1 is the number of references made to the institution in that year (period), and S_1 stands for the total number of characters in the documents for that year (period). To make the findings more easily understood, D_1 was multiplied by 10,000.

The comparison of the contribution to developing multilateralism on the key problems of global governance was based on the data on intensity and its dynamics over the period. The proportion of references to a certain institution to the total number of references was also compared.

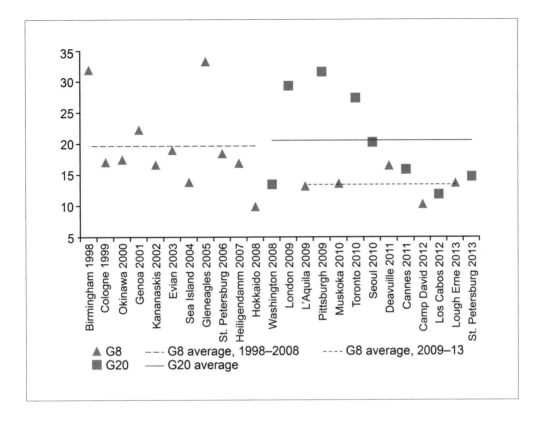

Figure 6.22 G8 and G20 references to international organizations, 1998–2013

The average intensity of G8 engagement with international institutions between 2009 and 2013 was 13, lower than the average of 20 between 1998 and 2008 (see Figure 6.22). In the 1998–2008 period the engagement trend was more or less even, except for the 1998 and 2005 summits, with enhanced cooperation under the presidency of British prime minister Tony Blair (2006) promoting 'a global alliance for global values'. The fluctuations reflected the preferences of the individual presidencies, the nature of the topic for cooperation, and G8 concern about the efficiency of multilateral institutions. However, from Gleneagles in 2005 to Hokkaido in 2007 there was a clear downward trend. After L'Aquila the G8 gradually expanded its engagement with international institutions, which peaked at 17 at Deauville.

The G20's increasing intensity of engagement reflects its imperative of reinvigorating efforts to reform the global architecture to meet the needs of the twenty-first century, an inability to substitute the old institutions with new ones, and the need to harness the capabilities of the existing institutions for generating strong, sustainable, and balanced growth. The intensity grew from Washington (13) to London (29), to Pittsburgh (32), which stands out as the pinnacle of engagement. However, then it slid down gradually from Toronto to Los Cabos and, although it recovered slightly at St Petersburg, remained well below the intensity of the first summits.

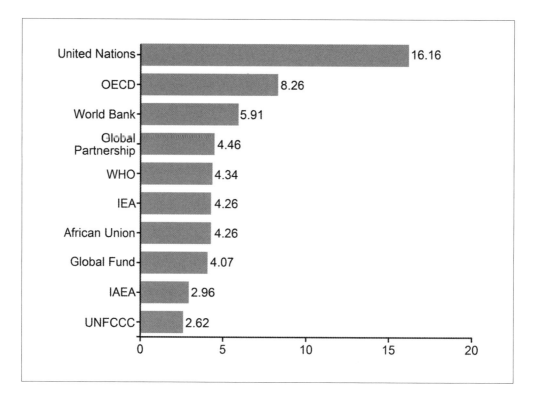

Figure 6.23 Top 10 international organizations in G8 documents, 2008–13

Note: IAEA = International Atomic Energy Agency; IEA = International Energy Agency; OECD = Organisation for Economic Co-operation and Development; UNFCCC = United Nations Framework Convention on Climate Change; WHO = World Health Organization.

The key partner institutions are determined by the G8 and G20 agendas. The G8's top 10 partners were defined by the prominence of development, energy, political, environment, and security issues on its agenda (see Figure 6.23). The UN's privileged position conformed both to the broad agenda the institution and its unique status.

The G20's core mission as the premier forum for economic cooperation foretold the intensity and its mode of engagement with international organizations. Hence, the G20's top 10 partners included the IMF, the World Bank, the FSB, the Basel Committee on Banking Supervision, the OECD, the Financial Action Task Force, and the International Organization of Securities Commissions (see Figure 6.24). The International Labour Organization became a key partner as job creation and employment moved to the core of the G20 agenda. The UN barely made it into the top 10, however, only referred to in relation to the call for ratification and implementation by all G20 members of the UN Convention against Corruption, engagement in UNFCCC negotiations, and commitments to the MDGs and shared growth. There is apparently scope for upgrading G20–UN coordination.

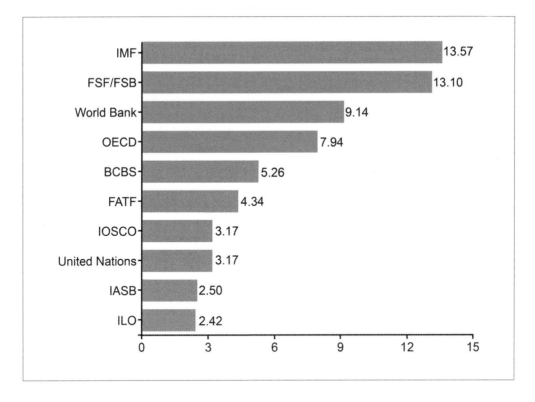

Figure 6.24 Top 10 international organizations in G20 documents, 2008–13
Note: BCBS = Basel Committee on Banking Supervision; FATF = Financial Action Task Force; FSF/FSB = Financial Stability Forum/Financial Stability Board; IASB = International Accounting Standards Board; ILO = International Labour Organization; IMF = International Monetary Fund; IOSCO = International Organization of Securities Commissions; OECD = Organisation for Economic Co-operation and Development.

Nevertheless, the G20's role in enhancing multilateralism was confirmed by an expanding number of organizations involved in cooperation and increasing references to international organizations from 44 at Washington to 310 at London, 395 at Pittsburgh, 443 at Toronto, 669 at Seoul, and 672 at Cannes. After dropping to 419 at Los Cabos, it shot up to 1,731 in St Petersburg. Another indication is the number of mandates delegated by the G20 to the organizations, which totalled 341 from Washington to St Petersburg. Over the same period the G8 agreed to 91 mandates. An important evidence of the G20's reliance on international institutions is the number of reports and recommendations it requested from the IMF, the World Bank, the FSB, the OECD, and the WTO.

An additional indicator of G8 and G20 contributions to multilateral cooperation is the nature of their engagement with each other. Most references have been made by the G8, particularly at L'Aquila (17 out of 25), and point to its disposition to cooperate with the G20. At Muskoka as well as Deauville there were only two references to the G20. At Camp David, the G8 acknowledged the G20 Anticorruption Action Plan as a basis for its Action Plan on Asset Recovery and emphasized the G20's role in addressing global economic and financial issues. The G8 made four references to the G20 at Lough Erne, stressing its contribution to international development, supporting its standstill commitment on trade, recognizing its role in financing for infrastructure in Africa, and committing to work in the G20 on the automatic exchange of tax information. At the same time, the first explicit mention of the G8 by the G20 was made at the 2013 St Petersburg Summit in the context of the recovery of stolen assets.

Thus, at the time of the global financial crisis the G8 enhanced its engagement with international organizations. It should not weaken its capacity to engage with international institutions and the G20. Simultaneously, the G20 has been moving toward enhancing multilateralism. This trend can produce several positive effects. First, it can reinforce the G20's legitimacy; second, it can consolidate the capacity of the G20 and its international partners for delivering on the decisions made at summits; and third, it can provide mechanisms for accountability and transparency. Reliance on key multilateral institutions also provides additional expertise in required policy areas, information-rich contexts for the activities of various working groups, pressure for compliance with decisions, and continuity on the G20's expanding agenda.

Conclusion

Claims of both the G20's inefficiency and the G7/8's demise are exaggerated. The two institutions share the functions of global governance. The G20 has proven its ability for direction setting, decision making, and developing global governance. The G7/8 retains its capacity as a concert for its leaders' deliberation and its good track record for delivering on the pledges they make. The G20 has substantially enhanced its delivery performance. Both institutions have been building accountability mechanisms.

The relationship between the G7/8 and G20 is cooperative rather than competitive. Although there is no clear division of labour on either policy areas or on global governance, both institutions have their own core agendas. At the same time, the G7/8 and G20 cooperate on certain priorities, and such cooperation should be consolidated. Both institutions have contributed to enhancing multilateralism through intense engagement with international institutions on the wide range of the issues pertaining to their respective agendas.

The G7/8's role in global governance has been overshadowed by the G20. However, it remains one of the key agents of the international community that would certainly benefit from a productive cooperation between a mature G7/8 as it turns 41 and a vibrant G20 as it turns eight.

References

Blair, Tony (2006). 'A Global Alliance for Global Values'. Foreign Policy Centre, London. http://fpc.org.uk/fsblob/798.pdf (December 2014).

G8 (2007). 'Growth and Responsibility in the World Economy'. Heiligendamm, June 7. http://www.g8.utoronto.ca/summit/2007heiligendamm/g8-2007-economy.html (December 2014).

G8 (2009). 'Responsible Leadership for a Sustainable Future'. L'Aquila, Italy, July 8. http://www.g8.utoronto.ca/summit/2009laquila/2009-declaration.html (December 2014).

G8 (2010). 'G8 Muskoka Declaration: Recovery and New Beginnings'. Huntsville, Canada, June 26. http://www.g8.utoronto.ca/summit/2010muskoka/communique.html (December 2014).

G8 (2011a). 'Declaration of the G8 on the Arab Springs'. Deauville, May 27. http://www.g8.utoronto.ca/summit/2011deauville/2011-arabsprings-en.html (December 2014).

G8 (2011b). 'G8 Declaration: Renewed Commitment for Freedom and Democracy'. Deauville, May 27. http://www.g8.utoronto.ca/summit/2011deauville/2011-declaration-en.html (December 2014).

G8 (2012). 'Camp David Declaration'. Camp David, May 19. http://www.g8.utoronto.ca/summit/2012campdavid/g8-declaration.html (December 2014).

G20 (2008). 'Declaration of the Summit on Financial Markets and the World Economy'. Washington DC, October 15. http://www.g20.utoronto.ca/2008/2008declaration1115.html (December 2014).

G20 (2011). 'Cannes Summit Final Declaration – Building Our Common Future: Renewed Collective Action for the Benefit of All'. Cannes, November 4. http://www.g20.utoronto.ca/2011/2011-cannes-declaration-111104-en.html (December 2014).

G20 (2013a). 'Annex 1: St Petersburg Fiscal Templates – G20 Advanced Economies'. St Petersburg, September 6. http://www.g20.utoronto.ca/2013/Annex_1_-_St_Petersburg_Fiscal_Strategies___AEs___FINAL.pdf (December 2014).

G20 (2013b). 'Annex 2: St Petersburg Fiscal Templates – G20 Emerging Market Economies'. St Petersburg, September 6. http://www.g20.utoronto.ca/2013/Annex_2_-_St_Petersburg_Fiscal_Strategies___EMEs_FINAL.pdf (December 2014).

G20 (2013c). 'Annex 3: MAP Policy Templates'. St Petersburg, September 6. http://www.g20.utoronto.ca/2013/Annex_3_MAP_Policy_Commitments_by_Members_September_5.pdf (December 2014).

G20 (2013d). 'Annex 4: St Petersburg Accountability Assessment'. St Petersburg, September 6. http://www.g20.utoronto.ca/2013/Accountabilty_Assessment_FINAL.pdf (December 2014).

Gilman, Martin (2010). 'What Comes after the G20?' *International Organisations Research Journal* (5): 121–22. http://iorj.hse.ru/data/2011/03/15/1211463629/13.pdf (December 2014).

Kirton, John J. (2006). 'Implementing G8 Economic Commitments: How International Institutions Help'. *International Affairs* (6): 31–58. http://ecsocman.hse.ru/hsedata/2011/02/28/1211519513/Implementing_G8_economic_commitments.PDF (December 2014).

Kirton, John J. (2013). *G20 Governance for a Globalized World*. Farnham: Ashgate.

Qureshi, Zia (2010). 'G20: Global Growth and Development Agenda'. *International Organisations Research Journal* (5): 25–30. http://iorj.hse.ru/data/2011/03/15/1211462180/6.pdf (December 2014).

Chapter 7
Working Together for G8–G20 Partnership: The Muskoka-Toronto Twin Summits of 2010

John J. Kirton

The Group of Eight's (G8) 36th summit in Muskoka, Canada, on June 25–26, 2010, and the Group of 20's (G20) fourth summit in nearby Toronto immediately after on June 26–27 were unusually significant events. This was the first and still the only time that a Group of Seven (G7) or G8 summit and a G20 one were held so closely together in time and space. They took place right after the G20 leaders had proclaimed at their Pittsburgh Summit in September 2009 that henceforth their new forum would serve as the permanent, premier body for their international economic cooperation. And the twin summits followed the disappointment produced by the 2009 G8 summit in L'Aquila, Italy, for its achievements beyond the field of food security.

Thus each of the twin 2010 summits was surrounded by unusually deep doubts on several fronts. Many observers felt that with the arrival of the G20 summit, the G8 was destined to disappear, dwindle to become a mere caucus group within the G20, or desperately search for a role in the diminishing development and security agenda it might retain in the evolving division of labour with a substantively expanding G20. The G20 itself aroused scepticism over whether it could live up to the standout successes of its three preceding summits in Washington in November 2008, London in April 2009, and Pittsburgh just nine months earlier, and transition from a crisis response committee to a crisis prevention and global steering committee now that the galvanizing force of great global financial disaster on the doorstep in 2008–09 was gone. Taken together, the two summits were often treated as the global governance equivalent of the final Olympic ice hockey game, where only one team could win the single gold medal at stake in a zero-sum game. Certainly, the local Canadian citizens had their doubts about whether the summits were worth it, as they watched the combined costs soar to an estimated $1.2 billion, and, as the G20 summit unfolded, saw a few of their cherished police cars, coffee shops, and storefront windows in downtown Toronto smashed and witnessed the largest mass arrests in Canadian history.

In the end, the doubters were disappointed. Each summit succeeded in its own right and, above all, together, as the twins worked in synergistic tandem to produce more than the sum of their parts. Muskoka's G8 delivered two signature outcomes, the Muskoka Initiative on Maternal, Newborn, and Child Health and the 'Muskoka Accountability Report'. It also combatted traditional macroeconomic challenges, the classic nuclear security threat from

Iran, a military attack from North Korea, and the human security threats from terrorism and from transcontinental drug trafficking across the Atlantic ocean north and south. Toronto's G20 summit contained the new euro crisis that had just erupted in Greece so it did not go global and sustained the still fragile economic recovery; it helped control future crises with a clear, credible message of stimulus now, exit soon, and fiscal consolidation in the medium term, with specific targets and timetables for the leading G8 members. The two summits together showed at a minimum that Canada – ranked low in terms of relative capability in the G8 and in the middle in the G20 – could physically mount two successful summits over a single weekend, arrange a division of labour that highlighted the acknowledged and applauded achievements of each, and partner with Korea, which could be counted on at the stand-alone G20 summit that it would chair in November to fill many of the gaps left by the June twins.

This trio of successes – from the G8, the G20, and the two together – was primarily the result of both the global demand for the two groups to work together in the face of the erupting euro crisis and the skill of the Canadian chair in finding a formula to supply that demand. The informal, free-flowing, flexible opening discussion of economics at the G8 helped forge the consensus that fuelled the larger, more divided G20 to produce the macroeconomic message that quelled the new European financial crisis before it could quickly become a global one. Conversely, the shortcomings arose where supplying the solution could safely be left to the G20 summit at Seoul five months later, where the chair had contradictory commitments and support coalitions, or where participation in the two short June summits was not arranged in the optimum way. The disappointing results on climate change and the environment at both scenic Muskoka and steamy Toronto were to be repaired at the G20's Seoul Summit in November and the United Nations Cancun climate conference in December. The G8 could treat a nuclear-armed North Korea more patiently than a soon-to-be-nuclear Iran. The G20 could leave the already long process of reforming the International Monetary Fund (IMF) and building better banking regulations to the Seoul Summit, and leave reforming the UN Security Council's 1945 formula to France when it hosted the G8 and G20 in 2011 – or perhaps forever, as far as the real world was concerned.

To examine how and why Canada's twin 2010 summits worked on the whole well separately and together, and how the future G7/8–G20 partnership can be improved to the benefit of both, this chapter first systematically compares the performance of the Muskoka G8 and Toronto G20 summits, identifying the synergistic convergence that was often hidden from public view. It next explores the causes of the successes and shortcomings of each alone and both together, by applying the closely related but distinct concert equality model of G7/8 governance and the systemic club model of G20 governance as analytical guides (Kirton 2013). It concludes with suggestions, on the basis of this analysis, for strengthening G7/8–G20 partnership, to the benefit of both summit-centred systems and the broader world, in the years ahead.

Comparing the Summits: Competition, Convergence, and Combination

The Cost–Benefit Calculus

The most obvious points of comparison between the two June 2010 summits were their physical characteristics, notably their financial and reputational costs, security presence, violent protests, and economic and soft power benefits for the community and country in which they were held.

The two summits were expected to cost a combined sum of more than $1 billion to mount. This sum was announced by the host government as an estimate before they took place, in order to secure appropriate budgetary approval for the maximum possible amount. Only several months after the summits was the actual total of about $857 million released. The initial headline-grabbing billion-dollar-plus sum attracted considerable attention, comment, and criticism before, during, and after the summits. Most of this expenditure was for the Toronto G20, as it involved many more leaders and was held in a downtown location in Canada's largest city, a venue that was more expensive to secure than the smaller, more remote G8 summit site. The Muskoka G8 was not the most expensive summit in G8 history, a distinction held by the 2000 Okinawa Summit and its estimated $750 million cost. The Toronto G20 was the most expensive G20 summit held, only if the event-dedicated costs – rather than routine, built-in costs – to government budgets are compared. But the G8 and G20 summits were each less expensive by being mounted together than the combined total would have been had they been held apart. Moreover, the parliamentary opposition, media commentators, and mass public treated the two together, rarely noting that the combined sum was for two events rather than one or dividing the costs in a reasonable portion between the two. Thus, by being held together, each summit was less expensive in reality but more expensive in the appearance of the twin single event.

Local security costs accounted for $675 million of the actual $857 million total costs known by early November 2010. Both summits proved to be completely secure events for their participants, as leaders were almost completely free to conduct their business without distraction from any threats from outside. Here the Muskoka G8 was fully free, while the Toronto G20 leaders were forced to pay some attention to the violent protests out on the street. There were no such protests at Muskoka, and only one day's worth at Toronto that produced limited property damage and virtually no serious personal physical harm, although it did result in the highest number of arrests in one day in Canadian history. Muskoka was a completely peaceful G8 summit, unlike many in the past two decades, notably Genoa in 2001 where a protester attacking security forces had been killed by them. The Toronto G20 demonstrations were also more peaceful than those at the second G20 summit in London, where property was also damaged and an innocent civilian was killed. While the G8 won the 2010 competition in this local peace and security category, the public image of property destruction and police reaction in downtown Toronto contaminated the media and public images of both events to a large degree among locals and to a very limited, short-lived degree among those abroad.

In regard to economic benefits, both summits performed adequately. This is especially the case as much of the international exposure came, as usual, in the lead-up to and long after the summit, before and after any violence at the event itself was visually available for broadcasting or worthy of repetition as news. Here the Muskoka G8 won again, as it was held in a small, relatively unknown location similar to Gleneagles in 2005 or Sea Island in 2004 and was not marred by violence at the site or terrorists attacks in the host's capital while the summit was taking place. Moreover, it had two named, normatively attractive summit successes – the Muskoka Initiative and the 'Muskoka Accountability Report' – to carry its name around the world indefinitely, much like the 1988 G7 summit's Toronto terms on debt relief. For the 2010 G20, there were no such 'Toronto terms', although the favourable references to the summit's signature achievement on medium-term fiscal consolidation remained substantial well after the event.

Dimensions of Policy Performance

On the six standard dimensions for assessing the summit's policy performance, the same pattern of separate and combined net success arose.

Domestic Political Management

On the first dimension of domestic political management, both summits performed adequately. On the initial indicator of attendance, Muskoka maintained the G7/8's 36-year-long perfect attendance record, as all the members saw it in their domestic political and policy interest and prestige to come, despite or because of political difficulties at home. This included the politically hard-pressed Japanese prime minister Naoto Kan. In sharp contrast, at only its fourth summit, the G20 lost its perfect attendance record, as the leaders of Brazil and Australia chose not to come to Toronto. However, 18 of the 20 leaders did, maintaining an equal balance between advanced and emerging members at the event. The two no-shows affected neither the balance of the summit nor the outcomes it produced.

In its impact on mass public approval, for host Canadian Prime Minister Stephen Harper, Muskoka probably provided some political benefit at home. The polls showed his public overwhelmingly approved his central Muskoka Initiative. Support for the fiscal austerity he featured at Toronto was less strong but still secure and broad, beyond his electoral base. Taking the two summits together, by late October 2010, public approval ratings for Harper's Conservative government positioned him to win a third consecutive minority government should an election be held.

And indeed, on the indicator of eventual electoral success, Harper called for a federal election in May 2011. His Conservative Party won its first majority government since its initial election with a minority government in January 2008. This time the Conservatives took 116 seats in the House of Commons, an increase of 23 seats from the last election in October 2008, which had left them with a stronger minority.

On the indicator of communiqué compliments, however, the G20 narrowly and weakly won. At the G8 Canada received none of the eight country-specific compliments issued in Muskoka's concluding communiqués. At the G20 Canada was one of five countries complimented, along with the United States, Japan, Turkey, and Mexico. In Canada's case, it was merely the routine expression of thanks for hosting a successful summit.

Deliberation

On the second dimension of deliberation, in their public component of communiqué conclusions, both summits performed substantially, if at lower levels than before. The G8's written conclusions contained 7,161 words in two documents: the main declaration and a separate statement on terrorism (see Chapter 2, Appendix 2.B). The G20 issued 11,078 words in five documents – the main declaration with three separate annexes plus a statement on 'Principles for Innovative Financial Inclusion'. The separate statements suggested that on the whole the twins faithfully followed the prearranged division of labour, whereby the G8 would deal with security and development and the G20 would do economics and finance.

However, the most striking feature of the two communiqués was their synergistic overlap, with both summits dealing with the same issue areas in a mutually supportive way. This was the case for trade and investment, climate change, development, the Millennium Development Goals (MDGs), corruption, and even terrorism (with the G20's component being terrorist finance).

In the private component of the conversations among the leaders on site, this overlapping, synergistic, substantive mutual support arose as well. G8 leaders devoted their opening luncheon session to a flexible and frank discussion of finance and economics, in response to the recent euro crisis, helping advance the G20's decisive public action two days later. They also discussed North Korea's recent sinking of South Korea's warship the *Cheonan*, an issue of central importance to the latter's President Lee Myung-bak whom they would meet at the G20 summit.

Direction Setting

On the third dimension of principled and normative direction setting, each summit focused on affirming principles flowing from its distinctive and foundational mission. The G8 took up open democracy, individual liberty, and, above all, social advance, the latter guiding its signature initiative on maternal, newborn, and child health (MNCH). The G20 focused on its first mission of financial stability, while extending a little to its second 'Montreal Consensus' mission of making globalization work for the benefit of all.

Yet synergistic, mutual support also arose. Both summits endorsed democratic principles – central to the G8's distinctive foundational mission – with 11 affirmations of democratic principles broadly defined at the Toronto G20 almost equal to the number produced at the first G20 summit in Washington in 2008. The G20 similarly supported the G8's mission of social advance. The dominant result was thus mutual mission reinforcement, rather than a separation of core global governance principles – let alone a competition.

Decision Making

On the fourth dimension of decision making, measured by the public production of precise, obligatory, future-oriented collective commitments, the performance of both summits was relatively low in quantity. The G8 produced 44 commitments and the G20 produced 61. Both were fewer than their respective predecessors. The combined total, while respectable, was also fewer than recent stand-alone G8 summits had produced.

On the component of money raised, the G8 won. Muskoka mobilized about $7.3 billion for its MNCH initiative, a sum that was raised to a pledged $40 billion at the UN MDG review summit three months later in September. The G20's major fundraising achievement was in the less direct category of debt relief, through its commitment to relieve the debt of Haiti, which had been struck by a devastating earthquake on January 12, 2010.

Delivery

On the fifth dimension of the subsequent delivery of summit decisions through compliance with their commitments, performance was modest for both.

On the component of accompanying accountability mechanisms, Stephen Harper had boldly declared that accountability would be the 'defining feature' of both summits. It was for the G8, where the 'Muskoka Accountability Report' was one of the two named signature initiatives. It was much less so for the G20, where no similar new broader self-assessment exercise was produced or initiated. This was despite the need for the compliance scores of the previous two G20 summits, at +0.42 at London and +0.28 at Pittsburgh (on a scale of −1.00 to +1.00), were lower than those of the G8 at +0.48 at Hokkaido and +0.53 at L'Aquila. Moreover, within the G20 compliance was higher from its G8 members than from the other ones. Where an advance on accountability was needed most, it was produced the least in June. Without such a serious internal accountability mechanism, it was likely that G20 members' compliance with their Toronto commitments by the time of the next G20 summit in Seoul in November would continue to lag that of the G8.

This it did. On the component of actual compliance, the G8 members complied with their priority commitments at Muskoka at an average of +0.46 by the time the next G8 summit was held in Deauville, France, almost a year later in May 2011. It was already +0.41 by the start of February 2011 (G8 Research Group 2011). In contrast, the G20 compliance with its Toronto commitments averaged +0.28 by the time of its subsequent Seoul Summit five months later in November 2010.

In general, each summit complied highly with its commitments in the subjects assigned to it according to the informally agreed division of labour. The G8 complied highly in security, development, and good governance and the G20 did so in macroeconomic policy and reform of international financial institutions. Both complied poorly in trade, food, energy, and climate change.

Development of Global Governance

On the sixth dimension of the institutionalized development of global governance, each of the June summits explicitly referred, in a supportive, complementary fashion, to the work of the other group. The Muskoka G8 (2010), in paragraph three of the preamble of its declaration stated: 'Progress is being made, through the work of the G20, towards the sustainable recovery of our global economic and financial system.' The Toronto G20 (2010), in paragraph 34 of its declaration, said: 'We call for the full implementation of the L'Aquila Initiative and the application of its principles.'

More broadly, the large overlapping agenda aroused no criticism or even comment from the participants and media about its apparent contradiction of the predefined division of labour. Most importantly, the G8's private action on finance and economics aroused no resentment on the part of G20-only members, in part because the G8 host and members kept the media focused on Muskoka's central communiqué-encoded achievements in the domains of development and security. This proved that the twin, tandem summits could work well together, despite earlier arguments from Russia that they should be separated by a decent interval in time, and from several Asian members that the G20 summit should take place before the G8 one.

In all, convergence and cooperation between the two summits rather than competition prevailed. Above all, the G8's informal, flexible conversation and emerging consensus on finance and economics, especially the balance between fiscal stimulus and consolidation, helped pave the way to the central achievement of the G20 Toronto Summit on a credible, crisis-calming macroeconomic message, with its new element of precise targets and timetables for fiscal consolidation in the medium term.

Causes of Summit Successes, Shortcomings and Synergies

The causes of this particular pattern of individual performance and joint partnership show the strengths and shortcomings of the concert equality model for explaining G8 governance, and of the closely related but distinctive systemic club model for explaining G20 governance (Kirton 2013).

The first cause, shared by both models, consists of successive shocks that show all members their equalizing vulnerability to old state threats and new non-state threats, especially by exposing the most powerful members to the most vulnerable ones. Here the Greek-catalysed euro crisis, coming so soon after the American and Atlantic financial crises of 2008–09, galvanized the major macroeconomic achievement of Toronto G20 and the important opening luncheon contribution of the Muskoka G8. Terrorist attacks against New York City and Detroit in the six months leading up to the summits also propelled the G8's actions on terrorism. However, the shock of the deadly attack on the Korean frigate *Cheonan* did not generate full G8 unity against North Korea, while the absence of a new shock from Iran or nuclear proliferation did not prevent the G8 from unifying to impose new sanctions on Iran. Above all, there were no issue-specific shocks that drove Muskoka's signature achievements on MNCH and accountability. The central shock of the euro crisis produced no such outcomes in any direct, traceable way, despite the argument that the failure of G20 members to comply with their earlier commitments had caused the crisis to erupt.

The old, state-centred economic and security shocks from the Greek and North Korean governments and the new, non-state shocks from terrorism were significant for inspiring both summits to act and to do so in a synergistic way. But they were by no means sufficient to explain most of the major results of the G8. Shocks were necessary and highly salient for getting the newer, larger, more diverse G20 to act. But they were less needed for the older, smaller, more similar, and more like-minded G8 club's achievements in June. Its causes came from forces lower down the list.

The second cause, also shared by both models and the 2010 summits, is the failure of the old multilateral organizations from the 1940s to respond adequately to the shocks, in a world where unilateral action by a hegemon or major power had long lost its potency as well. In the case of the G20, the IMF did not predict or prevent the Greek-catalysed crisis and its European contagion. Nor did the IMF have the resources to deliver the global lifeline from Washington that the Europeans asked for in the end. Only the G20 summit could deliver the credible macroeconomic message – containing medium-term fiscal consolidation – that would address the root cause of the crisis and calm markets as a result. For the G20, the systemic club model adds the component of G7/8 failure as a cause of G20 success. However, in June, it was G8 success, not failure, on finance and economics at Muskoka that propelled G20 success in Toronto over the next two days.

In the case of the G8, the failure of the UN and the World Health Organization (WHO) in regard to the three MDG health goals (MDGs 4, 5, and 6) caused the G8 to address and achieve the Muskoka Initiative (on MDGs 4 and 5) as its centrepiece. But here the G8 worked less as a competitor than as a partner with the relevant UN bodies such as the United Nations Children's Emergency Fund (UNICEF) before and after, as Muskoka helped drive the UN to greater achievements on MNCH at its long scheduled special summit in September in New York. Similarly, the failure of the UN Security Council (UNSC) on Iran caused the G8 to act effectively at Muskoka, but in ways that added not only Russia – a member of both the G8 and the Permanent Five (P5) countries on the UNSC – to the consensus but also China – a P5 member only – to produce a legally binding, non-vetoed UNSC resolution in the end.

The third cause, again shared between the two models, is predominant, equalizing capability. It worked very well in the case of the G20, as the collectively committed financial resources of a rising, less crisis-scarred Asia and G20-only members' coalition were necessary to rescue a crisis-afflicted Europe and a still struggling America, either through the IMF or through a smaller group. In the case of the G8 on MNCH, relatively well-off Canada took the lead in giving, followed by the United States, Japan, and others, which gave less than their traditional proportional burden-sharing part (Kirton, Kulik, et al. 2014). Contributions also came from Russia and other countries, such as Korea, the Netherlands and Norway, as well as from civil society actors.

The fourth cause, somewhat shared between the two models, is the embedded common principles among the members. For the G20's established and emerging economies, this is primarily the status quo principle of financial stability, which is precisely what the Toronto

Summit most produced. For the G8's established powers including Russia, those common principles are open democracy and individual liberty. These principles (unlike social advance in third place) had little direct relationship to MNCH. They did, however, drive the Muskoka achievement on accountability and arguably also on Iran, whose leader had been condemned by G8 leaders at their previous summit for his denial of the Holocaust. More broadly, the G20's focus on financial stability was to some degree driven by a common desire to preserve, in turn, the assumed causal consequences of social stability, political stability, and, thus, democracy in the newly democratic post-Cold War polities.

The fifth cause, still somewhat shared by both models, is political control, capital, continuity, professional competence, personal conviction, and public support. Here the average political control and capital of G20 leaders was greater than the G8-only ones. Continuity in the two was more equal, especially with the absence at the G20 of the leaders of Australia and Brazil. But the big unifier came on competence, where host Harper, a G8 and G20 veteran with experience and expertise in economics, guided both the G8's opening lunch and the G20 summit to their achievements in the macroeconomic field. Because many of the veteran sherpas, including the Canadian host sherpa Leonard Edwards, served their leaders at both the G8 and G20 summits, coordination and synergies between the two groups were enhanced.

The sixth cause, somewhat less shared by the two models, is constricted, controlled participation in a G8 club and a G20 hub of a global network with cross-cutting combinations of established and emerging systemically significant countries. With a 36-year history, only 10 members, five invited participants, no international organizations, and no ministers of finance or other ministries attending, the Muskoka G8 operated as a leaders-only club cherished by its members. Its informal, remote, resort setting enhanced the informality and the sense of equality and cohesiveness of the club. One result was the leaders' discussion of the G8's future and role now that the G20 summit had become a permanent part of global governance. All members enthusiastically endorsed the continuing value of their club, save for US president Barack Obama, who nonetheless seemed moved by the consensus of his colleagues to continue coming and indeed to host the G8 when America's turn arrived in 2012.

At the G20 there was much less constriction, as the 18 leaders (without Australia and Brazil) were joined by the finance ministers of all members, five invited country guests, and the heads of several multilateral organizations. In contrast to the free-flowing interactive exchanges at Muskoka, G20 discussions consisted largely of leaders reading or offering set-piece speeches in turn. Here the absence of the unusually direct Brazil's Lula da Silva and Australia's Kevin Rudd was felt. To be sure, the Toronto interventions were more focused, relevant, and shorter than at previous G20 summits. Moreover, the heads of the international organizations could intervene only on the topics where their expertise was relevant. Still, the format allowed for little spontaneity, interchange, or frankness. After four summits in two years, the 20 had become a group, but not yet a club in a social-psychological sense.

At the same time, the G20 served as the hub of a global network of transoceanic, plurilateral summit and ministerial institutions, where established and emerging power combinations of G20 members operated, along with many others in the global community as a whole. Such external expansiveness was accompanied at Toronto by the reduction of any internal caucuses or blocs, as Lula's absence meant that no summit of the leaders of Brazil, Russia, India, and China (BRICs) was held on the G20's eve. The external established-emerging equality was institutionalized for the first time in the leadership of the Toronto Summit, for which the leaders of Canada and Korea co-chaired politically if not physically. The two leaders had much in common, notably a commitment to open trade, as both their summits' solid but hardly spectacular work on trade liberalization showed.

Taken together, these configurations of causes suggest that the G8 was a cohesive club that needed only an internal sense of collective responsibility and equality and not an outside crisis to succeed. In contrast, the G20 remained a more diverse group that needed the standard financial-economic euro crisis, in the classic 1997–99 form of sovereign debt, to generate the singular success it had in the directly matched macroeconomic domain.

These causes are consistent with and may help account for some of the specific results obtained, with implications for how the summits will and should unfold in future years.

The differing personal commitments of the chairs took a toll. Harper had declared accountability to be a 'defining feature' of both the G8 and G20 summits. He succeeded where he chaired alone and was backed by most G8 members at Muskoka. But he failed at Toronto where he politically co-chaired with a less committed Korean president Lee, who was supported by the even less committed G20-only members such as China and Saudi Arabia. Adequate advances on accountability would thus come slowly from the G20, which produced its own equivalent to the 'Muskoka Accountability Report' for the St Petersburg Summit three years later in 2013.

Conversely, Lee Myung-bak had long been the green growth leader within the G20. He had taken important action at home to curb carbon dioxide emissions, even though his country was not part of the long advanced, industrialized, heavily polluting group. For Stephen Harper, who had long loved economics but had less expertise, experience, and personal interest in the environment, the macroeconomic and climate change outcomes at Muskoka and Toronto were consistent with his persona, his procedural leadership as chair, and the lack of enthusiasm of the most powerful members – the United States, China, and India – to prioritize climate change control.

The particular choice of participants in each summit also had an effect. Had Lee, already coming to Toronto for the G20 summit, been invited to Muskoka too, he could have made a more convincing case than the only other Asian representative, Japan, about who was responsible for sinking the *Cheonan* and what a united G8 could have usefully done in response. At the G20 Seoul Summit on the still divided Korean peninsula in November, Lee was in the lead, but the G8 summit was not. But all G8 leaders were available for a more spontaneous gathering to discuss proximate nuclear matters, in ways reminiscent of how, at the G20 Pittsburgh Summit in September 2009, Obama had assembled a few G8 colleagues, excluding Russia and Canada, to send a public message to Iran.

A second apparent anomaly in participation concerned UN secretary general Ban Ki-moon. He appeared at the G20, which focused on finance and economics, subjects on which the UN was not regarded as having a comparative advantage among multilateral organizations. He was not invited to the Muskoka G8, despite its assigned and accepted responsibility for security and development, and the UN's widely acknowledged charter-based lead in these subjects, including MDGs 4 and 5.

One cost came on climate change control, where the G8 had long ago first pioneered effective global governance at its summit in 1979. When Ban went to Canada just before the June 2010 summits, to meet privately with Harper and publicly with the Canadian people, he put climate change control as his number-one request of both the G8 and the G20. Absent from Muskoka, he was unable to make such a private pitch to the more empathetic G8 leaders. At Toronto he spoke again forcefully on the subject. But in the larger group of 20 leaders, with heads of multilateral organizations confined to a supporting role, and with too little time to deal with a long list of pressing subjects, Ban's pitch was squeezed in at the end of the summit at the end of a long lunch discussion largely devoted to trade. It was thus easily dismissed as a subject where serious G20 consensus and action were not possible at that time.

Similar effects came from Ban's absence at Muskoka in the security domain. At the G8's St Petersburg Summit in 2006, Ban's predecessor Kofi Annan was more easily able to convert the new G8 consensus on the Middle East, catalysed by Harper, into a unanimously approved UNSC resolution within a matter of days when he got back to New York. With Ban absent from Muskoka, post-summit progress was slower and more slender on North Korea, and even on Iran.

A further consequence of the missing UN at Muskoka could have come on the G8's signature initiative on MNCH, focused entirely on MDGs 4 and 5. The UN's special summit in September did build on Muskoka's advertised $7.3 billion to reach more than $10 billion in new money mobilized, raising it to a headline-friendly $40 billion. However, the actual delivery and effective use of the money to reach the goal could have benefited from having the UN present at the G8 summit start. The G8's experience at Okinawa and Genoa in producing the Global Fund on HIV/AIDS, Tuberculosis, and Malaria supports this claim. In Okinawa in 2000, the key figure was Gro Harlem Brundtland of WHO – a body key to meeting MDGs 4, 5 and 6 and to meeting multilateral goals on noncommunicable diseases (NCDs). The UN high-level meeting in September 2011 was devoted to NCDs and not the MDGs. The G8 dealt overwhelmingly with infectious diseases, rather than chronic or noncommunicable ones (Kirton, Guebert, et al. 2014). The G20 at Toronto and earlier had already put healthcare costs on its agenda. NCDs are the leading or rapidly rising health and economic burden in most G20 members – advanced, emerging, and developing countries alike. This enormous economic burden made it very difficult for the G20's advanced members to comply with their Toronto commitments on deficit and debt reduction by 2013 and 2016 respectively – unless the G20 acted specifically to control healthcare costs. Russia, which had made health comprehensively a planned presidential priority for the first G8 it hosted in 2006, had a special role and responsibility in this regard. But at its St Petersburg G20 Summit in 2013 it did not take up the cause of NCDs or healthcare costs.

Conclusion

From this analysis, several suggestive conclusions can be drawn.

First, crisis alone is not enough for G7/8, G20, or G7/8 and G20 combined success. To be sure, crisis – especially in the form of second and successive shocks – is the proven great galvanizer of G7/8 and G20 summit performance. Once again, the spring 2010 euro crisis, coming so soon after the 2007–09 American-Atlantic shocks, propelled Toronto on its core function and agenda, and Muskoka at its opening lunch, to their observed and acknowledged success. But there were no such shocks on MNCH or accountability to produce these named, signature achievements of the 2010 G8. Here other factors and actors were important: a smart, responsible civil society with expertise and capacity and a smart, strategic leader willing to use its prerogative of host and chair to work well with multilateral organizations, most directly with the IMF in the domain of finance.

Second, both summits need to work together at the same time and throughout the year. Together, the twin June summits brought two configurations of leaders together in close proximity for just over two days. Their achievements made the costs well worthwhile and were adequate to meet the global demand for global governance at the time. They should similarly work together in future years, should the global need arise.

Third, both summits need to work together, on the same issues if need be. Since its ministerial start in 1999 and continuing with its summits, the G20 has dealt regularly with development, including the MDGs and official development assistance, and with security in the hard form of fighting the financing of 9/11-like terrorism and once softer human security forms of corruption, starting with money laundering and tax havens. The Muskoka G8 dealt privately with finance and economics and publicly in its communiqués with trade and investment. Both dealt publicly with the MDGs, development more broadly, food security, Haiti, climate, corruption, health in different forms, and other pressing shared concerns.

Fourth, both summits need to work together on the same things for as long as needed and as often as needed – either once a year per the G8 norm, twice a year per the initial G20 norm or even more often should the global demand arise. Because of the long scheduled G8 in Muskoka, there was also a G20 summit in nearby Toronto in late June – both needed to contain the euro crisis. This crisis was unpredicted at the start of 2010, or even before when the tandem schedule was struck. But each summit added value and worked together to shared success in a quick financial crisis response.

Fifth, even two summits working well together are not enough to meet the great and growing demands for global governance in today's intensely globalized world. They need to work more closely with at least the major multilateral organizations and supportive civil society in several ways. One way is to invite the UN secretary general to both the G8 and the G20 summits. Another is to catalyse signature successes, as shown by the contribution of child-centred nongovernmental organizations in the Muskoka Initiative on Maternal, Newborn, and Child Health. On the second Muskoka initiative, on accountability, there are good grounds to conclude that a greater well-designed role for the multilateral organizations and civil society organizations in both the G7/8 and G20 can help convert their often impressive commitments into compliance by their members, effective solutions in the real world, and the legitimacy that will flow from such extended success.

References

G8 (2010). 'G8 Muskoka Declaration: Recovery and New Beginnings'. Huntsville, Canada, June 26. http://www.g8.utoronto.ca/summit/2010muskoka/communique.html (December 2014).

G8 Research Group (2011). '2010 Muskoka G8 Summit Interim Compliance Report'. February 21. http://www.g8.utoronto.ca/evaluations/2010compliance-interim (December 2014).

G20 (2010). 'The G20 Toronto Summit Declaration'. Toronto, June 27. http://www.g20.utoronto.ca/2010/to-communique.html (December 2014).

Kirton, John J. (2013). *G20 Governance for a Globalized World*. Farnham: Ashgate.

Kirton, John J., Jenilee Guebert and Julia Kulik (2014). 'G8 Health Governance for Africa'. In *Moving Health Sovereignty in Africa: Disease, Governance, Climate Change*, John Kirton, Andrew F. Cooper, Franklyn Lisk, et al., eds. Farnham: Ashgate, pp. 127–63.

Kirton, John J., Julia Kulik and Caroline Bracht (2014). 'The Political Process in Global Health and Nutrition Governance: The G8's 2010 Muskoka Initiative on Maternal, Child, and Newborn Health'. *Annals of the New York Academy of Sciences* 40: 1–15. doi: 10.1111/nyas.12494.

Chapter 8
G20: From Crisis Management to Policies for Growth

Zia Qureshi

Future global growth faces many challenges. The first is securing economic recovery from the global financial crisis and reviving strong growth. The euro area has experienced a double-dip recession. Growth remains subdued in other advanced economies. Emerging economies (including the BRICS countries of Brazil, Russia, India, China, and South Africa, as well as other major emerging economies) had been the driver of global growth, accounting for almost two thirds of global growth since 2008, but in 2013 they too were experiencing slowing growth. The second challenge is sustaining growth. Many countries have large and rising public debt, and face unsustainable debt dynamics (International Monetary Fund [IMF] 2012). Environmental stresses put the longer-term sustainability of growth at risk. The third challenge is promoting balanced growth. Large external imbalances between countries – China's surplus and the US deficit being the most notable – put global economic stability at risk and give rise to protectionist pressures. Unemployment has reached high levels in many countries, and there are concerns about a jobless recovery. And economic inequality within countries has been rising. More than two thirds of the world's people live in countries where income inequality has risen in the past few decades.

Thus, promoting strong, sustainable, and balanced growth is a central objective of the Group of 20 (G20). A core component of the G20 is the Working Group on the Framework for Strong, Sustainable, and Balanced Growth. Yet G20 policy actions since the onset of the global financial crisis in 2008 have focused mainly on short-term crisis response. Economic stabilization is necessary and risks to stability in the global economy, especially those in the euro area, call for firm actions to restore confidence. However, short-term stabilization only buys time and will not produce robust growth unless accompanied by structural reforms and investments that boost productivity and open new sources of growth. To be sure, several G20 members have announced or are implementing structural reforms. But the approach to strengthening the foundations for growth, meeting the jobs challenge, and assuring the longer-term sustainability of growth remains partial and piecemeal. Some elements of an approach are present, but the unrealized potential for a coherent and coordinated strategy and effort is significant. The G20 needs to move beyond a predominantly short-term crisis management role to focus more on the longer-term agenda for strong, sustainable, and balanced growth.

Key Elements of Agenda for Strong, Sustainable and Balanced Growth

The current slow growth in advanced economies is not just a cyclical phenomenon but has deeper structural roots. Some of the structural weaknesses are longstanding, such as labour market rigidities in Europe and deficiencies in the tax/expenditure structure in a broad range of advanced economies, including the United States, that have led to unsustainable fiscal trajectories. The global financial crisis added to the challenge by causing supply-side disruptions that lower potential growth, including increased structural unemployment, destruction of capital stock, and financial sector dislocations. Challenges also arise from the changing pattern of competitiveness and comparative advantage in the world economy as emerging economies increasingly penetrate global production and trade. So future growth will require not just supporting a recovery of demand but also reallocating resources to new sources of growth – new products and services and new jobs.

Emerging economies also face a challenging agenda in sustaining their growth momentum, including implementing further domestic reforms and boosting investment in infrastructure and human capital (World Bank 2013d). They need to adjust to an external environment marked by lower advanced-economy growth and more volatile capital flows. Lower advanced-economy growth means that emerging economies have to look more to other emerging economies and their own domestic markets for growth. For economies with large and persistent external imbalances, rebalancing demand and sources of growth are important for sustaining growth.

In meeting these growth challenges, structural reforms are a central element of the agenda – in advanced and emerging economies alike (Organisation for Economic Co-operation and Development 2012). As macroeconomic policy space has narrowed in many countries in the aftermath of the global financial crisis, productivity-enhancing structural reforms and investment will be even more crucial in supporting future growth. Structural reforms, such as tax and expenditure policy reform, regulatory reform, and labour and financial market reform, are also key to addressing the jobs challenge, the rise in inequality, and the challenge of environmental sustainability. Many of these reforms are cross-cutting, in that their effects cut across these objectives. Structural reform thus is a common thread that connects all the three dimensions of the growth challenge mentioned above – strong, sustainable, balanced.

With much of the action in response to the global financial crisis focused on short-term macroeconomic management, progress on structural reforms has been limited. The financial sector, closely connected to macroeconomic stabilization, has seen more reform, less so the real economy.

This chapter focuses on some key areas of structural reform in the longer-term agenda to strengthen the foundations for strong, sustainable, and balanced growth in the global economy. It argues that this agenda should receive increasing attention from the G20.

Restoring Fiscal Sustainability

A key area of reform is the restoration of fiscal sustainability, especially in advanced economies that have seen their public debts rise sharply in the aftermath of the global

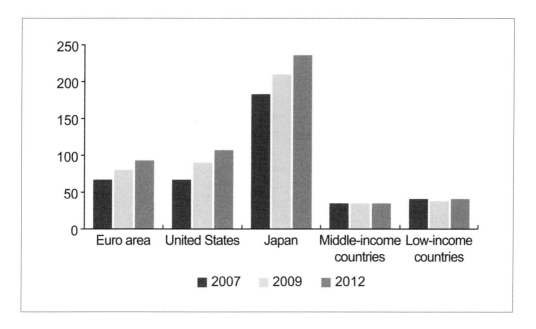

Figure 8.1 Government debt relative to gross domestic product (percentage)
Source: International Monetary Fund data.

financial crisis from levels that were already high (see Figure 8.1). Absent reform, many of the advanced economies of Europe as well as Japan and the United States face unsustainable debt dynamics. Much of the fiscal reform agenda is structural, with reform of tax systems and entitlement programs being key. The reform of entitlement programs (pensions, social security, and health) is especially important in aging economies. In Europe, reform of public finance and related labour market policies is a core issue in the agenda to revive strong and sustainable growth (Gill and Raiser 2012). The euro area crisis has triggered some fiscal reform actions in the region. Some reform action also started in the United States in the context of the 'fiscal cliff', the combination of expiring tax cuts and government spending cuts that threatened the US economy at the end of 2012. However, these are still small initial steps compared to the magnitude of the longer-term challenge that needs to be addressed. Deeper and sustained reform is required (IMF 2010).

While it is important to set out clear and credible medium-term fiscal reform frameworks, the pace of fiscal consolidation in the short run needs to be carefully calibrated given the still fragile economic recovery. And fiscal reform needs to be part of a broader reform agenda for growth, as growth is essential for durable fiscal sustainability; austerity alone is not enough.

Avoiding Middle-Income Traps

Emerging economies have posted impressive growth in the twenty-first century. Their growth performance is increasingly important for global growth. However, continued strong growth in these economies is not assured. Sustained structural reform and structural change are important for emerging, middle-income countries to renew the drivers of growth and avoid the so-called 'middle-income trap'. As countries reach middle-income levels, productivity gains from the reallocation of surplus labour from agriculture to industry and from technology catch-up are increasingly exhausted, while rising wage levels make labour-intensive products less competitive. If countries cannot increase productivity through innovation, they can get trapped. Historically, this transition has been difficult. Of the 101 middle-income countries in 1960, only 10 became high-income countries by 2008 (using 50 per cent of the US gross domestic product [GDP] per capita as the threshold). Latin America provides particularly compelling support for the difficulties of transition from middle- to high-income level. Most economies in the region reached middle-income status several decades ago and have remained there since (see Figure 8.2).

Recent research at the World Bank confirms the central role of structural reforms (Bulman et al. 2012). Countries that have successfully transitioned from middle- to high-income status typically have achieved stronger performance on structural transformation from agriculture to industry, growth in total factor productivity, human capital development and innovation, and openness. For example, at upper middle-income levels, countries making a successful transition had more than triple the growth in total factor productivity of those that failed. They had higher quality in education and more innovation as indicated by the number of patents acquired. Structural reform is the common element that connects these drivers of progress. A complementary attribute of successful escapees from the middle-income trap has been the avoidance of large external and internal imbalances – including macroeconomic imbalances and significant increases in inequality.

China's economic performance since 1983 has been exceptional, at average annual growth approaching 10 per cent. Its role in the global economy has risen sharply: it is now the second largest economy, contributing more than one third of global growth since 2008. The country's growth model, which has been so successful, will need to adapt to new challenges in the future: a shift from a reliance on exports and investment to domestic demand and consumption, an aging population, rising inequality, and environmental stresses. Continued progress and successful transition from a middle- to high-income country will depend on a range of structural reforms to address these challenges (World Bank 2013a).

Investing for Growth

The private sector is the main driver of growth. Investment by firms is a key means to innovation, productivity growth, and structural transformation. Governments play an important role by providing a conducive regulatory and institutional environment for private investment. The enabling environment for private enterprise and growth also depends crucially on investment in infrastructure (Bhattacharya et al. 2012).

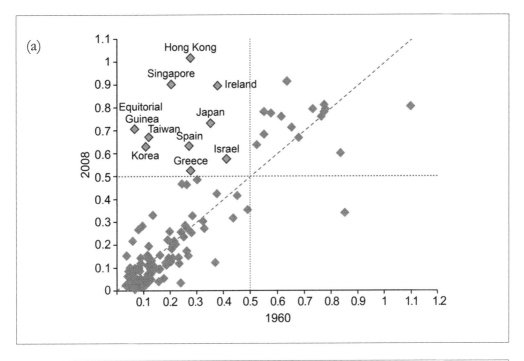

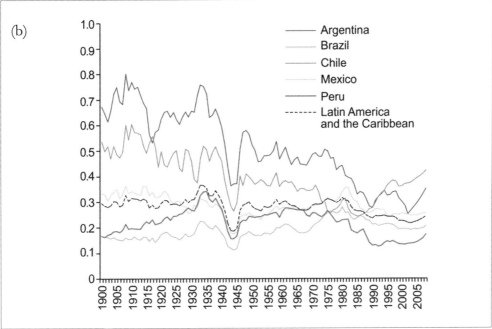

Figure 8.2 Middle-income traps

Note: a) Per capita gross domestic product relative to the United States (ratio); b) Countries in Latin America and the Caribbean.

Source: World Bank calculations based on Maddison data (http://www.ggdc.net).

Improving the Investment Climate

An important area of structural reform is the climate for private investment – which is a shorthand expression for the enabling environment for firms to invest and innovate, for competition to provide a level playing field to firms and spur change, and for markets to play their allocation role well. As measured by the World Bank's (2013b) Ease of Doing Business index, progress on reforms to improve the climate for private investment has in general accelerated somewhat since the onset of the global financial crisis, but much remains to be done.[1] Low-income countries remain farthest from the frontier on global best practice (see Figure 8.3). Nonetheless, they have achieved the largest improvement since 2005. The average index is higher in middle-income countries but still well short of the frontier, indicating a sizable unfinished reform agenda, including in several G20

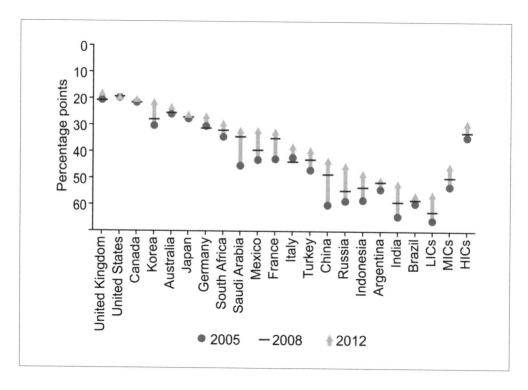

Figure 8.3 Ease of doing business: Distance to frontier, 2005–12

Note: The frontier (or best practice) is a synthetic measure based on the highest score achieved by any country on each of the nine component indicators of the World Bank's Ease of Doing Business index. The vertical axis represents the distance to the frontier, with n as the most efficient regulatory environment (frontier practice). LICs = low-income countries; MICs = middle-income countries; HICs = high-income countries.
Source: Based on 2013 data from the World Bank (2013b).

---

1 Progress is measured using indicators that capture different aspects of the regulatory and institutional environment for business. See World Bank (2013c).

members. There is considerable diversity across G20 members, both in the level of the index and progress since 2005. Even in some advanced economies, there is substantial room for further reforms. For example, Italy ranks 73rd out of 185 countries on the Ease of Doing Business index.

The areas in most need of reform can be identified by breaking the index down into its nine components (see Figure 8.4). Those components are divided into two groups: strength of corporate and financial institutional framework (enforcing contracts, resolving

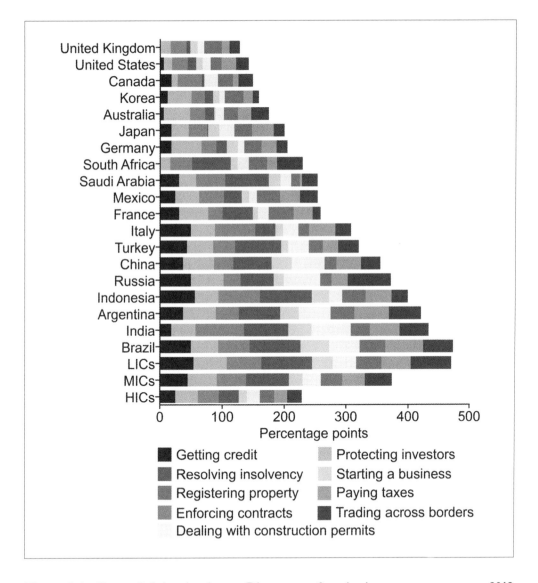

Figure 8.4 Ease of doing business: Distance to frontier in component areas, 2012
Note: LICs – low-income countries; MICs = middle-income countries; HICs = high-income countries.
Source: Based on 2013 data from World Bank (2013b).

insolvency, getting credit, and protecting investors) and efficiency of regulatory processes (starting a business, dealing with construction permits, registering property, paying taxes, and trading across borders). Typically, reforms to reduce the cost and complexity of regulatory processes, such as simplifying the process for starting a business or registering property, have seen the most progress, while deeper reforms of a more institutional nature have the farthest to go. Removing barriers to firms' entry, promoting competition, and strengthening the institutional underpinnings of product and factor markets are important not only for efficiency and productivity growth but also for the avoidance of a skewed industrial structure inimical to the growth of small and medium-sized enterprises and a broader sharing of economic opportunity.

Specific reform priorities vary across countries. For example, based on recent World Bank (2014) Enterprise Surveys, the constraint considered by the largest percentage of firms as a major obstacle to business was infrastructure in India, access to finance in Indonesia, formal/informal sector interface in Mexico, tax issues in Russia, and security and the legal framework in South Africa (see Figure 8.5). While priorities may differ across countries, there is much scope for improving the enabling environment for business in all G20 members.

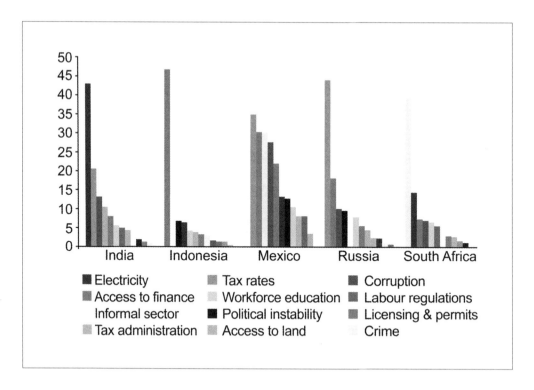

Figure 8.5   Major constraints to business, as reported by firms (percentage of firms)

Source: World Bank (2014).

G20: FROM CRISIS MANAGEMENT TO POLICIES FOR GROWTH

Investing in Infrastructure

Infrastructure is a key complement to reforms to improve the private investment climate. It is a crucial facilitator of growth and structural change. Infrastructure investment boosted growth in developing countries by an estimated 1.6 percentage points in the past decade (Calderón and Servén 2010). In the current global economic context, an increase in infrastructure investment could provide a welcome boost to demand and generate positive international spillovers, while strengthening the foundations for longer-term growth. For example, simulations show that a combination of successful fiscal consolidation in advanced economies and a redirection of global savings to support a matching increase in infrastructure investment in developing countries could raise GDP in developing countries by about 25 per cent and global GDP by 7 per cent over a 10-year period while also helping to reduce external imbalances – including the US deficit and China's surplus (see Figure 8.6). An alternative simulation whereby fiscal consolidation in advanced economies is accompanied by increased investment in key infrastructure in these economies produces a positive medium-term growth outcome for them (World Bank 2011; McKibbon et al. 2012).

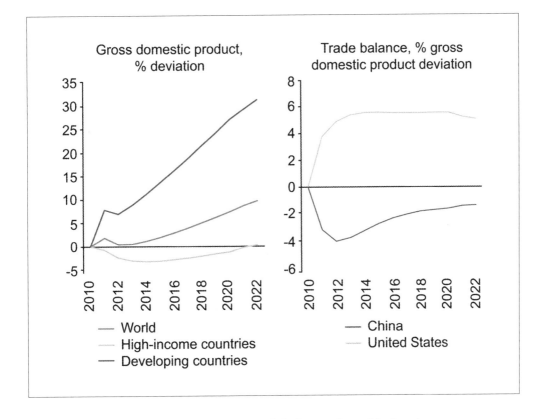

Figure 8.6 **Infrastructure investment, global growth and balancing**

Note: Simulations with G-cubed model. All results are expressed as percentage deviations from baseline.

Source: World Bank (2011).

Despite progress, infrastructure gaps in developing countries remain large. In many low-income countries, a lack of basic infrastructure acts as a major constraint to growth. For example, more than two thirds of the population in sub-Saharan Africa does not have access to electricity. In the rapidly growing middle-income countries, the infrastructure base is stronger but has strained to keep pace with the demands of dynamic growth. In India, almost one third of the population lacks access to electricity. The increasing role of global trade and supply chains, rapid urbanization, and the challenges of environmental sustainability have added to infrastructure needs. Even in many advanced economies, modernization of infrastructure needs to be part of a strategy for longer-term growth.

While potential returns to well-prepared and implemented infrastructure projects are high, a lack of financing keeps these opportunities from being exploited. Infrastructure investment needs in developing countries were estimated at $1.5 trillion in 2013, rising as high as $2.3 trillion by 2020 (World Bank 2012b). These estimates compare with current investment in infrastructure of around $0.8 trillion. In the medium term, therefore, incremental infrastructure investment needs in developing countries amount to about $1 trillion per year. Financing incremental investment of this order of magnitude presents a major challenge. More attention, therefore, needs to be paid to the availability of appropriate long-term financing for investment in infrastructure. Financing for infrastructure, and other long-term investments, appears to have become more difficult in the wake of the global financial crisis – not just for emerging and developing economies but advanced economies as well (World Bank 2013e). A deeper assessment is needed of policies to facilitate financing for infrastructure, including private capital, public financing, public-private partnerships, risk mitigation instruments, and innovative mechanisms to intermediate large pools of savings such as sovereign wealth funds. The agenda also includes actions to reform the regulatory and institutional framework for infrastructure investment and strengthen project preparation and implementation capacities.

Addressing the Jobs Challenge

Unemployment remains well above pre-crisis levels in most advanced economies. It continues to be a drag on economic recovery and will affect longer-term growth prospects if prolonged job losses lead to higher structural unemployment and destruction of skills. From an emerging economy perspective, the concerns are less cyclical and more structural and longer term. Some countries, such as India, continue to experience demographic trends causing rapid increases in the size of the labour force. Youth unemployment has been persistently high in many countries, such as those in the Middle East and North Africa. In some countries, job quality and underemployment are at the forefront: for example, informality soars above 50 per cent of employment in a number of emerging economies.

Growth-enhancing structural reforms are also central to job creation. The World Bank's (2012c) 'World Development Report 2013: Jobs' sets out a three-layered policy approach to job creation (see Figure 8.7). At the foundation are fundamentals that drive growth, including macroeconomic stability, a supportive investment climate, and human capital accumulation. The second layer of labour policies facilitates job creation from growth.

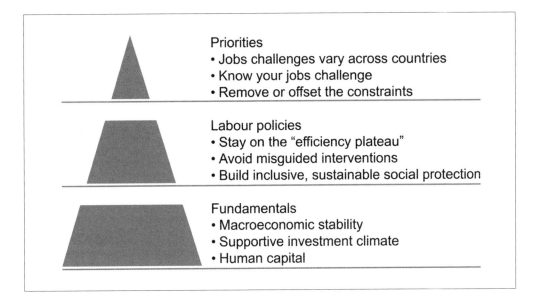

Figure 8.7 Three-layered approach to job creation
Source: World Bank (2012c).

The report finds that as long as labour market interventions remain on an efficiency plateau and avoid the cliffs of excessive or inadequate regulation, their effect on aggregate employment tends to be small compared to that of the fundamental drivers of growth. The third layer of priorities links specific, selective interventions to the particular nature of a country's jobs challenge, such as activation programs in economies with high youth unemployment, skill upgrading and worker retraining in economies experiencing rapid structural change, and social security reform in aging economies.

When labour policies are off the efficiency plateau, their effects on employment can be much greater. This is the case in some advanced European economies and some emerging economies such as India, Brazil, and South Africa, where labour market rigidities and distortions seriously hamper job creation and productive efficiency. In India, for example, labour market rigidities have contributed to a 'hollow middle' in manufacturing (see Figure 8.8) (World Bank 2012c). Medium-sized businesses, which typically generate most of the jobs in an economy, make up a disproportionately small share of total manufacturing firms in India. Labour market reform is an important part of the jobs agenda in these economies.

Global cooperation on migration can produce mutually beneficial outcomes for both sending and recipient countries by reconciling labour surpluses and shortages across national boundaries. Global agreements that facilitate cross-border investment can help in job creation and spur productivity growth (International Labour Organization et al. 2012).

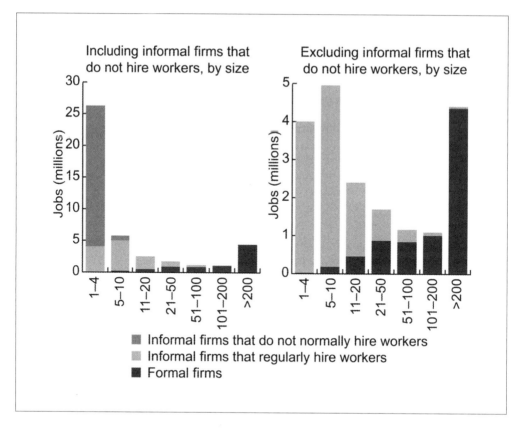

Figure 8.8 Labour policies off the efficiency plateau in India
Source: World Bank (2012c).

Advancing Trade Reform

Trade reform needs more attention – not only because of rising protectionist pressures but also because trade reform, by lowering existing barriers, can stimulate global growth. To date, in the policy response to the global financial crisis, the potential of trade reform remains untapped. Rather than open up trade and competition and boost market confidence and global growth, countries have for the most part resorted to trade-restrictive measures. G20 members account for the bulk of the trade-restrictive measures implemented since the onset of the global financial crisis. They were responsible for around three quarters of the trade-distorting measures implemented between November 2008 and November 2012, with their share in such measures rising from about 60 per cent in 2009 to 80 per cent in 2012 (see Figure 8.9).

All G20 members have resorted to trade-distorting measures, some more than others (see Figure 8.10). Overall, the new trade restrictions imposed since the start of the global financial crisis affect about 4 per cent of world trade, or about $750 billion. But that is not all. This is only the impact of the increase in trade restrictions. The opportunity cost of

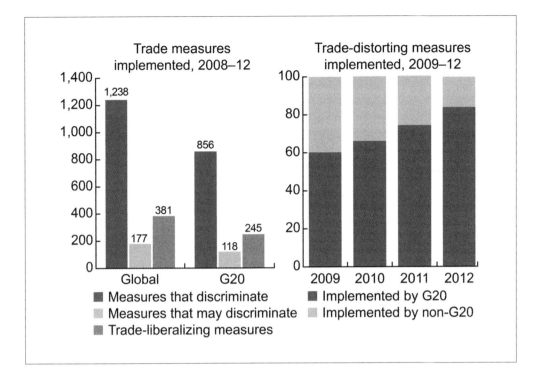

Figure 8.9 Rising protectionism
Source: Global Trade Alert (2013).

not lowering existing trade barriers, in terms of foregone gains from trade, is larger. And gains from liberalization of trade in services would be additional still.

There has been a rise in particular in the use of less transparent trade restrictions such as antidumping actions, countervailing duties, and safeguards. By 2011, the stock of imported products that G20 members subjected to such restrictions was about 50 per cent higher than before the global financial crisis. The largest increase was in South-South restrictions. Imported products restricted by G20 emerging economies rose by about 75 per cent between 2007 and 2011, covering at least 3.5 per cent of their total imported products. In contrast, imported product coverage of restrictions imposed by G20 advanced economies rose by about 20 per cent to a level of slightly more than 2 per cent of their total imported products. Most of the increase in these restrictions affected exports of emerging and developing economies, especially those of China, with the largest proportion of the impact arising from restrictions imposed by G20 emerging economies (see Figure 8.11).

The G20 needs to show more leadership on trade reform. G20 members should live up to the commitment they made at the start of the global financial crisis to refrain from protectionist measures, and should unwind such measures they have put in place since then. With progress on the World Trade Organization's Doha Round of trade negotiations stalled, the G20 (2011) should follow through on its leaders' call at the 2011 Cannes

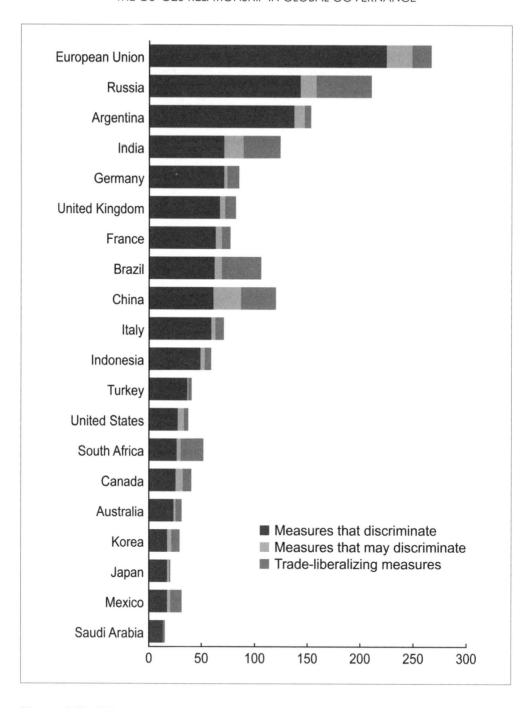

Figure 8.10 G20 trade measures, 2008–12

Note: Individual measures may have large or small trade coverage. Data on number of trade measures do not necessarily reflect trade coverage. Figures for the European Union are aggregate measures for all 27 members, including those shown separately in the chart.

Source: Global Trade Alert (2013).

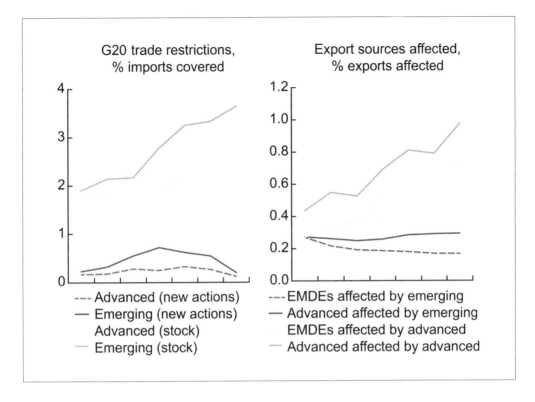

Figure 8.11 Increasing use of less transparent trade restrictions

Note: The chart on the left illustrates the percentage of imported products covered by the G20's use of antidumping actions, countervailing duties, and safeguards. The chart on the right illustrates percentage of exported products affected by the same measures. EMDEs = emerging market and developing economies.

Source: Temporary Trade Barriers Database Including the Global Antidumping Database (2013f).

Summit to pursue 'fresh, credible approaches' to multilateral trade negotiations. The reform agenda could also include trade matters of growing importance that were not part of the Doha negotiations, such as deeper disciplines for investment and export restrictions and trade-environment linkages.

Promoting Green Growth

There is also a need to better integrate environmental sustainability into the structural reform and investment agenda for growth. The greening of growth presents both challenges and opportunities. Green policies are necessary to address the threat of climate change but can also provide significant co-benefits in terms of growth and employment generation. They can spur innovation and investment in new technologies and foster new sources of growth. This is an agenda for emerging and advanced economies alike.

Well-designed green policies improve social welfare, taking into account present as well as future generations. Yet policy makers are naturally also concerned about potential

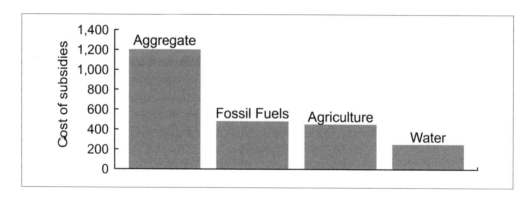

Figure 8.12 Environmentally harmful subsidies ($ billion)
Source: World Bank (2012a).

trade-offs and costs for near-term growth and employment. In some cases, the choice should be relatively straightforward in principle, such as when green objectives require the elimination of economic distortions such as energy subsidies, thus increasing economic efficiency and generating savings for potential use in other growth-promoting investments, such as green infrastructure. Removal of these subsidies can produce a win-win outcome not only for the environment and economic growth but also for equity, as they are often poorly targeted and their equity objectives can be better met through well-designed cash transfers to the poor – such as through cash transfers to poor families conditional on keeping children in school or making regular visits to the health clinic for maternal and child health care. Globally, the cost of environmentally harmful subsidies (in fossil fuels, agriculture, water, and fisheries) is estimated at upwards of $1.2 trillion annually (see Figure 8.12) (World Bank 2012a).

In other cases, the choice may be more difficult, as actions to combat climate change require economic costs today in return for environmental and economic benefits in the future. Such costs can be kept smaller if implemented using well-designed, market-based policies that create incentives for people to seek out the lowest-cost ways of protecting the environment. The economic costs can be further minimized when environmental damage is taxed and revenues are used to reduce other distorting taxes (or reduce a large fiscal deficit). For example, Turkey raises revenues equivalent to about 3.5 per cent of GDP from environmentally related taxes, while Germany, Korea, and the United Kingdom raise about 2.5 per cent. A key barrier to capturing the efficiency and sustainability benefits from green policies, even those that can be win-win, is a range of political economy and global collective-action constraints. The G20 process can help in the concentration of policies and addressing their global public good dimensions.

Conclusion

At the Pittsburgh Summit in 2009, G20 leaders designated the G20 as the 'premier forum' for their international economic cooperation. Much of the G20's attention since then has been focused on responding to the global financial crisis, in particular actions aimed at macrofinancial stabilization. Such actions are the first order of business in a crisis context – and much remains to be done to restore financial stability and secure the transition to an economic recovery. However, short-term crisis management alone will not produce a return to strong growth and job creation, much less assure the long-term sustainability of growth. Future global growth faces deeper structural challenges. The G20 will need to pay more attention to reforms that address these challenges. Many of these reforms require international peer interaction, policy coordination, or collective action, which the G20 can facilitate.

Cooperative actions by the G20 have helped steer the world economy from the depths of a severe crisis toward a path to recovery. The long-term structural reform agenda to strengthen the foundations for strong, sustainable, and balanced global growth will present a different challenge. This could arguably be a tougher challenge, as incentives to act and cooperate can weaken as the crisis recedes and the immediate pressures on policy makers diminish. But meeting this challenge will be an important test of the G20's ability to be effective beyond the firefighting phase of a crisis – and to live up to its aspirations as the premier forum for international economic cooperation.

References

Bhattacharya, Amar, Mattia Romani and Nicholas Stern (2012). 'Infrastructure for Development: Meeting the Challenge'. Centre for Climate Change Economics and Policy, Grantham Research Institute on Clmate Change and the Environment in collaboration with the Intergovernmental Group of 24, June. http://www.cccep.ac.uk/Publications/Policy/docs/PP-infrastructure-for-development-meeting-the-challenge.pdf (December 2014).

Bulman, David, Maya Eden and Ha Nguyen (2012). 'Transition from Low-Income Growth to High-Income Growth: Is There a Middle-Income Trap?' Background paper, World Bank, Washington DC.

Calderón, César and Luis Servén (2010). 'Infrastructure and Economic Development in Sub-Saharan Africa'. *Journal of African Economies* 19(Suppl 1): i13–i87.

G20 (2011). 'Cannes Summit Final Declaration – Building Our Common Future: Renewed Collective Action for the Benefit of All'. Cannes, November 4. http://www.g20.utoronto.ca/2011/2011-cannes-declaration-111104-en.html (December 2014).

Gill, Indermit S. and Martin Raiser (2012). *Golden Growth: Restoring the Lustre of the European Economic Model.* Washington DC: World Bank. http://documents.worldbank.org/curated/en/2012/04/16234385/golden-growth-restoring-lustre-european-economic-model (December 2014).

Global Trade Alert (2013). 'Statistics: Worldwide'. http://www.globaltradealert.org/ (December 2014).

International Labour Organization, Organisation for Economic Co-operation and Development, International Monetary Fund, et al. (2012). 'Boosting Jobs and Living Standards in G20 Countries'. A joint report prepared for the G20, June. http://www.ilo.org/wcmsp5/groups/public/---dgreports/---dcomm/documents/publication/wcms_183705.pdf (December 2014)

International Monetary Fund (2010). 'Navigating the Fiscal Challenges Ahead'. Fiscal Monitor, May, Washington DC. http://www.imf.org/external/pubs/ft/fm/2010/fm1001.pdf (December 2014).

International Monetary Fund (2012). 'World Economic Outlook: Coping with High Debt and Sluggish Growth'. October, Washington DC. http://www.imf.org/external/pubs/ft/weo/2012/02/ (December 2014).

McKibbon, Warwick J., Andrew B. Stoeckel and YingYing Lu (2012). 'Global Fiscal Adjustment and Trade Rebalancing'. Policy Research Working Paper 6044, World Bank, Washington DC. doi: 10.1596/1813-9450-6044.

Organisation for Economic Co-operation and Development (2012). 'Economic Policy Reforms: Going for Growth 2012'. Paris. http://www.oecd.org/eco/monetary/economicpolicyreformsgoingforgrowth2012.htm (December 2014).

World Bank (2011). 'Rebalancing, Growth, and Development: An Interconnected Agenda'. Paper prepared for the G20, October, Washington DC. http://siteresources.worldbank.org/DEC/Resources/84797-1320153303397/Rebalancing_Growth_and_Development-WB_paper_for_G20.pdf (December 2014).

World Bank (2012a). 'Inclusive Green Growth: The Pathway to Sustainable Development'. May, Washington DC. http://siteresources.worldbank.org/EXTSDNET/Resources/Inclusive_Green_Growth_May_2012.pdf (December 2014).

World Bank (2012b). 'Restoring and Sustaining Growth'. Paper prepared for the G20 finance ministers and central bank governors, June 19, Washington DC. http://go.worldbank.org/Q3U4L7U9L0 (December 2014).

World Bank (2012c). 'World Development Report 2013: Jobs'. Washington DC. http://go.worldbank.org/TM7GTEB8U0 (December 2014).

World Bank (2013a). 'China 2030: Building a Modern, Harmonious, and Creative Society'. Washington DC. http://documents.worldbank.org/curated/en/2013/03/17494829/china-2030-building-modern-harmonious-creative-society (December 2014).

World Bank (2013b). 'Doing Business'. Database, Washington DC. http://data.worldbank.org/data-catalog/doing-business-database (December 2014).

World Bank (2013c). 'Doing Business 2013: Smarter Regulations for Small and Medium-Size Enterprises'. Washington DC. http://www.doingbusiness.org/~/media/GIAWB/Doing%20Business/Documents/Annual-Reports/English/DB13-full-report.pdf (December 2014).

World Bank (2013d). 'Global Economic Prospects January 2013: Assuring Growth over the Medium Term'. January 15, Washington DC. http://go.worldbank.org/YF5N2YO550 (December 2014).

World Bank (2013e). 'Long-Term Investment Financing for Growth and Development: Umbrella Paper'. Prepared for the G20 finance ministers and central bank governors, February. http://en.g20russia.ru/load/781255094 (December 2014).

World Bank (2013f). 'Temporary Trade Barriers Database Including the Global Antidumping Database'. Washington DC. http://data.worldbank.org/data-catalog/temporary-trade-barriers-database (December 2014).

World Bank (2014). 'Enterprise Surveys'. Database, Washington DC. http://www.enterprisesurveys.org (December 2014).

Chapter 9
B20–G20 Engagement: Achievements and Challenges

Marina V. Larionova, Mark Rakhmangulov, Andrei Sakharov, and Andrey Shelepov[1]

Dialogue between the Group of 20 (G20) and the Business 20 (B20) should be instrumental in enhancing G20 efficiency both by responding to business interests and concerns and by engaging the private sector in generating growth and jobs. The B20 was first initiated by the Canadian Council of Chief Executives on the eve of the Toronto Summit in June 2010. By the beginning of 2014, five B20 meetings, including the one in Toronto, had been organized, each putting forward recommendations for G20 leaders: in Seoul in November 2010, in Cannes in November 2011, in Los Cabos in June 2012, and in St Petersburg in September 2013.

The investment made into the dialogue by both business and governments warrants an independent unbiased and rigorous analysis of what has been achieved and what lessons should be learned. This chapter reviews the progress in G20–B20 engagement in order to identify achievements and challenges.

Methodology

The primary focus here is on how B20 recommendations have translated into G20 decisions. The analysis was guided by three criteria: direct references to the B20, mentions of the keywords 'business' and 'private sector', and the degree to which G20 statements match B20 recommendations.

While the first two criteria were easily analysed, assessment of the third one was more complicated, given the differences in the language in B20 and G20 documents. To define the degree of B20 influence on G20 statements, the study examined whether the G20 documents contained text units matching B20 recommendations. Second, it identified whether the matching text unit in the G20 document was an expression of deliberation or direction setting or whether it contained concrete decisions (commitments and mandates).[2]

---

1   This chapter draws on the research project on 'Elaborating a Supply-Demand Model to Balance External Demand and National Priorities in the Presidency Proposals for Agenda in G20, G8, and BRICS', Project No. 12-03-00563, with financial support from Russian Foundation for Humanities.

2   A commitment is defined as a discrete, specific, publicly expressed, collectively agreed statement of intent: a promise or undertaking by summit members that they will undertake future

A scoring system was applied where +1 means the B20 recommendation is addressed in the G20 documents and G20 actions or mandates are in line with the B20 recommendations, 0 means the B20 recommendation is addressed in the G20 documents but there is no agreement on actions or mandates in line with the B20 recommendations, and −1 means the B20 recommendation is not addressed in the G20 documents.

The timeframe for this analysis is based on whether the B20 recommendations made within a certain G20 presidency were addressed in the documents issued by that same presidency. While this straightforward approach has its limitations, it cannot be assumed that a B20 recommendation can exert influence over several presidencies, especially if the B20 did not reiterate it in subsequent cycles, because too many variables can influence G20 decision making.

The review does not consider the effect of B20 recommendations on other international institutions unless there is a related G20 mandate. Thus, if an international institution acts in line with B20 recommendations or priorities but there is no evidence that it was guided by a G20 decision or mandate, no causal relationship is assumed.

The analysis does not include monitoring of G20 members' actions taken as the result of the B20-related commitments, unless such actions were reflected in the G20 documents.

As with any methodology, this one has certain limitations. First, in considering recommendations and documents produced within a single presidency, the review cannot include long-term proposals that could not be addressed within a short period but may be addressed over a longer period if the B20 continues to prioritize them in its dialogue with the G20. Such initiatives, although unheeded in G20 documents, can lay down the foundation for future decisions. Second, the B20 may make proposals despite knowing the G20 would find them too ambitious or concrete or not within the scope of its agenda or mandate. Hence it should be stressed that the scores do not assess either B20 or G20 performance, but characterize progress in their engagement. Therefore the scores indicate where the B20 may want to consolidate its efforts across presidencies to push G20 members to act.

The evidence base used in this study includes the recommendations made by B20 task forces in all policy areas from the 2010 Toronto Summit to the 2013 St Petersburg Summit. However, the recommendations contained in the B20's final documents are categorized according to policy areas as related to long-term G20 and B20 priorities, rather than according to the originating task force report. This approach is guided by two factors. First, the configuration of task forces changes significantly from presidency to presidency (see Appendix 9.A). Second, a task force's recommendations sometimes fall into a policy area beyond its stated focus. As the primary goal of the review is to look at G20–B20

---

action to move toward, meet, or adjust to an identified welfare target. Mandates include assignments to internal G20 structures, such as working groups or ministerial bodies, and external mechanisms, including international institutions. Commitments and mandates are drawn from the G20 leaders' documents issued at the summit according to a single methodology and consistent approach. See the G20 Information Centre at http://www.g20.utoronto.ca/analysis/index.html#commitments and the G8 and G20 Reference Manual for Commitment and Compliance Coding at http://www.hse.ru/en/org/hse/iori/G20_analytics#method.

engagement, B20 recommendations that required actions from the business community were not included, nor were they included in the catalogue of recommendations (see Appendix 9.B).

Advancing the Dialogue

Of the total of 403 recommendations, 145 (or 36 per cent) were reflected in the G20 documents between 2010 and 2013 as commitments or mandates (see Table 9.1). The Toronto kick-start proved the most productive with the caveat that its 11 B20 recommendations came in response to the G20 priorities on the eve of the summit, by which time G20 decisions by and large had been already agreed, and were not presented in a document but rather reported by the B20 chair (B20 2010a). Seoul and Cannes saw a substantive increase in the number of B20 recommendations, incorporating new areas of green growth, infrastructure development, health, and information and communications technologies (ICT), technology, and innovation in Seoul and, in Cannes, food security, anticorruption, global governance, and financing for development (B20 2010b, 2011). B20 recommendations expanded to new areas to reflect the G20's growing agenda. Under the Russian presidency in 2013, the expansionary trend was reversed, and the B20 focused only on six priorities directly related to the G20's core agenda (B20 2013). However, the total number of B20 recommendations to the leaders rose to 141.

The number and percentage of B20 recommendations that were translated into G20 decisions reached 16 in Seoul (28 per cent), 45 in Cannes (38 per cent), 25 in Los Cabos (33 per cent), and 52 in St Petersburg (37 per cent) (see Table 9.2). Thus the results across presidencies were mixed, although a positive trend emerged.

In terms of policy areas, the B20's recommendations on reform of the international monetary system, macroeconomic policies, and financial regulation, which all belong to the G20's core mission, have registered the greatest correlation with G20 decisions (with positive scores of 67 per cent, 58 per cent, and 58 per cent recommendations respectively) (see Table 9.3).

Recommendations on food security proposed at Cannes, Los Cabos, and St Petersburg also get a good track record in G20's decision making with the overall total positive score of 60 per cent, or 15 out of 25 recommendations.

Investment and infrastructure fare relatively well with a positive track record of 36 per cent (eight of 22 recommendations) and 31 per cent (four of 13 recommendations) in G20 decisions. The 2013 B20 Task Force on Investment and Infrastructure faced a special responsibility as these two policy areas, previously dealt with separately, were now combined. Ultimately, four of the eight recommendations on investment (50 per cent) and one of the three recommendations on infrastructure (33 per cent) found their way into the 2013 G20 documents as commitments or mandates.

Trade is a challenge: less than 30 per cent (15 of 52) of recommendations were reflected in G20 commitments.

The 2013 B20 Task Force on Job Creation, Employment, and Investment in Human Capital inherited 29 recommendations with only seven (24 per cent) positively reflected in

Table 9.1 B20 recommendations (by issue area and summit)

	Toronto		Seoul		Cannes		Los Cabos		St Petersburg		Total	
	Count	%	Count	%	Count	%	Count	%	Count	%	Count	%
Employment, human capital, social issues	1	9.1	8	14.0	8	6.8	12	15.8	26	18.4	55	13.6
Trade	2	18.2	6	10.5	10	8.5	11	14.5	23	16.3	52	12.9
Financial regulation	3	27.3	6	10.5	11	9.3	5	6.6	23	16.3	48	11.9
Corruption	0	0	0	0	6	5.1	15	19.7	17	12.1	38	9.4
Green growth	0	0	14	24.6	14	11.9	6	7.9	2	0.0	36	8.9
ICT, technology, and innovation	0	0	5	8.8	11	9.3	4	5.3	13	9.2	33	8.2
Food security	0	0	0	0	6	5.1	18	23.7	1	0.7	25	6.2
Macroeconomic	5	45.5	4	7.0	6	5.1	0	0.0	9	6.4	24	6.0
Investment	0	0	5	8.8	6	5.1	3	3.9	8	6.4	22	5.5
Energy	0	0	1	1.8	12	10.2	0	0	5	3.5	18	4.5
Global governance	0	0	0	0	8	6.8	0	0	8	5.7	16	4.0
Infrastructure	0	0	5	8.8	3	2.5	2	2.6	3	2.8	13	3.2
International monetary system	0	0	0	0	11	9.3	0	0	1	0.7	12	3.0
Financing for growth and development	0	0	3	5.3	6	5.1	0	0	2	1.4	11	2.7
Total	11	100	57	100	118	100	76	100	141	100	403	100

Table 9.2   Recommendation scores (by summit)

Score	Toronto		Seoul		Cannes		Los Cabos		St Petersburg		Total	
	Count	%	Count	%	Count	%	Count	%	Count	%	Count	%
0	4	36.4	11	19.3	26	22.0	23	30.3	23	16.3	87	21.6
1	7	63.6	16	28.1	45	38.1	25	32.9	52	36.9	145	36.0
−1	0	0.0	30	52.6	47	39.8	28	36.8	66	46.8	171	42.4
Total	11	100	57	100	118	100	76	100	141	100	403	100

Table 9.3   Recommendation scores (by issue area)

	−1		0		1		Total	
	Count	%	Count	%	Count	%	Count	%[a]
Employment, human capital, social issues	21	36.8	15	27.3	19	34.5	55	13.6
Trade	27	51.9	10	19.2	15	28.8	52	12.9
Financial regulation	12	25.0	8	16.7	28	58.3	48	11.9
Corruption	14	36.8	14	36.8	10	26.4	38	9.4
Green growth	17	47.2	7	19.4	12	33.3	36	8.9
ICT, technology, and innovation	30	90.9	3	9.1	0	0	33	8.2
Food security	6	24.0	4	16.0	15	60.0	25	6.2
Investment	9	40.9	5	22.7	8	36.4	22	5.5
Macroeconomic	5	22.7	5	20.8	14	58.3	24	6.0
Energy	9	50.0	3	16.7	6	33.3	18	4.5
Global governance	6	37.5	5	31.3	5	31.3	16	4.0
Infrastructure	4	33.3	4	33.3	4	33.3	12	3.0
International monetary system	3	25.0	1	8.3	8	66.7	12	3.0
Financing for development	7	63.6	3	27.3	1	9.1	11	2.7
Total	170	42.2	87	21.6	146	36.2	403	100

Note: Numbers may not add up to 100 due to rounding. [a] Percentage of total recommendations for all issues.

G20 documents. Close collaboration with the G20 Working Group on Employment as well as with the Labour 20 (L20) proved fundamentally important in crafting recommendations that would be well reflected in the G20 documents: 12 of the 26 recommendations (46 per cent) were drawn upon by the G20 in commitments or formulate mandates for future action.

Green growth, energy, and ICT, technology, and innovation, which in 2013 fell within the portfolio of the B20 Task Force on Innovation and Development as a Global Priority, had modest success on average, although 12 of the 36 recommendations on green growth could be traced in G20 commitments. For ICT, technology, and innovation, none of the B20's 20 recommendations was acted upon by the G20 before St Petersburg. This trend continued under the Russian presidency, with none of the 13 recommendations on innovation registered in the G20 documents.

Financial Regulation

Over the period from the Toronto Summit to the St Petersburg Summit, the B20 made 48 recommendations on financial regulation, which constituted 12 per cent of all B20 recommendations (see Table 9.3). In Toronto the B20 made three recommendations in the area of financial regulation, and two of them were reflected in the G20 commitments (see Figure 9.1). In Seoul, five of six B20 recommendations on financial regulation were translated into the G20 commitments and mandates. The B20 made 11 recommendations on financial regulation in Cannes, six of which were addressed in the G20's documents. In Los Cabos three of the B20's five recommendations were taken up by the G20. In St Petersburg, 23 recommendations were made on financial regulation, with 12 of them translated into G20 documents as commitments or mandates. Overall, 58 per cent (28 of 48) of B20 recommendations received a score of +1 for recognition in G20 decisions, which is the second highest score among all the issue areas on the B20 agenda.

The B20 recommendations on financial regulation for the Toronto Summit were generally in line with G20 priorities. As a result, recommendations on new requirements for banking capital ratios, leverage, and liquidity, and on 'not to tighten the requirements too quickly' were reflected in the G20 declaration (B20 2010a). However, the recommendation to impose taxes on the banking sector in some countries, which is not supported by some G20 members, was not addressed.

The B20's recommendations for the Seoul Summit focused on two broad issues: banking regulation and small and medium-sized enterprises (SMEs). The B20 reiterated its recommendation to strengthen the supervision of banks, while stimulating growth, which was again addressed by the G20. The B20 also made five recommendations on different aspects of stimulating the development of SMEs. Only one, very specific recommendation on establishing credit bureaus in emerging markets was not taken up by the G20.

At Cannes, no previous recommendation on financial regulation was taken up in the B20 report. Instead, the B20 focused on several new issues in this area. The G20 led the dialogue on developing local currency bond markets as one of the 'measures to increase companies' access to financial and non-financial currency hedges', and for the first time the

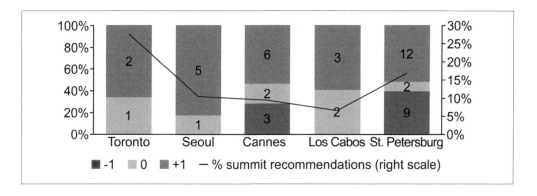

Figure 9.1 Recommendations on financial regulation

Note: The left scale indicates the total number of recommendations for the issue area. The line, which refers to the right scale, indicates the percentage of recommendations for that issue in relation to the total for each summit. The numbers in each column indicate the number of recommendations in that scoring category.

G20 made a commitment in this issue area (B20 2011). B20 recommendations on ensuring stable regulatory regimes, broadening capital markets, stimulating financial inclusion, preventing 'risk mutating into shadow banking', and defining 'tools and procedures to ensure consistent implementation of regulatory change' were reflected in the G20 Cannes documents. However, several important recommendations remained unaddressed, in particular, on reviewing whether 'Basel rules to ensure creditworthy SMEs have access to capital'; extending a regulatory approach to other economic policy areas, including fiscal policies; providing clear information to market participants; avoiding negative impacts from derivatives and banking regulations on international trade; and creating a structured roadmap for all financial reforms.

In the Los Cabos report, the B20 (2012) again reiterated previous recommendations on supporting SMEs. One recommendation to increase SME finance was translated into G20 decisions. More specific recommendations on improving SME access to finance through addressing 'barriers to entry and incentives to provide finance' and improving 'regulation, distribution channels and access' were deliberated upon in the G20 Los Cabos documents. As at Cannes, the B20 put forward new issues. Recommendations on improving financial education and consumer protection were reflected in the G20's Los Cabos documents, which was the first time the G20 leaders had made decisions on these issues.

The B20 proposed 23 recommendations on financial regulation in its St Petersburg report, which constitutes almost half of all B20 recommendations in this area made since its inception. The G20 acted on 12 and deliberated on two, thus reflecting about 61 per cent in its documents. The B20 reiterated some of its previous recommendations. One recurring recommendation on improving access to finance for SMEs was translated into the G20 decisions. However, an important recommendation on reforming tax systems to reduce compliance burdens for SMEs remained unaddressed. The B20 also put forward a number of new issues in the area of financial regulation. Recommendations on addressing shadow banking risks, establishing a mutual recognition process for national rules and practices, tackling base erosion and profit shifting, providing consistency among actions taken in the area of taxation and financial regulations, enhancing financial market infrastructures, and assessing the implications of financial reform on other areas were mainly reflected in the G20's St Petersburg documents as commitments and mandates, or were at least deliberated upon. The only exception was two very specific recommendations on financial market infrastructure that were not taken up by the G20.

At the same time, all six recommendations on trade finance made by the B20 were ignored, being very specific and relating more to the traditional activities of international financial institutions (IFIs), such as the Basel Committee on Banking Supervision. To ensure that these recommendations receive attention by the G20 in future, the B20 should make them less specific and call on the G20 to mandate relevant institutions to take concrete action.

Thus, financial regulation is an area where the B20 has consistently identified and promoted relevant issues in its dialogue with the G20. Given that financial reforms remain at the core of the G20 agenda, the B20 should augment cooperation in this particular area, with due regard of any newly emerging challenges and the relevance of previous B20 recommendations not addressed by the G20.

International Monetary System

At 3 per cent, the share of B20 recommendations on the international monetary system, made only to the Cannes and St Petersburg summits, is low (see Table 9.3). However, the level of their reflection in G20 documents is the highest (66.7 per cent were acted upon by the G20).

The 2011 B20 Task Force on the International Monetary System produced six recommendations focused on currency risks, reserve currencies and special drawing rights (SDRs), and International Monetary Fund (IMF) surveillance. The B20 Task Force on Global Economic Policy Imperatives working in the same year produced five more recommendations related to IMF governance reform and its surveillance mandate. Such a division seems unjustified as these issues are closely interconnected and should be dealt together. Moreover, the G20 usually includes IMF reform in its treatment of the international monetary system.

At the Cannes Summit the G20 leaders made commitments or mandates in line with seven B20 recommendations. The G20 continued to address strengthening the IMF surveillance and remitted mandates, supporting the IMF's work and delineating several reform features.

One B20 recommendation relates to the actions of a particular G20 member: increasing the convertibility of the Chinese renminbi, which 'is necessary to enhance the international importance of the nation's currency' (B20 2011). China confirmed its plans on convertibility through an individual commitment formulated in the G20's Cannes Action Plan for Growth and Jobs and thus this recommendation's reflection was assessed at a score of +1. The G20 leaders also reaffirmed their earlier commitments on reforming IMF governance and enhancing the exchange rate flexibility of their currencies and agreed that a broader SDR basket was 'an important determinant of its attractiveness ... as a global reserve asset' (G20 2011b). They also recognized the indicative guidelines, developed by the G20 finance ministers and central bank governors 'as a mechanism to assess progress in rebalancing, and the consistency of fiscal, monetary, financial sector, structural, exchange rate and other policies' and committed to continue using them (G20 2011a). However, they did not elaborate on the B20 proposal to require the IMF include 'a standardized table of key indicators to assess sustainability of policies' in its Article IV reports (B20 2011).

The G20 neither acted nor deliberated on B20-specific proposals to 'promote the production and communication of indicators ... about currency risks' and carry out studies of 'currency instability impact on individual companies and the global economy as a whole' (B20 2011).

Under the Russian presidency the B20 emphasized that the G20 should ensure the sustainability of public finances and global economy and make sovereign debt management plans an integral part of the prudent fiscal frameworks of all G20 members. This recommendation was broadly in line with Russia's G20 priorities, and was reflected in a mandate to the G20 finance ministers and the Organisation for Economic Co-operation and Development (OECD) to review the OECD's interim report on leading practices for raising, managing, and retiring public debt, including on state guarantees, as well as a request to the IMF and the World Bank to update the 'Guidelines for Public Debt Management' in light of recent experiences (G20 2013).

In fact, most of the B20 recommendations in this area corresponded to the G20 priorities that had emerged at previous summits. Thus, it might be assumed that the high level of correlation between B20 recommendations and G20 decisions on the international monetary system was not caused by the B20's influence on G20 decisions, but rather by the fact that the task force shared the G20 established agenda and reflected it in its recommendations.

Macroeconomic Issues

Between the Toronto and the St Petersburg summits, the B20 made 24 recommendations on macroeconomic issues, which constitute 6 per cent of all B20 recommendations (see Table 9.3). At 58 per cent (14 recommendations), the level of their reflection in G20 documents is relatively high. This is due to the fact that macroeconomic issues have remained a G20 priority since the 2008 Washington Summit, and thus some B20 recommendations supported already agreed decisions.

Five of 11 B20 recommendations made in Toronto focused on macroeconomic policy, and three were addressed by the G20 (see Figure 9.2). In Seoul the B20 made four macroeconomic recommendations, with only one reflected in the G20 decisions. In Cannes half of the six B20 macroeconomic recommendations were addressed in the G20 documents. The B20 produced no macroeconomic recommendations at the Los Cabos Summit.

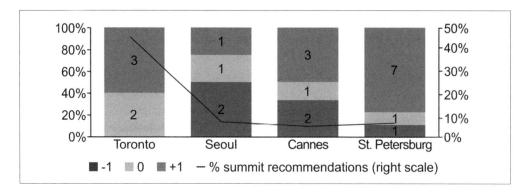

Figure 9.2 Recommendations on macroeconomic issues
Note: The left scale indicates the total number of recommendations for the issue area. The line, which refers to the right scale, indicates the percentage of recommendations for that issue in relation to the total for each summit. The numbers in each column indicate the number of recommendations in that scoring category.

The B20 recommendations reflected in the G20's Toronto commitments focused on implementing structural reforms, supporting the development of SMEs, and pursuing fiscal consolidation. Recommendations on ensuring access to credit for SMEs and on promoting 'open trade and competition, innovation and entrepreneurship' as growth drivers were not directly addressed by the G20 (B20 2010a).

The only B20 recommendation on macroeconomic issues translated into commitments in Seoul focused on addressing current account and financial account imbalances. Three relevant recommendations were not taken up by the G20. These included recommendations on exiting from financial sector support with a focus on cutting spending rather than increasing taxes, and on making monetary policy more neutral (B20 2010b).

In Cannes the B20 reiterated its recommendation on fiscal consolidation and also recommended that G20 members set 'mid-term economic objectives, specifically for fiscal, monetary and exchange policies' (B20 2011). Both recommendations were reflected in the G20 documents, along with a new recommendation on reforming entitlement programs, which translated in an individual commitment made by the United States. Again, the recommendation on reducing public spending rather than increasing taxes was not taken up by the G20. Two new B20 recommendations on developing 'policies in emerging economies to facilitate economic convergence with developed countries' and encouraging 'countries to adopt sound public finance as a best practice' were also not addressed.

Under the Russian presidency, B20 recommendations on macroeconomic issues focused on fiscal consolidation and structural reforms. The B20 proposed that the G20 prioritize public debt management instruments that could contribute positively to the productive potential of both advanced and emerging economies avoiding hikes in corporate and personal income tax and social contribution, as well as cuts in public infrastructure spending. It stated that fiscal consolidation plans should be growth-friendly, provide for investment into structural reforms, prioritize business and consumer confidence, and encourage enterprise and private investment. The G20 should reinforce its efforts on structural reforms, with a focus on liberalizing markets generally and strengthening labour markets in particular. These recommendations were fully reflected in the G20 Leaders' Declaration and the St Petersburg Action Plan and its annexes.

Two of the St Petersburg macroeconomic recommendations focused on SME-related issues. The recommendation on developing a common SME definition was addressed in the 'G20 Study Group on Financing for Investment Work Plan' (2013). However, the recommendation on the coordination of public entities to optimize support programs for SMEs was not translated into G20 decisions.

In sum, those B20 macroeconomic recommendations addressed by the G20 deal mainly with the traditional issues on the G20 agenda. Given the limited value of reiterating recommendations already being dealt with by G20, the B20 should focus on priorities that retain their relevance, but were previously neglected by the G20, and consolidate the push for structural reforms that are key for generating growth and jobs with due regard of the members' individual national circumstances.

Food Security

Between the Toronto Summit and the Los Cabos Summit the B20 made 25 recommendations related to food security, which is 6.2 per cent of all B20 recommendations (see Table 9.3). The issue was included in B20 priorities after the Seoul Summit, although food security had been on the G20 agenda since London when the leaders committed to making available resources for social protection for the poorest countries, including through investing in long-term food security. At Cannes the B20 made six recommendations on food security, of which five were addressed by the G20 (see Figure 9.3). At Los Cabos 10 of 18 B20 recommendations were reflected in the G20 documents. At St Petersburg the B20 made only one recommendation on food security, which was not reflected, receiving a score of 0. Thus, 60 per cent (15 of 25) of the B20 recommendations received a score of +1 for being translated into G20 commitments.

Six recommendations made by the B20 for the Cannes Summit were devoted to the issues of agricultural technology transfer, environmental sustainability of agricultural policies, increased public and private investment in agriculture, agricultural policy coordination, and improved functioning of agricultural markets.

The B20 recommendations on food security to the Los Cabos Summit were more numerous and addressed more specific issues, such as strengthening countries' capacities to achieve national food security goals, improving value chains in agriculture, managing risks in agriculture, producing biofuels, improving water management and efficiency, and establishing property rights. In their recommendations to the Los Cabos Summit the B20 also touched upon other areas of the G20 agenda connected with food security. For instance, the recommendations addressed such issues as improving trade policy, developing rural industries and employment, empowering women farmers, managing price volatility risks, expanding access to agricultural information, establishing land rights, increasing public investment, and creating an enabling environment for private investment in agriculture.

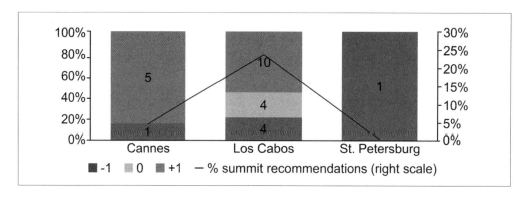

Figure 9.3 Recommendations on food security
Note: The left scale indicates the total number of recommendations for the issue area. The line, which refers to the right scale, indicates the percentage of recommendations for that issue in relation to the total for each summit. The numbers in each column indicate the number of recommendations in that scoring category.

These issues were extensively addressed in the Action Plan on Food Price Volatility and Agriculture issued by the G20's French presidency (G20 Agriculture Ministers 2011). At the Cannes Summit the G20 (2011b) 'decided to act on the five objectives of this Action Plan: (i) improving agricultural production and productivity; (ii) increasing market information and transparency; (iii) reducing the effects of price volatility for the most vulnerable; (iv) strengthening international policy coordination; and (v) improving the functioning of agricultural commodity derivatives' markets'. Because the B20 recommendations clearly supported the objectives set out by the G20 in the previous year, it is difficult to determine any impact the B20 might have had on the G20 decisions.

The B20 recommendation to the St Petersburg Summit called upon the G20 to increase agricultural productivity through promoting advanced information technologies among farmers. It was ignored in the G20 documents, perhaps due to its emphasis on the ICT aspects of agricultural productivity, which, despite the prominent position held by food security issues on the G20 agenda, could not be addressed by the G20, as it falls beyond the scope of the institution's core agenda.

Several notable B20 recommendations were not taken up by the G20:

- the recommendation to enable affordable and easier technology transfer and capacity building from developed to developing countries in the area of food and nutritional security (Cannes);
- the recommendation to strengthen capacity for achieving national food security goals (Los Cabos);
- the recommendation to build capacity along the value chain (Los Cabos);
- the recommendation to manage the approach to biofuels (Los Cabos); and
- the recommendation to reduce waste and optimize value chains (Los Cabos).

Some of these proposals remain relevant. Given the G20's extensive and demanding agenda on food security, the B20 could add value by focusing on the specific aspects of implementation, and agreeing on its own commitments that would support G20 efforts. Thus, the B20 could transform its recommendations on value chains into commitments. The B20 should align its recommendations more closely to the G20's core agenda in order to achieve greater responsiveness in the future.

Trade

From the Toronto Summit to the St Petersburg Summit the B20 made 52 trade-related recommendations, amounting to 12.9 per cent of all the recommendations made by the B20 (see Table 9.3). In Toronto the B20 made two recommendations on trade, both reflected in the G20 commitments (see Figure 9.4). In Seoul four of six recommendations were addressed by the G20 in their documents. In Cannes four of 10 were addressed, and in Los Cabos only two of 11 were addressed. Under the Russian presidency the Task Force on Trade agreed on 23 recommendations – more than half of the total number. However, only three were reflected in the G20 commitments and mandates at St Petersburg, and only one was deliberated upon. Because of this slump, only 28.8 per cent (15 of 52) of the B20 recommendations received a score of +1 for being translated into G20 commitments.

The core of the B20 trade recommendations covered facilitating trade, completing the Doha Development Round of the negotiations at the World Trade Organization (WTO), and combatting protectionism. All these issues were included in the B20 recommendations to the St Petersburg Summit.

The recommendations on trade facilitation were made in the B20 documents for the Toronto, Seoul, Cannes, Los Cabos, and St Petersburg summits, but none was converted into G20 commitments. The St Petersburg B20 report contained four recommendations

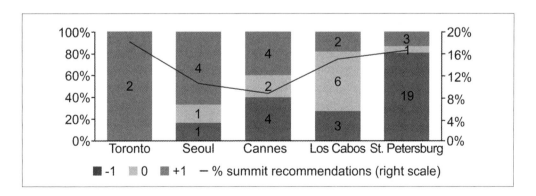

Figure 9.4 Recommendations on trade

Note: The left scale indicates the total number of recommendations for the issue area. The line, which refers to the right scale, indicates the percentage of recommendations for that issue in relation to the total for each summit. The numbers in each column indicate the number of recommendations in that scoring category.

on trade facilitation, including a call to commit to concluding the WTO Trade Facilitation Agreement – the cornerstone of the trade facilitation agenda. The leaders confirmed that a successful outcome at the WTO ministerial conference in Bali in December 2013 on trade facilitation, and some elements of agriculture and development issues, would be a stepping stone to further multilateral trade liberalization and progress in the Doha negotiations.

The recommendations on completing Doha were made for the Toronto, Seoul, Cannes, and St Petersburg summits. All the recommendations were reflected in G20 commitments. However, the G20 stated its intention 'to reach agreement on modalities that leads to a successful conclusion to the WTO's Doha Development Agenda with an ambitious and balanced outcome' at its first summit in Washington in 2008 and reiterated it at every subsequent summit, with no noticeable outcomes (G20 2008).

The issue of combatting protectionism in international trade and investment was addressed in the B20 reports to the G20 summits in Seoul, Cannes, Los Cabos, and St Petersburg. Respective G20 commitments were expressed in summit documents, although once again the leaders had committed to resist raising new barriers to investment or to trade in goods and services, as well as resist imposing new export restrictions in their first declaration. Thus any impact of B20 recommendations on G20 decisions is questionable.

On trade finance, the B20 made recommendations to the Seoul, Los Cabos, and St Petersburg summits. In Seoul, the B20 focused on regulating trade finance under the new capital framework (in the Basel III accord). In Los Cabos the B20 urged the G20 to encourage trade finance in non–dollar-denominated products and asked the Financial Stability Board, the IMF, and the World Bank to consider the effects of regulation on provision of trade finance. In the St Petersburg report the B20 called upon the G20 to avoid overregulating trade finance in order to ensure its availability. Overall, three of the five recommendations on trade finance were partially reflected in G20 commitments, receiving a score of 0; one was addressed fully by the G20, receiving a score of +1; and the St Petersburg recommendation was not addressed at all.

The recommendations to put trade and investment permanently on the G20 agenda, made for the Seoul and Los Cabos summits, were broadly in line with the G20 core agenda, as the leaders make commitments on trade and investment issues at each summit. Thus, although these recommendations scored positively for being addressed by the G20, their impact is limited to the reiteration and support of G20 priorities.

Several notable recommendations have not been taken up by the G20:

- the recommendation to establish a public-private task force under G20 leadership, to help facilitate business actions (Seoul);
- the recommendation to pay attention to the problem of maritime piracy (Cannes);
- the recommendation to enforce the WTO's Government Procurement Agreement (Cannes);
- the recommendation to expand the WTO's Information Technology Agreement (Los Cabos);
- the recommendation to eliminate agricultural export subsidies (Los Cabos); and
- the recommendation to carry out joint research on the best practices of trade regulation (St Petersburg).

None of these proposals has been built upon by the B20 in its subsequent documents.

The evidence base leads to four simple conclusions. First, the value of continued emphasis on completing the Doha Development Round, liberalizing trade, and combatting protectionism is limited given that they constitute an inherent part of the G20 core agenda and the B20 thus simply reinforces its support for the commitments made. Second, those B20 recommendations that were not taken up by the G20 tend to be dropped from subsequent B20 reports, which raises questions of consistency and continuity among B20 priorities and the coordination process across presidencies. Third, the G20 fails to translate some of the more specific recommendations into commitments for obvious reasons: they fall short of the leaders' level, or belong to the mandates of specialized organizations. Moreover, it is always more complicated to reach consensus on concrete commitments than it is on broad decisions. Thus, the B20 needs to balance between the broad recommendations that form the core G20 agenda and the specific recommendations, which it prioritizes in a consistent way that consolidates its position across presidencies.

Investment

The number and share of B20 recommendations on investment, made for the first time for the Seoul Summit, decreased from Seoul to Los Cabos (8.8 per cent in Seoul, 5.1 per cent in Cannes, and only 3.9 per cent in Los Cabos) (see Figure 9.5). However, given the significance of this issue as a priority during Russia's G20 presidency, 5.5 per cent of recommendations made by the B20 to the St Petersburg Summit focused on investment (see Table 9.3). The share of all B20 investment-related recommendations that were not addressed by the G20 equals almost 41 per cent, while those that were acted upon in the form of commitments and mandates constitute 36 per cent.

The only recommendation reflected in the Seoul Summit documents called for the reaffirmation of the commitment to global capital flows, consistent global regulatory

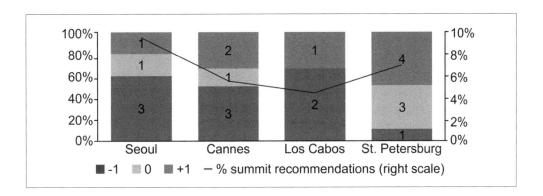

Figure 9.5 Recommendations on investment

Note: The left scale indicates the total number of recommendations for the issue area. The line, which refers to the right scale, indicates the percentage of recommendations for that issue in relation to the total for each summit. The numbers in each column indicate the number of recommendations in that scoring category.

standards, and the development of 'capital markets while highlighting the risks of financial protectionism' (B20 2010b). Given that these issues have been on the G20 agenda since the Washington Summit, and financial protectionism appeared at the following summit in London, it was easy for the G20 leaders to repeat existing commitments and once again pledge to avoid financial protectionism. It might be assumed that more specific recommendations on this issue, if reflected by the G20, could have been more important for the B20 than just the reaffirmation of a traditional agenda.

Other recommendations focused on ensuring 'a clear and enforceable legal framework' on 'principle-based' regulation of foreign direct investment with 'developing a non-binding International Model Investment Treaty as an interim step' and eventually working 'toward a Multilateral Framework for Investment reflecting all interests (host and home countries)' (B20 2010b). These were not acted upon nor were they reflected by the G20. At least two reasons could be identified: first, the B20 did not reinforce its final recommendations with background materials and specific detailed proposals; second, the G20 was not ambitious enough to take on this new issue, which would eventually lead to legally binding international commitments under a new treaty.

A recommendation to 'broaden monitoring of changes in conditions for private investment to areas affecting all private investment' was not addressed (B20 2010b). The OECD and the United Nations Conference on Trade and Development (UNCTAD), mandated by the G20 to monitor investment-related measures, had already included liberalization measures in a wide range of areas in their regular reports.

The level of inclusion of B20 recommendations in the Cannes Summit documents was much higher: the G20 acted upon two of the six recommendations and deliberated on one. The G20 reaffirmed its traditional commitment on 'refraining from raising barriers or imposing new barriers to both outward and inbound investment' until the end of 2013 and reaffirmed the mandate of OECD and UNCTAD to monitor and report on the situation (B20 2011).

In 2011, the B20 made a recommendation on an issue that had not previously been discussed: strengthening project design and preparation to ensure the availability of quality projects. It recommended the G20 'design a model of a 'Well-Prepared Project' (e.g., taking into account whole life-cycle cost analysis) and create conditions for successful PPP [public-private partnership] projects' (B20 2011). This recommendation partly coincided with G20 pledges in the Multi-Year Action Plan on Development adopted at the Seoul Summit, when the High-Level Panel for Infrastructure Investment was established 'to mobilize support for scaling up infrastructure financing', including through private-public cooperation (G20 2010). At the Cannes Summit the panel was commissioned to set 'criteria to identify exemplary investment projects' and highlighted 11 specific projects developed by the program with 'the potential to have a transformational regional impact' (G20 2011b). However, the G20's actions were limited to recognizing these projects and calling on the multilateral development banks (MDBs) to 'pursue the implementation of such projects that meet the [panel's] criteria'. Thus, aside from the participation of private sector representatives in the panel's activities, the B20's influence on this issue was not significant and was, in fact, limited to supporting the G20's own plans and actions.

Another B20 recommendation – to 'adopt a G20 statement in favor of open investment as a tool for growth, development and job creation' – was addressed by the G20 in the form of deliberation (B20 2011). Although the G20 did not make a separate statement on this issue, it emphasized investment's link to growth, jobs, and development in its documents. However, the G20 did not articulate the relationship between development and investment at that time, so it could be perceived as different from the B20 concept. For example, the G20 mentioned development as 'a key element of our agenda for global recovery and investment for future growth' (G20 2011b). It also mainly focused on infrastructure investments in developing countries, especially in low-income countries as an instrument of achieving the Millennium Development Goals, while business pursued promoting investments in a wider group of countries, including the advanced economies.

Recommendations on negotiating an international investment treaty, similar to ones made in 2010, were not reflected by the G20. The B20 considered the G20's position on this issue at the previous summit and amended its proposals. The B20 report noted that 'the G20 has no legal standing and, for this reason, is not able to negotiate an investment treaty' (B20 2011). It suggested that 'the G20, as a powerful political instrument, must open discussions to find a common vision and approach to this issue', noting that the WTO was 'the best option among the international organizations to serve as the multilateral platform for cross-border investment rules and standards'. Nevertheless, the G20 did not mention this issue in its summit documents.

Only three investment-related recommendations were made by the B20 to the Los Cabos Summit and only one was addressed by the G20 at the summit. The B20 repeated its call for the G20 to 'reiterate its support for open cross-border investment as an essential contributor to growth, development and job creation' (B20 2012). The G20 easily reaffirmed its standstill commitments on open investment and deliberated on the links of investment with growth, jobs, and development.

B20 recommendations on international investment treaty were watered down to the following ambiguous wording: 'strengthening the framework of rules for international investment in the interest of all stakeholders' (B20 2012). The concept moved away from the central role of the WTO in these negotiations. The B20 suggested it should be done 'in partnership with international organizations where dialogue is already underway – such as the OECD, UNCTAD and the WTO'. However, it was not able to convince the G20 to include this topic in the summit documents.

At the Los Cabos Summit, the B20 for the first time made a recommendation on investment, concerning the creation of a new G20 internal structure and strengthened it with a proposed catalyst of a specific deadline: 'a working group on investment to advance this agenda and report back to the next G20 summit in Russia in 2013' (B20 2012). It was neither mentioned in the summit documents nor realized in practice. Investment issues were still addressed in the framework of the trade agenda on the sherpas' track (with regard to cross-border flows) and within the Development Working Group with the focus on infrastructure investment.

Most of the B20 recommendations on investment made under the Russian presidency were translated into the G20 decisions or deliberated upon. The only one that remained unaddressed was very specific and focused on the establishment of the G20 Project Preparation Fund 'to foster capital market financing of real economy assets' (B20 2013).

The B20 reiterated its recommendation on removing restrictions to the free flows of capital, which was translated into the G20 commitment. However, more specific recommendations in this sub-area, focused on the G20 multilateral investment framework and financial reporting standards that are more conducive to long-term investments, were only discussed.

The B20 recommendation to stimulate private investment in real economy assets across the G20 was fully in line with Russia's G20 priorities and, consequently, was taken up. Again, the G20 only partially addressed the more specific recommendation on improving the mandate and funding of the Multilateral Investment Guarantee Agency. Still, recommendations in both sub-areas were heard by the G20, as reflected in the G20 Study Group on Financing for Investment Workplan. It agreed to consider the results of the work of the B20 and relevant international organizations and then decide whether to undertake further analysis on foreign direct investment. Thus, the abovementioned recommendations will likely be fully reflected in future G20 decisions.

The recommendation on ensuring favourable conditions for long-term investments for both consumers and providers of capital was also acted upon. However, given that this issue was among the priorities of the Russian G20 agenda, the B20's influence on corresponding G20 decisions seems questionable.

Progress in the G20-B20 dialogue on investment issues has been slow. The analysis of the reflection of B20 recommendations in G20 documents shows a very low level of B20 influence on G20. Recommendations on developing an international legal framework on investment were not reflected, despite the fact that B20 changed the wording and approaches from summit to summit, trying to adapt it to the G20 mandate and principles. This fact suggests that the G20 does not intend to include this issue on its agenda.

The only core sub-area where B20 recommendations are constantly reflected in G20 documents is freedom of international investment flows. Given that this is a traditional issue on the G20 agenda, the degree of B20 influence on G20 decisions here can be questioned.

The success of other recommendations from different sub-areas was mixed. Under the Russian presidency the G20-B20 dialogue on investment significantly advanced due to the G20's prioritization of the issue at various levels of its decision making on the one hand and the B20's dedication to develop actionable recommendations on the other hand.

Infrastructure

From the Toronto Summit to the St Petersburg Summit the B20 has made 12 recommendations on infrastructure development, which constitutes 3 per cent of all B20 recommendations (see Figure 9.6). Two of four B20 infrastructure-related recommendations made in Seoul were addressed by the G20 leaders (see Figure 9.6). In Cannes, only one of three recommendations was translated into the G20 decisions. In Los Cabos the B20 produced two recommendations in the area, and both were neglected by the G20. The B20's infrastructure recommendations were most successfully reflected in

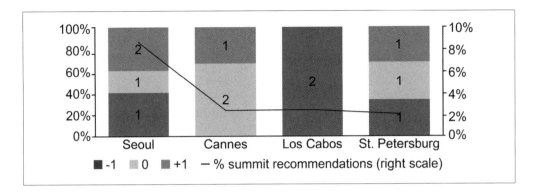

Figure 9.6 Recommendations on infrastructure

Note: The left scale indicates the total number of recommendations for the issue area. The line, which refers to the right scale, indicates the percentage of recommendations for that issue in relation to the total for each summit. The numbers in each column indicate the number of recommendations in that scoring category.

the G20 documents in St Petersburg, with one of three recommendations addressed in the G20 decisions. The overall level of reflection equals 30.0 per cent (4 of 12).

In its Seoul report the B20 made five recommendations on infrastructure, all focused on promoting private sector participation in infrastructure development projects through different incentives. The level of these recommendations' reflection in the G20 documents differs, with more general recommendations taken up by the Seoul Summit and more targeted recommendations neglected.

In Cannes, the B20 reiterated its recommendation on stimulating private investment in infrastructure and made it less specific, merging previous recommendations from Seoul into one. Two new recommendations were agreed upon, focused on improving the availability of information through designing an infrastructure-attractiveness index, and addressing environmental and societal concerns when implementing infrastructure projects (B20 2011). New recommendations were not reflected in any G20 decisions at the Cannes Summit.

In its Los Cabos report the B20 made two new infrastructure-related recommendations, but did not pick up any previous recommendations from Seoul or Cannes. Those two recommendations urged the G20 to provide 'funding dedicated ... to improving pre-project feasibility and assembly studies' and to 'prioritize 'brownfield' infrastructure investments that modify or upgrade existing structures to increase their scale or quality while creating jobs at a lower cost than equivalent 'greenfield' investments' (B20 2011). However, none of them was addressed in the Los Cabos G20 documents.

Recommendations on infrastructure made to the St Petersburg Summit focused on different issues. The general recommendation on stimulating infrastructure financing by promoting a range of instruments and sources was in line with Russia's G20 priority of financing for investment and thus was reflected in several G20 mandates.

Two more specific B20 recommendations establishing an 'infrastructure network', including a Moscow based Infrastructure Productivity Institute, and developing a 'PPP

Toolbox' within this network remained unaddressed (B20 2013). The G20 fully ignored the first one and deliberated upon the second one by committing to explore ways to improve the design of PPP arrangements.

Thus, as with many other policy areas, general recommendations are reflected more in G20 decisions than targeted ones. B20 proposals on new issues tend to be ignored. It does not follow that the B20 should not pursue innovative issues in its dialogue with the G20. Reiterating recommendations that are already on the G20 agenda does not add significant value to the G20–B20 dialogue. The B20 should be both selective and consistent in defining its priorities, coordinating positions, and consolidating efforts across presidencies.

Employment, Human Capital and Social Issues

The B20 began including recommendations on employment, human capital development, and social issues at its first meeting in Toronto (see Figure 9.7). By the St Petersburg Summit it had made 55 recommendations on employment and social issues, or 13.6 per cent of all recommendations (the highest number among all areas) (see Figure 9.7). In Toronto the B20 made one related recommendation, which was not addressed by the G20. Only one of the eight recommendations on employment was translated into the G20 commitments in Seoul. The B20 made eight recommendations in Cannes, and this time three of them were addressed in the G20 documents. In Los Cabos three out of 12 B20 recommendations were reflected in the G20 documents. The highest number of recommendations on this issue was made at St Petersburg (26 or 18.4 per cent), with 12 reflected in the G20 documents. Overall, 34.5 per cent (19 out of 55) of the B20's recommendations on employment received a score of +1 for being translated into the G20 commitments, which is a medium score compared to other areas.

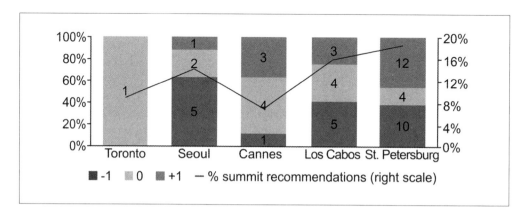

Figure 9.7 Recommendations on employment, human capital and social issues

Note: The left scale indicates the total number of recommendations for the issue area. The line, which refers to the right scale, indicates the percentage of recommendations for that issue in relation to the total for each summit. The numbers in each column indicate the number of recommendations in that scoring category.

B20 recommendations for the Toronto Summit contained one focused on providing employment opportunities for youth through stimulating self-employment and entrepreneurship. This recommendation was not reflected in any G20 commitments or mandates.

Recommendations for the Seoul Summit were more specific. In particular, the B20 made two on training and internships for young people and two on fostering entrepreneurship. These recommendations reiterated and built on the single recommendation on employment for the Toronto Summit. Again, they were not reflected in G20 decisions. The B20 also agreed on several recommendations on new issues, such as supporting social protection floors and reporting on job scenarios to monitor progress in the area of labour and employment. These were also neglected by the G20. The only B20 employment-related recommendation reflected in the Seoul documents stated that the G20 should 'create effective unemployment, welfare and social-protection systems' (B20 2010b). Thus, certain progress can be registered and it can be assumed that B20 consistency was instrumental in influencing G20 positions.

Recommendations on supporting entrepreneurship and creating job opportunities for youth were taken up in the Cannes B20 report, which were addressed in G20 decisions. However, the B20 did not reiterate any of the previously neglected recommendations. Instead, new recommendations were formulated, dealing with facilitating labour mobility, combatting informal employment, and encouraging cooperation between governments, international institutions, and business with regard to employment. These recommendations received varying degrees of attention from the G20, with the one on tackling informal employment translated into a G20 decision, the one on private sector involvement in the labour market deliberated upon, and the one on skill transfer not addressed at all.

In its Los Cabos report the B20 again reiterated previous recommendations on supporting entrepreneurship and SMEs and on improving employment opportunities for young people. All these recommendations were translated into G20 decisions or mandates, or at least deliberated upon in the G20 Los Cabos documents. A number of new recommendations were made, all neglected by the G20 except a general one that linked labour market reforms with general regulatory reforms 'designed to support economic growth and improve the climate for investing and doing business as a foundation for further employment' (B20 2012).

In 2013 the B20's Task Force on Job Creation, Employment, and Investments in Human Capital presented 26 recommendations grouped into three categories: developing education and training systems, creating enabling environment for entrepreneurship, and addressing the demographic challenge. Most of the recommendations in the first category were included in the G20 documents in the form of commitments, including member-specific commitments in the St Petersburg Action Plan. The G20 took note of the proposals from the B20–L20 Joint Understanding of Key Elements on Quality Apprenticeships and committed to encouraging better cooperation between different stakeholders, including businesses, to ensure 'a successful matching of skills and qualifications with the current and future job requirements' (G20 2013). However, the G20 neither acted upon nor mentioned the need to ensure access to education for vulnerable groups and provide support for people with special needs. The G20 fully shared the B20's message of fostering entrepreneurship as an important source of good-quality jobs, but it did not make specific commitments on supporting entrepreneurs, including start-ups, through introducing tax incentives, adopting flexible labour legislation, and promoting a diversity of forms of employment. The G20 did not act upon the three recommendations on adapting pension systems and immigration policies to the new needs of the economy, opting not to expand the G20 agenda.

Overall, during the Russian presidency the inclusion of the B20's recommendations into G20 decisions was the highest to date (46.2 per cent compared to 34.5 per cent for all summits).

Employment is a good example of the B20 leading the dialogue, rather than following the G20, on its core areas of coordination. The task forces' track record on employment and social policies provides evidence that the B20 is capable of identifying key challenges that G20 members face and pursuing its priorities consistently in dialogue with the G20, together with the L20, to get issues addressed by the leaders. However, proposals on new areas such as pension systems and migration were largely ignored in G20 documents, indicating the limitations of B20 leadership. Hopefully, the B20's commitments on monitoring national responses to G20 commitments on employment implemented together with current and future G20 presidencies will consolidate the dialogue in this area.

Green Growth

From the Toronto Summit to the Los Cabos Summit the B20 made 36 recommendations on issues related to green growth, amounting to 9 per cent of all B20 recommendations (see Figure 9.8 and Table 9.3). The B20 made 14 recommendations on green growth in the run-up to the Seoul Summit, where for the first time the G20 committed to support country-led green growth policies. In Cannes six of 14 recommendations were addressed in G20 documents. In Los Cabos two of six B20 recommendations were addressed. Thus, G20 responsiveness to B20 recommendations was mixed. For the most part the G20 addressed the core recommendations, while more specific issues were not mentioned in summit documents. Overall only 33 per cent (12 of 36) of the B20 recommendations received a score of +1 for being translated into G20 commitments.

Two green growth recommendations were made in St Petersburg, both reflected in the G20's documents. In particular the B20 recommended encouraging the implementation of best practices to increase the productivity of investments in infrastructure and green energy and the establishment of a working group to identify and support sharing best practices on the effective integration of energy and environmental policies. On the first recommendation, the G20 endorsed a work plan to assess factors that affect the availability and accessibility of long-term financing for investment and committed to start implementing measures to improve domestic investment environments. The leaders also mandated their finance ministers to continue identifying approaches to climate finance, building on the report of the G20 Climate Finance Study Group. On the second recommendation, the leaders called for a dialogue between the private sector, the MDBs, and the G20 Energy Sustainability Working Group to be launched in 2014. This dialogue

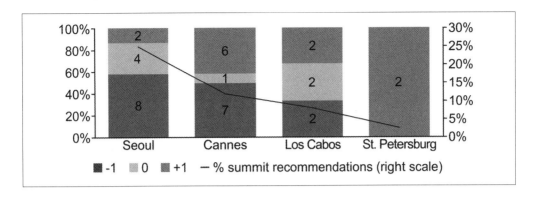

Figure 9.8 Recommendations on green growth
Note: The left scale indicates the total number of recommendations for the issue area. The line, which refers to the right scale, indicates the percentage of recommendations for that issue in relation to the total for each summit. The numbers in each column indicate the number of recommendations in that scoring category.

discuss the factors hindering energy investment, including investment in clean and energy-efficient technologies, and ways to promote sustainable, affordable, efficient, and secure energy supplies.

The B20 recommendations on green growth, made prior to the Seoul, Cannes, and Los Cabos summits, included proposals for free trade in environmental goods and services, but were not reflected in the G20's Seoul commitments. Recommendations for market-based pricing on carbon also were not taken up by the G20 at either Seoul or Cannes. The recommendations to promote green technologies and innovation, including by facilitating technology transfer, were addressed by the G20 at the Cannes Summit, where the leaders made commitments on different aspects of promoting green technology, including encouraging investment and creating enabling environments. However, although the B20 expressed support for these issues, they received little attention from the G20 leaders in Seoul and Los Cabos.

Recommendations to phase out or rationalize fossil fuel subsidies made for the Seoul, Cannes, and Los Cabos summits were regularly addressed by the G20 since the 2009 Pittsburgh Summit. The B20's impact on G20 decision making in this area is thus a matter of debate.

The G20's overall response to B20 recommendations on green growth can be regarded as insufficient, even though some proposals fall within the G20's stated priorities and remain relevant. Several notable recommendations have not been taken up by the G20:

- the recommendation to promote PPPs for achieving universal access to energy (Seoul);
- the recommendation to mandate regular meetings of energy-related ministers (Seoul);
- the recommendation to provide new financing solutions to help companies make long-term investments necessary for improved energy efficiency (Seoul);
- the recommendation to introduce an energy market framework in developing countries to incentivize the provision of energy services on a universal basis (Cannes); and

- the recommendation to radically cut energy consumption in the real estate sector with a real transformation in design, use of technology, and change in behaviour (Cannes).

Ample B20 recommendations on green growth were reiterated in each subsequent B20 report. Their impact on reducing fossil fuel subsidies is unclear, as the issue had been on the G20 agenda long before the B20 made any pertinent recommendations. The G20's responsiveness to the B20 proposals on green growth is most visible in the area of green technologies and innovation promotion. The B20 could consider revisiting some of its recommendations that retain their relevance and re-emphasize the need for new financing solutions to facilitate long-term investments in new energy-efficient technologies.

ICT, Technology, and Innovation

The B20 has made recommendations on ICT, technology, and innovation since the Seoul Summit (see Figure 9.9). They represent a relatively considerable share of 8.2 per cent of all the B20 recommendations made to five summits, reaching a maximum of 9 per cent at the Cannes Summit (see Table 9.3). However, the rate of inclusion in G20 documents is the lowest of all issue areas. None of recommendations was acted upon by the G20 and only 9 per cent was reflected in summit documents in the form of deliberation. This poor performance can be explained by the fact that neither ICT nor innovation has been on the G20 agenda. Russia's G20 presidency did not include it as a separate priority either.

In Seoul a special B20 Working Group on Unleashing Technology-Enabled Productivity Growth worked out three recommendations (create a task force to identify opportunities to drive public sector productivity; create a G20 clearinghouse to identify best practices in workforce development and innovation; and develop a joint commission connecting G20, relevant organizations, and business to identify barriers to productivity). The B20 Working Group on Funding and Nurturing the Small and Medium-Sized Enterprise Sector recommended promoting the value of intellectual property and establishing SME Innovative Technology Development Funds. None of these recommendations was reflected in G20 documents.

In 2011 the B20 continued to prioritize technology and innovation and formed the Working Group on ICT and Innovation. This group emphasized that 'innovation is critical for growth, employment and economic recovery' and urged the G20 to include ICT and the internet as 'key elements of innovation' on its agenda (B20 2011). While the G20 did not take any decisions that fully corresponded, several commitments were partially in line with B20 proposals: support to large-scale innovation in the sphere of energy and support to SMEs through innovative solutions.

In 2012 a special working group on ICT and innovation was created as well, although this did not improve the G20's recognition of B20 recommendations. The G20 addressed only one partially: the development of applications for harnessing social inclusion. However, the Los Cabos Summit supported the 'knowledge sharing platform (KSP) on skills for employment, a project led by the ILO [International Labour Organization] in coordination with OECD, UNESCO [United Nations Educational, Scientific, and

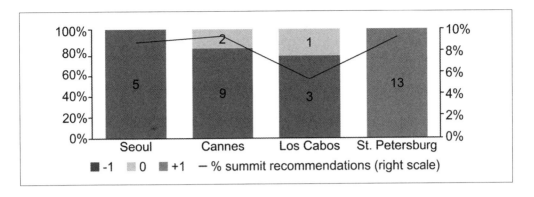

Figure 9.9 Recommendations on ICT, technology, and innovation

Note: The left scale indicates the total number of recommendations for the issue area. The line, which refers to the right scale, indicates the percentage of recommendations for that issue in relation to the total for each summit. The numbers in each column indicate the number of recommendations in that scoring category.

Cultural Organization] and the WB [World Bank]' (Development Working Group 2012). This support reflected the B20's recommendation to the Seoul Summit to 'create a G20 clearinghouse to identify best practices in workforce development and innovation' made to the Seoul Summit (B20 2011). Because the G20's recognition occurred two years after the B20's proposal, it is difficult to assess the degree of influence of the B20. However, the B20 had clearly anticipated the relevance of this work.

In 2013 the B20 formed the Task Force on Innovation and Development as a Global Priority. Its agenda encompassed the issues of ICT, intellectual property rights, innovation, energy, and health care with a special emphasis on biotechnology. The task force came up with 13 recommendations, none of which translated into G20 commitments or mandates. One reason for such a low rate of responsiveness may be the nature of the recommendations, which were characterized by a high degree of specificity for a leader-level event. Another reason is that many of the task force's recommendations fell beyond the G20 agenda.

As ICT, technology, and innovation are not included specifically in the G20 agenda, the effectiveness of a separate B20 task force is questionable. The approach adopted by the B20 in 2013, uniting several issue areas under one group, did not improve the G20's responsiveness. The B20 might consider the alternative of integrating the issues of technology and innovation into the recommendations of other task forces, such as on green growth, structural reforms, or food security.

Energy

Between the Toronto Summit and the St Petersburg Summit the B20 made 18 recommendations on energy issues, amounting to 4.5 per cent of all recommendations made by the B20 (see Table 9.3 and Figure 9.10). In Seoul the B20 made one

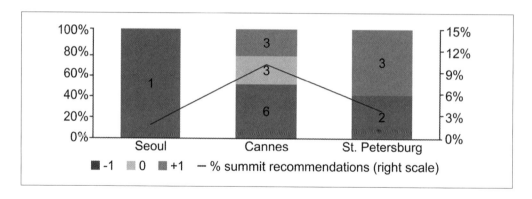

Figure 9.10 Recommendations on energy

Note: The left scale indicates the total number of recommendations for the issue area. The line, which refers to the right scale, indicates the percentage of recommendations for that issue in relation to the total for each summit. The numbers in each column indicate the number of recommendations in that scoring category.

recommendation on energy, with no response from the G20. In Cannes three of 12 B20 recommendations were addressed by the G20 leaders. In Los Cabos there were no recommendations on energy. In St Petersburg the B20 made five recommendations, three of which translated into G20 decisions. The G20's overall responsiveness to these recommendations has been modest. Only 33.3 per cent (six of 18) of the B20 recommendations received a score of +1 for being translated into G20 commitments.

For the purposes of the analysis in this chapter, several energy-related issues from the previous summits, most notably fossil fuel subsidies and carbon prices, were considered in the green growth area and were excluded from the calculations on energy. However, in 2013 these issues were integrated under the auspices of the G20 Energy Sustainability Working Group and the B20 Task Force on Innovation and Development as a Global Priority, and hence are considered within the energy area.

At Cannes, the B20 recommendations on energy that were translated into the G20 commitments included ones on implementation of the Joint Oil Data Initiative, strengthening the dialogue between producing and consuming countries, and increasing market transparency and visibility through dialogue in appropriate international forums. Thus, the G20 tended to promote international cooperation and information exchange in the area.

The B20's St Petersburg recommendations that were translated into G20 decisions included those on increasing energy efficiency, improving energy access, and enhancing energy sustainability and reliability. The G20 did not respond to recommendations to enhance energy sustainability and ensure energy balance through natural and shale gas.

Several notable recommendations, which retain their relevance, were not taken up by the G20:

- the recommendation to 'clarify rules on sustainable development goals such as greenhouse gas mitigation, and promote transparency and predictability of energy availability through a strengthened cooperation with the International Energy Forum (IEF) and International Energy Agency (IEA)' (Seoul) (B20 2010b);

- the recommendation to establish genuine market mechanisms to encourage investments and facilitate access to energy in developing countries (Cannes);
- the recommendation to harmonize nuclear safety standards (Cannes);
- the recommendation to develop dialogue between producers and consumers including governments and business (Cannes);
- the recommendation to ensure timely information on supply, demand, and storage flows (Cannes); and
- the recommendation to create a global level playing field for commodities and raw materials (Cannes).

The evidence reveals no clear focus in B20 recommendations on energy issues. Attention is spread among multiple areas such as regulation of energy markets, safety standards, information exchange, and efficiency promotion. The consolidation of the energy and green growth agendas by both the G20 and the B20 at St Petersburg produced a much higher rate of responsiveness compared to previous summits. However, this result was also due to the broad nature of the recommendations containing multiple actions. The impact of the B20 on G20 deliberation and decision making can be enhanced by focusing on the G20's priorities, limiting the number of recommendations, and following up on them across presidencies.

Corruption

Between the Toronto and the St Petersburg summits the B20 made 38 recommendations on fighting corruption, constituting 9.4 per cent of all B20 recommendations made over that period (see Table 9.3). In Cannes the B20 made six recommendations on anticorruption, two of which were subsequently addressed by the G20 – by which time the G20 had made 15 commitments on anticorruption (see Figure 9.11). In Los Cabos only four of 15 B20 recommendations were reflected in G20 documents. The G20 acted on five of 17 at St Petersburg. Overall, 26.3 per cent (10 of 38) of B20 recommendations were translated into G20 decisions, which is a relatively low score in comparison with other areas on the B20 agenda.

The B20's recommendations on anticorruption for the Cannes Summit focused on several issues, including providing incentives for companies to prevent corruption, supporting 'negotiations within the WTO for a multilateral agreement on standards for procedures and transparency in government procurement', creating a G20–B20 joint platform addressing corruption, and 'promoting education on ethics and business integrity at all level of public and private education' (B20 2011). None of these recommendations was reflected in any G20 commitments or mandates. The B20 also made two recommendations to recognize the role of public leaders in fighting corruption, and to enforce and monitor the implementation of international anticorruption conventions. Both of these recommendations were reflected in G20 decisions with the caveat that both

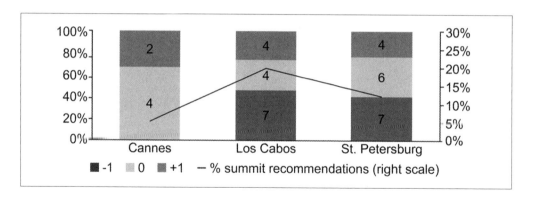

Figure 9.11 Recommendations on corruption
Note: The left scale indicates the total number of recommendations for the issue area. The line, which refers to the right scale, indicates the percentage of recommendations for that issue in relation to the total for each summit. The numbers in each column indicate the number of recommendations in that scoring category.

issues have been consistently addressed by the G20 since the Pittsburgh Summit, and B20 noted that its recommendations were derived from the G20 Seoul Anti-Corruption Action Plan. Thus, the B20 recommendations were taking a supportive role rather than a leading one.

In the Los Cabos report, the B20 reiterated almost all its previous recommendations on fighting corruption but addressed the issues more specifically. Four recommendations focused on incentives for business to combat corruption including certifying and self-reporting by companies on their anticorruption practices and making the adoption of such practices a condition for participating in public tenders. None of these recommendations was reflected in the G20 documents. The G20 also did not address the two reiterated B20 commitments on strengthening transparency in public procurement. Similarly, the recommendation on raising awareness of the risks of corruption through 'anti-corruption training programs tailored to SMEs' was not reflected in the G20's documents (B20 2012). The recommendation to promote the G20–B20 dialogue on anticorruption was, however, translated into the G20 commitment. But the G20's decisions did not align with the more specific recommendations on possible engagement processes and a model review approach for the review mechanism for the United Nations Convention against Corruption (UNCAC). The issues of asset disclosure by private officials, the fight against solicitation, the enforcement of foreign bribery legislation, and certain articles of the OECD Anti-Bribery Convention and UNCAC were also put forward by the B20. As in Toronto, Seoul, and Cannes, the G20 deliberated on these issues and made several commitments. The only proposal put forward by the B20 that was new for the G20 was on extending the mandate of the Anti-Corruption Working Group. In Los Cabos, the G20 decided to extend its mandate to the end of 2014.

The recommendations of the 2013 Transparency and Anti-Corruption Task Force were divided into four areas: enhancing B20–G20 dialogue on anticorruption, combatting the solicitation of bribes, training company personnel and public officials, and setting up a collective-action hub and anticorruption centres of excellence. All four areas were included on the G20 agenda, although the level of inclusion varied considerably.

The engagement between the G20 Anti-Corruption Working Group and the B20's task force was intense throughout the presidency: the B20 participated in all the working group's meetings and Russia's G20 presidency organized the Third Annual High-Level Anti-Corruption Conference for G20 Governments and Business. G20 leaders agreed that the working group would have the same status as other G20 working groups, and the support of both the B20 and the Civil 20 (C20) was mentioned specifically in G20 documents. However, the G20 did not note the need to involve the private sector in the UNCAC review.

Although the G20 adopted Guiding Principles to Combat Solicitation, it did not refer to the B20's specific proposals on transparency in government procurement in global trade talks, fair procurement practices through external trade and development programs, the use of World Bank indicators to assess procurement, and the introduction of a high-level reporting mechanism.

Despite the G20's emphasis on the importance of anticorruption education programs 'to build and reinforce a culture of intolerance towards corruption', there were no specific commitments on this issue except to endorse the St Petersburg Strategic Framework for the G20 Anti-Corruption Working Group, which included a commitment to promote awareness of the overview of educational and training tools in G20 countries (G20 2013; G20 Anti-Corruption Working Group 2013).

The G20 welcomed the B20's proposal of creating a collective-action hub but neither made any commitments nor expressed direct support for this initiative. The B20–G20 dialogue on combatting corruption was mentioned positively in the G20 documents several times and the G20 committed to continue it. Despite a relatively low level of inclusion of B20 recommendations, the G20 acted on several of the most important messages and included all working areas proposed by the B20 in its agenda. Thus the B20 proved its ability to engage constructively with the G20 on critical anticorruption issues. The B20 could consider more emphasis on the implementation of G20 decisions given that the anticorruption priority is fully established as a high priority on the G20 agenda. The St Petersburg Strategic Framework declared the need to 'cooperate closely with business community' through 'keeping an open dialogue with the Business 20' (G20 Anti-Corruption Working Group 2013).

Financing for Development

Appearing at the Seoul, Cannes, and St Petersburg summits, the issue of financing for development accounts for a mere 3 per cent of all the B20 recommendations (see Table 9.3). The level of those recommendations' inclusion is the lowest after the issues of ICT, technology, and innovation (64 per cent of the recommendations were not addressed by the G20 at all). The recommendations made by the B20 Task Force on Financing for

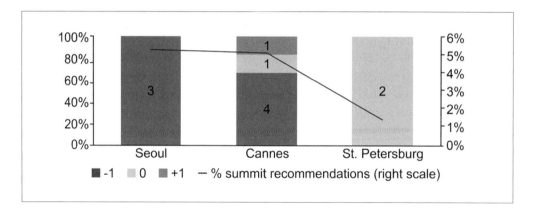

Figure 9.12 Recommendations on financing for development
Note: The left scale indicates the total number of recommendations for the issue area. The line, which refers to the right scale, indicates the percentage of recommendations for that issue in relation to the total for each summit. The numbers in each column indicate the number of recommendations in that scoring category.

Growth and Development during the Mexican presidency focused on 'how the financial sector can support growth, job creation and economic opportunity' and were categorized under other areas (B20 2012).

The B20 included the issue of development assistance into the discourse for the first time in the run-up to the Seoul Summit, when the B20 Working Group on Increasing Access to Healthcare in Developing Countries was created. Health had not been on the G20 agenda and the leaders ignored the B20's call to include 'global health as a permanent agenda item at G20 Summits' at Seoul (B20 2010b). Nor did the G20 address the recommendations to invest a significant proportion of developing countries' annual budgets in health and channel health assistance 'through novel financing mechanisms'. However, health issues, while not linked directly to developing countries' needs, were mentioned in the Seoul Summit documents as a part of strengthening social safety nets and enhancing employable skills (the impact of noncommunicable diseases on skills development).

All six recommendations on development finance to the Cannes Summit were elaborated by the B20 Working Group on Development and Food Security. They included the issues of enhancing corporate social responsibility, including by IFIs and bilateral development institutions, and creating a public-private dialogue to define national development guidelines. Only one recommendation was acted upon: the one on changing the procurement rules of the MDBs to 'facilitate the private sector's involvement in project development and implementation' (B20 2011). The G20 called on MDBs 'to harmonize their procurement rules and practices' (G20 2011b). The B20 also recommended prioritizing 'financing and project development and implementation over an increase in ODA [official development assistance]', including through improving 'the relevance, quality and management of the projects to be implemented' and reducing 'the differences between contracts and their implementation' (B20 2011). This was partially acted upon in the High-Level Panel for Infrastructure Investment recommendations on support to 'development of local capacities to improve supply and quality of projects and make them bankable' (G20 2011b).

At the same time the B20 recommendations to the Cannes Summit did not include a position on innovative financing for development, although in 2011 the G20 discussed such options as a financial transaction tax, which could have substantially affected the business community if implemented. However, this topic was addressed in the report presented by Bill Gates (2011) to G20 leaders on 'Innovation with Impact: Financing 21st Century Development'.

The 2012 B20 Task Force on Financing for Growth and Development made recommendations in areas different from the priorities of similar task forces in 2010 and 2011: SME finance, financial inclusion and education, the impact of regulation on trade finance, and trade finance in non–dollar-denominated products. Thus, in the analysis its recommendations were assigned to other areas used in this chapter (see the discussions on financial regulation and trade).

At the St Petersburg Summit the B20 made two recommendations on development finance. Both were partially addressed by the G20, receiving a score of 0. The first proposed shifting the G20 emphasis from further increases in ODA to project financing, development, and implementation, while the second urged the G20 to change the way MDBs operated so they would concentrate on facilitating private sector involvement in development projects in the most vulnerable countries. The G20 responded by deliberating upon these issues in the summit's official documents.

Given that development, including innovative approaches to private sector participation, was an important topic on the G20 agenda and one of the major priorities of Russia's presidency, the B20's inclusion of the recommendations on these issues was a step in the right direction. Debate and recommendations in this area could promote the better reflection of private sector interests in the post-2015 development agenda. Priorities of almost all 2013 task forces included development-related issues. A need to convene a task force on development issues in future should be contemplated on the basis of balance between the G20 presidency's priorities and business community interests.

Global Governance

The B20's Global Governance Task Force was created in response to the G20's contemplation of its role in the future of global governance, led by British Prime Minister David Cameron (2011) in the run-up to the Cannes Summit. The task force produced eight recommendations, most focused on improving G20 coordination and communication with business and other stakeholders, and also enhancing G20 transparency and legitimacy (see Table 9.3). Two recommendations were reflected in the G20 commitments. The G20 leaders agreed to hold themselves accountable for commitments they made and to review progress at the next summit. They also stated that the G20 must remain efficient, transparent, and accountable and must pursue consistent and effective engagement with non-members, regional and international organizations, and other actors. The B20 was

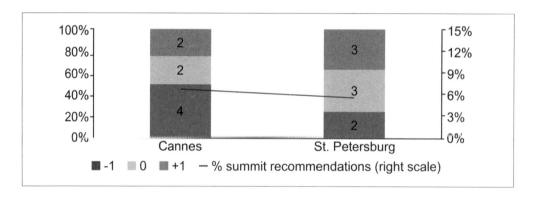

Figure 9.13 Recommendations on global governance
Note: The left scale indicates the total number of recommendations for the issue area. The line, which refers to the right scale, indicates the percentage of recommendations for that issue in relation to the total for each summit. The numbers in each column indicate the number of recommendations in that scoring category.

thus instrumental in the emergence of the G20's accountability process. However, four of the eight recommendations were neglected by the G20, and two were deliberated upon (see Figure 9.13).

For Los Cabos, the B20's Task Force on Impact and Accountability addressed its recommendations to enhance efficiency and capacity in the dialogue with the G20. This crucial transition resulted from reflection on previous experiences.

The B20 Task Force on G20–B20 Dialogue Efficiency under the Russian presidency built on this work. With the hindsight of accumulated collaboration and planning for a G20–B20 partnership, the B20 agreed on a balanced set of recommendations addressed to the G20 and the B20. Three of the recommendations were ignored by the G20, two were deliberated upon, and three were reflected in actions or mandates. The ones ignored related to setting up joint G20–B20 working groups and encouraging international organizations to foster cooperation with the B20. On anticorruption the G20 committed to build on the enhanced dialogue between the G20 Anti-Corruption Working Group and the B20 and C20. The investment study group declared its preparedness to explore the scope for deeper dialogue with private sector participants to better understand their perspectives on financing for investment.

The B20's recommendation to the G20 to improve its transparency and monitoring of outcomes was supported by the G20's reiterated commitment to improve working practices for more effective outcomes by implementing an accountability process to improve monitoring and coordination, and by ensuring greater transparency. The B20's aspirations for continued and structured dialogue with the G20 was acknowledged in the leaders' declaration, which expressed an appreciation of the contribution of the B20 and the L20 and recognized the crucial role of social dialogue as a means to achieving its objectives of fostering growth, employment, and social cohesion. It was also recognized in the leaders' fifth anniversary vision statement pledging to strengthen engagement with the social partners, including the B20.

Conclusion

B20–G20 engagement advanced unevenly in different policy areas. The B20 consistently identified and promoted relevant issues in its dialogue with the G20 on financial regulation. There was a high level of correlation between B20 recommendations and G20 decisions on the international monetary system and macroeconomic policy, although it may be due to the fact that most recommendations on these issues aligned with the G20 priorities. The B20 consistently upheld the objectives of completing the Doha Development Round, liberalizing trade, and combatting protectionism, thus reiterating its support for the G20 commitments on trade. Surprisingly, progress in the G20–B20 dialogue on investment issues was slow despite the need for engagement and the B20's continued dedication to the topic. It was only under the Russian presidency that it advanced significantly thanks to the G20's prioritization of investment at various levels of its decision making and a systemic dialogue between the G20 and the relevant task force.

On green growth the G20's response to the B20 recommendations was insufficient, even though many B20 proposals remained relevant. The consolidation of the energy and green growth agendas for both the G20 and the B20 led to a much higher responsiveness. The advance was most pronounced on the promotion of green technologies and green innovation. The least progress was on ICT, technology, and innovation, for the simple reason that these issues were not usually included on the G20 agenda.

On employment the B20 pursued its priorities consistently, often together with the L20, to get crucial issues on the business and global agendas addressed by the G20 leaders. The B20–G20 engagement on employment is a good case of the B20 leading the dialogue, rather than following the G20. The B20 has also proven its ability to engage constructively with the G20 on anticorruption.

Overall, the B20 has transformed from an ad hoc, leader-inspired meeting into a reliable stakeholder in the G20-led process of steering the world to strong, sustainable, and balanced growth. Given that this process is indeed led by the G20, it comes as no surprise that the B20 has been more successful in getting its recommendations heard when they relate to the G20 core agenda. Proposals on that do not fit neatly with the conventional G20 agenda stand little chance of getting the leaders' attention. Under the Russian presidency in 2013, the B20 advanced its engagement with the G20, consolidated its contribution to G20 decision making and direction setting, and made substantive progress toward establishing the B20 as a global governance actor.

Nonetheless, there remains much to be done for the B20 to become recognized as a true global governance actor. It ought to ensure its own transparency, efficiency, legitimacy, and accountability. To this end, B20 members must develop a mid-term strategy, communicate it clearly to other stakeholders, including the international organizations and SMEs, and agree on a mid-term engagement strategy with the G20. The B20 needs to increase its representativeness. It must share with the G20 the responsibility for delivering on commitments, and account for its own actions in a transparent, coherent, and unbiased way. The B20 process cannot afford to stall. Future presidencies have an opportunity to consolidate the B20's status as a recognized global governance actor in line with its ambitious goals and with international relations theory.

References

B20 (2010a). 'Chairman's Summary: Report to G20 Ministers of Finance'. B20 Business Summit, June 26, Toronto. http://www.hse.ru/en/org/hse/iori/B20_Toronto_Recommendations (December 2014).

B20 (2010b). 'Joint Statement by Participating Companies'. G20 Business Summit, November 11, Seoul. http://www.hse.ru/data/2013/01/23/1306478418/Seoul_G20_Business_Summit_Joint_Statement.pdf (December 2014).

B20 (2011). 'Final Report, with Appendices'. G20 Business Summit, November 3, Cannes. http://www.hse.ru/data/2013/01/23/1306477802/Cannes_B20_Report.pdf (December 2014).

B20 (2012). 'B20 Task Force Recommendations'. June, Los Cabos. http://www.hse.ru/data/2013/01/23/1306477584/Los_Cabos_B20_Report.pdf (December 2014).

B20 (2013). 'B20–G20 Partnership for Growth and Jobs: Recommendations from Business 20'. G20 Business Summit, September 5, St Petersburg. http://b20russia.com/B20_WhiteBook_web.pdf (December 2014).

Cameron, David (2011). 'Governance for Growth: Building Consensus for the Future'. Report submitted to the 2011 G20 Cannes Summit, November. www.g20.utoronto.ca/2011/2011-cameron-report.pdf (December 2014).

Development Working Group (2012). '2012 Progress Report of the Development Working Group'. June. http://www.international.gc.ca/g20/2012/progress_report-progres_rapport.aspx (December 2014).

G20 (2008). 'Declaration of the Summit on Financial Markets and the World Economy'. Washington DC, October 15. http://www.g20.utoronto.ca/2008/2008declaration1115.html (December 2014).

G20 (2010). 'Annex II: Multi-Year Action Plan on Development'. November 12, Seoul. http://www.g20.utoronto.ca/2010/g20seoul-development.html (December 2014).

G20 (2011a). 'Cannes Action Plan for Growth and Jobs'. Cannes, November 4. http://www.g20.utoronto.ca/2011/2011-cannes-action-111104-en.html (December 2014).

G20 (2011b). 'Cannes Summit Final Declaration – Building Our Common Future: Renewed Collective Action for the Benefit of All'. Cannes, November 4. http://www.g20.utoronto.ca/2011/2011-cannes-declaration-111104-en.html (December 2014).

G20 (2013). 'G20 Leaders Declaration'. St Petersburg, September 6. http://www.g20.utoronto.ca/2013/2013-0906-declaration.html (December 2014).

G20 Agriculture Ministers (2011). 'Action Plan on Food Price Volatility and Agriculture'. June 23, Paris. http://www.g20.utoronto.ca/2011/2011-agriculture-plan-en.pdf (December 2014).

G20 Anti-Corruption Working Group (2013). 'St Petersburg Strategic Framework for the G20 Anti-Corruption Working Group'. http://www.g20.utoronto.ca/2013/G20_ACWG_St_Petersburg_Strategic_Framework.pdf (December 2014).

G20 Study Group on Financing for Investment (2013). 'G20 Workplan on Financing for Investment Study Group's Findings and Ways Forward'. July, G20 Russian presidency. http://en.g20russia.ru/load/782804292 (December 2014).

Gates, Bill (2011). 'Innovation with Impact: Financing 21st Century Development'. Report to G20 leaders at the Cannes Summit, November. http://www.gatesfoundation.org/~/media/GFO/Documents/2011%20G20%20Report%20PDFs/Full%20Report/g20reportenglish.pdf (December 2014).

Appendix 9.A: B20 task forces, 2010–13

2010 Seoul (12)	2011 Cannes (12)	2012 Los Cabos (8)	2013 St Petersburg (7)
Closing the Gap in Infrastructure and Natural Resource Funding	Trade and Investment	Trade and Investment	Investments and Infrastructure
Encouraging Foreign Direct Investment			Trade as a Growth Driver
Revitalizing World Trade			
Supporting Economic Growth and the Implications for Financial Sector Policy and Regulatory Reforms	Financial Regulation		Financial System – Restoring Confidence and Growth
	International Monetary System		
Unleashing Technology-Enabled Productivity Growth	Information and Communication Technologies and Innovation	Information and Communication Technologies and Innovation	Innovation and Development as a Global Priority
Addressing the Impact of Youth Unemployment	Employment and Social Dimension	Employment	Job Creation, Employment and Investments in Human Capital
	Anti-Corruption	Improving Transparency	Transparency and Anti-Corruption
		Advocacy and impact	G20–B20 Dialogue Efficiency
Creating Green Jobs	Green Growth	Green Growth	
Increasing Access to Healthcare in Developing Economies	Development and Food Security	Financing for Growth and Development	
		Food Security	
Improving Energy Efficiency	Energy		
Encouraging Substantial Use of Renewable and Low-Carbon Energy			
Reducing Monetary and Fiscal Stimulus	Economic policies		
	Global Governance		
	Commodities and Raw Materials		
Funding and Nurturing the Small and Medium-Sized Enterprise Sector			

Appendix 9.B: 2013 task force priorities by summit

	Toronto		Seoul		Cannes		Los Cabos		St Petersburg		Total	
	Count	%	Count	%	Count	%	Count	%	Count	%	Count	%
Innovation and Development as a Global Priority	0	0	19	33.3	36	30.5	14	18.4	18	12.8	87	21.6
B20 (no task force)	2	18.2	11	19.3	34	28.8	16	21.1	13	9.2	76	18.9
Financial System – Restoring Confidence and Growth	5	45.5	6	10.5	19	16.1	5	6.6	25	17.7	60	14.9
Job Creation, Employment and Investments in Human Capital	2	18.2	8	14.0	8	6.8	11	14.5	26	18.4	55	13.6
Trade as a Growth Driver	2	18.2	5	8.8	7	5.9	11	14.5	23	16.3	48	11.9
Transparency and Anti-Corruption	0	0	0	0	6	5.1	17	22.4	17	12.1	40	9.9
Investments and Infrastructure	0	0	8	14.0	0	0	1	1.3	11	7.8	20	5.0
G20-B20 Dialogue Efficiency	0	0	0	0	8	6.8	1	1.3	8	5.7	17	4.2
Total	11	100	57	100	118	100	76	100	141	100	403	100

Note: The full catalogue of B20 recommendations is available from the International Organisations Research Institute at the National Research University Higher School of Economics at http://www.hse.ru/org/hse/iori/B20. It lists all B20 recommendations by summit, broken down into issue areas for each summit, with an indication of the originating task force where applicable and its position in the configuration of 2013 task forces.

PART IV
Accountability

Chapter 10
The Muskoka Accountability Report: Assessing the Written Record

Ella Kokotsis

The annual G7/8 summits produce written, publicly available communiqués, declarations, statements, and action plans that bind leaders to hard commitments across a breadth of policy issues (Hajnal 1989). Are there limits to how much or how often the G7/8 members comply with their summit commitments, particularly given that each is a sovereign, autonomous state, operating in a structurally anarchic system, with leaders driven by divergent domestic and international demands? How can compliance with these commitments be measured once the summit is over, the journalists have dispersed, and the leaders have returned home to their national constituencies?

Whether leaders comply with their summit commitments generates much debate in political, academic, policy, and media circles. Summit sceptics routinely question the ability, and indeed capacity, of the G7/8 to keep its promises under conditions of ongoing domestic political constraint and conflicting international demands. But scholars and practitioners alike agree that it makes little sense for leaders to invest their time and resources while potentially risking their political and personal reputations to generate commitments that they have neither the ability nor will to comply with after the summit's end. And pioneering scholars have developed a method to systematically chart the compliance performance of member states (von Furstenberg and Daniels 1992; Kokotsis and Kirton 1997; Daniels 1993; Kokotsis and Daniels 1999).

The importance of assessing progress in implementing these commitments and ultimately holding leaders to account has long since been recognized by the G8 Research Group, based at the University of Toronto. Since 1996, it has produced and published annual compliance assessments of the progress made by the G7/8 in meeting the commitments reached at the annual summits, using the framework and methodology developed by George von Furstenberg and Joseph Daniels and enhanced by Ella Kokotsis (von Furstenberg and Daniels 1992; Kokotsis and Daniels 1999). These reports monitor and assess each member's compliance on a carefully chosen selection of priority summit commitments. They provide policy makers, scholars, civil society, the media, and other stakeholders with transparent and accessible information. They also offer systemic data that enable the social science analysis of this highly unique international forum to determine patterns of compliance over time, by member and issue area, and to determine what causes the patterns that arise.[1]

The G8 Research Group's collaboration on these compliance reports has expanded to include an important partnership since 2005 with the National Research University Higher School of Economics (HSE), adding to the strength and robustness of this annual analytic exercise by the inclusion of Russian-language translation, access to information provided by key Russian government officials involved in the G8 process, greater reliability and observational balance, and analytical advances.

G8 governors themselves began conducting increasingly systematic compliance assessments of their own in 2007. They took a major step forward at the Muskoka Summit in 2010. For those around the world engaged in the exercise of tracking and assessing the G7/8's annual commitments, as well as follow-through with these promises, the release of the first full and comprehensive 'Muskoka Accountability Report' in 2010 was a highly anticipated and much-welcomed event.

This chapter examines how the Muskoka report came to be and how it fared in its delivery, impact, contribution, and limitations. Although the report represented a breakthrough in summit leadership and accountability, the reporting process itself can and must be improved through a number of prescriptive recommendations, allowing for the delivery of a more tangible, coherent, results-driven accountability process.

An Overview of the Muskoka Accountability Report

The timing of the release of the 'Muskoka Accountability Report' was not accidental, given the rapid ascension of the Group of 20 (G20) as the permanent, pre-eminent forum of global economic cooperation. In an era of rising G20 prominence, the issue of legitimacy and the restoration of confidence in the G8 process were major drivers in the report's timing and delivery. Despite the G7/8's 36-year history, it was necessary to prove its good faith and effective global leadership in order to retain its continued credibility. Assessing progress in implementing commitments was therefore essential in keeping the leaders on track while demonstrating a commitment to transparency and open reporting.

This is not to suggest, however, that the question of G8 accountability did not exist prior to Muskoka. In fact, the G8 had seen a noticeable surge in the number of remit mandates over the years, with leaders publicly promising in their summit documents to report back at subsequent summits on their progress in achieving key economic, environmental, security, and development commitments.[2]

Modest accountability reports had been released by the G8 in 2008 and 2009. The first, issued at the 2008 Hokkaido Summit, included an implementation review of the G8's anticorruption commitments (G8 2008). The following year in Italy, as part of their

---

1   Compliance assessments and the methodology used are available on the G8 Information Centre website at http://www.g8.utoronto.ca/compliance.

2   Between 1975 and 2003, the G7/8 produced 74 such remit mandates.

summit declaration, the G8 leaders released the G8 Preliminary Accountability Report, focused on food security, water, health, and education (G8 2009a).

Also at the 2009 L'Aquila Summit, the leaders committed – for the first time – to adopt a full and comprehensive accountability mechanism, to task a senior-level working group to devise a consistent methodology for reporting on key commitments, and to deliver the report at the 2010 Muskoka Summit. In doing so, they noted:

> Guided by our common values, we will address global issues and promote a world economy that is open, innovative, sustainable and fair. To this end, effective and responsible leadership is required. We are determined to fully take on our responsibilities, and are committed to implementing our decisions, and to adopting a full and comprehensive accountability mechanism by 2010 to monitor progress and strengthen the effectiveness of our actions. (G8 2009b)

And deliver they did, as promised, at Muskoka: a glossy, 88-page, magazine-format document that included a CD-ROM of reporting annexes and supporting documentation. The release of this report represented a key development in the G8's (2010, 3) desire to provide what it called 'a candid assessment on what the G8 has done'.

Substantively, the 'Muskoka Accountability Report' aimed to report on G8 progress in a number of key development-related commitments, assess the results of G8 action, and identify lessons learned for future reporting. It clearly acknowledged at the outset that it was neither an exhaustive review nor an assessment of global progress on meeting international development commitments. It noted, similar to what the G8 Research Group and the HSE have known for years, that this type of reporting presented a number of important empirical and scientific challenges. In overall terms, however, the report rightly argued that it signified a 'major step forward in assessing the extent to which the G8 has lived up to its promises' (G8 2010, 3).

The report assessed 10 thematic areas, reflecting the range of development-related issues on which the G8 had focused its attention over the years. These consisted of aid effectiveness, debt relief, economic development, health, water and sanitation, food security, education, governance, peace and security, and the environment and energy.

Given this roster, why was the exclusive focus on development chosen? The answer lies in several related factors.

First, the G7/8 has played a leading role in drawing attention to, and catalysing action for, the development of poor countries and people in the world. Development issues have consistently and systematically been on the agenda since the inception of the G7 in 1975 (see Appendix 10.A). It generated 478 commitments from 1975 to 2013 (see Appendix 10.B). The number of development-related commitments has risen since 2000, with an unprecedented amount of discussion and number of commitments in this area made since then.

Second, the G8 has been able to shape and influence the policy direction of international development issues to a large degree, committing to work with the developing world and the broader international development community on an extensive breadth of development-related issues. These include, among others, aid, debt relief, food security, health and infectious diseases, energy conservation, and water and sanitation.

Third, the summit has been very successful in raising financial resources from its members, and from other partners as well. The Muskoka Initiative on Maternal, Newborn, and Child Health is a clear example of this effort. In 2010, the G8 mobilized $5 billion in new funds to support maternal, newborn, and child health, along with an additional $2.3 billion in contributions from various international organizations, aid agencies, and foundations.

And, fourth, a few months following the Muskoka Summit, the September 2010 United Nations Summit on the Millennium Development Goals (MDGs) offered the G8 an opportunity to flex its global muscle, proving that it could exercise strong leadership and assemble key resources on those MDGs to which maternal, newborn, and child health were key. This placed the G8 members in a particularly prominent position going into the UN summit, ultimately enabling a further mobilization of $40 billion over five years from the private sector, foundations, international organizations, civil society, and research organizations – all aimed at accelerating progress on maternal, newborn, and child health, the subject of MDGs 4 and 5.

These leadership attributes and strengths, coupled with a general recognition following L'Aquila and Muskoka that significant challenges remained on both the 2005 Gleneagles commitments and in achieving the 2015 MDGs, led to development issues becoming the focus of this first, systematic, official G8 accountability report.

Africa was a particular focus in the report, as the G8 recognized that its development agenda continued to be very closely tied to the continent. Much of the report therefore focused on commitments that supported Africa's goals of achieving social progress, sustainable economic growth, good governance, and security.

The 'Muskoka Accountability Report' identified 56 development-related commitments on which G8 progress was assessed. Four criteria were applied to identify a commitment:

- Was it over-arching? (Did it encompass more detailed and specific commitments in the same sector?)
- Was it measurable? (Did it include financial resource allocations?)
- Was it within the G8's control?
- Did it represent a multi-year commitment expiring in 2010?

The Muskoka report concentrated on commitments made between 2005 and 2009, paying particular attention to the ambitious 2005 Gleneagles development commitments. Within each thematic area, three basic questions were addressed:

- What key G8 commitments were made?
- What action did the G8 take to implement these commitments?
- What results had been achieved?

Strengths and Limitations of the Muskoka Accountability Report

Strengths

This type of reporting was clearly a landmark move. Being the first of its kind, it represented a clear departure from previous G8 reports, which focused primarily on identifying and reporting on G8 inputs – such as resources allocated, programs developed, and working groups established.

A report of this nature demonstrated a clear recognition on the part of the G8 that leadership begins with promises being kept, that regular, clear, and transparent reporting is an important first step in this process, and that the need for the newly created Accountability Working Group (AWG) was essential in ensuring this work stays on track.

The report also acknowledged that the G8 should continue to improve how it develops, implements, monitors, and reports on its commitments. It recognized that the G8 needs to make commitments that are clear, transparent, measurable, and time-bound, because measurable objectives make future tracking and reporting on results less complicated.

Important, also, was the fact that this type of reporting added an additional element of peer pressure, which ultimately played a critical role in the G8 members' desire to keep up with their counterparts, as few countries wanted to be publically acknowledged as failing to deliver on their international commitments and obligations.

A final strength of the report was that it acknowledged its own limitations.

Limitations

The first limitation was one of attribution. On most development-related initiatives, the G8 does not and cannot act alone, requiring partner organizations, nongovernmental organizations (NGOs), private foundations, civil society, and the private sector to contribute to the successful outcome of its development goals. G8 interventions and implementation successes are therefore clearly influenced by how all these partners and groups come together to ultimately deliver on results.

The second issue is that of data limitations. Many activities identified in the report are in sectors where data quality is poor. Therefore activities are carried out without adequate attention to the need for baseline data or a consistent methodology that would allow for rigorous assessments.

The third limitation relates to the general lack of adequate monitoring systems on the ground. Such systems would provide timely and reliable information for results-oriented reporting.

Given these limitations, the AWG recognized that a significant amount of work had to be done in terms of improving the overall quality of these evaluations in the future. Beyond the report's self-professed limitations, several other limitations existed in this type of reporting format.

First, the report failed to specify why these 56 commitments were selected and not other development commitments. In so doing, it failed to outline its selection criteria.

Second, the report generally lacked standard and quantifiable terms, common benchmarks, and baselines. The lack of a clearly established set of interpretive guidelines resulted in a commitment selection process void of any standard terms or definitions.

Third, the report lacked any kind of specified scoring metrics. Information was presented in the narrative, with limited tables and graphs, but there was no overall view of how G8 members stacked up against each other. Without a comprehensive, country-specific scorecard to outline overall achievements across the various issues areas, a comparative assessment of how members performed relative to each other became difficult to discern.

Fourth, related to this third point, some country assessments were much richer in detail than others. For example, more robust information was provided on Canada and the United States than on Italy and Russia.

Fifth, certain financial numbers included both bilateral aid as well as multilateral donations. This made it difficult to distinguish if double-counting factored into the reporting process.

Sixth, the report drew its financial data from the Development Assistance Committee of the Organisation for Economic Co-operation and Development, of which Russia is not a member. The report contained no indication of how Russian data were treated and interpreted.

Seventh, progress in the report was measured in current dollars, as opposed to constant dollars adjusted to the rate of inflation. Without an accurate assessment of the impact on price increases on the real value of every dollar spent, G8 aid expenditures were artificially inflated, creating larger funding gaps than the report acknowledged (Sachs and Killelea 2011, 1).

Eighth, although the report acknowledged the importance of working with NGOs on the ground to implement G8 commitments, it failed to specify a clear path for NGO input into the framework. A similar argument can be made for civil society and foundations, all of which are required to work together both within the boardroom and on the ground to deliver development results.

Ninth, the report failed to produce a clear plan of action on how to rectify lagging progress on past commitments. Nor was there a strategy to speed progress in areas deemed to be falling short. These primarily included universal access targets for HIV/AIDS and the provision of sanitation, which the report acknowledged were falling 'dangerously behind' (G8 2010, 38).

Impact: Did the G8 Muskoka Summit Make a Difference?

A year following the release of the 'Muskoka Accountability Report', and with France preparing for its 2011 Deauville Summit, questions loomed as to whether the Canadian-hosted Muskoka G8 made a real difference. If so, did the release of the G8's first accountability report play a role?

THE MUSKOKA ACCOUNTABILITY REPORT

Delivery by Deauville 2011

The accountability trend initiated at Muskoka had a notable impact at the French-hosted G8 the following year. Issues of accountability fared high on the French agenda with the release of the 'Deauville Accountability Report – G8 Commitments on Health and Food Security: State of Delivery and Results' (G8 2011a). Noting that members 'remain strongly committed to meeting our commitments and to tracking their implementation in a fully transparent and consistent manner', the report tracked progress on several commitments related to health (G8 2011b). These included commitments from both the 2010 Muskoka Initiative, as well as the 2009 L'Aquila Food Security Initiative.

Successful in its intent but limited to health and food security, the Deauville report lacked the overall robustness in assessing the broad range of commitments made at the Muskoka Summit. It noted only that 'in order to track this commitment and monitor its implementation, the G8 will work in coordination with a range of stakeholders involved in the Global Strategy for Women's and Children Health' (G8 2011a, 3).

By contrast, in going one step beyond, the '2010 Muskoka G8 Summit Final Compliance Report', produced by the G8 Research Group (2011) and HSE, assessed how well, and to what extent, the G8 lived up to 18 priority commitments made at the Muskoka Summit. These commitments spanned a much broader range of issues than those covered by the 'Deauville Accountability Report', but included those commitments made on key health and development issues.

The results of this compliance report indicated that the G8 had lived up to their priority commitments 73 per cent of the time – lower than the scores achieved in 2008 and 2009 (see Appendix 10.C). Canada and Russia led their G8 partners, followed by the United States, with Germany and the United Kingdom tied in third place. Then came France and the European Union in fourth place, Japan in fifth, and Italy in last.

On the summit's signature Muskoka Initiative – a cornerstone of the 'Muskoka Accountability Report' – Canada led its G8 partners with $284 million in contributions (G8 Research Group 2011, 44). Despite Canada's leadership, its G8 partners fell behind, with Germany the only other country to honour this pledge in the year following the Muskoka Summit. With US allocations at less than a quarter of its promised $1.3 billion, and little progress from France, Japan, Russia, or the UK, the G8 would need to more than quintuple its funding by the end of 2011 to meet this key summit target.

Official development assistance (ODA), another key component of the Muskoka report, yielded above average compliance at 84 per cent. The G8 committed to increase its ODA levels and enhance aid effectiveness through more inclusive partnerships and better transparency mechanisms.

Climate change, on the other hand, integrally connected to the development agenda, failed to produce concrete results from the G8. The G8's pledges to undertake robust individual mid-term emissions reductions and to implement all provisions of the stalled Copenhagen Accord from the 2009 Conference of the Parties to the UN Framework Convention on Climate Change, including those provisions on reporting and verification, fell dangerously short in their delivery

On the political-security front, in areas of traditional high compliance, including regional security issues (Afghanistan and civilian security systems), nonproliferation, and terrorism (enhancing security and capacity building), the G8 once again fared very well. Its compliance averaged between 89 per cent and 100 per cent across these issue areas. Commitments to reduce trade barriers and strengthen or create new trade agreements, however, garnered only 61 per cent, well below the overall compliance average.

Delivery by Camp David 2012

As the G8 leaders prepared for their annual summit gathering at Camp David in 2012, the momentum on accountability was not lost. The Camp David Accountability Report: Actions, Approach, Results focused on the performance and action of the G8 (2012) in the areas of food security, agricultural markets, trade, and nutrition. It also included a section on the G8's performance and actions related to health.

Building on the recommendations of the Muskoka and Deauville accountability reports, Camp David added two new tools: a self-reported scorecard 'intended to catalogue indicators of progress in specific focus areas' and in-depth reporting tables, provided to 'give a fuller picture of G-8 members' agricultural development and food security activities in a set of developing countries' (G8 2012, 4).

The Camp David report concluded that the G8 (2012, 4) is 'generally on track in realizing the commitments its leaders have made to food security and health and in increasing the broader effectiveness of development assistance'. The report noted that although the global economic downturn had resulted in lower overall volumes of ODA, the G8 had largely met individual targets for increased aid volumes to African countries. However, in offering detailed disbursement updates for only the Muskoka commitments, the Camp David report failed to provide a clear progress update on the G8's Deauville commitments made in 2011.

In contrast, the G8 Research Group (2012) and HSE's final compliance report on selected priority commitments made at Deauville provided detailed evidence on the G8's progress in meeting its Deauville pledges. The compliance report offered further insight on whether the G8's new accountability reporting mechanism did, in fact, make a difference.

The average Deauville compliance score of 77 per cent showed signs of improvement over both the 2010 Muskoka score of 73 per cent (see Appendix 10.C). Full compliance was awarded in the areas of good governance (Afghanistan) and nuclear nonproliferation (national systems effectiveness). Generally high scores of 84 per cent and 95 per cent came on reinforcing the Nuclear Non-Proliferation Treaty (NPT) and Comprehensive Test Ban Treaty respectively. Compliance was also very strong on macroeconomic policy (unemployment), with the G8 scoring 95 per cent for efforts to tackle jobless rates.

On the environment, compliance was substantial: the G8 scored 84 per cent for emissions reductions, up from 61 per cent in 2010. Trade-related commitments saw an upward swing at Deauville with a score of 84 per cent, up from only 61 per cent the year before, and 11 per cent in 2009. Development assistance showed moderate overall improvement over the compliance average, with the G8 scoring 78 per cent on its ODA pledges. Terrorism also scored 78 per cent, just slightly above the overall average. Ensuring protection of intellectual property scored 89 per cent.

Delivery by Lough Erne 2013

Momentum on accountability reporting continued in 2013, with G8 leaders releasing their 'Lough Erne Accountability Report: Keeping Our Promises', covering 61 development-related commitments made since 2002. The report assessed nine key development challenges: aid effectiveness and debt, economic development, health, water and sanitation, food security, education, governance, peace and security, and environment and energy. Based on a scorecard approach, the five-point rating system used a combination of publically available, independently verifiable data and G8 members' self-assessments.[3]

By moving to country-specific reporting, and by including case studies highlighting the individual efforts of members, the Lough Erne report demonstrated how the G8 (2013, 119) 'catalysed action, influenced global policies and mobilised resources … in addressing the challenges of poverty reduction and sustainable development'. The report, however, also acknowledged the G8's limitations, by recognizing that 'not all efforts were successful' and that 'some commitments were missed or are off-track', most notably those related to aid effectiveness, remittances and the protection of biodiversity (G8 2013, 119). It concluded by noting that future G8 accountability assessments would be issued to monitor progress, but effectiveness in meeting current and future development challenges would require focus, relevance, and clarity of commitments assessed (G8 2013, 12).

Contrasting the qualitative reporting style of the Lough Erne report, the G8 Research Group and HSE's 2013 compliance assessment used a quantitative evaluation of 17 priority commitments made at Camp David relative to the G8's compliance in the past. These findings showed strong compliance with the G8's priority commitments at 80 per cent, an increase from 77 per cent at Deauville in 2011, 73 per cent at Muskoka in 2010, and 77 per cent at L'Aquila in 2009 (see Appendix 10.C). This rising record was led by the United States with 94 per cent, followed by Germany with 88 per cent, Canada with 86 per cent, and the United Kingdom and France both with 83 per cent. As the UK, US, and France served as hosts in 2011, 2012, and 2013, this finding confirms the compliance-boosting effect of hosting these annual summit gatherings.

By issue area, complete 100 per cent compliance came in the realm of public-private partnerships, food and agriculture, health, and the NPT. Higher than average compliance scores (95 per cent) also came in the area of export control policies regarding NPT and on macroeconomics and productivity. These high compliance levels 'matched reasonably well the agenda of the Lough Erne Summit, notably the stress on private sector–led growth, food and nutrition, and health (in the form of dementia)' (Kirton 2013).

---

3   The five-point rating system used colour coding to represent 'excellent, good, satisfactory, below expectations, or off track' (G8 2013, 3).

Recommendations for Future Reporting

As the G7/8 leadership prepares for future summits, this momentum on accountability must not be lost. With the G7/8 so heavily focused on transparency and the delivery of results, future summits offer excellent opportunities to move the accountability agenda forward. To do so, however, the AWG will have to ensure that the work done to date stays on track. This means that several aspects of the G7/8's reporting mechanism will need to be further refined.

First, the use of measurable objectives will ensure that future tracking and reporting on results are less difficult and complex. Second, data limitations will need to be addressed in a more comprehensive manner, as baseline data and consistent methodologies allow for more rigorous assessments. Third, monitoring systems on the ground will need to be improved, allowing for timely and reliable information to enhance results-oriented reporting. Fourth, the G7/8 will need to rely more on the ongoing support of its partner organizations – NGOs, foundations, civil society, and private sector association – to ensure the successful delivery of its commitments and monitoring of their implementation and actual results.

Fifth, with a large number of expert working groups at the G7/8's disposal, including those on Africa, health, education, water, sanitation, education, and corruption, reliance on these expert working groups is critical. But these working groups should be mandated to seek and receive inputs from civil society and other international organizations in their monitoring and reporting process. To execute their mandates effectively, these working groups also require the capacity to evaluate results against a consistent and specific set of indicators. This is critical to the evaluation process. Reports produced by these expert working groups should also include a systematic, reliable, and consistent framework for on-the-ground monitoring and program implementation, as well as specific timetables and options for future action.

Conclusion: A New Era in Summit Accountability

The 2010 'Muskoka Accountability Report' represents a landmark change. Being the first of its kind, it signified a clear departure from previous G7/8 documents where the focus was primarily on identifying and reporting on inputs – such as resources allocated, programs developed, and working groups established.

A report of this nature demonstrated a clear recognition on the part of the G8 that leadership begins with promises being kept, that regular reporting is an important first step in this process, and that the ongoing AWG is essential in ensuring that this work stays on track.

Certain limitations initially revealed in the Muskoka report have subsequently been improved, most notably the efforts of the AWG to include civil society, NGOs, and partner organizations in development-related compliance activities. This trend is illustrated by the compliance results following the Muskoka Summit – with increasing compliance scores across most development-related issue areas assessed by the G8 Research Group and HSE, and a general increase in overall compliance trends over the mid term.

Holding G7/8 leaders to account, in an open and transparent manner, suggests that pressure to comply with their global commitments on key policy areas is positively affected through this form of self-reporting and accountability. Such reporting has inspired similar accountability assessments by other forums, most notably the G20. Just after the release of the 'Muskoka Accountability Report', at the outset of the 2010 Muskoka G8 and Toronto G20 summits, Canadian Prime Minister Stephen Harper announced that the issue of accountability would be the 'defining feature', not only of the G8, but of his G20 as well, which he would both host. Indeed, at the Toronto Summit, G20 leaders established the G20 Development Working Group, with the aim of implementing a development agenda. Later that year at the Seoul Summit, G20 leaders (2010) adopted the Seoul Development Consensus for Shared Growth to 'add value to and complement existing development commitments'. This work culminated in the release of the first ever G20 accountability exercise on the 67 development-related commitments from the Seoul Development Consensus in the lead-up to the G20 St Petersburg Summit in September 2013. Similar to the approach adopted by the G8, the G20's accountability reporting recognized the importance of policy coordination across different G20 workstreams, encouraged private-public partnerships between non-G20 members, and noted the value in leveraging different funding sources to support and promote development initiatives. As with the G8's AWG, the G20 (2013, 7) sees the value-added of the Development Working Group in 'delivering tangible development outcomes through high level political leadership and a more coherent, results-driven and long term approach'.

To stay on track for future summits, the G7/8 (and now, by extension, the G20), should continue to improve the way it develops, implements, monitors, and reports on its commitments by making promises that are clear, transparent, measurable, and time-bound. By continuing to candidly assess its own accomplishments, and by involving others in that assessment process, the G7/8 can enhance its credibility as the centre of effective global governance, shaping and influencing the policy direction of the world's most demanding political, security, and development issues.

References

Daniels, Joseph P. (1993). *The Meaning and Reliability of Economic Summit Undertakings*. New York: Garland Publishing.

G8 (2008). 'Accountability Report: Implementation Review of G8 on Anti-corruption Commitments'. July, Hokkaido. http://www.g8.utoronto.ca/summit/2008hokkaido/2008-corruptionreport.pdf (December 2014).

G8 (2009a). 'G8 Preliminary Accountability Report'. Annex to the L'Aquila G8 2009 Declaration, L'Aquila, Italy, July 8. http://www.g8.utoronto.ca/summit/2009laquila/2009-accountability.pdf (December 2014).

G8 (2009b). 'Responsible Leadership for a Sustainable Future'. L'Aquila, Italy, July 8. http://www.g8.utoronto.ca/summit/2009laquila/2009-declaration.html (December 2014).

G8 (2010). 'Muskoka Accountability Report'. June 20. http://www.g8.utoronto.ca/summit/2010muskoka/accountability (December 2014).

G8 (2011a). 'Deauville Accountability Report – G8 Commitments on Health and Food Security: State of Delivery and Results'. May 18. http://www.g8.utoronto.ca/summit/2011deauville/accountability.html (December 2014).

G8 (2011b). 'G8 Declaration: Renewed Commitment for Freedom and Democracy'. Deauville, May 27. http://www.g8.utoronto.ca/summit/2011deauville/2011-declaration-en.html (December 2014).

G8 (2012). 'Camp David Accountability Report: Actions, Approach, Results'. Camp David, May 19. http://www.g8.utoronto.ca/summit/2012campdavid/g8-cdar.html (December 2014).

G8 (2013). 'Lough Erne Accountability Report: Keeping Our Promises'. June 7. http://www.g8.utoronto.ca/summit/2013lougherne/lough-erne-accountability.html (December 2014).

G8 Research Group (2011). '2010 Muskoka G8 Summit Final Compliance Report'. May 24. http://www.g8.utoronto.ca/evaluations/2010compliance-final (December 2014).

G8 Research Group (2012). '2011 Deauville G8 Summit Final Compliance Report'. May 18. http://www.g8.utoronto.ca/evaluations/2011compliance-final (December 2014).

G8 Research Group (2013). '2012 Camp David G8 Summit Final Compliance Report'. 14, June. http://www.g8.utoronto.ca/evaluations/2012compliance/2012compliance.pdf (December 2014).

G20 (2010). 'Annex I: Seoul Development Consensus for Shared Growth'. Seoul, November 12. http://www.g20.utoronto.ca/2010/g20seoul-consensus.html (December 2014).

G20 (2013). 'St Petersburg Accountability Report on G20 Development Commitments'. August 28. http://www.g20.utoronto.ca/2013/Saint_Petersburg_Accountability_Report_on_G20_Development_Commitments.pdf (December 2014).

Hajnal, Peter I. (1989). *The Seven-Power Summit: Documents from the Summits of Industrialized Countries, 1975–1989.* Millwood NY: Kraus International Publishers.

Kirton, John J. (2013). 'A Summit of Significant Success: Prospects for the G8 Leaders at Lough Erne'. June 12. http://www.g8.utoronto.ca/evaluations/2013lougherne/kirton-prospects-2013.html (December 2014).

Kokotsis, Eleanore and John J. Kirton (1997). 'National Compliance with Environmental Regimes: The Case of the G7, 1988–1995'. Paper prepared for the annual convention of the International Studies Association, 18–22 March, Toronto.

Kokotsis, Ella and Joseph P. Daniels (1999). 'G8 Summits and Compliance'. In *The G8's Role in the New Millennium*, Michael R. Hodges, John J. Kirton and Joseph P. Daniels, eds. Aldershot: Ashgate, pp. 75–91.

Sachs, Jeffrey and Steve Killelea (2011). 'Holding G8 Accountability to Account'. Institute for Economics and Peace and the Earth Institute, Columbia University. http://economicsandpeace.org/wp-content/uploads/2011/10/Holding-G8-Accountability-to-Account.pdf (December 2014).

von Furstenberg, George M. and Joseph P. Daniels (1992). *Economic Summit Declarations, 1975–1989: Examining the Written Record of International Cooperation* (Princeton Studies in International Finance No. 72). Princeton: Princeton University Press.

Appendix 10.A: G7/8 communiqué conclusions on development, 1975–2012

Year	# words	% total words	# paras	% total paras	# docs	% total docs	# dedicated docs
1975	164	14.5	1	6.6	1	100	0
1976	270	16.6	3	12	1	100	0
1977	491	18.3	5	12.8	1	50	0
1978	585	19.5	12	24.4	1	50	0
1979	330	15.6	4	11.7	1	50	0
1980	654	16.3	6	12.5	1	20	0
1981	589	18.6	10	19.2	1	33.3	0
1982	290	16.1	1	5	1	50	0
1983	233	10.8	2	5.4	1	50	0
1984	109	3.3	1	2	1	20	0
1985	528	16.8	3	7.1	1	50	0
1986	394	10.9	4	12.5	1	25	0
1987	373	7.3	4	5.4	1	14.2	0
1988	824	16.9	9	13.8	1	33.3	0
1989	858	12	18	15	1	9	0
1990	1,066	14	15	12.1	1	25	0
1991	705	8.7	13	23.2	1	20	0
1992	510	6.7	5	2.9	1	25	0
1993	334	9.8	3	7.1	1	33.3	0
1994	913	22.1	8	11.7	1	50	0
1995	711	9.8	7	5.2	2	66.6	0
1996	3,129	20.4	46	20.1	2	50	1
1997	848	6.5	8	5.7	1	20	0
1998	407	6.6	5	7.8	1	25	0
1999	1,460	14.5	23	26.7	2	66.6	0
2000	1,974	14.5	21	14.4	2	40	0
2001	1,003	16.1	14	19.1	2	28.5	1
2002	6,693	55.9	64	56.1	3	42.8	2
2003	695	4.1	11	6.5	1	7.6	0
2004	461	1.1	3	0.89	3	14.2	2
2005	6,105	27.3	63	29.7	2	10	0
2006	3,234	10.5	46	18.7	1	5.8	1
2007	1,766	6.8	17	6.1	5	41.6	2
2008	1,661	9.8	12	6.8	2	18.1	0
2009	3,815	22.9	31	9.4	4	30.7	2
2010	1,839	17.3	17	17.3	3	100	0
2011	5,498	36.4	69	37.3	3	100	1
2012	620	17.0	6	15.0	1	50	0
Average	1,372.1	15.1	15.5	13.8	1.6	40.2	0.3

Note: Compiled by John Kirton, Zaria Shaw, and Sarah Cale. Data are drawn from all official English-language documents released in the G7/8 leaders' name at a summit. '# words' is the number of words referring to development for the year specified, excluding document titles and references. '% total words' refers to the percentage of the total number of words in all documents for the year specified. '# paras' is the number of paragraphs containing references to development for the year specified. Each bullet point is recorded as a separate paragraph. '% total paras' refers to the percentage of the total number of paragraphs in all documents for the year specified. '# docs' is the number of documents that contain development-related subjects and excludes dedicated documents.

Appendix 10.B: G7/8 development commitments, 1975–2013

Year	# commitments
1975	2
1976	2
1977	2
1978	3
1979	5
1980	5
1981	8
1982	3
1983	8
1984	8
1985	3
1986	4
1987	4
1988	4
1989	3
1990	12
1991	1
1992	4
1993	6
1994	4
1995	5
1996	21
1997	18
1998	16
1999	7
2000	24
2001	41
2002	23
2003	3
2004	4
2005	13
2006	25
2007	57
2008	35
2009	36
2010	4
2011	29
2012	16
2013	10
Total	478
Average	12.3

Note: Compiled by Zaria Shaw and Caroline Bracht.

THE MUSKOKA ACCOUNTABILITY REPORT

Appendix 10.C: G8 research group compliance, 2010–2012

2010 Muskoka Summit

Commitment	Canada	France	Germany	Italy	Japan	Russia	United Kingdom	United States	European Union	Average	
Official development assistance	1	1	0	0	1	1	1	1	0	0.67	84%
Health: healthcare funding	1	−1	1	−1	−1	−1	−1	−1	−1	−0.56	22%
Health: HIV/AIDS	1	0	0	−1	1	0	−1	1	1	0.22	61%
Neglected tropical diseases	1	0	1	−1	−1	0	1	1	−1	0.11	56%
Food and agriculture: L'Aquila	0	0	0	0	0	0	0	0	0	0.00	50%
Food and agriculture: principles for investment	0	0	0	1	1	1	0	1	0	0.44	72%
Good governance: Kimberley Process	1	1	0	0	0	1	1	1	0	0.56	78%
Climate change: mid-term emissions reductions	−1	1	1	0	−1	1	1	−1	1	0.22	61%
Climate change: Copenhagen Accord	0	0	0	−1	−1	0	0	0	0	−0.22	39%
Trade	0	0	0	0	0	1	0	0	1	0.22	61%
Nonproliferation	1	1	1	0	1	1	1	1	1	0.89	95%
Nuclear safety	0	1	1	0	0	1	1	1	1	0.67	84%
Regional security: Afghanistan	1	1	1	1	1	1	1	1	1	1.00	100%
Regional security: civilian security systems	1	1	0	1	1	1	1	1	1	0.89	95%
Terrorism: international cooperation	1	0	1	1	0	1	0	1	1	0.67	84%
Terrorism: enhancing security	1	0	1	1	1	1	1	1	1	0.89	95%
Terrorism: capacity building	1	1	1	1	1	1	1	0	0	0.78	89%
Natural disasters	1	1	0	1	1	0	1	1	1	0.78	89%
Average	0.61	0.44	0.50	0.17	0.28	0.61	0.50	0.56	0.44	0.46	73%
	81%	72%	75%	59%	64%	81%	75%	78%	72%	73%	

Note: Compliance scores are based on a three-point scale, where +1 constitutes full compliance, 0 constitutes a work in progress or no action taken, and −1 constitutes failure to comply or contrary action taken.
Source: G8 Research Group (2011).

2011 Deauville Summit

Commitment	Canada	France	Germany	Italy	Japan	Russia	United Kingdom	United States	European Union	Average	
Green growth	0	0	0	0	+1	+1	+1	0	+1	+0.44	72%
Macroeconomics: unemployment	+1	+1	+1	+1	+1	+1	0	+1	+1	+0.89	95%
Climate change: emissions reductions	+1	+1	0	0	+1	+1	+1	+1	0	+0.67	84%
Maternal, newborn, and child health	+1	−1	+1	−1	−1	+1	−1	−1	+1	−0.11	45%
Food and agriculture	+1	0	0	0	0	0	0	0	0	0.11	56%
Accountability on development	+1	0	+1	0	+1	0	0	+1	0	+0.44	72%
Nuclear non-proliferation	0	0	+1	0	+1	+1	+1	+1	+1	+0.67	84%
Nuclear non-proliferation	+1	+1	+1	+1	+1	+1	+1	0	+1	+0.89	95%
Good governance: Afghanistan	+1	+1	+1	+1	+1	+1	+1	+1	+1	+1	100%
Crime and corruption: stolen asset recovery	0	+1	−1	−1	−1	−1	0	+1	0	−0.22	39%
Supporting sustainable and inclusive growth	0	+1	+1	+1	+1	0	+1	+1	+1	+0.78	89%
Trade	+1	+1	0	+1	0	0	+1	+1	+1	+0.67	84%
Internet economy: intellectual property	+1	+1	0	+1	+1	+1	+1	0	+1	+0.78	89%
Regional security: Somalia	0	0	0	+1	+1	0	0	0	0	+0.22	61%
Terrorism	+1	0	0	+1	0	+1	+1	+1	0	+0.56	78%
Development	0	0	+1	0	0	0	+1	+1	+1	+0.44	72%
Official development assistance	+1	+1	0	−1	+1	+1	+1	+1	0	+0.56	78%
Nonproliferation: national systems effectiveness	+1	+1	+1	+1	+1	+1	+1	+1	+1	+1	100%
Average	0.67	0.50	0.44	0.33	0.56	0.56	0.61	0.61	0.61	0.54	77%
	84%	75%	72%	67%	78%	78%	81%	81%	81%	77%	

Note: Compliance scores are based on a three-point scale, where +1 constitutes full compliance, 0 constitutes a work in progress or no action taken, and −1 constitutes failure to comply or contrary action taken.
Source: G8 Research Group (2012).

2012 Camp David Summit

Commitment	Canada	France	Germany	Italy	Japan	Russia	United Kingdom	United States	European Union		Average
Macroeconomics: fiscal consolidation	0	+1	0	+1	0	+1	0	0	0	+0.33	67%
Macroeconomics: productivity	+1	+1	+1	+1	0	+1	+1	+1	+1	+0.89	95%
Macroeconomics: public-private partnership	+1	+1	+1	+1	+1	+1	+1	+1	+1	+1	100%
Trade: regulatory coherence	+1	+1	+1	−1	+1	+1	−1	+1	+1	+0.56	78%
Food and agriculture: L'Aquila	+1	+1	+1	+1	+1	+1	+1	+1	+1	+1	100%
Food and agriculture: food security	+1	0	+1	−1	0	0	+1	+1	+1	+0.44	72%
Nuclear nonproliferation: Non-Proliferation Treaty	+1	+1	+1	+1	+1	+1	+1	+1	+1	+1	100%
Nuclear nonproliferation: export controls	+1	+1	+1	+1	+1	0	+1	+1	+1	+0.89	95%
Energy: free trade	0	0	0	0	+1	−1	+1	+1	+1	+0.33	67%
Energy: transparency	+1	+1	+1	0	0	+1	0	+1	+1	+0.67	84%
Climate change	+1	0	+1	−1	0	−1	0	0	+1	+0.11	56%
Development: capital markets	0	0	−1	0	+1	−1	0	+1	−1	-0.11	45%
Labour and employment	+1	+1	+1	+1	+1	−1	+1	+1	+1	+0.78	89%
Crime and corruption: recovery	+1	0	+1	+1	+1	−1	+1	+1	−1	+0.44	72%
Health	+1	+1	+1	+1	+1	+1	+1	+1	+1	+1	100%
IFI reform	+1	+1	+1	−1	+1	+1	+1	+1	+1	+0.78	89%
Good governance	−1	0	+1	0	0	−1	+1	+1	−1	0	50%
Average	0.71	0.65	0.76	0.29	0.65	0.18	0.65	0.88	0.59	0.60	80%
	86%	83%	88%	65%	83%	59%	83%	94%	80%	80%	

Note: Compliance scores are based on a three-point scale, where +1 constitutes full compliance, 0 constitutes a work in progress or no action taken, and −1 constitutes failure to comply or contrary action taken.
Source: G8 Research Group (2013).

Chapter 11
G7/8 and G20 Accountability and Civil Society

Peter I. Hajnal[1]

This chapter examines the role and impact of civil society in increasing the accountability of the Group of Seven (G7), Group of Eight (G8), and Group of 20 (G20). It first clarifies the key concepts of civil society and accountability, then discusses for what and to whom the G7/8 and the G20, as global governance institutions, are accountable, and, third, looks at the kinds of civil society organizations (CSOs) that play a role in the nexus between the G7/8 and G20. Fourth, it considers the motivations for, and range of, civil society interaction with the G7/8 and G20. Finally, it analyses how and to what extent civil society engagement has (or has not) had an impact on G7/8 and G20 accountability.

The chapter argues that the G7/8 and G20 have increasingly recognized the crucial role of accountability in gauging progress and building legitimacy. It further asserts that the Mutual Assessment Process (MAP), conducted through a series of reports published by the International Monetary Fund (IMF) with other intergovernmental organizations also playing a role, has an important accountability dimension. Civil society groups have tracked G7/8 and G20 performance, using a variety of methods that all contribute to enhancing accountability by exposing various strengths and weaknesses.

Introduction

G8 accountability has long been a concern for CSOs, think tanks, some G7/8 governments, and, more recently, for the G7/8 and the G20 themselves. The 'Gs' have come to realize that much of their claim to legitimacy rests on the fulfilment of their promises and that they will be held accountable for their actions or lack of actions as the case may be – not just in their member countries but also for global populations, including the marginalized.

Definitions and Dimensions

The term 'civil society', as used in this chapter, denotes not-for-profit groups of citizens engaging in collective action on particular public issues of concern. Another way of

---

1   The author wishes to thank the civil society activists, academics and former and present government officials who generously offered advice and shared their insight.

characterizing civil society is as a 'political space where associations of citizens seek, from outside political parties, to shape societal rules' through collective action in 'groups that share concerns about, and mobilise around, a particular problem of public affairs' (Scholte 2011, 34). Civil society associations include formally structured nongovernmental organizations (NGOs) as well as social movements, campaigns and coalitions. CSOs are very diverse: they vary in size, geographic extent, ideological orientation, available resources, and strategies and tactics. CSOs engage in anti-poverty activities, peace and disarmament activities, development, environment and climate change, human rights, gender issues, financial rules, and many other issues. Faith-based groups, labour unions, and research institutes are also included under this broad umbrella.

Some observers include business sector groups in overall civil society, but a good case can be made to exclude the private sector from civil society because the former's objectives, modus operandi, and close ties with governmental and intergovernmental bodies are quite distinct from those of nonprofit civil society associations. The related but not synonymous private philanthropies and foundations, celebrities, and parliamentarians have, at best, tenuous identities as civil society entities.

Accountability, particularly democratic accountability, means that an actor is answerable for its actions or inactions to all those affected by such actions and inactions. Or, in a different phrasing, accountability means that 'if A takes an action that impacts upon B, then by the principle of accountability A must answer to B for that action and its consequences' (Scholte 2011, 16). Accountability may be considered to have four main aspects or manifestations: transparency, consultation, evaluation, and correction or redress. Obtaining redress or remedy for inaction or wrong action is problematic in the G7/8 and G20, given their nature as informal institutions. This, however, has not stopped civil society and other stakeholder groups from advocating remedies for unjust or unfair action (or lack of necessary action) on the part of the G7/8 and G20. Further questions arise concerning accountability: Accountability for what? Accountability to whom? Accountability by what means, what mechanisms? What is democratic accountability?

Accountability: For What and To Whom?[2]

For what is the G7/8 accountable? The mandate, activities, and evolving agenda lead to the assertion that leaders can be held accountable for their actions and lack of actions on a wide range of economic, political, environmental, and other global issues: political and security issues, the environment and climate change, the fight against terrorism and organized crime, development, alleviation of the debts of poor countries, infectious diseases, food security, energy, education, intellectual property issues, corruption, and so forth.

To whom is the G7/8 accountable? Certainly to G7/8 members' own citizens but, more broadly, also to the global community, including marginalized populations, since all are affected by G7/8 decisions and initiatives. Internally, within the G7/8, leaders are also accountable to their peers, and sub-summit entities such as task forces, expert groups, and

---

2   For a more detailed G8-related treatment of these ideas see Peter I. Hajnal (2011).

other such bodies owe accountability to their principals. There is also mutual accountability between the G7/8 and other actors, particularly with respect to Africa.

The G20, as with the G7/8, can also be held accountable for its actions and inactions on all issues on its agenda: financial and economic coordination, sustainable development, green growth, anticorruption, climate change finance, trade, terrorist finance, food security, and so forth. The G20's original agenda, since its establishment at the leaders' level in 2008, centred on economic and financial concerns, but, inevitably, linkages became apparent almost from the beginning. The economic and financial crisis that became global by late 2008 has had deleterious effects on food prices, development assistance, climate change action, poverty, health care, and new indebtedness. G20 leaders at their summits have gradually begun to take notice of such related issues, albeit cautiously. G20 summit declarations have referred to trade (if only in a formulaic manner) and the financing of climate change mitigation and adaptation. The Canadian host of both the G8 Muskoka and G20 Toronto summits in June 2010 insisted on a sharp division of labour, thus finding justification for the continued existence and notionally continued relevance of the older G8 forum. And yet agenda expansion in the G20 is inevitable. The G20 Seoul Summit in November 2010 made this clear by placing development firmly on the agenda, alongside the financial and economic issues that have been the hallmark of the G20 forum from the start (the Korean host later added the issue of financial safety nets to the continuing financial concerns).

G20 leaders can be called to account by the populations of their own countries. Indeed, since one of the core missions of the G20 is to make globalization work for the benefit of all, the G20 is accountable to the whole global community affected by its decisions and initiatives. Internally, G20 leaders' accountability to their peers operates as well. G20 accountability to financial markets is clearer than in the case of the G7/8. This accountability can be seen as mutual, as the G20 also expects accountability from markets and their regulators. Sub-summit entities owe accountability to the G20 leaders, including the obligation to report back to them.

Civil Society Actors Interacting with the G7/8 and G20

A very broad range of CSOs cultivate a nexus with the official G7/8 and G20. CSOs embrace environmental and climate change NGOs and campaigns, human rights NGOs, development and relief agencies, anti-poverty groups and movements, faith-based groups, and CSOs focusing on various other economic, social, and political issues such as financial regulation, health, sustainable economic growth, and education. As well, the G7/G8/G20 have built relations, beyond business and young entrepreneurs, with trade unions, professional bodies, research groups and think tanks, youth groups, and, to a more limited extent, women's groups and, occasionally, indigenous groups (Lewallen 2008).

As indicated earlier, the business sector is a special case and its inclusion within civil society is problematic. Indeed, G7/8 and G20 officials themselves distinguish between business players and nonprofit civil CSOs. If the business sector in civil society is included, then the overall impact of civil society on the G7/8 would greatly increase. For example, most G8 and G20 leaders have attended the World Economic Forum (WEF) since 2005 and 2008 respectively, to flesh out their agendas for their annual presidencies at this exclusive annual business gathering. This close relationship is also evident with the G20 Business 20 (B20). The first formal B20 was convened on June 25–26, 2010, at the request of Canadian prime minister Stephen Harper and finance minister Jim Flaherty.

The host of the following summit in Seoul integrated the B20 (held on November 10–11, 2010) even more closely into the leaders' summit, which overlapped on November 11–12. In 2011, the B20, which was preceded by a meeting with B20 representatives and French president Nicolas Sarkozy at the Elysée Palace in Paris, met in Cannes on November 2–3, once again overlapping with the official G20 summit on November 3–4. The B20 consolidated its proposals with those of the WEF and the International Chamber of Commerce. They addressed, in a final report, the business sector priorities of adjusting global governance to strengthen confidence, unlocking the levers of economic growth, and ensuring that the benefits of growth are shared in a sustainable fashion. The association was strengthened at Los Cabos on June 17–18, 2012, where the B20 convened some 150 chief executive officers and presidents of major businesses from the 19 G20 member countries, with heads of various international organizations, including the IMF, the World Bank, and the Organisation for Economic Co-operation and Development (OECD). On June 19 the chairs of B20 task forces met with G20 officials over breakfast. Each task force was devoted to a particular issue: food security, green growth, employment, transparency and anticorruption, trade and investment, information and communication technologies and innovation, and financing for growth and development (B20 2012).

The Russian host of the 2013 St Petersburg Summit mounted an outreach program that, in addition to broad civil society outreach, involved the B20. The Russian-hosted B20 first met in Moscow on December 12, 2012, and then convened its summit on June 20–21, 2013, at the St Petersburg International Economic Forum. Its detailed recommendations to the G20 were published as a 'White Book' (B20 2013). Another report prepared by the G20-B20 Dialogue Efficiency Task Force (2013) examined the progress of engagement between the two groups. Australia continued the tradition, with a B20 summit held in Sydney on July 16–18, 2014.

Celebrities, like business, are a special case (Cooper 2007). In the context of the G8, Bono and Bob Geldof staged 'Live 8' concerts around the world before the 2005 Gleneagles Summit. Their engagement with the G8 led to the creation of DATA (Debt, AIDS, Trade, Africa) and One (the two advocacy organizations joined forces in 2007). Following their custom of co-editing issues of major newspapers before G8 summits, in 2010 Bono and Geldof were guest editors of the May 10 issue of Canada's national newspaper, *The Globe and Mail*. The entire issue was devoted to Africa (Bono and Geldof 2010).

In April 2013 Angelina Jolie joined British foreign minister William Hague to announce the G8 Declaration on Preventing Sexual Violence in Conflict at the foreign ministers meeting in the lead-up to the Lough Erne Summit later that year.

Bill Gates (in his personal capacity, not on behalf of the Bill and Melinda Gates Foundation) played a celebrity role in the G20 at Cannes and (less so) in Los Cabos. At Cannes, after careful preparation that included consultations with CSOs and other stakeholders, he presented the G20 leaders with a report containing substantial proposals on development, health, and domestic resource mobilization (Gates 2011). Many NGOs welcome such highly visible support from famous people, but some activists are concerned about the potential of celebrities stifling the voices of civil society itself. This is an ambiguous relationship.

Parliamentarians from the G7/8 and G20 are another special case. Parliaments themselves are essential for ensuring democratic accountability of elected governments. There have been G8 initiatives around legislatures for some years, in the form of the G8 Parliamentarians' Group of speakers of legislatures. As an extension of this process in 2010, the Halifax Initiative and other CSOs organized three parliamentary roundtables in Ottawa, on April 20 at the time of the G20 finance ministers' meeting in Washington on April 20, on April 26 at the time of the G8 development ministers' meeting in Halifax, and on April 27 at the time of the Africa Partnership Forum meeting in Toronto. The roundtables dealt, respectively, with climate change and climate financing, the financial crisis and the Millennium Development Goals (MDGs) – issues also on the agenda of the G8 and G20 summits. Civil society representatives and opposition members of the Canadian parliament participated. Although the organizers designed the roundtables to be nonpartisan, the governing Conservative Party did not accept the invitation to participate in or co-sponsor the events. Other parliamentary events in 2010 included a meeting of the speakers of the lower houses of G8 countries, held in Ottawa on September 9–12 and a consultation, also in Ottawa, of G20 parliamentary speakers on September 2–5. G20 parliament speakers met in Seoul on May 18–20, 2011, in Riyadh on February 24–26, 2012, and in Mexico City on April 4–5, 2013.

Other civil society groups quickly realized the broad implications of the financial and economic crisis and took action vis-à-vis the G20. With the G20 agenda beginning to expand to development, trade, climate financing, and food security, it was natural for an increasing range of CSOs to become active in advocating, responding to, and otherwise interacting with the G20. These CSOs include anti-poverty groups and campaigns (for example, the Jubilee Movement, the Make Poverty History campaign, and the Global Call to Action against Poverty [GCAP]), labour union organizations (such as the International Trade Union Confederation, climate- and environment-centred CSOs (for instance, the Climate Action Network, the World Wildlife Fund [WWF], and Greenpeace), human rights NGOs (for example, Amnesty International and Human Rights Watch), and development NGOs (such as Oxfam, Save the Children, ActionAid, and World Vision). CSOs advocate on a whole range of issues that are in the purview of the G7/8 and the G20, such as the G8/G20 Global Working Group formed in 2010 (although its roots go back to 2006) and are still active with both forums. The working group prepares common lobbying positions on a set of policy demands for the G7/G8/G20. In 2011 these positions covered governance, accountability, corruption, human resource development (including aid, education, gender, and health), climate change, financial issues (including debt, financial transaction tax, tax havens, and financial inclusion), growth, food security and food prices, infrastructure, jobs and decent work, and trade. Part of the working group's annual preparation is a strategy planning meeting.

Several academic groups and think tanks focus exclusively, partly, or occasionally on the G20 as an institution. Examples include the Centre for Global Studies at the University of

Victoria in Canada, the Centre for International Governance Innovation, the Brookings Institution, Chatham House, the G20 Research Group, the Peter G. Peterson Institute for International Economics, the Friedrich-Ebert-Stiftung, the Heinrich Böll Foundation North America, and the Lowy Institute for International Policy. Other CSOs have interacted with the G20, such as faith-based groups (World Vision and many others). Some CSOs have focused on other social and political issues; the Halifax Initiative, the FIM-Forum for Democratic Global Governance, and Transparency International are examples. In 2012 the Mexican host took advantage of CSO expertise by convening a 'Think 20' meeting. In a related development in 2012, the Council on Foreign Relations (2012) in the United States established the Council of Councils, and brought together 24 major foreign policy think tanks, including 18 G20 members, at its inaugural conference on March 12–13, 2012, in Washington DC. It has continued to meet annually.

These diverse groups have in common the desire to promote social and economic justice, but there are huge variations among CSOs in ideological orientation, tactics, and priorities. Those CSOs that choose to engage the G7/8 and the G20 (and some groups explicitly reject such engagement) also wish to have an impact on policies, governance, and accountability. Moreover, they look for media exposure and an increased public profile – as, indeed, do G7/8 and G20 governments themselves. More radical groups, which generally do not care to have anything to do with either the G7/8 or the G20, wish to change political and economic systems, for example by ending capitalism and creating a different world.

Types of Civil Society Action

The G7/8 and the G20 are both cognizant of the problem of legitimacy. Establishing and maintaining relations with the global community enhances that legitimacy, and civil society – as part of that community – plays an important role in this process. Successful interaction improves the legitimacy of both CSOs and the G7/G8/G20, increasing the potential impact of civil society on the summits, and can be of mutual benefit.

Over the history of G7/8 and G20 summits, CSOs have had multifaceted interaction with the groups. The civil society nexus with the G7/8 and G20 has taken various forms, all contributing to accountability. They include dialogue, evaluation and monitoring, alternative summits, policy papers, and other forms of interaction. Andrew F. Cooper (2013) argues that the G20-CSO interaction exhibits both similarities to and distinctive differences from the G7/8-civil society template.

Dialogue

The dialogue/consultation process is an important instrument of G7/8 and G20 accountability. It serves to convey civil society's concerns about crucial global issues to officials; it also allows CSO representatives to learn more about government negotiations, and about what can and cannot be accomplished in the political milieu in which those negotiations take place.

Among NGOs, environmental groups such as Greenpeace, Friends of the Earth, and WWF have engaged the G7/8 for many years. As well, human rights NGOs – for example Amnesty International and Human Rights Watch – have interacted with the G7/8 for a long time. So have development and relief agencies such as Oxfam, Tearfund, ActionAid, and the World Development Movement. Several mass campaigns have also targeted the G7/8, including the Jubilee Debt Campaign, GCAP, and the Make Poverty History movement. Faith-based groups from Christian, Jewish, Muslim, Buddhist, Hindu, and other traditions as well as CSOs focusing on various social and political issues (such as Social Watch, the Halifax Initiative, FIM, Transparency International, and Consumers International) have also conducted dialogue. Youth groups have participated in the Junior Eight (J8) forum that began around the Gleneagles Summit, although the civil society status of this initiative was problematic as it was organized by the United Nations Children's Fund (UNICEF) and the G8 host government. Other civil society assemblies have focused on the G7/8; these include the 'poor people's summits' that have convened in Mali since 2002 and the Civil G8 that began during the Russian G8 presidency in 2006.

Civil G8

The dialogue process known as Civil G8 began during Russia's G8 presidency in 2006. It was preceded by long, careful preparations, with impressive resources and substantial support from the Russian host government. The Civil G8 had an ambitious program, including the development of proposals based on NGO positions on the three main topics of the G8's St Petersburg agenda (energy security, health and infectious diseases, and education). The Civil G8 also facilitated input on additional issues of civil society interest: organized national and international discussions in order to set priorities and approaches to the G8, evaluation of projects, and recommendations of social significance for the G8. It also generated ideas and recommendations for subsequent G8 summits (Hajnal 2007, 125–8).

Until 2013, the Civil G8 was repeated yearly in one form or another, but more modestly and with fewer resources (see, for example, G8 Research Group 2007b; 2012).

Civil G20

For the G20, a dialogue in Korea in 2010 was the first consultation bearing the name Civil G20 (although there was a civil society consultation with the G20 host sherpa in Ottawa prior to the Toronto Summit earlier that year). The Korean Civil G20 took place on October 15 in Inchon, following a G20 sherpa meeting. It brought together some 100 representatives from 70 NGOs from 40 countries. The GCAP campaign was one of the main organizers of this event, which was jointly hosted by G20 preparation committee vice-chief Lee Chang-yong and GCAP preparation committee chief Lee Seong-hun. The consultation covered trade, financial regulation, and G20 governance; it also touched on food security, job creation, and G20 cooperation with international organizations. The resulting recommendations were delivered to the sherpas, who elaborated on the G20 agenda and, significantly, called for active cooperation with NGOs (Choi 2010).

Before the 2011 Cannes Summit, the French ministry of foreign affairs hosted a dialogue presented as the Civil G20. Because the meeting was called on very short notice, it was not carefully prepared and French and international NGO attendance was therefore limited. Another meeting was held, with 100 NGOs and civil society coalitions participating, among them major NGOs such as Oxfam, WWF, One, and World Vision, and French CSOs such as CCFD-Terre Solidaire and Coordination SUD, and the US civil society umbrella group InterAction.

There was no real Civil G20 dialogue with G20 sherpas before the 2012 Los Cabos Summit. Instead, several seminars and forums took place.

A Civil 20 conference (a continuation of the Civil G20 stream around earlier G20 summits) took place in Moscow on December 11–13, 2012, with the participation of 140 representatives of NGOs, academics, and think tanks. The program, entitled 'G20 Civil Society Vision for the Russian Presidency', focused on civil society's role in the global political dialogue, CSO expectations from the Russian presidency, accountability, and other issues. The Civil 20 Summit (a first for CSO-G20 interaction) was held in Moscow on June 13–14, 2013, and prepared recommendations for the G20 leaders (Civil 20 Task Force on Inequality 2013). Australia's presidency also included a Civil 20 summit in Melbourne on June 20–21, 2014.

Think 20

Experts from 19 think tanks from around the world gathered on February 27–28, 2012, in Mexico City for the first Think 20 meeting. This was called at the initiative of the Mexican host government of the Los Cabos Summit in order to make the G20 dialogue an 'open, transparent, innovative and inclusive' process and to use it 'to gather practical and innovative ideas for improving the G20 processes and policies' (Mexico, Secretaría de Relaciones Exteriores 2012). The meeting was organized by the Mexican Council on Foreign Relations together with other think tanks. Several former and current high-level G20 officials participated. The Think 20 (2012a) submitted a report and recommendations to the Mexican G20 presidency.

The Russian host government's outreach program for the St Petersburg Summit involved a Think 20, in addition to the Civil 20, Youth 20, Labour 20 (L20), and B20. The Russian-hosted Think 20 met on December 11, 2012, in Moscow to discuss economic growth, macroeconomic issues, fiscal sustainability, trade, foreign direct investment, and sustainable development (Think 20 2012b).

In December 2013, soon after Australia assumed the presidency of the G20 for the Brisbane Summit, the Lowy Institute (2014) hosted a Think 20 meeting in Sydney and subsequently released a progress report based on the discussions held there.

Other consultations

In addition to the Civil G8 and Civil G20 processes, other types of consultations have taken place. Several NGOs held separate consultations with government officials that resulted in exchanges useful to both government officials and the participating NGOs in the lead-up to the G8 Muskoka Summit in 2010. Maternal, newborn, and child health was a focal point of that summit. Another example was the dialogue with the Canadian G20 sherpa team prior to the Toronto Summit that same year. It was pioneered by the Montreal-based FIM, a civil society think tank that built on its experience of initiating a similar dialogue in 2002, when Canada hosted the G8 Kananaskis Summit, between the host government and three other G8 governments on the one hand and civil society representatives from about a dozen countries from the global economic North and South on the other. In 2010, the focus was on 'accountability of the G20 to the citizens of the world' (FIM 2010). Apart from a roundtable discussion held at the British consulate in Istanbul prior to the April 2009 G20 London Summit, the Ottawa dialogue was the first such major event in the G20 setting. It gave civil society representatives from the North and South a voice that called on the G20 to 'deepen democratization of global governance institutions, processes, and decision-making' (FIM 2010).

Before the Seoul Summit, similarly, there were consultations other than the Civil 20. In October 2010, Korean and international civil society representatives held a workshop on G20 and development. It featured civil society discussions and a presentation by the Korean sherpa on his government's position on the major items on the summit agenda. In a separate dialogue, trade union leaders arranged bilateral high-level talks with G20 leaders before the Seoul Summit, giving the unions direct access to the top. The content and results of this and similar high-level consultations are generally not available to the public (the need for confidentiality sometimes trumps transparency). NGOs and G20 officials also consulted in other parts of the world before the Seoul Summit. Civil society representatives met with the Russian, Japanese, and German sherpas or their assistants to discuss the summit and exchange views.

At the 2011 Cannes Summit, some 100 NGOs and civil society coalitions were represented at the summit media centre at the Palais des Festivals, among them major NGOs such as Oxfam, WWF, One, and World Vision; French CSOs CCFD-Terre Solidaire, Coordination SUD, and others; and InterAction from the US. On November 2, Sarkozy met with L20 representatives at the Elysée Palace for a working lunch. The L20 Summit, which took place in Cannes on November 4, issued a joint statement with the B20 (B20 and L20 2011). The 2014 L20 Summit was held in Brisbane on November 13–14, just ahead of the leaders' summit on November 15–16.

The most important idea behind regular consultations between civil society and the G20 is not the particular type of dialogue (Civil 20, think tanks, and others), but rather the regular relationship and the continuous flow of ideas among CSOs as well as between CSOs and the G20 before, during, and after summits. The precise makeup of the CSO presence for any given event is not the most crucial element, as long as a group with the relevant expertise is brought together. This process worked well at the time of the summits of 2009 (London), 2010 (Seoul), 2011 (Cannes), and 2012 (Los Cabos). Civil society impact on actual summit outcomes is difficult to gauge; for such impact on any initiative, there has to be a convergence of all forces, including consensus within the G20 itself.[3]

---

3   Interviews with Colin I. Bradford (2012).

Alternative Summits

Alternative or parallel summits convened by civil society groups have a long tradition in CSO relations with the G7/8 and now with the G20. The first such alternative summit, called the 'Popular Summit', took place around the time of the G7's 1981 Montebello Summit near Ottawa. Such events are another form of democratic activity through which CSOs, if they choose to engage, can influence the G7/G8/G20. Some parallel summits collaborate with G7/8 or G20 officials and have transmitted recommendations to such officials. This may be considered a form of consultation. Alternative summits that reject dialogue with the G7/8 and G20 can still demand the rectification of harmful effects of any action or inaction.

People's summits

The G8 System and the G20: Evolution, Role, and Documentation contains a detailed discussion and analysis of the G7/8 alternative summits (2007). In the G20 context, the People's Summit, sponsored by educators and peace- and social justice-oriented advocacy groups, met in Pittsburgh in September 2009, with more than 700 participants. Signalling local official endorsement, the Pittsburgh City Council issued a proclamation supporting the People's Summit, which discussed economic, social, and political problems worldwide. This gathering, in the *altermondialiste* tradition, issued a vision statement titled 'Another World Is Possible', expressing the ideals of eliminating hunger and poverty, ending racism, ensuring rights and dignity of labour, empowering women, providing education for all, ensuring adequate health care as a basic human right, creating safe and inclusive communities, ending war, preserving the planet's ecosystem, and protecting the human rights of refugees, immigrants, the disabled, and other vulnerable groups (People's Summit 2009). Also on November 7, 2009, in London and St Andrews, Scotland (the venue of the G20 finance ministers' and central bank governors' meeting), a coalition of labour unions and development, climate change, and faith-based groups called 'Put People First' (2009) held the 'G20 Counter Conference' on jobs, justice, and a safer climate.

In 2010, the 'People's Summit: Building a Movement for a Just World' took place in Toronto on June 18–20, just before the back-to-back G8–G20 summits in Muskoka and Toronto. It brought together a diverse group of CSOs, campaigns, and coalitions, and built on a preparatory process that had begun well in advance, in late April 2009, with input from all participating groups and coordinated by a steering committee on which labour unions, NGOs, and civil society coalitions and campaigns were represented. The stated aims of the People's Summit (2010a) were to 'educate, empower and ignite the positive change we would like to see in our world'. It did not wish to engage with G8 and G20 officials – a strategy in common with similar alternative summits in the *altermondialiste* tradition. The slogan '*un autre monde est possible*' (another world is possible) was used at the first World Social Summit in Porto Allegre in Brazil, and has been taken up ever since.

The 2010 People's Summit program had the following themes:

- global justice (defined by the organizers as the 'struggle against the global expansion of corporate and national imperialism in order to build a better world based on equity, respect and dignity');
- environment and climate change (land, water, climate change, resource use, pollution, and food security issues);
- human rights and civil liberties ('working in solidarity for dignity and justice for all, against all war and occupation, racism and patriarchy, repression and the police state');
- economic justice (alternatives to neo-liberalism: 'community control over resources, resistance to free trade, anti-poverty organizing, taxing the rich to support the poor');
- building the movement ('Skills for CHANGE!'); and
- 'Holding Canada Accountable' for its policies and practices at home and abroad (People's Summit 2010b).

Thus this event, too, had an accountability dimension. The program included film showings, group discussions, panel discussions, speaker presentations, and workshops.

During the 'Joint Action Week' before the Seoul Summit, major Korean CSOs organized events related to the People's Summit on November 8–10, hosted by the People's G20 Response Preparation Committee. The agenda covered financial regulation and taxation on speculative capital, decent work and basic labour rights, the environment and climate change, alternative trade agreements different from those under neo-liberal policies, food security and agriculture, democracy and human rights, poverty and development, forced migration, peace and security, gender and G20, cultural diversity and intellectual property rights, and public services.

At the margins of the Cannes Summit, on November 1–4, 2011, an alternative summit named 'alter-forum' or Forum of the Peoples (Forum des Peuples) met in Nice, with more than 40 CSOs participating, including trade unions and social movements. This *altermondialiste* event began with a large demonstration, with the slogan 'people first, not finance'. This was followed by workshops and discussions on six themes: inequality and austerity, quality of life, systemic change for environmental protection, food security, solidarity among the indignant and the revolutionaries, and G20 legitimacy.[4] The main organizing body was Coordination SUD, a French umbrella group of CSOs. The forum closed with a press conference (Coordination SUD 2011).

For Los Cabos in 2012, a 'Summit of the People' (Cumbre de los Pueblos frente al G20) convened in Mexico City on June 12–15 and in La Paz, Baja California Sur, on June 16–19, overlapping with the G20 summit on June 18–19. It brought together CSOs from Mexico and 30 other countries. It was preceded by the International Seminar on Alternatives to G20 in Mexico City on June 14–15, which featured a panel on 'Illicit Flows of Capital, Financial Transaction Tax and Tax Havens'. The agenda included democratic alternatives for a new legitimacy; governance, corruption, and financial regulation; alternatives to the financial policies of banks and speculators, a financial transaction tax and illicit flows of

---

4   The themes in their original French were as follows: '*Inégalités, austérité: y'en a marre*'; '*La vie, pas la bourse*'; '*Changer le système, pas la planète*'; '*Ne jouez pas avec notre nourriture*'; '*Indignés, révoltés, solidarité*'; '*Ils sont 20, nous sommes des milliards*' (Mobiliations G8 G20 2011).

capital; workers against structural adjustment under neo-liberal politics; and alternatives to free trade. The People's Summit issued an anticapitalist, anti-G20 declaration (Coalición Mexicana frente al G20 2012a).

A counter-summit was held in St Petersburg on 3–4 September 2013, just before the G20 summit there. It issued a declaration, asserting that 'the G20 is not legitimate, democratic or transparent' and that it 'continues promoting failed neoliberal policies' (G20 Counter-Summit 2013; see also Post Globalization Initiative 2013).

Religious leaders' summits

Are religious groups an integral part of civil society? Karen Hamilton (2010, 308) answers in the affirmative: 'faith communities ... are not only a part of civil society but are also grounded in divine imperatives to be so for the sake of the world's peoples and indeed for the sake of the globe itself'. A case can thus be made for including these faith-based groups in the wide range of civil society activities around the G7/8 and G20 summits.

The first such event was convened at Lambeth Palace in London in 2005 just before the Gleneagles Summit. Subsequent faith leaders' summits met in 2006 in Moscow, in 2007 in Cologne, in 2008 in Sapporo and another in Kyoto and Osaka, in 2009 in Rome, in 2010 in Winnipeg, in 2011 in Bordeaux, and in 2012 in Washington DC. An International Continuance Committee ensures that each meeting builds on the experiences of, and lessons learned from, previous meetings and then passes the torch to the hosts of next year's meeting, although there was a hiatus among the G8 in 2014. A G20 interfaith summit was being organized by Griffith University for November 16–18, 2014, immediately following the Brisbane Summit. These religious leaders' summits have all had the objective of reminding the G7/8 and the G20 of their responsibilities to address poverty, care for the Earth, and invest in peace – common values of faith communities around the world. This process, too, is thus part of overall accountability efforts.

The 2010 gathering (which will serve as a detailed example) took place on June 21–23, just before the Muskoka G8 and Toronto G20 summits, on the campus of the University of Winnipeg. Lloyd Axworthy, the university's president and former Canadian foreign minister, gave it his full support. The meeting was the culmination of a year-and-a-half-long process under the aegis of the Interfaith Partnership chaired by the Reverend Dr Karen Hamilton, general secretary of the Canadian Council of Churches. The main task of the partnership was to draft a statement for the religious leaders to consider at their summit; the draft was then circulated to various faith communities and other supporting organizations for comment. The partnership also organized a series of interfaith dinner and dialogue sessions across Canada with members of Parliament in order to take the interfaith message on poverty, the environment, and peace to the Canadian government for action. As well, it conducted various public awareness activities.[5] It circulated a petition urging G8 and G20 political leaders 'to take courageous and concrete actions to address poverty, care for our Earth, and invest in peace' and, in particular, to commit to put the MDGs back on track (Faith Challenge G8 2010).

---

5   These included, among others, hosting a website at http://www.faithchallengeg8.com.

The meeting brought together 80 senior leaders of religions and faith-based organizations from more than 20 countries from all regions of the world, representing aboriginal, Baha'i, Buddhist, Christian, Hindu, Jewish, Muslim, Shinto, and Sikh traditions. Thirteen youth delegates also participated, and a number of observers were present. The opening ceremonies were hosted by David Courchene, an Anishnabe elder from the Canadian province of Manitoba. This was followed by working sessions dealing with extreme poverty and the economy, peace and security, and the MDGs. A panel of youth delegations also addressed the themes of the environment, poverty, and peace. The last session finalized the statement entitled 'A Time for Inspired Leadership and Action' (Interfaith Leaders Summit 2010). It urged the G8 and G20 political leaders to alleviate poverty and injustice; to promote care for the Earth and its environment; to attend to the needs of the most vulnerable, especially children; and to halt the arms race, reduce nuclear weapons, and support a culture of peace and the rule of law. It asked for a transparent and effective dialogue between international organizations and faith communities. The statement was presented at the end of the summit to Stephen Fletcher, Minister of State for Democratic Reform, who accepted it on behalf of the government of Canada and promised to pass it on to the prime minister. Because of its emphasis on transparency and dialogue, the 2010 World Religions Summit had an important accountability dimension.

The 2011 Bordeaux event produced a statement focusing on the global macroeconomic situation, global governance, climate change, development, and peace. The 2012 Washington religious summit's statement asked for economic justice; food, health and human security; and poverty reduction. These statements were again intended for transmission to the G8 and G20 summits, respectively in 2011 and 2012 (Interfaith Leaders Summit 2011a, 2011b). In 2013 there was an 'Interfaith Leaders' Initiative' rather than a religious leaders' summit. It consisted of an open letter signed by 83 faith leaders from around the world, urging G8 leaders to do more to accomplish the MDGs (Hamilton and Reed 2013; ENS Staff 2013).

Other alternative summits

A 'Gender Justice Summit' was held in Toronto in 2010, simultaneously with the People's Summit, under the aegis of Oxfam Canada. As well, the G(irls) 20 Summit has met each year since 2010, the latest convening in Sydney, Australia, in 2014. Each meeting brought together young women aged 18–20, representing each G20 member plus the African Union, with an agenda that reflected the annual G20 summit agenda. The 2013 communiqué from the G(irls)20 Summit in Moscow addressed the role of technology in economically empowering girls and women, particularly in the mining, oil and gas, high tech industries and agriculture (G(irls)20 Summit 2013).

The four-day Indigenous Peoples' Summit was held in Sapporo, Japan, ahead of the G8 summit in 2008, with participants from five continents and the Pacific region. The only such occasion in G8 summit history, it released the Nibutani Declaration, which spelled out various concerns of indigenous peoples and addressed 22 proposals to the G8 (Indigenous Peoples Summit 2008; Lewallen 2008). Although no other indigenous peoples' summit has since taken place, aboriginal peoples have been represented in various other CSO activities, and there was limited dialogue in 2012 with the Mexican hosts of the G20 Los Cabos Summit.

G7/8 and G20 'Global University Summits' of university presidents and officials have met for several years: in Sapporo (2008), Turin and Palermo (2009), Vancouver (2010), Dijon (2011), Chicago (2012), London (2013), and Moscow (2014). These have issued reports and statements for transmission to the G7/8 and G20 leaders (see, for example, Université de Franche-Comté 2010; Global University Summit 2013).

G7/8 and G20 youth summits are usually co-sponsored by the host governments so they cannot be considered true civil society events. They began with the J8 youth forum at Gleneagles in 2005. G7/8 and G20 youth summits have continued to meet annually: in St Petersburg, Berlin, Yokohama, Milan, Paris (the first G20 youth summit), Vancouver and again in Paris in 2011, Puebla, Mexico, in 2012, St Petersburg in 2013, and Sydney in 2014. During some of these events, youth representatives had the opportunity to meet with G20 leaders.

Policy Papers

Publishing policy papers is another way for CSOs to influence the G7/8 and G20 on pressing global issues. For example, a 2009 Friedrich-Ebert-Stiftung study noted that the rapid rescue of the global financial system spurred by the G20 leaders, national governments, central banks, and international financial institutions (IFIs) was not accompanied by equally vigorous efforts to reform global financial governance (Rude and Burke 2009). It called for full transparency and accountability in the global economic system, underlined the need for radical reforms of domestic and international financial institutions, and argued for a socially responsible and democratic global economic system.

For the Seoul Summit, Oxfam (2010) issued 'The Making of a Seoul Development Consensus: The Essential Development Agenda for the G20'. In late 2012, InterAction (2012) released a policy paper containing recommendations for the 2013 G8 Lough Erne Summit, concerning, among other issues, the G8 Accountability Working Group; it encouraged the G8 to '1) direct the Accountability Working Group (AWG) to collect input from international organizations, recipient governments and civil society; 2) mandate the AWG to initiate transparent practices by publicly identifying all G8 working groups; 3) make public the AWG annual report 30 days before the G8 summit'. In 2013 Oxfam (2013a) issued 'Fixing the Cracks in Tax: A Plan of Action', a policy brief that was the result of the collaboration of 34 CSOs.

The Heinrich Böll Foundation has published several policy papers, including 'The G20: Playing Outside the Big Tent – Implications for Rio+20' (Alexander and Riggs 2012). It compared the development agendas of the Los Cabos Summit and the subsequent United Nations Rio+20 conference, and offered recommendations on G20 accountability and transparency, development financing, and the G20 Development Action Plan.

Demonstrations and Other Action

Protests and other street demonstrations have been a recurring feature of summits since the G7 Montebello Summit in 1981. In the G20 context, there was little protest at the Washington Summit in 2008, with only several hundred peaceful street demonstrators. But before the next summit, in London in April 2009, 35,000 people marched in Hyde Park under the theme 'Put People First', demanding more and better jobs, and climate justice and action. During the G20 summit itself, protests were organized by the G20 Meltdown group and others, and stressed a number of concerns including the Iraq war, globalization, human rights, and climate change. These, too, were largely peaceful, but the police overreacted, resulting in serious injury of an innocent non-protester, Ian Tomlinson, who happened to be in the wrong place. He later died (Dobson 2011).

The G20 Pittsburgh Summit also saw street protests in September 2009. Among the organizers were the Bail Out the People movement, the tcktcktck climate justice campaign, and the Pittsburgh G20 Resistance Project. Despite fears of violence, these protests were largely peaceful around the summit venue, but outside that area there were some skirmishes and road blocks (Dobson 2011).

The events around the G8 and G20 summits in June 2010 in Canada serve to illustrate this type of action. The Toronto street scene was tumultuous in June 2010. The People's Summit was accompanied by a number of demonstrations, most of them peaceful but a few less so. The grassroots, radically oriented Community Mobilization Network staged a range of activities: the June 21–24 Themed Days of Resistance focused on justice for migrants, income equality, community control over resources, gender justice, rights for the disabled, environmental and climate justice, and justice for indigenous peoples. These events led to Days of Action in opposition to the G8 and G20: a feminist picnic on June 25, a Free the Streets march and a forum, a march with the theme of 'People's First: We Deserve Better', and another march on the theme of 'Get Off the Fence'. The stated aim of the Mobilization Network (also referred to as G20 Convergence) was 'to challenge, disrupt and abolish the G8/G20' (Community Solidarity Network 2010). This radical approach went further than non-engagement with the G8 and G20. Cooper (2013) posits a dichotomy of delivery-oriented versus resistance-oriented civil society approaches to the G20.

These radicals did indeed challenge the G20, but did not disrupt it and certainly did not abolish it. Nonetheless, they claimed victory in various ways:

- by organizing 'Toronto's community struggles against the impact of colonial, capitalist policies that seek to weaken us every day';
- through the 'nearly 40,000 people [who] took to the streets, gathered in discussion, watched movies, set up a tent city, danced and fought';
- by marching in the 'thousands against colonization and for Indigenous sovereignty', through supporting 'actions … for Environmental Justice …, for Income Equity and Community Control Over Resources …, for Gender Justice and Disability Rights …, for Migrant Justice and an End to War and Occupation';
- by the Days of Action;

- by ensuring (as the Mobilization Network claimed) 'that actions with conflicting tactics took place separately'; and
- by continuing the demonstrations in the face of being 'followed, intimidated, arrested … [and] infiltrated by state thugs' (Community Solidarity Network 2010).

Such claims of victory are not persuasive, and the strident rhetoric of the Mobilization Network put off many people. Some of these actions did indeed highlight issues of social and economic justice, but unfortunately such actions were conflated with disruptive activities, wanton destruction of property, and other 'uncivil' acts. If the aim of the Mobilization Network was to garner maximum media attention, it achieved that – but to the detriment of the peaceful majority of civil society focusing on important messages on poverty, the environment, and other burning global issues. Not unexpectedly, there were confrontations between protesters and security personnel. Police appeared on foot, bicycles, horseback, and motorcycles and in cars. Secure areas were surrounded by three-metre-high fences. On the other side, protesters had earplugs, masks of various description, gloves, and other gear.

The specifics of the confrontation are still being debated, long after the event. But observers assert that on Saturday, June 26, when those protesters who used Black Bloc tactics burned several police cars, broke windows, and looted some stores on the streets of Toronto, the police were notably absent from the scenes of the worst violence. By contrast, on Sunday, June 27, the police overreacted when, for example, they used the 'kettling' tactic familiar from the London Summit – surrounding protesters, passers-by, tourists, and others, and preventing anyone from entering or leaving the area. They also arrested or detained some 1,100 people; most arrests took place in the streets but some at people's homes. The majority of those arrested were released within a few hours or days. Only a relatively small number remained charged with offences or crimes; others were not charged or charges against them were dropped. Perversely, these police actions were used by the violent protesters and their supporters to demonstrate police 'brutality', but they were also used by the Canadian host government to justify the extravagant summit expenses (Salutin 2010; Harper 2010). Repercussions from the summit security measures and the confrontation on Toronto streets have continued for years after the 2010 summits, with more than half a dozen inquiries, including into police behaviour and court cases.

Several demonstrations took place around the 2011 Cannes Summit, with thousands participating. They advocated for the financial transaction tax ('Robin Hood tax'), better protection of the environment, and fair labour laws, among other causes. The largest of these street demonstrations took place in Nice on November 1, at the start of the Forum of the Peoples. A couple of days later, several hundred activists marched to the nearby Monaco border to protest tax havens for the rich. Some 12,000 security personnel were deployed around the Riviera, including in Cannes where the G20 leaders were meeting.

Some protests took place around the time of the 2012 Los Cabos Summit, in La Paz, Mexico, in connection with the People's Summit held there. Also before the summit, CSOs led by Oxfam continued the long tradition of advocating a financial transaction tax by staging a Global Week of Action on May 15–22.

There were protests around the G8 Lough Erne Summit in 2013, some in London in the weeks leading up to the summit, organized by the Stop G8 Movement. The main event was called 'Carnival against Capitalism'. Several hundred police were in the streets and forcibly removed anti-G8 demonstrators who squatted in an abandoned building. Street stunts included demonstrators disguised as G8 leaders who protested against tax avoidance and world hunger. Smaller protests took place at Lough Erne itself, with some protesters breaking through the wire fence outside the security wall surrounding the summit site, but very few arrests were made.

Petitions

Petitions are another common peaceful tactic of CSOs. In March 2010 the Make Poverty History coalition and other Canadian and global CSOs launched the At the Table campaign. They called for 'bold and concrete action on poverty, climate change, and economic recovery for all in the G8 and G20 summits' (At the Table 2010). The campaign aimed to convince as many people as possible to sign a declaration with those three objectives. The campaign also initiated a 'flat leader photo petition' with cut-out images of G8 leaders to serve as interlocutors for civil society supporters.

A similar type of action unfolded before the Seoul Summit, in the form of a letter to the Korean president, asking him to put in place a civil society consultation along the lines of the B20. This letter was drafted by the Global Campaign for Climate Action, a coalition of environmental, development, labour, and faith-based groups. Such an initiative, if ever acted on by the G20, would greatly raise the profile and increase the impact of civil society. But, in any event, the G20–B20 relationship remains much closer.

A third example: the Mexican civil society umbrella group Coalición Mexicana frente al G-20 (Mexican Coalition on the G20) addressed a letter to Mexican government officials, proposing a public debate between social movements and G20 governments during the Los Cabos Summit (Coalición Mexicana frente al G20 2012b). As far as is known, such a debate did not materialize.

Monitoring and Evaluation

Outside assessments

CSOs play an important role in holding the G7/8 and G20 accountable for fulfilling their promises. A number of NGOs, including academic groups and NGO-centred think tanks have initiated systematic evaluations either across a range of issues or concentrating on specific sectors, such as development. Examples include the G8 and G20 Research Groups at the University of Toronto, the International Organisations Research Institute (IORI) at the National Research University Higher School of Economics, New Rules for Global Finance, One, and Transparency International.

Several CSOs (including think tanks and academic bodies) were evaluating the performance of the G7/8 for some time before the G8's self-assessment exercise started, beginning as far back as 1990. As Ella Kokotsis describes elsewhere in this book, the G8 Research Group at the University of Toronto has issued annual compliance reports on selected summit commitments since 1996. These are based mostly on the precise language used in the text of the principal documents of summits. The recent annual reports, prepared in collaboration with IORI in Moscow, assess G8 compliance with its commitments; the most recent one assesses compliance with commitments made at the 2013 Lough Erne Summit, covering from June 2013 to the eve of the G7 Brussels Summit in June 2014.[6]

The G20 Research Group – again in cooperation with IORI – has prepared similar reports since the first G20 summit in Washington. Its first full G20 compliance study covered actions taken to comply with Toronto Summit commitments between June 28, 2010, and October 31, 2010, just before the Seoul Summit.[7]

The commitments are defined on the basis of methodology developed by the G8 Research Group (2007a). It 'uses a scale from -1 to $+1$, where $+1$ indicates full compliance with the stated commitment, -1 indicates a failure to comply or action taken that is directly opposite to the stated goal of the commitment, and 0 indicates partial compliance or work in progress, such as initiatives that have been launched but are not yet near completion and whose results can therefore not be assessed. Each member assessed receives a score of -1, 0 or $+1$ for each commitment' (G20 Research Group and IORI 2012, 5).

In 2012 IORI and the G20 Research Group (2012) released 'Mapping G20 Decisions Implementation: How G20 Is Delivering on the Decisions Made'. The report analyses the implementation of commitments made by G20 members at their summits in the areas of structural reform and overcoming imbalances, IFI reform, financial markets regulation, and development. The analysis includes infrastructure, private investment, job creation, human resource development, trade, financial inclusion, growth with resilience, food security, domestic resource mobilization, and knowledge sharing. Nancy Alexander and Aldo Caliari (2013) produced a critical commentary on this report. A similar implementation report was prepared by the two groups on development, and both were discussed with the G20 sherpas at their first preparatory meeting for the G20 St Petersburg Summit (IORI and G20 Research Group 2013).

Another evaluation of the fulfilment of the Gleneagles commitments has been undertaken since 2006 by the One campaign. Its 2012 DATA report recalls that these reports have 'held the world's wealthiest countries accountable for their commitments to the world's poorest countries. For the … [previous] six years, it has tracked progress against the Gleneagles commitments made by the G7 in 2005. However, with those commitments expiring in 2010, key donors such as the United States, Canada and Japan no longer have overall official development assistance (ODA) targets' (One 2012, 5). The report notes that 'the G20, despite their growing significance on the world stage, have not presented clear and measurable targets in development finance to which member countries can be held to account' (5). Therefore, this report focuses on the EU's commitments to increase development assistance to Africa, but includes figures for development assistance by G20 countries that are not members of the OECD's Development Assistance Committee (DAC).

---

6   G8 Research Group compliance reports are available on the G8 Information Centre website at http://www.g8.utoronto.ca/compliance.

7   G20 Research Group compliance reports are available on the G20 Information Centre website at http://www.g20.utoronto.ca/compliance.

DATA reports are based mostly on statistics derived from the DAC and the OECD's Creditor Reporting System Database, as well as the Quality of Official Development Assistance Database developed by the Brookings Institution and the Center for Global Development. These data are highly reliable, but they tend to be up to a year late, so the DATA reports have a time lag.

Another case is Transparency International, which has monitored the G7/8's and G20's role on fighting corruption. This NGO has published its well-regarded annual Corruption Perception Index since 1995. A recent edition, measuring the perceived levels of public sector corruption in 177 countries and territories, was issued in 2013 (Transparency International 2013).

G8 accountability assessments

Previous steps on the part of the G8 itself toward accountability included an accountability report on G8 anticorruption commitments at the 2008 Hokkaido Summit and the 'Preliminary Accountability Report' at the 2009 L'Aquila Summit, which took a sectoral approach, tracking commitments and their fulfilment on food security, water, health, and education (G8 2008, 2009). At L'Aquila the G8 leaders established the G8 Accountability Senior Level Working Group, tasking it with identifying key development-related G8 commitments since Gleneagles, identifying indicators for assessing those commitments, developing a reporting methodology, exploring ways of measuring the impact of G8 commitments beyond merely assessing progress, consulting with the OECD and other organizations with expertise in data manipulation and reporting, preparing a report for G8 leaders in time for the Muskoka Summit the following year, and making recommendations on regularizing ('institutionalizing') accountability practices after Muskoka. The Muskoka Summit had been dubbed in advance the 'accountability summit' by the Canadian host. Indeed, accountability was a principal theme at the summit, along with Prime Minister Stephen Harper's maternal, newborn, and child health initiative.

Subsequent G8 accountability reports have been less ambitious and less comprehensive, as already indicated by the G8 Muskoka Declaration: Recovery and New Beginnings, in which the leaders, despite referring numerous times to accountability, signalled their intention to devote future accountability reports to specific sectors rather than treating accountability comprehensively (G8 2010).

Indeed, the 2011 'Deauville Accountability Report' focused only on health and food security, and the 2012 'Camp David Accountability Report' focused on food security, markets and trade, nutrition, and global health (G8 2011, 2012). Yet, although the scope of the 2011 and 2012 reports is less comprehensive than the Muskoka report, the 'Camp David Accountability Report' not only built on the previous two summit's accountability recommendations but also introduced two advances: a scorecard to show indicators of progress and more detailed tables showing G8 members' food security and agricultural activities, with further focus on aid effectiveness in the sectors covered. The 2013 'Lough Erne Accountability Report' builds on the Muskoka, Deauville, and Camp David reports, covering 56 development commitments (G8 2013).

G20 accountability assessments

With the G20, (democratic, open) accountability is more problematic than in the G8, but there are encouraging signs. One is a series of IMF reports (with the World Bank and other intergovernmental organizations also playing a role) commissioned by the G20. These are part of the G20's MAP (IMF 2010). MAP was launched by the 2009 G20 Pittsburgh Summit as a crucial component of the Framework for Strong, Sustainable, and Balanced Growth (G20 2009). It would further enhance accountability if the G20 were to allow full public reporting of the MAP.

The G20 has advanced in its accountability in recent years. The G20 Seoul Summit Leaders' Declaration states: 'We will continue to monitor and assess ongoing implementation of the commitments made today and in the past in a transparent and objective way. We hold ourselves accountable. What we promise, we will deliver' (G20 2010c).

The G20 Seoul Summit Document called for 'strong, responsible, accountable and transparent development partnerships between the G20' and less-developed countries (G20 2010b). It added: 'The G20 will hold itself accountable for its commitments. Beyond our participation in existing mechanisms of peer review for international anti-corruption standards, we mandate the Anti-Corruption Working Group to submit annual reports on the implementation of our commitments to future Summits for the duration of the Anti-Corruption Action Plan'.

More specifically, on corruption, Annex III of the G20 Seoul Summit Document asserted:

> Leading by example, the G20 holds itself accountable for its commitments. Beyond our participation in existing mechanisms of peer review for anti-corruption standards, reports, agreed within the working group, on individual and collective progresses [sic] made by G20 countries in the implementation of the Action Plan will be submitted on an annual basis to the G20 Leaders for the duration of this Action Plan. In this context, the Anti-Corruption Working Group will prepare a first monitoring report for the Leaders at [the] next Summit in France. (G20 2010a)

Policy Commitments by G20 Members, a 49-page document released as a supporting document at the Seoul Summit, is significant for transparency, and for facilitating subsequent monitoring and evaluation (G20 2010d). It consists entirely of a table of policy commitments, in order to facilitate subsequent monitoring and evaluation.

The Cannes Action Plan for Growth and Jobs 'draws on the IMF Staff's independent assessments of the root causes of ... imbalances and recommended policies to address them' (G20 2011b). Annexed to the action plan is a detailed list of commitments by members, with timeframes for implementation (G20 2011a).

The Los Cabos Summit took a further step. Through The Los Cabos Growth and Jobs Action Plan, which included an accountability assessment framework, the leaders agreed to use third-party evaluations, especially by the IMF, in moving forward with the Los Cabos accountability framework (G20 2012b). The peer review would include reports by the IMF, OECD, the Financial Stability Board (FSB), the World Bank, International Labour Organization, United Nations Conference on Trade and Development, and the World Trade Organization. The framework 'will be used to prepare reports on progress in meeting past commitments, which will inform the development of future action plans and domestic policies' (G20 2012b). The framework also mandates 'short progress reports prepared for Ministerial meetings and regular Annual Accountability Assessments for Ministers, Governors and Leaders', which is an example of internal accountability. It thus established a regular, systematic process of assessments to 'provide critical input to inform the range of concrete policy commitments that should be included in the G20 Action Plans'.

'Toward Lasting Stability and Growth: Umbrella Report for G20 Mutual Assessment Process', the MAP report prepared for the Los Cabos Summit, assessed the G20's global risks, policies, and progress, and provided a scenario for the Los Cabos Summit (IMF 2012). The report stated that 'to attain their growth objectives, G-20 members must effectively manage rising risks, deliver on past commitments, and enact more complete and collective policies', including effective crisis and risk management, implementing previous commitments, and undertaking additional steps for the mutual benefit of all members. The enhanced assessment portion is of special interest; it concludes that although members have made progress in implementing their policy commitments made in the Cannes Action Plan on financial policy, fiscal policy, monetary and exchange rate policies, and structural reform, they need to take further action on financial sector reform, sound public finances, rebalancing global demand, and employment and growth. This shows some improvement in transparency. Another marked innovation was the reissuance of 'Policy Commitments by G20 Members' (G20 2012c).

In September 2013, the IMF (2013) issued for 'Imbalances and Growth: Update of Staff Sustainability Assessments for G20 Mutual Assessment Process', which was prepared in accordance with the Los Cabos 2012 decision to produce biennial assessments to identify large and persistent imbalances against indicative guidelines. Also in 2013, the St Petersburg Summit produced the rather full 'St Petersburg Accountability Report on G20 Development Commitments' and the St Petersburg Accountability Assessment, issued as an annex to the St Petersburg Action Plan (G20 2013a, 2013c, 2013b).

Commitments to accountability have been made not only by the leaders but also by several sub-summit G20 entities. For example, at their meeting on November 4–5, 2012, G20 finance ministers and central bank governors (2012) stated that they had 'made progress in strengthening our Accountability Assessment framework by agreeing on a set of measures to inform our analysis of our fiscal, monetary and exchange rate policies … [including considering] a range of indicators and approaches to assess spillover effects, progress towards commitments on structural reforms, and our collective achievement of strong, sustainable and balanced growth'.

At the working group/expert group level, the G20 Framework for Strong, Sustainable, and Balanced Growth Working Group (Framework Working Group) made accountability one of its priorities for 2013. It promised to 'further enhance the Accountability Assessment Process … [by examining] how to assess progress against structural reform commitments and the implications of policy spillovers'; turning to 'outside experts/academics to assess overall progress towards SSB [strong, sustainable, and balanced] growth … [thereby obtaining] an additional perspective on the issue, supplementing the work of the IMF, World Bank, OECD and other IFIs, without jeopardizing the country-led nature of the exercise'; and preparing 'a report on overall progress towards SSB growth, drawing on experts' report (if provided) and inputs from IFIs' (Framework Working Group 2012). The working group also undertook to 'assess members' progress against past policy commitments … based on a peer-review process'.

Another example is the G20 Development Working Group. It promised in its report to the leaders at the Cannes Summit to 'monitor progress on the reduction of the global average cost [of remittances] through the World Bank, including on actions undertaken in reaching the quantitative target' (G20 Development Working Group 2011, 12). The working group has also expressed its willingness to contribute further in the area of regional and global trade in cooperation with intergovernmental organizations: 'We would welcome an invitation from the African Union and the African Development Bank to jointly review progress at their annual meeting. This could include assessing the support we are providing at different levels, including to the national level and to the Regional Economic Communities and how best to strengthen that support' (G20 Development Working Group 2011, 4). In their 2012 report to G20 leaders at Los Cabos, the working group undertook to 'report back on progress by the end of 2012' on inclusive green growth (G20 Development Working Group 2012). The Los Cabos leaders declaration invited 'the Development Working Group to explore putting in place a process for ensuring assessment and accountability for G20 development actions by the next Summit' (G20 2012a). The Development Working Group [DWG] duly prepared its accountability assessment on development commitments to the St Petersburg Summit; this assessment forms part of the 'St Petersburg Accountability Report on G20 Development Commitments'. In it, the Development Working Group examined '67 commitments originating from the Seoul MYAP [Multi-Year Action Plan on Development] and 2011–2012 Leaders' Declarations relevant to the DWG's work. The DWG assessed progress on the nine pillars of the MYAP and on inclusive green growth. This process examined implementation, identified lessons learned, drew conclusions and determined next steps for the G20 development agenda' (G20 2013b, 6–7).

Post-Summit Reactions and Other Shorter Assessments

The media, civil society groups, and academic observers often voice their immediate reaction at the end of summits. Although not amounting to systematic evaluation, such reactions convey thoughts sparked by the summit just ended.

The One campaign, like many other NGOs, has compared its pre-summit 'asks' with summit outcomes. For example, after the Los Cabos Summit, One's reaction included faint praise as well as criticism: 'Good intentions continue at G20, but promises on development are not being kept'; 'G20 is getting a reputation for over-promising and under-delivering' (Powell 2012a, 2012b).

Also after Los Cabos, New Rules for Global Finance (2012) noted that the FSB's expanded charter represented steps forward, and singled out as 'most noteworthy' the call for expanding public consultation. New Rules released the text of the revised FSB Charter, with annotations indicating progress achieved and further progress needed.

After the St Petersburg Summit, Oxfam praised the G20 commitment to increase humanitarian aid for Syria, but on tax evasion its representative, Carlos Zarco, stated that 'the G20 have put their first nail in the coffin of corporate tax dodging, but n given no guarantees how or when the rip-off of the poorest countries will stop' (Oxfam 2013b). Zarco criticized the leaders for having 'failed entirely to confront the growing problem of income inequality'.

Academic and other observers have also offered brief assessments of G20 performance, either immediately following a summit or at other times. For example, Fen Osler Hampson and Paul Heinbecker (2011, 304) argued that G20 members 'were effective in cooperating to stabilize financial markets, coordinate regulatory reform, and launch a global economic stimulus' but were less successful in resolving problems of current accounts, trade, and budget imbalances. John J. Kirton and Julia Kulik (2012b) underlined the successes of the Los Cabos Summit in controlling the euro crisis, in setting a strategy to enhance growth and jobs, improving financial regulation and inclusion, and addressing food security issues, G20 accountability, and other sectors. But in another contribution, they commented on the summit's shortcomings on fossil fuel subsidies, health issues, youth entrepreneurship, the role of women, and the role of the academic community (Kirton and Kulik 2012a).

An example of media reaction to Los Cabos is Helene Cooper (2012) who, writing in the *New York Times*, pinpointed the summit's handling of the euro crisis, remarking that 'world leaders pronounced themselves united in the effort to increase growth and employment in the global economy ... but appeared to make only modest headway in persuading Chancellor Angela Merkel of Germany to drop her opposition to more government spending to alleviate Europe's debt crisis'. She added that the G20 leaders 'eschewed' specific commitments, instead limiting themselves to more generalized promises to invest in public works, overhaul labour markets and use innovation, education and infrastructure investment to fuel economic growth. Elsewhere, the *New York Times* (2012) editorialized that although the leaders 'managed to say some of the right things' by pledging 'to do more to spur growth, ensure financial stability and support a stronger European fiscal union', the question remained 'whether these words will ever translate into effective action'.

Conclusions

This chapter examined the role of civil society in enhancing the accountability of the G7/8 and G20. Both of these powerful transgovernmental networks have significant accountability. Both have made important strides toward greater accountability. But much remains to be accomplished, and the correction/redress dimension of accountability is largely lacking.

Civil society has played, and is continuing to play, a major role in enhancing G7/8 and G20 accountability, especially in the areas of consultation and evaluation. But much more needs to be done, particularly in respect of democratic accountability. One structural problem is that the push to achieve greater accountability is complicated by the informal nature of the G7/8 and G20.

Continuous and substantive consultations between CSOs and G7/G8/G20 officials play an important role in enhancing accountability, particularly when both sets of players treat the give-and-take of dialogue seriously and constructively. When consultations play out in a ritualistic manner or as one-time opportunities, their impact will be minimal.

Civil society's experience in interacting with the G7/8 and G20 points to the need and benefits of maintaining systematic, transparent monitoring and evaluation of G7/8 and G20 commitments. This is a crucial component of accountability.

Policy papers are also useful in conveying civil society concerns and priorities to broader society and, optimally, to G7/8 and G20 officials. Alternative summits, when they choose to engage with the G7/8 and G20, can also have an accountability benefit. It is doubtful, however, whether the accountability potential of these types of gatherings can match the relative success of the consultation or dialogue mode. More generally, civil society groups' willingness to engage with the G7/8 and G20 in various types of interaction is essential for achieving positive results.

Parliaments are an essential means for obtaining democratic accountability of elected governments. There have been G8 initiatives around legislatures for some years, in the form of the G8 parliamentarians' group of speakers of legislatures. In 2010, further advances were made in both the G8 and G20 context. Greater use of parliamentary channels to enhance democratic accountability would benefit all stakeholders: CSOs, the G7/8, the G20, and the global community.

Finally, civil society can be more effective in influencing the G7/8 and G20 by timely preparations, thorough knowledge of the official summit preparatory process including sherpa and ministerial meetings, and subject expertise. Steering close to the agenda of the official G7/8 and G20 also contributes to receptivity by officials, although it is equally important to voice other concerns.

Consultations, alternative summits, policy papers and petitions, and participation in peaceful demonstrations all benefit civil society itself. G20 acceptance of regular, systematic consultations with CSOs is a particularly significant advance. Such dialogue can increase (and occasionally has done so) civil society influence on G20 processes, negotiations, and accountability.

References

Alexander, Nancy and Aldo Caliari (2013). 'Commentary on the Report: "Mapping G20 Decisions Implementation"'. January, Heinrich Böll Stiftung, Washington DC. http://us.boell.org/2013/02/01/commentary-report-mapping-g20-decisions-imple mentation-group-20 (December 2014).

Alexander, Nancy and Peter Riggs (2012). 'The G20: Playing Outside the Big Tent – Implications for Rio+20'. June, Heinrich Böll Stiftung, Washington DC. http://ke.boell. org/2012/06/15/g20-playing-outside-big-tent-implications-rio20 (December 2014).

At the Table (2010). 'Take Your Place at the Table'. http://www.puttingfarmersfirst.ca/ at_the_table/ (December 2014).

B20 (2012). 'B20 Global Business Leaders Announce Their Prioritized Recommendations for Global Economic Recovery and Growth'. May 29, Mexico City. http://www.prnewswire.com/news-releases/b20-global-business-leaders-announce-their-prioritized-recommendations-for-global-economic-recovery-and-growth-155411765.html (December 2014).

B20 (2013). 'B20-G20 Partnership for Growth and Jobs: Recommendations from Business 20'. G20 Business Summit, September 5, St Petersburg. http://b20russia.com/B20_WhiteBook_web.pdf (December 2014).

B20 and L20 (2011). 'B20 L20 Joint Statement'. November 4, Cannes. http://www.g20.utoronto.ca/2011/2011-b20-l20-en.pdf (December 2014).

Bono and Bob Geldof (2010). 'The African Century'. *Globe and Mail*, May 10.

Choi, Jessica Seoyoung (2010). 'Civil G20 Dialog Held in Incheon'. October 19, Korea.net. http://www.korea.net/NewsFocus/Policies/view?articleId=83509 (December 2014).

Civil 20 Task Force on Inequality (2013). 'Civil 20 Proposals for Strong, Sustainable, Balanced and Inclusive Growth'. Civil 20, Moscow. http://www.g20.utoronto.ca/c20/C20_proposals_2013_final.pdf (December 2014).

Coalición Mexicana frente al G20 (2012a). 'Declaración de la Cumbre de los Pueblos contra el G20'. June 19, La Paz, Mexico. http://www.coaliciong20.org/?p=1166 (August 2012).

Coalición Mexicana frente al G20 (2012b). 'G20 Cumbre del Capital, Anticapitalismo y Altermundismo'. May 21, La Paz, Mexico. http://www.coaliciong20.org/?s=Carta+dirigida+al+presidente+pro+tempore+&x=0&y=0 (August 2012).

Community Solidarity Network (2010). 'June 2010: The People Won!', July 26, Toronto. http://g20.torontomobilize.org/node/432 (December 2014).

Cooper, Andrew F. (2007). *Celebrity Diplomacy*. Boulder: Paradigm Publishers.

Cooper, Andrew F. (2013). 'Civil Society Relationships with the G20: An Extension of the G8 Template or Distinctive Pattern of Engagement?' *Global Society* 27(2): 179–200. doi: 10.1080/13600826.2012.762346.

Cooper, Helene (2012). 'World Leaders Make Little Headway in Solving Debt Crisis'. *New York Times*, June 19, p. A3. http://www.nytimes.com/2012/06/20/world/leaders-make-little-headway-in-solving-europe-debt-crisis.html?_r=0 (December 2014).

Coordination SUD (2011). 'Alter-forum de Nice: Les peuples d'abord, pas la finance!', November 4. http://www.coordinationsud.org/actualite/alter-forum-de-nice-les-peuples-d%E2%80%99abord-pas-la-finance/ (December 2014).

Council on Foreign Relations (2012). 'CFR Convenes 'Council of Councils' Linking Leading Foreign Policy Institutes from around the World'. March 12, New York. http://www.cfr.org/global-governance/cfr-convenes-council-councils-linking-leading-foreign-policy-institutes-around-world/p27612?co=C03920 (December 2014).

Dobson, Hugo (2011). 'The G8, the G20, and Civil Society'. In *Global Financial Crisis: Global Impact and Solutions*, Paolo Savona, John Kirton, and Chiara Oldani, eds. Farnham: Ashgate, pp. 245–60.

ENS Staff (2013). 'Global Religious Leaders Call on G8 to "Strike at Causes of Poverty"'. Episcopal News Service, April 5. http://episcopaldigitalnetwork.com/ens/

2013/04/05/global-religious-leaders-call-on-g8-to-strike-at-causes-of-poverty (December 2014).

Faith Challenge G8 (2010). 'Petition: A Time for Inspired Leadership and Action'. https://web.archive.org/web/20100823050155/http://petition.faithchallengeg8.com/ (December 2014).

FIM-Forum for Democratic Global Governance (2010). 'Civil Society Dialogue with the Host Sherpa to the Toronto 2010 G20 Summit: Communiqué'. June 11, Ottawa. http://www.g8.utoronto.ca/evaluations/2010muskoka/fim-sherpas.pdf (May 2014).

G8 (2008). 'Accountability Report: Implementation Review of G8 on Anti-corruption Commitments'. July, Hokkaido. http://www.g8.utoronto.ca/summit/2008hokkaido/2008-corruptionreport.pdf (December 2014).

G8 (2009). 'G8 Preliminary Accountability Report'. Annex to the L'Aquila G8 2009 Declaration, L'Aquila, Italy, July 8. http://www.g8.utoronto.ca/summit/2009laquila/2009-accountability.pdf (December 2014).

G8 (2010). 'G8 Muskoka Declaration: Recovery and New Beginnings'. Huntsville, Canada, June 26. http://www.g8.utoronto.ca/summit/2010muskoka/communique.html (December 2014).

G8 (2011). 'Deauville Accountability Report – G8 Commitments on Health and Food Security: State of Delivery and Results'. May 18. http://www.g8.utoronto.ca/summit/2011deauville/accountability.html (December 2014).

G8 (2012). 'Camp David Accountability Report: Actions, Approach, Results'. Camp David, May 19. http://www.g8.utoronto.ca/summit/2012campdavid/g8-cdar.html (December 2014).

G8 (2013). 'Lough Erne Accountability Report: Keeping Our Promises'. June 7. http://www.g8.utoronto.ca/summit/2013lougherne/lough-erne-accountability.html (December 2014).

G8 Research Group (2007a). 'Background on Compliance Reports: Methodology'. http://www.g8.utoronto.ca/evaluations/methodology/g7c2.htm (December 2014).

G8 Research Group (2007b). 'The G8 Presidency and Civil Society: An Overview of German and Russian Efforts to Engage Civil Society and Civil Society Organization around the G8'. June. http://www.g8.utoronto.ca/evaluations/csed/g8-cs.pdf (December 2014).

G8 Research Group (2012). 'Report on Civil Society and the 2011 Deauville Summit'. March. http://www.g8.utoronto.ca/evaluations/csed/2011-deauville-civilsociety-post.pdf (December 2014).

G20 (2009). 'G20 Leaders Statement: The Pittsburgh Summit'. Pittsburgh, September 25. http://www.g20.utoronto.ca/2009/2009communique0925.html (December 2014).

G20 (2010a). 'Annex III: G20 Anti-Corruption Action Plan'. G20 Agenda for Action on Combating Corruption, Promoting Market Integrity, and Supporting a Clean Business Environment, Seoul, November 12. http://www.g20.utoronto.ca/2010/g20seoul-anticorruption.html (December 2014).

G20 (2010b). 'The G20 Seoul Summit Document'. Seoul, November 12. http://www.g20.utoronto.ca/2010/g20seoul-doc.html (December 2014).

G20 (2010c). 'The G20 Seoul Summit Leaders' Declaration'. Seoul, November 12. http://www.g20.utoronto.ca/2010/g20seoul.html (December 2014).

G20 (2010d). 'Policy Commitments by G20 Members'. Seoul, November 12. http://www.g20.utoronto.ca/2010/g20seoul-commitments.pdf (December 2014).

G20 (2011a). 'Annex to the Cannes Action Plan for Growth and Jobs'. Cannes, November 4. http://www.g20.utoronto.ca/2011/2011-cannes-action-annex-111104-en.pdf (December 2014).

G20 (2011b). 'Cannes Action Plan for Growth and Jobs'. Cannes, November 4. http://www.g20.utoronto.ca/2011/2011-cannes-action-111104-en.html (December 2014).

G20 (2012a). 'G20 Leaders Declaration'. Los Cabos, June 19. http://www.g20.utoronto.ca/2012/2012-0619-loscabos.html (December 2014).

G20 (2012b). 'Los Cabos Growth and Jobs Action Plan'. Los Cabos, June 19. http://www.g20.utoronto.ca/2012/2012-0619-loscabos-actionplan.html (December 2014).

G20 (2012c). 'Policy Commitments by G20 Members'. Los Cabos, June 19. http://www.g20.utoronto.ca/2012/201-0619-loscabos-commitments.pdf (December 2014).

G20 (2013a). 'Annex 4: St Petersburg Accountability Assessment'. St Petersburg, September 6. http://www.g20.utoronto.ca/2013/Accountabilty_Assessment_FINAL.pdf (December 2014).

G20 (2013b). 'St Petersburg Accountability Report on G20 Development Commitments'. August 28. http://www.g20.utoronto.ca/2013/Saint_Petersburg_Accountability_Report_on_G20_Development_Commitments.pdf (December 2014).

G20 (2013c). 'St Petersburg Action Plan'. St Petersburg, September 6. http://www.g20.utoronto.ca/2013/2013-0906-plan.html (December 2014).

G20 Counter-Summit (2013). 'Declaration of the G20 Counter-Summit'. St Petersburg, September 4. http://www.canadians.org/blog/declaration-g20-counter-summit (December 2014).

G20 Development Working Group (2011). '2011 Report of the Development Working Group'. October 28. http://www.g20.utoronto.ca/2011/2011-cannes-dwg-111028-en.pdf (December 2014).

G20 Development Working Group (2012). '2012 Report of the Development Working Group'. June 19, Los Cabos. http://www.g20.utoronto.ca/2012/2012-0619-dwg.html (December 2014).

G20 Finance Ministers and Central Bank Governors (2012). 'Communiqué of Meeting of G20 Finance Ministers and Central Bank Governors'. Mexico City, November 5. http://www.g20.utoronto.ca/2012/2012-121105-finance-en.html (December 2014).

G20 Framework Working Group (2012). 'Proposal: Framework Working Group's 2013 Work Plan'. November 1. http://en.g20.ria.ru/load/780982134 (December 2014).

G20 Research Group and International Organisations Research Institute (2012). '2011 Cannes G20 Summit Final Compliance Report'. June 16. http://www.g20.utoronto.ca/compliance/2011cannes-final/ (December 2014).

G20–B20 Dialogue Efficiency Task Force (2013). 'From Toronto to Saint Petersburg: Assessing G20-B20 Engagement Effectiveness'. June, International Organisations Research Institute and G20 Research Group. http://www.g20.utoronto.ca/g20-b20 (December 2014).

G(irls)20 Summit (2013). 'Communiqué'. June 19, Moscow. http://www.girls20summit.com/wp-content/uploads/2013-communique-english.pdf (December 2014).

Gates, Bill (2011). 'Innovation with Impact: Financing 21st Century Development'. Report to G20 leaders at the Cannes Summit, November. http://www.gatesfoundation.org/~/media/GFO/Documents/2011%20G20%20Report%20PDFs/Full%20Report/g20reportenglish.pdf (December 2014).

Global University Summit (2013). 'Universities and Economic Growth: Pre-summit Report'. May 28–30, London. http://gus2013.org/files/9513/6938/2184/Global_University_Summit_-_pre-Summit_report.pdf (December 2014).

Hajnal, Peter I. (2007). *The G8 System and the G20: Evolution, Role, and Documentation.* Aldershot: Ashgate.

Hajnal, Peter I. (2011). 'Civil Society and G8 Accountability'. In *Building Global Democracy? Civil Society and Accountable Global Governance,* Jan Aart Scholte, ed. Cambridge: Cambridge University Press, pp. 182–205.

Hamilton, Karen (2010). 'Inspired Leadership'. In *G8 & G20: The 2010 Canadian Summits,* John J. Kirton and Madeline Koch, eds. London: Newsdesk, p. 308. www.g8.utoronto.ca/newsdesk/g8g20 (December 2014).

Hamilton, Karen and Charles Reed (2013). 'After 13 Years, The Millennium Development Goals Are Still Pertinent'. In *The UK Summit: The G8 at Lough Erne 2013,* John J. Kirton and Madeline Koch, eds. London: Newsdesk, pp. 234–5. http://www.g8.utoronto.ca/newsdesk/lougherne (December 2014).

Hampson, Fen Osler and Paul Heinbecker (2011). 'The "New" Multilateralism of the Twenty-First Century'. *Global Governance* 17(3): 299–310.

Harper, Stephen (2010). 'Statement by the Prime Minister at the Clsoing of the G20 Summit'. Toronto, June 27. http://www.g20.utoronto.ca/2010/to-harper-en.html (December 2014).

Indigenous Peoples Summit (2008). 'Nibutani Declaration of the 2008 Indigenous Peoples Summit in Ainu Mosir'. July 4, Ainu Mosir (Hokkaido), Japan. http://www.galdu.org/govat/doc/nibutani_declaration_of_indigenous_peoples_final_copy3.pdf (December 2014).

InterAction (2012). '2013 G8 Summit Recommendations: Lough Erne, United Kingdom'. Washington DC, December. http://www.interaction.org/document/2013-g8-summit-recommendations-lough-erne-united-kingdom (December 2014).

Interfaith Leaders Summit (2010). 'A Time for Inspired Leadership and Action'. 23, June, Winnipeg. http://www.faithchallengeg8.com/pdfs/2010%20Interfaith%20Statement%20-%20English.pdf (December 2014).

Interfaith Leaders Summit (2011a). 'The Bordeaux G8 Religious Leaders' Summit'. 23–24, May, Bordeaux. http://www.g8.utoronto.ca/interfaith/2011-interfaith-leaders-en.pdf (December 2014).

Interfaith Leaders Summit (2011b). 'Statement of the Bordeaux Religious Leaders Summit'. May 23–24, Bordeaux. http://www.g8.utoronto.ca/interfaith/2011-interfaith-leaders-en.pdf (December 2014).

International Monetary Fund (2010). 'G20 Mutual Assessment Process: Alternative Policy Scenarios'. June 26, Washington DC. http://www.imf.org/external/np/g20/pdf/062710a.pdf (December 2014).

International Monetary Fund (2012). 'Toward Lasting Stability and Growth: Umbrella Report for G20 Mutual Assessment Progress'. Washington DC. http://www.imf.org/external/np/g20/pdf/062012.pdf (December 2014).

International Monetary Fund (2013). 'Imbalances and Growth: Update of Staff Sustainability Assessments for G20 Musual Assessment Process'. September, Washington DC. http://www.imf.org/external/np/g20/pdf/map2013/map2013.pdf (December 2014).

International Organisations Research Institute and G20 Research Group (2012). 'Mapping G20 Decisions Implementation: How G20 Is Delivering on the Decisions Made'. National Research University Higher School of Economics, Moscow. https://www.hse.ru/data/2012/12/13/1301054564/Mapping_G20_Decisions_Implementation_full_report.pdf (December 2014).

International Organisations Research Institute and G20 Research Group (2013). 'Tracking Progress on the G20 Development Commitments'. https://www.hse.ru/data/2013/02/26/1307405287/Development%20Report%20130226.pdf (December 2014).

Kirton, John J. and Julia Kulik (2012a). 'The Shortcomings of the G20 Los Cabos Summit'. G20 Research Group, June 27. http://www.g20.utoronto.ca/analysis/120627-kirton-kulik-shortcomings.html (December 2014).

Kirton, John J. and Julia Kulik (2012b). 'A Summit of Significant Success: G20 Los Cabos Leaders Deliver the Desired Double Dividend'. G20 Research Group, June 19. http://www.g20.utoronto.ca/analysis/120619-kirton-success.html (December 2014).

Lewallen, Ann-Elise (2008). 'Indigenous at Last! Ainu Grassroots Organizing and the Indigenous Peoples Summit in Ainu Mosir'. *Asia-Pacific Journal: Japan Focus* 48 (November). http://www.japanfocus.org/-ann_elise-lewallen/2971 (December 2014).

Lowy Institute on International Policy (2014). 'Think20 2014: A Progress Report on Australia's g20 Presidency'. Sydney. http://www.lowyinstitute.org/files/think20-2014-a-progress-report.pdf (December 2014).

Mexico. Secretaría de Relaciones Exteriores (2012). 'Think 20 Meeting Concludes Successfully'. Press release 64, Mexico City, February 29. http://saladeprensa.sre.gob.mx/index.php/es/comunicados/1208-064 (December 2014).

Mobiliations G8 G20 (2011). 'Propositions clés portées au sein de la Coalition G8G20'. October 24. https://web.archive.org/web/20120227090340/http://www.mobilisationsg8g20.org/la-coalition/article/propositions-cles-portees-au-sein-de-la-coalition-g8g20.html (December 2014).

New Rules for Global Finance (2012). 'Revised FSB Charter: Shift Toward Improved Transparency and Inclusion'. Washington DC. http://www.new-rules.org/news/program-updates/411-revised-fsb-charter-shift-toward-improved-transparency-and-inclusion (December 2014).

New York Times (2012). 'The Troupble with Mrs. Merkel'. June 19. http://www.nytimes.com/2012/06/20/opinion/the-trouble-with-ms-merkel.html?_r=0 (December 2014).

One (2012). 'The 2012 Data Report: Europe's African Promise'. July 6. http://one-org.s3.amazonaws.com/us/wp-content/uploads/2012/11/dr2012.pdf (December 2014).

Oxfam (2010). 'The Making of a Seoul Development Consensus: THe Essential Development Agenda for the G20'. October 7. http://www.oxfam.org/en/policy/making-seoul-development-consensus (December 2014).

Oxfam (2013a). 'Fixing the Cracks in Tax: A Plan of Action'. September 3. http://www.oxfam.org/en/policy/fixing-cracks-tax-plan-action (December 2014).

Oxfam (2013b). 'Oxfam Verdict on the G20 Russia Summit'. Press release, September 6. http://www.oxfam.org/en/pressroom/pressrelease/2013-09-06/oxfam-verdict-g20-summit-russia (December 2014).

People's Summit (2009). 'Vision Statement of the People's Summit: "Another World Is Possible"'. Pittsburgh. https://web.archive.org/web/20120227011442/http://www.peoplessummit.com/page/peoples-summit (December 2014).

People's Summit (2010a). 'The 2010 People's Summit: Building a Movement for a Just World'. https://web.archive.org/web/20100612154338/http://peoplessummit2010.ca/section/2 (December 2014).

People's Summit (2010b). 'The 2010 People's Summit: Program'. http://peoplessummit2010.ca/section/18 (June 2010).

Post Globalization Initiative (2013). 'St Petersburg Counter Summit Opposes US Plans'. September 13. http://www.pglobal.org/news/548/ (December 2014).

Powell, Joseph (2012a). 'G20 Is Getting a Reputation for Over-Promising and Under-Delivering'. (Blog). One. 21 June. http://www.one.org/international/blog/g20-is-getting-a-reputation-for-over-promising-and-under-delivering (December 2014).

Powell, Joseph (2012b). 'Good Intentions Continue at G20, But Promises on Development Are Not Being Kept'. (Blog). One. 20 June. http://www.one.org/international/blog/good-intentions-continue-at-g20-but-promises-on-development-are-not-being-kept (December 2014).

Put People First (2009). 'Put People First G20 Counter Conference Report and Audio'. November 7–8. http://www.putpeoplefirst.org.uk/2009/12/put-people-first-g20-counter-conference-report-and-audio/ (December 2014).

Rude, Christopher and Sara Burke (2009). 'Towards a Socially Responsible and Democratic Global Economic System: Transparency, Accountability, and Governance'. Briefing Paper 15, November, Friedrich Ebert Stiftung, New York. http://library.fes.de/pdf-files/bueros/usa/06778-20091105.pdf (December 2014).

Salutin, Rick (2010). 'What Happened at Jailapalooza?' *Globe and Mail*, August 27. http://www.theglobeandmail.com/globe-debate/what-happened-at-jailapalooza/article1378333/ (December 2014).

Scholte, Jan Aart (2011). 'Global Governance, Accountability, and Civil Society'. In *Building Global Democracy? Civil Society and Accountable Global Governance*, Jan Aart Scholte, ed. Cambridge: Cambridge University Press, pp. 8–41.

Think 20 (2012a). 'Report to G20 Sherpas'. March, Mexico City. http://think20.consejomexicano.org/?page_id=69 (December 2014).

Think 20 (2012b). 'Think 20 Summary Report by Co-chairs'. Moscow, December 13. http://en.g20russia.ru/docs/think_20/summary_report.html (December 2014).

Transparency International (2013). 'Corruption Perceptions Index'. http://www.transparency.org/cpi2013 (December 2014).

Université de Franche-Comté (2010). 'Welcome to University Summit 2011'. April 26, Dijon, France. https://web.archive.org/web/20140509011323/http://www.univ-fcomte.fr/download/partage/document/actualite/lettre-flash/10-ufc-lettre10.pdf (December 2014).

Chapter 12
Mapping G7/8 and G20 Accountability

Marina V. Larionova and Andrei Sakharov

Introduction

Global governance is the reality of the contemporary world. The Group of Seven (G7), the Group of Eight (G8) and the Group of 20 (G20) are indispensable institutions of contemporary global governance, and global governance institutions should be answerable for their actions (or inactions) (Scholte 2011a). Accountability processes should thus be inherent to global governance and can improve governance.

In the global governance system, the G7/8 and G20 stand out as powerful informal institutions, and much of the critique of their accountability deficit derives from the fact that they were established and act without any formal authorization. Another reason for the claim of the accountability gap is that the three components of accountability – namely, standards for accountability, sanctions, and information – do not work properly (Grant and Keohane 2005). The G7/8's standards of accountability behaviour have a longer and better track record than those of the G20; however, the lack of a sanction mechanism and the lack of information or transparency make demands for improving accountability fully valid. Instead, G7/G8/G20 summitry is a case of transnational accountability with two main sources of accountability: reputational and peer pressure. For the G7/8, the third source of accountability is shared norms and democratic values.

Nevertheless, both the G7/8 and the G20 submit their performance to accountability mechanisms, although there is no 'authorized or institutionalized accountability relationship when the requirement to report, and the right to sanction, are mutually understood and accepted' (Keohane 2002, 12). The leaders mandate their internal structures in the form of ministerial meetings, experts groups, and working groups to report on the progress made on decisions. G20 leaders also ask relevant international organizations to monitor and report publicly on G20 compliance with their pledges. There are also examples of actors (such as nongovernmental organizations [NGOs], academic institutions, or international organizations) seeking to hold the G7/8 and G20 accountable on the normative justifications of the impact of their decisions on the societies and economies of their member states and global society. Such a claim is valid if 'accountability is a condition and process whereby an actor answers for its conduct to those whom it affects' (Scholte 2011b, 16).

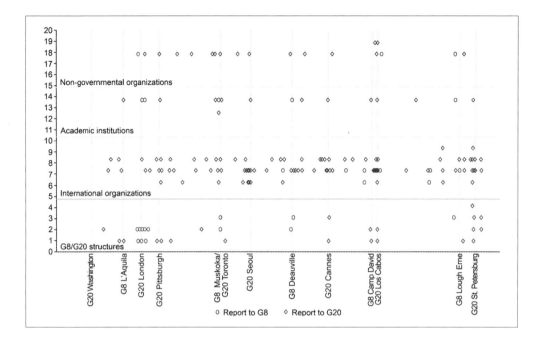

Figure 12.1 Mapping G8 and G20 accountability reports

Note: A report's position within the sector (between 0 and 3) is determined by its score on the three quality dimensions: transparency, consultation, and evaluation.

These considerations have underwritten this review of a flow of 'accountability' reports made public in the G8/G20 process between 2008 and 2013.[1] By October 2013 a total of 206 such reports had been published for both institutions. That number grew rapidly, especially pertaining to the G20, with 53 accountability reports released between July 2012 and October 2013 alone. The two main types of reports were those authorized by the G7/8 or G20 and those initiated by actors seeking to hold them accountable. Report authors can be classified broadly as G7/G8/G20 structures, international institutions, academic institutions, and NGOs.

This chapter examines how these reports addressed the four accountability aspects of transparency, consultation, evaluation, and correction (see Scholte 2011a). Several features of the reports were used as indicators of these four qualities. The provision of an evidence base and data for each of the members individually, rather than in an aggregated form, enhances transparency, and hence illustrates the quality of transparency. Recommendations provided by the report's authors to the G8/G20 promote consultation. Scorings or ratings give clear signals of the evaluation results, and were regarded as indications of evaluation. Each report was assessed against these three functions, with one score for transparency, one score for evaluation, and one score for consultation (see Figure 12.1). As the fourth

---

1 This period begins with the first summit of G20 leaders in 2008 and ends in 2013 before the G7 leaders began meeting without Russia in 2014.

function, quality of correction, is the prerogative of the actors affected – namely the G8 and G20 – the reports could not be assessed on this aspect of accountability. Documents were included in the analysis if they contained elements of accountability, even if they were not formally positioned as accountability reports.

Accountability in the Galaxy of G8/G20 Summitry

Most of the 206 reports assessed G20 compliance: 27 assessed the G8 and 179 assessed the G20. This disparity is due to at least three reasons. First, the G20's role as the anti-crisis manager necessitated monitoring of its actions. Second, as the G20 initially had no self-accountability mechanisms, other institutions were tasked with assessing its performance, or took the initiative to do so. Third, the expansion of the G20's agenda raised questions of the institution's effectiveness and legitimacy, spurring monitoring activities among other actors. Some of the reports included countries beyond the G20's membership but focus on the G20 commitments, such as the reports on trade and environment protection produced by the Organisation for Economic Co-operation and Development (OECD), the World Trade Organization (WTO), and the United Nations Conference on Trade and Development (UNCTAD), and by Global Trade Alert.

The majority of reports (131 or 64 per cent) were prepared by international organizations (WTO, OECD, the Financial Stability Board [FSB], etc.). Of those, 130 assessed G20 compliance, and only one assessed G8 accountability (see African Union Commission [AUC] and NEPAD Planning and Coordinating Agency 2011). The share of reports prepared by G8/G20 structures (such as the chair, finance ministers and central bank governors, or working and experts groups) amounted to 38 or 19 per cent, with the G8 totalling 14 and G20 amounting to 24. The number of the reports and delegation of authority for monitoring and evaluation to international organizations is a clear signal of the G8 and G20's pursuit of legitimacy and transparency.

About 72 per cent of the reports by international organizations were prepared within the mandates given by the G8/G20 through public calls, made in official documents (mainly to international organizations) or internal procedures (mainly to G8/G20 structures). Of the 130 reports, 108 were mandated by the G20 and 22 were initiated by various organizations within their respective mandates and assessed G20 members' compliance with a wide range of commitments. The first trade-related report issued by the WTO director general, published in January 2009 and monitoring compliance with the anti-protectionist commitment made at the G20 Washington Summit, was not requested by the G20 – at least not publicly – but at the next summit in London the G20 leaders called on the WTO to monitor their adherence to the commitment.

Only one of the self-initiated reports produced by international organizations provides recommendations (see AUC and NEPAD 2011). Among the mandated reports, 66 provided a basis for further consultation and possible correction. For example, 'Toward Lasting Stability and Growth', prepared by the International Monetary Fund ([IMF] 2012) for the G20 Los Cabos Summit, analyses G20 members' compliance with the Cannes Action Plan commitments and recommendations on collective action to restore economic growth. The FSB also produced a number of reports containing policy options for G20 members (see, for example, FSB 2013a, 2013c, 2013b).

G8 members did not mandate any international organizations, relying instead on their own institutions for monitoring. However, they turned to the OECD and other organizations for support in preparing their accountability reports. The AUC/NEPAD document reviewed the mutual commitments of African countries and the G8 under the framework of the G8's Africa outreach from 2001 to 2010: 'The report accounts for progress made by Africa in meeting its commitments, highlighting the remaining challenges, while also examining specific G8 pledges to the Continent. The monitoring and evaluation of development-related commitments agreed to at G8 Summits, including Kananaskis, Gleneagles, L'Aquila and Muskoka, form the central focus of the assessment' (AUC and NEPAD 2011, 7). It was a unique accountability review that systemizes and institutionalizes the partnership between African countries and the G8.

The World Bank, OECD, IMF, and Bank for International Settlements on the G20's action plan on local currency bond markets stands out as it assessed the actions of these organizations in response to the G20's mandate, rather than the performance of the G20 or its members (IO Working Group 2013). The report was submitted to the G20 finance ministers and central bank governors.

The reports produced by G8/G20 structures focus mostly on the progress made. However, 10 of the 38 reports contain recommendations. Notably, recommendations were presented in the reports of the Trade Finance Experts Group, the Development Working Group, and the Anti-Corruption Working Group. The G8's 2010 and 2011 reports on the Global Partnership against the Spread of Weapons and Materials of Mass Destruction can also be included in this category as they perform both accountability and direction-setting functions (G8 2010, 2011).

At 130, the overwhelming majority of the international organization reports are on G20 performance. Fewer than half (56) provide an assessment of progress made by individual G20 members (53 of them provide an evidence base to support their findings), as do 11 of the 14 G8 self-assessment reports. The reports by G20 structures mostly provide data in an aggregated form (16 of 25). Until recently the G8/G20 structures did not include scores in their reports. However, this element was introduced in the G8's 2013 Lough Erne and the G20's 2013 St. Petersburg accountability reports on development commitments, although they used different methodologies that do not facilitate cross-institutional comparisons.

There were 17 reports produced by academic institutions, which account for 8 per cent of the total. All were compiled by the University of Toronto G8 and G20 Research Groups and the Higher School of Economics (HSE), using a methodology that enables cross-institutional comparison. This methodology's scoring system and ratings were not used in any other accountability reports.

NGOs, including One and the Global Trade Alert, produced 19 reports. As with the reports produced by academic institutions, these were initiated by the NGOs rather than the G8 or G20. All but one provided an evidence base and track members' individual compliance, thus contributing to the institutions' transparency and the credibility of the assessments themselves. The only exception is the ICC G20 Business Scorecard produced by the International Chamber of Commerce, which assessed the G20 aggregate performance on the commitments, proposed by the business community.

Most of the reports were issued immediately before or during the G8/G20 summits. The number produced by international organizations on the G20 steadily increased: two were prepared for the London Summit, six for the Toronto Summit, eight for the Seoul Summit, eight for the Cannes Summit, 12 for the Los Cabos Summit, and 19 for the St. Petersburg Summit. Several international organizations published reports according to their own schedule, which may not correspond to summit dates. Such was the case with the WTO's reports on G20 trade- and investment-related measures. Releasing data well in advance of the summit provides an opportunity and time for engagement, especially when the international organizations have a counterpart structure in the G20/G8. Such is the case with the FSB and the IMF, as well as the OECD in its collaboration with the finance ministers, the International Labour Organization in its work with the G20 Task Force on Employment, and the World Bank working with the G20 Development Working Group. However, the international organizations attract the attention of the leaders, the media, and the international community by presenting their reports on the eve of the summits.

The number of reports produced by the G8 itself decreased between 2009 and 2013, partly because earlier reports on different aspects of development were superseded by more comprehensive reports, such as the accountability reports issued for the Muskoka, Deauville, Camp David, and Lough Erne summits. The G8 also published the 'Report on the G8 Global Partnership against the Spread of Weapons and Materials of Mass Destruction' for the Deauville Summit. Also in 2011, the G8 Roma/Lyon Group prepared a report on the measures to implement the priorities set out in the G8 Statement on Counter-Terrorism adopted at the Muskoka Summit, but it was not made public. The AUC/NEPAD report was also considered at the summit.

The trend in G20 self-reporting was the opposite, with the number of reports steadily growing. While there were six reports prepared by G20 structures in 2009, the number dropped to two in 2010 and 2011. However, in 2012 the G20 produced six self-accountability reports. In 2013 nine self-accountability reports were produced. This trend was due partly to the broadening of the G20 agenda. G20 self-reporting covered a broader spectrum of issues than the G8's, which tended to report almost exclusively on development, non-proliferation, and nuclear safety and security. The G20 carried out self-assessment on the main elements of the Framework on Strong, Sustainable, and Balanced Growth, covering such areas as economy, finance, investment, energy, and climate change. Major attention was also paid to fighting corruption, with four of the 25 G20 reports on that issue (three during 2012–13). After the Seoul Summit, the Development Working Group regularly published reports. With employment becoming a priority for the G20, the G20 Task Force on Employment also released a report on G20 members' job creation policies.

About 19 per cent of all reports were devoted to trade and investment (most of them produced by the OECD, WTO, and UNCTAD, and Global Trade Alert on protectionism). Economic growth and financial regulation accounted for almost 42 per cent. Six out of 25 G20 self-accountability reports tracked compliance with commitments in several areas (mainly financial reform, monetary policies, structural reforms, and reform of international financial institutions), while most of the G8 reports were more area-specific (with separate reports on water management, health, education, and peacekeeping).

The compliance reports by the University of Toronto and HSE can be considered comprehensive because the monitored commitments were selected according to several criteria, including a balanced representation of the agenda.

Conclusion

At the centre of global governance and in the spotlight of international community attention, the G20 generated a proliferation of external monitoring and gradually produced its own accountability mechanisms. While the number of the G8's reports decreased, with multiple specific reports superseded by comprehensive ones, the G20's self-reporting trend was the opposite, with the number of reports growing steadily. The 2013 St. Petersburg Summit resulted in nine self-accountability reports compared to six in 2012 and only two in 2011 and 2010.

Despite such progress, however, the reviews did not yield an evidence base that would allow an assessment using the accountability framework developed by Jan Aart Scholte (2011b). First, the G8 and G20 should be sufficiently transparent about their efforts to deliver on the commitments made. Second, the effectiveness of their consultative processes in providing a global public good should be improved. Third, the evaluation of G8/G20 performance in furthering that global public good should be enhanced. These steps would allow the institution to correct their shortcomings effectively and would enhance their effectiveness in promoting the global public good.

The findings indicate that accountability is being practised in a shared but dispersed way. The multitude of formats renders it difficult to make a comprehensive judgement about the implementation of decisions and the fulfilment of institutional missions. Accountability procedures are indirect. The absence of a clear connection between commitments, results, and further decision making decreases the effectiveness of monitoring. The technocratic nature of the accountability reports makes them inscrutable to the public. Only two of the 206 reports received a top score for providing evidence base, data for individual members, having a scoring system, and making recommendations.

The reports produced by academic institutions and NGOs tended to lack recommendations. International organizations did not provide an evidence base or data by member or did not offer recommendations. Reports by G20 structures rarely offered recommendations or assessments. G8 reports would benefit from assessments and more recommendations. None of these shortfalls is insurmountable.

The accountability mechanisms require strengthening. Despite a growing number of reports, it is not the quantity but the quality of the accountability mechanisms that should be addressed. The following steps could be taken to improve accountability for both the G7/8 and the G20.

1. An evidence base on individual members' compliance could be provided. Such evidence is currently missing in many reports commissioned by the G20 from international

organizations and in most of the progress reports produced by G20 structures. It would improve transparency and provide the foundation for evaluation, peer pressure, and enhanced effectiveness.

2. Evaluation can be made more explicit through the use of a scoring system or ratings. As 'naming and shaming' is a sensitive process, the responsibility for such scorings can rest with independent monitors (namely, NGOs and academic institutions).

3. Recommendations, which are currently missing in most of the reports published by international organizations, NGOs, and academic institutions, would promote consultation.

4. Monitoring reports should not be the end of the process, but the beginning of an open dialogue.

5. Regularly released reports using consistent methodology would improve the epistemic quality of accountability tracking, as well as increase its impact on decision making.

In addition, all these steps could promote the engagement of the G7/8 and G20 with civil society, including NGOs and the academic networks.

Is There a Role for the Academic Institutions and NGOs?

Academia and civil society can try to respond to the powerful call made by Robert Keohane in 2006, before the start of the global financial crisis and the emergence of G20 summitry:

Rather than abandoning democratic principles, we should rethink our ambitions. First, we should emphasize, in our normative as well as our positive work, the role played by information in facilitating international cooperation and democratic discourse. Second, we should define feasible objectives such as limiting potential abuses of power, rather than aspiring to participatory democracy and then despairing of its impossibility. Third, we should focus as much on the powerful entities that are the core of the problem, including multinational firms and states, as on multilateral organizations, which often are the focus of criticism. Finally, we need to think about how to design a pluralistic accountability system for world politics that relies on a variety of types of accountability: supervisory, fiscal, legal, market, peer and reputational. (Keohane 2006, 75)

The G7/8 and G20 are powerful entities. Of all the aforementioned accountability types, evaluations by academia and civil society can most significantly contribute to reputational accountability of the G7/8 and the G20. Academia should build on its strengths in information assessment and quality. NGOs could harness their advocacy and lobbying capabilities. Rigorous, consistent, and interactive monitoring can promote transparency, provide expertise, and enhance epistemic quality and information. Developing relevant recommendations will improve the chance that they will be received and could possibly improve the consultation aspects of G7/G8/G20 accountability. NGOs and academic institutions can help build a pluralistic accountability system through a network of epistemic groups coming together as independent monitoring agents.

References

African Union Commission and NEPAD Planning and Coordinating Agency (2011). 'Assessing Africa-G8 Partnership Commitments: Accountability Report on Africa-G8 Commitments, 2001–2010'. http://can-mnch.ca/wp-content/uploads/2011/10/Assessing-Africa-G8-Partnership-Commitments.pdf (December 2014).

Financial Stability Board (2013a). 'A Narrative Progress Report on Financial Reform: Report of the Financial Stability Board to G20 Leaders'. September 5, Basel. http://www.financialstabilityboard.org/wp-content/uploads/r_130905a.pdf (December 2014).

Financial Stability Board (2013b). 'Strengthening Oversight and Regulation of Shadow Banking: Policy Framework for Strengthening Oversight and Regulation of Shadow Banking Entities'. August 29, Basel. http://www.financialstabilityboard.org/wp-content/uploads/r_130829c.pdf (December 2014).

Financial Stability Board (2013c). 'Update on Financial Regulatory Factors Affecting the Supply of Long-Term Investment Finance: Report to G20 Finance Ministers and Central Bank Governors'. August 29, Basel. http://www.financialstabilityboard.org/wp-content/uploads/r_130829g.pdf (December 2014).

G8 (2010). 'Report on the G8 Global Partnership 2010'. June 26, Huntsville, Canada. http://www.g8.utoronto.ca/summit/2010muskoka/globalpartnership.html (December 2014).

G8 (2011). 'Report on the G8 Global Partnership Against the Spread of Weapons and Materials of Mass Destruction'. May 27, Deauville. http://www.g8.utoronto.ca/summit/2011deauville/2011-globalpartnership-en.html (December 2014).

Grant, Ruth W. and Robert O. Keohane (2005). 'Accountability and Abuses of Power in World Politics'. *American Political Science Review* 99(1): 29–43. doi: 10.1017.S0003055405051476.

International Monetary Fund (2012). 'Toward Lasting Stability and Growth: Umbrella Report for G20 Mutual Assessment Progress'. Washington DC. http://www.imf.org/external/np/g20/pdf/062012.pdf (December 2014).

IO Working Group (2013). 'G20 Action Plan on the Development of Local Currency Bond Markets: Implementation Report to G20 Ministers and Central Bank Governors'. January. http://en.g20russia.ru/load/783432293 (December 2014).

Keohane, Robert O. (2002). 'Global Governance and Democratic Accountability'. Chapter prepared for a volume to be edited by David Held and Mathias Koenig-Archibugi from the Miliband Lectures, London School of Economics, Durham NC. http://unpan1.un.org/intradoc/groups/public/documents/apcity/unpan034133.pdf (December 2014).

Keohane, Robert O. (2006). 'Accountability in World Politics'. *Scandinavian Political Studies* 29(2): 75–87.

Scholte, Jan Aart, ed. (2011a). *Building Global Democracy? Civil Society and Accountable Global Governance*. Cambridge: Cambridge University Press.

Scholte, Jan Aart (2011b). 'Global Governance, Accountability, and Civil Society'. In *Building Global Democracy? Civil Society and Accountable Global Governance*, Jan Aart Scholte, ed. Cambridge: Cambridge University Press, pp. 8–41.

Chapter 13
Advancing G8 and G20 Effectiveness through Improved Accountability Assessment

John J. Kirton

Just how effective are global governance institutions? How would one measure and monitor what they do and, on this basis, offer recommendations to improve their performance, especially their implementation, compliance, and accountability regarding their commitments to solve the pressing global problems of today's world?

These questions have long been of central concern to both scholars and practitioners for several reasons. Scholars have charted the extraordinary proliferation of intergovernmental institutions over the past century on the assumption that they make some difference to the otherwise autonomous behaviour of even the most powerful states, but scholars still disagree profoundly about how much, how and why those institutions make a difference (Keohane and Nye 1977; Kirton 2009; Krasner 1983). Citizens regularly criticize the failure of institutions to solve major problems and to meet their proudly proclaimed, high-profile public commitments. Even when the institutions seem to succeed, there is much dispute about which ones did best and which or what caused such success and thus can claim credit for it. Practitioners confront the cruel choice of where to invest increasingly scarce resources among the ever larger array of institutions available to help meet their goals abroad and at home. Now that the reform of international institutions and their overall architecture has risen to the top of the G20 and global governance agenda, spawning proliferating proposals for reform, a better understanding of which ones are effective and why is needed to arbitrate the competing claims. And in a world now crowded with international institutions of both 'hard' and 'soft' kinds, it is important to identify and share what has worked to enhance effectiveness in one body so that others can benefit as well (Kirton et al. 2010; Raustiala and Slaughter 2002).

The importance of assessing effectiveness is enhanced by additional concerns. In an era of America's rising relative vulnerability and declining relative capability, at least in relation to its once hegemonic past, America may increasingly need help from others through international institutions and from the effective international institutions themselves to address challenges it can no longer solve on its own. In this post–September 11 period, more 'after vulnerability' than 'after victory', the United States has pioneered new summit-level international institutions such as the three-member North American Leaders Summit in 2005, the 17-member Major Economies Meeting on Energy Security and Climate Change (later the Major Economies Forum) in 2007, the G20 summit in 2008 and the

44-member Nuclear Security Summit in 2009 (Ikenberry 2001, 2011). It is especially important to know how they are effective in meeting American, allied, and global goals and needs. This is especially so at a time when apparent rivals have arisen, notably the summit of the BRIC countries of Brazil, Russia, India, and China since 2009 (adding South Africa in 2013 to become the BRICS), and when investments in international institutions, starting with the International Monetary Fund (IMF), have become very expensive, just as the US government has fewer funds at home to spend on anything aboard. If others are to bear a bigger burden, as they appear willing to do, they also want to know how and why the institutions work, including in adjusting the actions of America as the world's most powerful country, in response to others and everyone's views and needs.

Moreover, improving the accountability of these institutions is important for their legitimacy, as their many stakeholders want to know not only if they have complied with the letter and spirit of their commitments but also if they have delivered the intended and desired results, done so synergistically with simultaneous and sequential co-benefits for other goals, and are willing to have their performance inclusively and transparently measured, monitored, constructively criticized, and corrected, so that the many not at the table can understand and contribute to what those institutions do.

This chapter thus asks two questions: In universities, think tanks, governments, and international institutions themselves, how and how well has 'effectiveness' been conceptualized, operationalized, and assessed? How can this be improved through accountability processes from all, and for all, with the greatest stake? It offers four arguments in response. First, the effectiveness of international institutions has largely been conceptualized and operationalized as first-order implementation by the member governments with their public, written commitments over the short term or their achievement of authorized expenditures and conditions in specific programs and projects. Second, assessments of actors' conformity with behaviour caused by their public commitments, and compliance with their decisional commitments need to be extended to assess compliance with principled and normative consensus; they also need to be extended from implementation to outcomes and results, from linear calculations of impacts on a single goal to synergistic co-benefits in sequential or simultaneous form, and from individual institutions' actions to their interaction with other institutions, as they affect effectiveness overall. Third, assessments of effectiveness require better measurements of consensus, commitment, and compliance, as well as better concepts about the institution's overall 'mission accomplished', 'human lives improved', and 'problem solved'. Fourth, such assessments require better mechanisms, by expanding the mandates of multilateral organizations, mobilizing members' legislatures and auditors general, establishing an independent accountability institute, foundation, and network, and creating a multistakeholder compliance consortium for all the assessors to share, compare, improve, and be accountable to their peers for what they do.

The Conceptualization and Operationalization of Effectiveness

In the context of international institutions, there is a gap between how the term 'effectiveness' is conceptualized in the ideal, ideational, cost-free world and how it is operationalized in the real world where resources are required to measure and monitor what is done. The concept thus runs the full gamut, from having an institution create a new world that only the author or advocate has imagined, through solving individual problems recognized by very few and achieving optimum outcomes never obtained before, to making progress in controlling current problems that many accept as real. However, in moving to operationalization and measurement, the vision constricts considerably, to compliance with the commitment by those that made it or their targets outside, their implementation through commitment-consistent action, and their progress toward achieving the specified goals. Even more narrowly, there is a considerable concern with whether particular programs or projects mounted by international organizations achieve their intended and authorized results in the way specified by the organization.

There has been much concern with regime effectiveness and even legitimacy, and considerable innovation (Breitmeier 2008). Yet scholarly assessments still concentrate on first-order compliance with concrete commitments encoded in public collective communiqués, especially commitments endowed with the high degree of precision, obligation, and delegation that the legalization literature highlights (Abbott et al. 2000). The commitments are treated, in the fashion of strict constructionists, rather literally, as they are written. Assessment focuses on the manageably measurable first-order compliance through implementing action by those making the commitment, rather than the extended results and broader consequences of what they do. Here a premium is placed on fighting the good fight rather than on winning the battle or the broader war. Moreover, the dominant approach of first-order implementation with public, written commitments tends to be done individually by commitment, communiqué, or institution, in isolation, or at best in a comparative mode as distinct from an interactive one. Less reliable evidence and analytical consensus have been obtained about the actual causes of the compliance that comes by institution, communiqué, or country. Attention focuses more on compliance over the short term, as longer periods make it more difficult to claim that the result has been caused by a commitment made so long ago.

In formal, heavily legalized international organizations such as the multilateral World Trade Organization (WTO) or the regional North American Commission for Environmental Cooperation, one data set and one analytical procedure flow from these organizations' dispute resolution mechanisms. The record of disputes taken up, processed, and ruled on through these mechanisms offers some systematic, easily available, well-used evidence of which countries are complying with their commitments under the governing treaties. This approach has the practical advantages of the comprehensibility and credibility coming from its legalization and its close relationship with 'enforcement' action for redress or deterrence.

Within informal, plurilateral international institutions without a secretariat such as the Group of Seven (G7), Group of Eight (G8), the Group of 20 (G20), and the BRICS – as distinct from those with a small secretariat such as the Commonwealth and the Asia-Pacific

Economic Cooperation forum – the measurement of effectiveness concentrates more broadly on the overall, ongoing commitments by the highest level political authorities that make them. In the case of the G8, after occasional experimentation, a process emerged through which a member-owned Accountability Working Group assesses members' performance in meeting their commitments in the domain of development and in specific issues areas such as health contained therein. Reports used a standard framework applied across all issue areas and a multi-year medium-term period for assessment of five to ten years (G8 2010, 2013).

Independent comprehensive assessments of G7/8, G20, and BRICS compliance have, since the start of serious, non-advocacy assessment in the early 1990s, focused on first-order compliance with individual commitments for a period beginning immediately after they were made until the leaders meet at their next summit to make new commitments as they choose. Attention has recently turned to compliance with multi-year commitments, as well as to the causes of compliance, including the compliance catalysts that leaders can consciously or otherwise embed in their commitments to increase the compliance that comes, and, much more tentatively, to co-benefits and the impact of interactive commitments by the same or fellow international institutions (von Furstenberg 2008; Kirton 2006; Kirton and Guebert 2011; Kirton et al. 2012).

The state of the art is well reflected in the 2010 compliance report by the G20 Research Group and the work of Marina V. Larionova and her team at the National Research University Higher School of Economics (G20 Research Group and International Organisations Research Institute 2013; Larionova 2011). The highly efficient approach of content analysis of public communiqués can provide systematic, reliable evidence to measure indicators of the performance functions or dimensions of domestic political management (e.g., communiqué compliments to individual countries), direction setting (e.g., affirmations of democratic, distributional, or embedded liberal principles and norms), decision making (e.g., commitments), and the development of global governance (e.g., reference to institutions inside and outside the one issuing the communiqué) (Kirton 2013).

The Adequacy of the Existing Metrics

The existing metrics and assessment processes that put them into practice are inadequate in many ways. Indeed, there is continuing experimentation, intellectually and operationally, to find a better way. To begin with, the written record that is relied upon heavily is but a partial reflection of what the leaders actually discuss and do at their summits, often with much added by lower level officials without the leaders themselves ever reading it in advance or afterwards (Kirton 1989). Some of what the leaders themselves do, including the most important things, remains the modern equivalent of 'secret agreements, secretly arrived at'.

The need to go well beyond textual analysis is especially important on the dimension of delivery or compliance, which is arguably one of the most important ways by which an institution's effectiveness, and hence credibility, can be assessed. It is not the communiqué-encoded declared intention to comply or implement or even the reflections on how well an institution has done in this regard that is critical, but the actual commitment-consistent and ideally commitment-caused and thus compliant behaviour of the member states whose leaders have bound themselves to do or not do particular things.

Assessing such state behaviour directly requires a great investment of resources, to assess the compliance of the five to 20 members with the more than 300 commitments that a single Gx summit can make. Thus far systematic compliance assessments for the G7/8 have generated a considerable data base of more than 416 assessments dating back to 1975. That data base has provided comparable evidence across many years, members, countries, and the G7/8 itself, as well as the individual commitments with different combinations of compliance catalysts. In the case of the G20, compliance assessments have been completed for 107 of the commitments the first seven summits have made. About 15 assessments have been completed for the BRICS. There is thus an understandable resistance to altering the approach to G7/8, G20, and BRICS accountability and effectiveness assessment, lest the legacy advantages of comparability be lost and of the great expense of creating anything new that is similarly robust.[1]

In the case of the G8, its intergovernmental self-assessment with a public reporting of the results has several shortcomings (Guebert and Bracht 2010; Kokotsis 2010). It covers only the policy field of development, but not that of security, which is now the G7/8's second core competence in a world where G20 summitry has arrived. Multi-year or five-year assessments, such as the 'Muskoka Accountability Report', make it difficult to measure or use the results on a timely one-year schedule when G7/8 leaders and their citizens presumably want to know on the eve of a summit whether the promises made at the last one have been kept. And it is difficult to find the data detailing which members have complied and which have not.

In the case of the G20, its dominant approach has been to ask its own finance ministers and increasingly other international organizations to selectively monitor the compliance of G20 members with their specified G20 commitments. However, the admittedly limited data currently available suggest that this approach has not had the desired compliance-enhancing effect. In the case of trade, where compliance data are available, the request of the 2009 London Summit to the WTO regarding G20 commitments on antiprotectionism was followed by a G20 compliance score on these commitments of +0.50, higher than the summit's overall compliance average of +0.42. However, its repetition at the Pittsburgh Summit five months later produced compliance of only +0.10, which was lower than the summit's overall compliance average of +0.28. Similarly, its repetition at Toronto in June 2010 produced trade compliance of only +0.15, which was again lower that the summit's overall compliance average of +0.28.[2]

---

1 These compliance assessments have been completed by the G8 Research Group, the G20 Research Group, and the BRICS Research Group. Many of them have been published on the G8 Information Centre website at http://www.g8.utoronto.ca, the G20 Information Centre website at http://www.g20.utoronto.ca, and the BRICS Information Centre website at http://www.brics.utoronto.ca.

2 For the issue-specific scores, see International Organizations Research Institute (IORI) (2009), IORI and the G20 Research Group (2010). For overall average scores, see Appendix 2.C in Chapter 2.

This suggests that the initial apparent success of this approach at London on trade led G20 leaders to expand their reliance upon this approach at future summits, even as it had diminishing value in the trade field itself. However, the trend may be due to the fact that the antiprotectionist commitments became more ambitious, by adding a 'redress' component to the core 'refusal' one. More research is required on the compliance effects of the expansion of this approach in other fields.

In the case of accountability assessment through an international organization's dispute settlement mechanisms, the evidence relates only to the subset of obligations that are legalized, largely from the founding treaty or treaties, rather than to the many other and often more important commitments made by the parties, especially at subsequent ministerial meetings. Moreover, there is high selectivity and skewing from the particular cases that are chosen by parties to take to and through the mechanism. Finally, the resulting record is only that of noncompliance, rather than compliance, and noncompliance is difficult to assess against all the cases of compliance and the potential, relevant universe of cases overall.

Enhancing Effectiveness Assessment and Its Effects

To enhance effectiveness through improved monitoring and accountability, several steps stand out as requiring immediate action, both by the institutions themselves and by those outside with a critical contribution to make in this domain. These 11 steps involve better measures, better concepts, and better mechanisms.

Better Measures

In regard to better measures, four steps stand out. The first is to measure compliance with the direction-setting consensus over principles and norms, inspired by John Ruggie's (1983) initial constructivist insight that shared social purpose was as autonomously important as relative power in shaping a regime's life and work, and the subsequent rise of constructivist scholarship in this domain. Here it is feasible to start with those principles presented in preambles or permeating the texts of collectively agreed outcome documents from which the decisional commitments themselves are identified, proceed to identify which commitments have been directly produced and bought into being by the leaders themselves, and what their shared meaning of those commitments is. Particularly in the case of soft law institutions, it may be that compliance with general principled consensus is higher than that with specific commitments on regime rules and that such soft law summit institutions do not follow a linear logic where they begin by doing something first for domestic political management and then progressively for direction setting, then decision making, then delivery, and, ultimately, the development of global governance as time goes by.

A second step is to spend more time on the commitments themselves, assessing whether they are timely, well targeted, significant and ambitious, so the compliance finding can be weighed according to the varying importance of the commitments themselves.

Early proof-of-concept work showed that such measurements were feasible, but it is a highly resource-intensive task (Juricevic 2000). Beyond lies the question of whether the commitments made are consistent, coherent, and synergistic with the others in the same communiqué. In all cases it is useful to discover, based on the preparatory and negotiating history, the 'intention of the founders' to assess, inter alia, if a country's compliance comes primarily with the commitments it has invented and initiated, or with those from the most powerful member of the club (Juricevic 2000).

A third step is to consider the cumulative and interactive context, not just among commitments in the same communiqué, but also commitments from the same institutions over time and above all by different institutions in the same field. Beyond the existing concerns with regime nests and countries' forum shopping (or forum creation), do institutions at work on the same issue come to the same, different, or antithetical consensus and commitments? How do combinations affect compliance? Do the commitments of one summit receive support from subsequent, surrounding summits? Depending on the answers, in a world where the demand for global governance exceeds the supply, having G7/8, G20, and BRICS summits cover the same subjects and in the same way could enhance the effectiveness of all.

A fourth step is to explore more carefully the causes of compliance, especially those that rest within the leaders' or practitioners' own control. The recent work on compliance catalysts could be extended both empirically and conceptually, to consider whether the addition or accountability of monitoring mechanisms of different sorts enhances or erodes compliance and does so just on the same or other subjects and with what impacts over time. More intra-institutional accountability means a potential diversion or resources from performing the main six performance functions. It may also mean, as the 2010 G8 Muskoka Summit suggested, that the prospect of more accountability monitoring means a reduced desire to make ambitious commitments in the first place.

Better Concepts

In regard to better concepts, the major thrust is to move from a focus on compliance and implementation to a focus on results. Here three steps stand out.

Here the first step is to conceive, in a measurable way, of the institution's 'mission accomplished' as that mission applies to the international institution overall and the distinctive, core collective purpose it was created and continued to achieve. Here one needs to go beyond specific decisional commitments to core, foundational principles and norms. For the G7/8 this mission is to promote among its members and globally the values of 'an open, democratic society, dedicated to individual liberty and social advancement' (G7 1975). For the G20 it is to promote financial stability and make globalization work for all. For the BRICS, it is to strengthen collaboration among its members, support the G20 summit in the face of global financial crises, and, less clearly, support the common interest of emerging countries in their economic development.

A second step is improved concepts of outcomes, especially the results obtained against referents ranging from the intent of the creators to the demand for global governance of key problems, as independently assessed. In some cases standard data sets provide sound, over-time data specific to the core of a commitment that measure changing welfare outcomes in the state of the world. These could potentially be converted and aggregated into an overall measure of deaths delayed or human lives enhanced as a result of what the international institution does. This would require attention to causality, starting with the performance dimensions themselves to ask if the individual institution is responding to the proper domestic political pressures, discussing the right subjects, setting the appropriate directions, and so on. Then one would consider international institutions in interaction with one another and how this interaction shapes the observed changes in the outcomes.

A third step is to ask if problems are actually solved by institutions or simply shifted to a lower level or different track as they are redefined or fade away. This raises the larger question of how well today's international institutions, largely conceived in the hierarchical, static, slow-moving Westphalian world of the nineteenth century, match the fluid, fast-moving, networked world of the twenty-first century and the complex adaptive system that generates the problems it confronts (Kirton 2013).

Better Mechanisms

Of the many improved mechanisms that offer the promise of improved accountability assessment and thus effectiveness, four stand out.

Expand the mandates of multilateral organization mechanisms
The first improvement is available to and appropriate for those major multilateral organizations with a large, professional staff that already regularly assesses members' performance on behaviour related to the members' current, cumulating, highest level commitments to and at the organization itself and to the same subject ones made at the G7/8, G20, and BRICS summits. Thus the IMF could add to its Article IV consultations and reports a systematic assessment of how each member is complying with the commitments made at the ministerial level at the semi-annual IMF meetings, including at related meetings such as those of the International Monetary and Finance Committee. The WTO could do the same as part of the Trade Policy Review Mechanism's periodic assessments of members, with the largest countries most consequential for the system and its overall level of compliance and 'defection dynamic' being reviewed most frequently. For summit commitments on subjects without a core multilateral organization similarly equipped, compliance and accountability assessments would need to be done elsewhere.

Assess member governments' extra-executive branches
The second improvement is to have the member countries of the international institution use components of their own governments beyond the core executive branch more systematically to assess compliance with the countries' international commitments, just as they do with the operations of their own government at home. Legislatures play the key role here, especially with the well-established legislative components or companions of many international institutions, such as the United Nations, the North Atlantic Treaty Organization, the Summit of the Americas and the Organization of American States, the

G7/8 since 2002, and the G20 since 2010. It would also be useful to mobilize governments' auditors general, in general or in the environmental field, to assist with this task.

Establish an autonomous accountability institute, foundation, network or foundation

The third improvement is to establish an institute, network, or foundation for independent, third-party compliance and implementation assessment, by those without a specific stake as owners of the commitments or advocates for further action. In the case of the G20's use of the WTO as an external accountability assessor on trade, the WTO's public results were less specific and more favourable than those of the fully independent Global Trade Alert Project, perhaps because the WTO was understandably bound by its own legally defined definitions and sensitive to the potential costs of publicly naming noncompliant members. Moreover, it is unreasonable to expect, or arguably even ask, the WTO to assess the compliance of G20 members with their repeated commitment to get the Doha Development Round done, if only because in the case of such delicate ongoing negotiations, publicly identifying the noncompliance of individual members' could be counterproductive to the WTO secretariat's more important role in achieving the intended result of completing the negotiations. Finally, an independent institute, backed by a foundation, could mobilize more resources than the secretariats of international organizations or intergovernmental working groups themselves would devote to this task, especially if the institute were assisted by a global network of academics and others contributing to the work on an ongoing basis.

Such an exercise, with input from advocacy organizations but led and controlled by those only with an analytic rather than advocacy stake, could have considerable appeal to the international institutions and governments under scrutiny, if only to offset the well-publicized findings and criticism that the advocacy organizations understandably and appropriately tend to make. Furthermore, as British prime minister David Cameron (2012) publicly recognized in his remarks at the end of the Los Cabos Summit, timely, independent third-party monitoring and reporting are above all valuable to those individuals who made the commitment and who thus most want to know if those commitments are being kept: 'I think this is important; we come to these summits, we make these commitments, we say we are going to do these things and it is important that there is an organisation that checks up on who has done what.' In the minds of citizens, such independent assessments would have the credibility inevitably lacking in the institutions, their member governments' own individual or delegated second-hand self-assessments, and the assessments of advocacy nongovernmental organizations and private sector players (Kirsch 2013). That is why the institutions and governments under assessment, as well as philanthropists and others, could be expected to contribute to the endowment that supports such an independent institute's assessment work.

Create a multistakeholder accountability consortium

The fourth step is to create an ongoing multistakeholder compliance consortium and regular conference for all the assessors to share, compare, improve, and advance and to be accountable to their peers for what they do. This should foster some agreement on best practices, an appropriate division of labour and mutual understanding of the different purposes and thus methods that guide different parties' work.

References

Abbott, Kenneth W., Robert Keohane, Andrew Moravcsik, et al. (2000). 'The Concept of Legalization'. *kirtonk* 54(3): 401–20.

Breitmeier, Helmut (2008). *The Legitimacy of International Regimes*. Farnham: Ashgate.

Cameron, David (2012). 'Prime Minister's Press Conference at Mexico G20'. Los Cabos, June 19. https://www.gov.uk/government/speeches/prime-ministers-press-conference-at-mexico-g20 (December 2014).

G7 (1975). 'Declaration of Rambouillet'. Rambouillet, November 17. http://www.g8.utoronto.ca/summit/1975rambouillet/communique.html (December 2014).

G8 (2010). 'Muskoka Accountability Report'. June 20. http://www.g8.utoronto.ca/summit/2010muskoka/accountability (December 2014).

G8 (2013). 'Lough Erne Accountability Report: Keeping Our Promises'. June 7. http://www.g8.utoronto.ca/summit/2013lougherne/lough-erne-accountability.html (December 2014).

G20 Research Group and International Organisations Research Institute (2013). '2012 Los Cabos G20 Summit Final Compliance Report'. September 4. http://www.g20.utoronto.ca/compliance/2012loscabos-final (December 2014).

Guebert, Jenilee and Caroline Bracht (2010). 'Assessing the Results and Impacts of G8 Accountability Reports to Help Pave the Way Forward'. Paper prepared for Partnership for Progress: From the 2010 Muskoka-Toronto Summits to the Seoul Summit, 27–28 October, Moscow.

Ikenberry, G. John (2001). *After Victory: Institutions, Strategic Restraint, and the Rebuilding of Order after Major Wars*. Princeton: Princeton University Press.

Ikenberry, G. John (2011). *Liberal Leviathan: The Origins, Crisis, and Transformation of the American World Order*. Princeton: Princeton University Press.

International Organizations Research Institute (2009). 'G20 London Summit Commitments Compliance Report 2009'. September 18, Moscow. http://www.g20.utoronto.ca/analysis/hse/2009-london-compliance.pdf (December 2014).

International Organizations Research Institute and G20 Research Group (2010). '2009 Pittsburgh G20 Summit Compliance Report'. June 21. http://www.g20.utoronto.ca/analysis/Pittsburgh_G20_compliance_report.pdf (December 2014).

Juricevic, Diana (2000). 'Controlling for Domestic-Level Commitments: An Analysis of the Authoritative National Commitments Made in Canada and the United States from 1995 to 2000'. G8 Research Group. http://www.g8.utoronto.ca/scholar/juricevic2000/juricevic.pdf (December 2014).

Keohane, Robert O. and Joseph S. Nye (1977). *Power and Interdependence: World Politics in Transition*. Boston: Little, Brown.

Kirsch, David (2013). Accountability in Children's Development Organizations, PhD thesis, Institute of Medical Science, University of Toronto, Toronto. Unpublished.

Kirton, John J. (1989). 'Introduction'. In *The Seven-Power Summit: Documents from the Summits of Industrialized Countries, 1975–1989*, Peter I. Hajnal, ed. Millwood NY: Kraus International Publishers.

Kirton, John J. (2006). 'Explaining Compliance with G8 Finance Commitments: Agency, Institutionalization, and Structure'. *Open Economies Review* 17(4): 459–75.

Kirton, John J., ed. (2009). *International Organization*. Farnham: Ashgate.

Kirton, John J. (2013). *G20 Governance for a Globalized World*. Farnham: Ashgate.

Kirton, John J., Caroline Bracht and Leanne Rasmussen (2012). 'Implementing the G20 Seoul Development and Employment Commitments: An Assessment'. Paper produced with the financial support of the International Labour Office through the ILO–Korea Partnership Program, G20 Research Group, Toronto. http://www.g20.utoronto.ca/biblio/SDC_Assessment.pdf (December 2014).

Kirton, John J. and Jenilee Guebert (2011). 'Shaping a United Nations High-Level Meeting on Non-communicable Diseases that Delivers'. Paper commissioned by the Pan American Health Organization/World Health Organization, Global Health Diplomacy Program, Toronto. http://www.ghdp.utoronto.ca/pubs/shaping-un-hlm.pdf (December 2014).

Kirton, John J., Marina V. Larionova and Paolo Savona, eds (2010). *Making Global Economic Governance Effective: Hard and Soft Law Institutions in a Crowded World*. Farnham: Ashgate.

Kokotsis, Ella (2010). 'The Muskoka Accountability Report: Assessing the Written Record'. Paper prepared for Partnership for Progress: From the 2010 Muskoka-Toronto Summits to the Seoul Summit, 27–28 October, Moscow.

Krasner, Stephen (1983). 'Structural Causes and Regime Consequences: Regimes as Intervening Variables'. In *International Regimes*, Stephen Krasner, ed. Ithaca NY: Cornell University Press, pp. 1–21.

Larionova, Marina V. (2011). 'Assessing G8 and G20 Effectiveness in Global Governance So Far'. Paper prepared for Princeton Global Governance Conference on Rivalry and Partnership: The Struggle for a New Global Governance Leadership, 14–15 January, Princeton NJ.

Raustiala, Kal and Anne-Marie Slaughter (2002). 'International Law, International Relations, and Compliance'. In *Handbook of International Relations*, Walter Carlsnaes, Thomas Risse, and Beth A. Simmons, eds. London: Sage Publications, pp. 538–58.

Ruggie, John G. (1983). 'International Regimes, Transactions, and Change: Embedded Liberalism in the Postwar Economic Order'. In *International Regimes*, Stephen D. Krasner, ed. Ithaca: Cornell University Press, pp. 195–232.

von Furstenberg, George M. (2008). 'Performance Measurement under Rational International Overpromising Regimes'. *Journal of Public Policy* 28(3): 261–87.

PART V
Conclusion

Chapter 14

Conclusion

John J. Kirton

This volume has explored the performance, strengths and limitations, and division of labour emerging during the first five years of coexistence between the Group of Eight (G8) and the Group of 20 (G20). It has examined their evolving relationship and involvement with the BRICS group of Brazil, Russia, India, China, and South Africa, as well as with civil society and multilateral organizations. It considers how the future partnership between the G20 and the Group of Seven (G7) or G8 can be improved to their benefit and for the global community as a whole.

Taken together, the contributions in this volume offer a clear consensus on some key issues and the basis for a rich, progressive debate on several others. They provide a basis for several conclusions and resulting recommendations to strengthen the G7/8 and the G20 and their relationships in future years.

The Analytical Consensus and Debate

Comparing G7/8 and G20 Summitry

The first task of this volume was to chart and compare, using a common analytic framework, the older G7/8 and newer G20 summits, especially during their first five years of coexistence from 2008 to 2013. This comparison covered their creation, characteristics, performance of global governance functions, and the causes that determine why and how they perform.

Creation
There is great consensus on the creation of the G7/8 and the G20, based on the similarities between the two foundational processes. John Kirton, Dries Lesage, and Martin Gilman on the G20 agree that both were created as a response to globalization and multipolarity, first as finance ministers' forums that were then elevated at European initiative to the leaders' level. Kirton emphasizes the role of crisis in their creation at the summit level and the co-leadership of the United States with France in both the G7/8 and G20 and with Canada's Paul Martin for the finance G20 in 1999.

Core characteristics
There is also considerable consensus on the core characteristics of the G7/8 and G20. Lesage sees several striking similarities between the institutions and Kirton uses a common

comparative framework based on those similarities (Kirton 2013). Both authors emphasize the character of the G7/8 and G20, and of the BRICS, as informal, plurilateral summit institutions (PSIs) and note the expansion of their agendas. Lesage claims the often cited differences between the G7/8 and G20 are less significant than they first appear to be. Kirton, however, also notes a core difference between the G7/8's status as a modern democratic concert and the G20 as the hub at the centre of a network of systemically significant states in an intensely interconnected world.

Performance

There is also consensus, along with contestation, on the performance of the G7/8 and G20 summits, challenging the prevailing outside view of the demise of the G7/8 and the decline of the G20. Kirton, with support from Lesage, argues that each group, including the BRICS, has a rising performance record across most of its global governance functions. Marina V. Larionova, Mark Rakhmangulov, and Andrey Shelepov more modestly conclude that the G7/8 is strong on deliberation and delivery and the G20 is strong in direction setting, decision making, developing global governance, and, increasingly, delivery.

In the case of the twin G8 and G20 summits of 2010, Kirton argues that the G8 Muskoka Summit successfully brought the G8 'back to basics' as a leaders-driven process centred on informal direct dialogue. It produced the Muskoka Initiative on Maternal, Newborn, and Child Health, a counter-terrorism action plan, and the decision to carry on the Global Partnership against the Spread of Weapons and Materials of Mass Destruction in its current form. The G20 Toronto Summit generated commitments on fiscal consolidation, reform of international financial institutions (IFIs), and the commencement of country reviews to implement the Framework on Strong, Sustainable, and Balanced Growth.

However, Gilman, in sharp contrast, sees a decline in post-crisis G20 summit performance on its core economic functions of ensuring global financial stability, promoting sustained economic growth, and reducing imbalances. Zia Qureshi argues less strongly that G20 policy actions since the start of the 2008 global financial crisis have emphasized short-term crisis management, which, while necessary, is insufficient to restore robust economic growth. No one, however, argues that the G7/8 is in decline.

Causes of performance

There is considerable consensus on the causes of G7/8 and G20 performance. Most authors generally rely on the variables contained in the concert equality model of G7/8 governance and the systemic hub model of G20 governance (Kirton 2013). They agree, as do these models, that the most salient causes lie at the international level of analysis.

At the international level, all highlight crisis, or shock-activated vulnerability, as a key contributing cause but neither a necessary nor a sufficient one. They see relative capability and connectivity, and the cohesiveness and club-like character of the groups as consequential as well. Thus, Kirton emphasizes shifting relative capabilities among rising and retreating powers; globalized connectivity, complexity, and uncertainty; and equal vulnerability for all to new non-state threats. Lesage and Gilman agree on the causal role of crisis. But Lesage specifies that the G7/8 is a cohesive club that needs an internal sense of collective responsibility and equality to succeed, while the more diverse G20 depends

CONCLUSION

more on an external crisis for success. Marina Larionova, Mark Rakhmangulov, Andrei Sakharov, Andrey Shelepov, and Vitaly Nagornov go beyond crisis to identify more broadly the chronic and periodic global problems that generate a demand for global governance, which should be met by the available supply of international institutions.

At the international and transnational levels, Kirton adds as a cause of Canada's 2010 G8 and G20 successes a smart, responsible civil society containing expertise and capacity and a smart, strategic host willing to use its prerogative of host and chair and to work well with multilateral organizations, notably the United Nations and the International Monetary Fund (IMF). At the domestic level, Larionova, Rakhmangulov, Sakharov, Shelepov, and Nagornov add the members' priorities as factors that shape the demand for collective action and confront the institution's capacity for forging consensus and making collective decisions.

Connecting G7/8 and G20 Summitry

The second task of this volume was to consider the connection between G8 and G20 summitry during their first five years together. Here the central concern was with the closeness of the connection, its cooperative, convergent, or competitive character, and the combined capacity to cope with the challenges of the contemporary world.

Most authors see a considerable connection that became close only with the twin Canadian-hosted G8 and G20 summits in June 2010. And all emphasize the cooperative and convergent character of the connection, rather than a competitive one.

Cooperation, not competition, is affirmed by Larionova, Rakhmangulov, and Shelepov, who acknowledge the two groups have no clear division of labour on global governance functions or on policy areas, but conclude that each has a distinctive core agenda and cooperate on certain priorities. Kirton emphasizes the increasing overlap in their agendas and their cooperative relationship that extends to the BRICS.

Convergence is highlighted by Lesage, who notes the division of labour between the two as the G20 moved from the level of finance ministers and central bank governors to the leaders' level. Scenarios for future coexistence are based on the application of functional and pragmatic approaches and on representing the interests of different countries through mechanisms already developed as the groups' agendas deepen. Their likely relationship is thus a very complex pragmatic one, without a rigid division of labour.

Most authors confirm or concede that the combined capacity of the G7/8 and G20 for global governance is considerable but not enough to cope by themselves with the challenges of the contemporary world. Kirton emphasizes that both offer mutual support to produce summit-level global governance at least twice a year, in order to counter and control the new vulnerabilities that all now confront. But almost all authors add many reforms that would enable both to do a better job and suggest that other actors must contribute as well.

The Contribution of Other Actors

The third task was to consider the performance and relationship of the G7/8 and G20 in the context of the other consequential new actors importantly involved in global governance. These include in particular an empowered civil society, led by the business community in the Business 20 (B20), and the new BRICS summit, amid broader forces at work in the contemporary world.

Civil society's contribution is identified by some and denied by none. Kirton highlights the critical contribution of children's nongovernmental organizations (NGOs) to the Muskoka G8's success on maternal, newborn, and child health (MNCH). In the case of the G20, Larionova, Rakhmangulov, Sakharov, and Shelepov conclude that since its start at Toronto in 2010 the B20 has become a reliable stakeholder in the G20-led process of generating strong, sustainable, and balanced growth. Its recommendations that relate to the G20's core agenda are more likely to be heard than recommendations that come from outside. The B20 under the 2013 Russian presidency advanced its engagement with the G20, consolidated its contribution to G20 decision making and direction setting, and substantially moved to establish the B20 as a global governance actor.

The BRICS summit also contributes in several ways. Kirton concludes its rising performance is mutually supportive with the G7/8 and G20. Larionova, Rakhmangulov, Sakharov, Shelepov, and Nagornov agree that it contributes to the convergent division of labour and combined capacity of the three central global PSIs to cope with global risks. On issues such as health, BRICS governance is becoming critical as the G7/8 and G20 have largely abandoned the field.

The contribution made by multilateral organizations is noted by several authors. Larionova, Rakhmangulov, and Shelepov argue that both the G7/8 and G20 enhance multilateralism through their intense engagement with international institutions on a wide range of issues. Kirton shows how the UN's Millennium Development Goals helped cause and were in turn strengthened by the G8's Muskoka success on MNCH. And several authors affirm many multilateral organizations' contribution to compliance monitoring and accountability within the G20.

Compliance and Accountability

The fourth task was to assess the compliance and accountability of G7/8 and G20 members, as an essential element in the effectiveness and legitimacy of both bodies. This analysis covered the compliance monitoring and accountability mechanisms employed by and effective in each group, the learning and borrowing from each other, and the resulting competitive and cooperative quest to provide the effective, legitimate global governance the world now needs.

Mechanisms employed

All authors analyzing this subject agree that a wide and increasing variety of mechanisms has been used by the G7/8 and G20. Peter Hajnal notes that civil society groups have tracked G7/8 and G20 performance, using various methods.

Larionova and Sakharov highlight the G20's greater reliance on invited reports from an ad hoc array of multilateral organizations, reflecting in part the fact that the IMF and World Bank have been members of the G20 since the start. Hajnal specifies the Mutual Assessment Process, conducted through a series of IMF reports (with other intergovernmental organizations also contributing), as having an important accountability dimension.

Ella Kokotsis argues that the 'Muskoka Accountability Report' in particular was a landmark that moved the G8 from its earlier focus on inputs toward a concern with outcomes. It showed that G8 leaders understood that accountability begins with compliance, that regular, clear, transparent reporting is important for compliance, and that an ongoing accountability working group is essential.

Effectiveness

The effectiveness of these mechanisms is open to debate. On the one hand, Hajnal concludes that all mechanisms contribute to enhancing accountability by exposing the strengths and weaknesses of the groups. Kokotsis adds that the 'Muskoka Accountability Report' was effective, as seen in the G7/8's increasing compliance scores across most assessed development-related issues and a general rise in its overall compliance over the mid term.

On the other hand, Larionova and Sakharov, supported by Kirton and others, suggest there is still a great gap. G7/8–G20 accountability is not sufficiently developed to allow its performance and impact to be assessed along all key dimensions. By conducting accountability in a shared but dispersed way in a multitude of formats, effectiveness is decreased because of indirect procedures and the absence of a clear connection between the commitments, results monitoring, and further decision making. Technocratic accountability reports render them incomprehensible to the broad public. The assessments of academics and NGOs tend to lack recommendations. Those of international organizations do too, and often lack their evidence base and data by member.

Learning and borrowing

Few authors see the G7/8 and G20 learning or borrowing from each other in the realm of compliance monitoring and accountability. The exception is Kokotsis, who argues that the 'Muskoka Accountability Report' inspired similar accountability assessments by other G-x forums, most notably the G20 with its first development accountability report in 2013.

Effective, legitimate global governance

Similarly weak claims come in regard to how G7/8 and G20 compliance monitoring and their accountability mechanisms have increased the effectiveness and legitimacy of these bodies and global governance as a whole. Hajnal argues that the G7/8 and G20 have increasingly recognized the crucial role of accountability in gauging progress and building legitimacy. But no one asserts that either group has achieved this result in the judgement or behaviour of the many stakeholders and citizens involved and affected by what the G7/8 and G20 do and do not achieve.

The Policy Consensus and Debate: Recommendations

The fifth task of the contributors to this volume was to come to conclusions for strengthening the connection between the G7/8 and G20 and the other actors involved in their work. They sought to identify, on the basis of their individual and shared empirical and analytical foundation, how the G7/8–G20 relationship could realistically be improved to better meet the needs of citizens in today's tightly wired world. Together, they have produced a rich, multifaceted cornucopia of recommendations, with consensus prevailing and contradictions limited indeed.

Comparing G7/8 and G20 Summitry

Almost all authors agree that the G7/8 and G20 summits should continue to coexist. The one exception, Gilman, concludes from the initial creation and decade-long work of the G20 at the finance ministers' level and the capacity of the IMF, that G20 governance should be maintained at the ministerial level until more representative and effective mechanisms can be introduced or until a new crisis erupts. Qureshi recommends that the G20 add to its economic stabilization activities a deep, long-term agenda of structural reforms and investments that boost productivity and bolster the extended sustainability of growth. Larionova, Rakhmangulov, and Shelepov recommend that, given the diversity of the G20 economies' situation, any one-size-fits-all formula should often be replaced by a list of individual commitments aimed to meet agreed objectives, as stated in the Seoul supporting document. Such individual commitments must be balanced across countries and new commitments and past actions should not be combined.

To strengthen their contributions, Lesage and several others recommend that both groups should continue to build their respective institutional capabilities and reform their processes. No one recommends that either the G7/8 or the G20 add a secretariat to cause their performance to improve.

Connecting G7/8 and G20 Summitry

Almost all authors concur that the G7/8 and G20 should work together to reinforce the system of global governance. They need to do so in many ways throughout the year, with their cooperation consolidated in several ways.

Larionova, Rakhmangulov, Sakharov, Shelepov, and Nagornov provide a formula for convergence upon which more active cooperation could and should be built. Here each group's work should address the risks, challenges, and global governance failures most relevant to its mission and capabilities, with the G20 focusing on economic risks, the G7/8 on geopolitical and technological ones, and the BRICS on innovative long-term societal ones. The country occupying the chair should align the demands from global risks and national priorities with the capacity of that group and the chair's own national priorities, interests, and capabilities. The chair should be guided by a comparative assessment of each group's effectiveness for dealing with specific global governance problems.

CONCLUSION

Coexistence would start from the principle of comparative advantage. Both the G7/8 and the G20 should have their own core agenda but could cooperate on the same things if need be. Such cooperation built on the comparative advantages of the two groups can yield productive complementarity. In the economic and finance realm, the G20 should complete IFI reform and discuss reforming the system of reserve currencies. In energy and climate change, financing adaptation can be dealt with within the G7/8, whereas phasing out fossil fuel subsidies or setting post-Kyoto climate targets should be done in the G20 where the major emerging economies are represented. The G7/8 is better placed to work on energy security and nuclear energy, while the G20 is needed to coordinate actions to achieve transparency and to facilitate technology transfers.

Political and security issues should remain within the G7/8. It should have full respect for and coordination with the UN, especially the UN Security Council. The G7/8 should also continue to deal with education, health, and migration, based on work it launched in 2006. Development assistance should come through the G20's contribution to economic growth, eventually adding aid from emerging donors. The G7/8 should continue to bear responsibilities for both economic growth and official development assistance.

Importantly, systemic risks such as severe income disparity, the unforeseen negative consequences of regulation, the prolonged neglect of infrastructure, and the extreme volatility in energy and agriculture prices demand cooperation and coordination among both the G7/8 and the G20, and the BRICS too.

Kirton recommends even more strongly that both summits need to work together at the same time, throughout the year, and on the same things if necessary. Moreover, both the G7/8 and the G20 need to work together on the same things for as long and as often as needed – either once a year per the G7/8 norm, twice a year per the initial G20 norm, or even more often should the global demand arise.

The Contribution of Other Actors

There is complete consensus that even two G summits working well together are not enough to meet the great and growing demands for global governance in today's globalized world. Both must work more closely with the BRICS, the major multilateral organizations, supportive academic communities, and civil society in several ways.

Larionova, Rakhmangulov, Sakharov, Shelepov, and Nagornov thus recommend that the G20 further institutionalize and structure its dialogue with both internal and external stakeholders, but not by creating a secretariat. Internally, it should reinforce the troika system of cooperation among the outgoing, current, and incoming presidencies and clearly define the rotation principle for hosting, in order to facilitate summit preparation and ensure long-range planning, agenda continuity, and accountability. With the B20, G20 chairs can consolidate the B20's status as a partner responsible for generating strong, sustainable, and balanced growth. The B20, in line with its own ambitious goals, should ensure its own transparency, efficiency, legitimacy, and accountability. It should develop a mid-term strategy, communicate it clearly to stakeholders including international organizations and small and medium-sized enterprises, and agree on its mid-term engagement with the G20.

It should become more representative, share with the G20 responsibility for delivering on commitments, and account for its own actions in a transparent, coherent, and unbiased way.

In regard to broad outreach, Larionova, Rakhmangulov, Sakharov, Shelepov, and Nagornov argue that the G7/8 has greater outreach potential than the G20 despite the latter's large membership. The G7/8 should realize this potential and include into its dialogue the countries that have been formerly part of the process, were 'qualified' to become members of the G14 in case of expansion, and now feel resentment about their non-inclusion in the G20. G20 engagement with international organizations and non-member countries should be more structured and transparent. This will ensure the division of labour among the international organizations mandated by G20.

Compliance and Accountability

There is also great consensus among the contributors to this volume on strengthening compliance and accountability. All are comfortable with the inclusive approach of using mechanisms within the groups, delegated to related multilateral organizations, and conducted by independent advocacy, academic, and civil society groups. Most agree that more quality, not quantity, is required, as is a will to move forward on a set of simple, realistic reforms to improve the mechanisms already in place.

Kokotsis as well as Larionova and Sakharov start by recommending more measureable objectives, better baseline data, and on-the-ground monitoring. Kirton adds compliance monitoring over an extended time, a move from commitment-implementation consistency and conformity to tighter causality by tracing the process, and compliance with principled direction setting as well as decisional commitments. He also adds the impact of implementation on outcomes and results, including synergistic co-benefits in sequential or simultaneous form, as well as benefits from individual institutions' actions to their interaction as it affects effectiveness overall. Monitoring requires better measurements of consensus, commitment, and compliance, and better concepts about the institution's overall 'mission accomplished', 'human lives improved', and 'problem solved'. Hajnal recommends more emphasis on correction and redress and on democratic accountability.

There is considerable consensus on the particular contribution that each accountability community should make. Kokotsis as well as Larionova and Sakharov recommend that the G7/8's and G20's many working groups engage in improved monitoring with a consistent methodology. Kirton suggests expanding the mandates of multilateral organizations for monitoring and assessment.

Larionova and Sakharov as well as Kirton recommend that academics and NGOs help build the needed pluralistic accountability system through a network of epistemic groups aspiring to become an independent monitoring agent. Academics should build on their strengths in terms of information and analytic quality. Experts can help to provide public-oriented data on agenda items. This system has a special relevance, given the highly sophisticated and technical nature of G20 topics and the need to communicate outcomes to the public in the G20 members and beyond in order to make the process more transparent and address legitimacy and efficiency concerns. NGOs should harness their advocacy and lobbying capabilities. Academics and NGOs should both develop recommendations. Kirton and Hajnal suggest other actors get involved, by mobilizing members' legislatures and auditors general and establishing an independent accountability institute, foundation, and network.

Finally, most authors recommend that all actors come together at times in the compliance monitoring and accountability task. Hajnal suggests continuous and substantive consultations between civil society organizations and officials in the G7/8 and G20, as well as independent monitoring by such organizations, the publication of policy papers, alternative summits, and well-prepared civil society expertise relevant to the groups' priorities. Other authors recommend rendering systematic the interaction of the G7/8 and G20 governors with civil society, including academia, and the establishment of an international experts network. Kirton calls for the creation of a multistakeholder compliance consortium for all the assessors to share, compare, improve, and be accountable to their peers.

Conclusion

On all its tasks, this volume has come to conclusions, pointed the way ahead, and clarified many outstanding issues to guide future research. It has advanced the epistemic consensus about G7/8–G20 governance in a policy relevant way. The analysis and recommendations in this volume should be used to help strengthen the G7/8–G20 governance and the partnership of these two groups to the benefit of their members, international cooperation, and growth.

References

Kirton, John J. (2013). *G20 Governance for a Globalized World*. Farnham: Ashgate.

Bibliography

Abbott, Kenneth W., Robert Keohane, Andrew Moravcsik, et al. (2000). 'The Concept of Legalization'. *kirtonk* 54(3): 401–20.

African Union Commission and NEPAD Planning and Coordinating Agency (2011). 'Assessing Africa-G8 Partnership Commitments: Accountability Report on Africa-G8 Commitments, 2001–2010'. http://can-mnch.ca/wp-content/uploads/2011/10/Assessing-Africa-G8-Partnership-Commitments.pdf (December 2014).

Alexander, Nancy and Aldo Caliari (2013). 'Commentary on the Report: "Mapping G20 Decisions Implementation"'. January, Heinrich Böll Stiftung, Washington DC.http://us.boell.org/2013/02/01/commentary-report-mapping-g20-decisions-implementation-group-20 (December 2014).

Alexander, Nancy and Peter Riggs (2012). 'The G20: Playing Outside the Big Tent – Implications for Rio+20'. June, Heinrich Böll Stiftung, Washington DC. http://ke.boell.org/2012/06/15/g20-playing-outside-big-tent-implications-rio20 (December 2014).

Alpert, Daniel, Robert Hockett and Nouriel Roubini (2011). 'The Way Forward: Moving from the Post-Bubble, Post-Bust Economy to Renewed Growth and Competitiveness'. October, New America Foundation. http://newamerica.net/sites/newamerica.net/files/policydocs/NAF--The_Way_Forward--Alpert_Hockett_Roubini.pdf (December 2014).

At the Table (2010). 'Take Your Place at the Table'. http://www.puttingfarmersfirst.ca/at_the_table/ (December 2014).

B20 (2010). 'Chairman's Summary: Report to G20 Ministers of Finance'. B20 Business Summit, June 26, Toronto. http://www.hse.ru/en/org/hse/iori/B20_Toronto_Recommendations (December 2014).

B20 (2010). 'Joint Statement by Participating Companies'. G20 Business Summit, November 11, Seoul. http://www.hse.ru/data/2013/01/23/1306478418/Seoul_G20_Business_Summit_Joint_Statement.pdf (December 2014).

B20 (2011). 'Final Report, with Appendices'. G20 Business Summit, November 3, Cannes. http://www.hse.ru/data/2013/01/23/1306477802/Cannes_B20_Report.pdf (December 2014).

B20 (2012). 'B20 Global Business Leaders Announce Their Prioritized Recommendations for Global Economic Recovery and Growth'. May 29, Mexico City. http://www.prnewswire.com/news-releases/b20-global-business-leaders-announce-their-prioritized-recommendations-for-global-economic-recovery-and-growth-155411765.html (December 2014).

B20 (2012). 'B20 Task Force Recommendations'. June, Los Cabos. http://www.hse.ru/data/2013/01/23/1306477584/Los_Cabos_B20_Report.pdf (December 2014).

B20 (2013). 'B20-G20 Partnership for Growth and Jobs: Recommendations from Business 20'. G20 Business Summit, September 5, St Petersburg. http://b20russia.com/B20_WhiteBook_web.pdf (December 2014).

B20 and L20 (2011). 'B20 L20 Joint Statement'. November 4, Cannes. http://www.g20.utoronto.ca/2011/2011-b20-l20-en.pdf (December 2014).

Bailin, Alison (2005). *From Traditional to Group Hegemony: The G7, the Liberal Economic Order, and the Core-Periphery Gap.* Aldershot: Ashgate.

Baker, Andrew (2006). *The Group of Seven: Finance Ministries, Central Banks, and Global Financial Governance.* London: Routledge.

Bayne, Nicholas (2005). *Staying Together: The G8 Summit Confronts the 21st Century.* Aldershot: Ashgate.

Bhattacharya, Amar, Mattia Romani and Nicholas Stern (2012). 'Infrastructure for Development: Meeting the Challenge'. Centre for Climate Change Economics and Policy, Grantham Research Institute on Clmate Change and the Environment in collaboration with the Intergovernmental Group of 24, June. http://www.cccep.ac.uk/Publications/Policy/docs/PP-infrastructure-for-development-meeting-the-challenge.pdf (December 2014).

Blair, Tony (2006). 'A Global Alliance for Global Values'. Foreign Policy Centre, London. http://fpc.org.uk/fsblob/798.pdf (December 2014).

Bono and Bob Geldof (2010). 'The African Century'. *Globe and Mail*, May 10.

Boorman, Jack T. and André Icard (2011). 'Reform of the International Monetary System: A Cooperative Approach for the 21st Century'. In *Reform of the International Monetary System: The Palais Royal Initiative*, Jack T. Boorman and André Icard, eds. Thousand Oaks CA: Sage Publications.

Breitmeier, Helmut (2008). *The Legitimacy of International Regimes.* Farnham: Ashgate.

BRIC (2009). 'Joint Statement of the BRIC Countries' Leaders'. Yekaterinburg, June 16. http://www.brics.utoronto.ca/docs/090616-leaders.html (March 2014).

BRICS (2013). 'BRICS and Africa: Partnership for Development, Integration, and Industralisation'. Durban, March 27. http://www.brics.utoronto.ca/docs/130327-statement.html (December 2014).

Bulman, David, Maya Eden and Ha Nguyen (2012). 'Transition from Low-Income Growth to High-Income Growth: Is There a Middle-Income Trap?' Background paper, World Bank, Washington DC.

Calderón, César and Luis Servén (2010). 'Infrastructure and Economic Development in Sub-Saharan Africa'. *Journal of African Economies* 19(Suppl 1): i13–i87.

Cameron, David (2011). 'Governance for Growth: Building Consensus for the Future'. Report submitted to the 2011 G20 Cannes Summit, November. www.g20.utoronto.ca/2011/2011-cameron-report.pdf (December 2014).

Cameron, David (2012). 'In Fight for Open World, G8 Still Matters'. *Globe and Mail*, November 20. http://www.theglobeandmail.com/report-on-business/economy/david-cameron-in-fight-for-open-world-g8-still-matters/article5508595/ (December 2014).

Cameron, David (2012). 'Prime Minister's Press Conference at Mexico G20'. Los Cabos, June 19. https://www.gov.uk/government/speeches/prime-ministers-press-conference-at-mexico-g20 (December 2014).

BIBLIOGRAPHY

Cecchetti, Stephen G. (2011). 'Global Imbalances: Current Accounts and Financial Flows'. Remarks repared for the Myron Scholes Global Markets Forum, University of Chicago, September 27, Bank for International Settlements, Basel. http://www.bis.org/speeches/sp110928.pdf (December 2014).

Choi, Jessica Seoyoung (2010). 'Civil G20 Dialog Held in Incheon'. October 19, Korea.net. http://www.korea.net/NewsFocus/Policies/view?articleId=83509 (December 2014).

Civil 20 Task Force on Inequality (2013). 'Civil 20 Proposals for Strong, Sustainable, Balanced and Inclusive Growth'. Civil 20, Moscow. http://www.g20.utoronto.ca/c20/C20_proposals_2013_final.pdf (December 2014).

Coalición Mexicana frente al G20 (2012). 'Declaración de la Cumbre de los Pueblos contra el G20'. June 19, La Paz, Mexico. http://www.coaliciong20.org/?p=1166 (August 2012).

Coalición Mexicana frente al G20 (2012). 'G20 Cumbre del Capital, Anticapitalismo y Altermundismo'. May 21, La Paz, Mexico. http://www.coaliciong20.org/?s=Carta+dirigida+al+presidente+pro+tempore+&x=0&y=0 (August 2012).

Community Solidarity Network (2010). 'June 2010: The People Won!', July 26, Toronto. http://g20.torontomobilize.org/node/432 (December 2014).

Cooper, Andrew F. (2007). *Celebrity Diplomacy*. Boulder: Paradigm Publishers.

Cooper, Andrew F. (2013). 'Civil Society Relationships with the G20: An Extension of the G8 Template or Distinctive Pattern of Engagement?' *Global Society* 27(2): 179–200. doi: 10.1080/13600826.2012.762346.

Cooper, Andrew F. and Ramesh Thakur (2013). *Group of Twenty (G20)*. London: Routledge.

Cooper, Helene (2012). 'World Leaders Make Little Headway in Solving Debt Crisis'. *New York Times*, June 19, p. A3. http://www.nytimes.com/2012/06/20/world/leaders-make-little-headway-in-solving-europe-debt-crisis.html?_r=0 (December 2014).

Coordination SUD (2011). 'Alter-forum de Nice: Les peuples d'abord, pas la finance!', November 4. http://www.coordinationsud.org/actualite/alter-forum-de-nice-les-peuples-d%E2%80%99abord-pas-la-finance/ (December 2014).

Council on Foreign Relations (2012). 'CFR Convenes 'Council of Councils' Linking Leading Foreign Policy Institutes from around the World'. March 12, New York. http://www.cfr.org/global-governance/cfr-convenes-council-councils-linking-leading-foreign-policy-institutes-around-world/p27612?co=C03920 (December 2014).

Daniels, Joseph P. (1993). *The Meaning and Reliability of Economic Summit Undertakings* New York: Garland Publishing.

Development Working Group (2012). '2012 Progress Report of the Development Working Group'. June. http://www.international.gc.ca/g20/2012/progress_report-progres_rapport.aspx (December 2014).

Dobson, Hugo (2006). *Group of 7/8*. London: Routledge.

Dobson, Hugo (2011). 'The G8, the G20, and Civil Society'. In *Global Financial Crisis: Global Impact and Solutions*, Paolo Savona, John Kirton, and Chiara Oldani, eds. Farnham: Ashgate, pp. 245–60.

ENS Staff (2013). 'Global Religious Leaders Call on G8 to 'Strike at Causes of Poverty''. Episcopal News Service, April 5. http://episcopaldigitalnetwork.com/ens/2013/04/05/global-religious-leaders-call-on-g8-to-strike-at-causes-of-poverty (December 2014).

Faith Challenge G8 (2010). 'Petition: A Time for Inspired Leadership and Action'. https://web.archive.org/web/20100823050155/http://petition.faithchallengeg8.com/ (December 2014).

FIM-Forum for Democratic Global Governance (2010). 'Civil Society Dialogue with the Host Sherpa to the Toronto 2010 G20 Summit: Communiqué'. June 11, Ottawa. http://www.g8.utoronto.ca/evaluations/2010muskoka/fim-sherpas.pdf (May 2014).

Financial Stability Board (2012). 'Identifying the Effects of Regulatory Reforms on Emerging Market and Developing Economies: A Review of Potential Unintended Consequences'. Report to the G20 Finance Ministers and Central Bank Governors, June 19, Basel. http://www.financialstabilityboard.org/publications/r_120619e.pdf (December 2014).

Financial Stability Board (2013). 'A Narrative Progress Report on Financial Reform: Report of the Financial Stability Board to G20 Leaders'. September 5, Basel. http://www.financialstabilityboard.org/wp-content/uploads/r_130905a.pdf (December 2014).

Financial Stability Board (2013). 'Strengthening Oversight and Regulation of Shadow Banking: Policy Framework for Strengthening Oversight and Regulation of Shadow Banking Entities'. August 29, Basel. http://www.financialstabilityboard.org/wp-content/uploads/r_130829c.pdf (December 2014).

Financial Stability Board (2013). 'Update on Financial Regulatory Factors Affecting the Supply of Long-Term Investment Finance: Report to G20 Finance Ministers and Central Bank Governors'. August 29, Basel. http://www.financialstabilityboard.org/wp-content/uploads/r_130829g.pdf (December 2014).

Fitoussi, Jean-Paul and Joseph Stiglitz, eds (2011). *The G20 and Recovery and Beyond: An Agenda for Global Governance for the Twenty-First Century*. Paris: Paris Group. http://www.ofce.sciences-po.fr/pdf/documents/ebook2011.pdf (December 2014).

G7 (1975). 'Declaration of Rambouillet'. Rambouillet, November 17. http://www.g8.utoronto.ca/summit/1975rambouillet/communique.html (December 2014).

G7 (1988). 'Toronto Economic Summit Economic Declaration'. Toronto, June 21. http://www.g8.utoronto.ca/summit/1988toronto/communique.html (March 2014).

G8 (2007). 'Growth and Responsibility in the World Economy'. Heiligendamm, June 7. http://www.g8.utoronto.ca/summit/2007heiligendamm/g8-2007-economy.html (December 2014).

G8 (2008). 'Accountability Report: Implementation Review of G8 on Anti-corruption Commitments'. July, Hokkaido. http://www.g8.utoronto.ca/summit/2008hokkaido/2008-corruptionreport.pdf (December 2014).

G8 (2009). 'G8 Preliminary Accountability Report'. Annex to the L'Aquila G8 2009 Declaration, L'Aquila, Italy, July 8. http://www.g8.utoronto.ca/summit/2009laquila/2009-accountability.pdf (December 2014).

G8 (2009). 'Responsible Leadership for a Sustainable Future'. L'Aquila, Italy, July 8. http://www.g8.utoronto.ca/summit/2009laquila/2009-declaration.html (December 2014).

G8 (2010). 'G8 Muskoka Declaration: Recovery and New Beginnings'. Huntsville, Canada, June 26. http://www.g8.utoronto.ca/summit/2010muskoka/communique.html (December 2014).

BIBLIOGRAPHY

G8 (2010). 'Muskoka Accountability Report'. June 20. http://www.g8.utoronto.ca/summit/2010muskoka/accountability (December 2014).

G8 (2010). 'Report on the G8 Global Partnership 2010'. June 26, Huntsville, Canada. http://www.g8.utoronto.ca/summit/2010muskoka/globalpartnership.html (December 2014).

G8 (2011). 'Deauville Accountability Report – G8 Commitments on Health and Food Security: State of Delivery and Results'. May 18. http://www.g8.utoronto.ca/summit/2011deauville/accountability.html (December 2014).

G8 (2011). 'Declaration of the G8 on the Arab Springs'. Deauville, May 27. http://www.g8.utoronto.ca/summit/2011deauville/2011-arabsprings-en.html (December 2014).

G8 (2011). 'G8 Declaration: Renewed Commitment for Freedom and Democracy'. Deauville, May 27. http://www.g8.utoronto.ca/summit/2011deauville/2011-declaration-en.html (December 2014).

G8 (2011). 'Report on the G8 Global Partnership Against the Spread of Weapons and Materials of Mass Destruction'. May 27, Deauville. http://www.g8.utoronto.ca/summit/2011deauville/2011-globalpartnership-en.html (December 2014).

G8 (2012). 'Camp David Accountability Report: Actions, Approach, Results'. Camp David, May 19. http://www.g8.utoronto.ca/summit/2012campdavid/g8-cdar.html (December 2014).

G8 (2012). 'Camp David Declaration'. Camp David, May 19. http://www.g8.utoronto.ca/summit/2012campdavid/g8-declaration.html (December 2014).

G8 (2013). 'Lough Erne Accountability Report: Keeping Our Promises'. June 7. http://www.g8.utoronto.ca/summit/2013lougherne/lough-erne-accountability.html (December 2014).

G8 (2013). 'Lough Erne Declaration'. June 18, Lough Erne, Northern Ireland, United Kingdom. http://www.g8.utoronto.ca/summit/2013lougherne/lough-erne-declaration.html (December 2014).

G8 Research Group (2007). 'Background on Compliance Reports: Methodology'. http://www.g8.utoronto.ca/evaluations/methodology/g7c2.htm (December 2014).

G8 Research Group (2007). 'The G8 Presidency and Civil Society: An Overview of German and Russian Efforts to Engage Civil Society and Civil Society Organization around the G8'. June. http://www.g8.utoronto.ca/evaluations/csed/g8-cs.pdf (December 2014).

G8 Research Group (2011). '2010 Muskoka G8 Summit Final Compliance Report'. May 24. http://www.g8.utoronto.ca/evaluations/2010compliance-final (December 2014).

G8 Research Group (2011). '2010 Muskoka G8 Summit Interim Compliance Report'. February 21. http://www.g8.utoronto.ca/evaluations/2010compliance-interim (December 2014).

G8 Research Group (2012). '2011 Deauville G8 Summit Final Compliance Report'. May 18. http://www.g8.utoronto.ca/evaluations/2011compliance-final (December 2014).

G8 Research Group (2012). 'Report on Civil Society and the 2011 Deauville Summit'. March. http://www.g8.utoronto.ca/evaluations/csed/2011-deauville-civilsociety-post.pdf (December 2014).

G8 Research Group (2013). '2012 Camp David G8 Summit Final Compliance Report'. 14, June. http://www.g8.utoronto.ca/evaluations/2012compliance/2012compliance.pdf (December 2014).

G20 (2008). 'Declaration of the Summit on Financial Markets and the World Economy'. Washington DC, October 15. http://www.g20.utoronto.ca/2008/2008declaration1115. html (December 2014).

G20 (2009). 'G20 Leaders Statement: The Pittsburgh Summit'. Pittsburgh, September 25. http://www.g20.utoronto.ca/2009/2009communique0925.html (December 2014).

G20 (2010). 'Annex I: Seoul Development Consensus for Shared Growth'. Seoul, November 12. http://www.g20.utoronto.ca/2010/g20seoul consensus.html (December 2014).

G20 (2010). 'Annex II: Multi-Year Action Plan on Development'. November 12, Seoul. http://www.g20.utoronto.ca/2010/g20seoul-development.html (December 2014).

G20 (2010). 'Annex III: G20 Anti-Corruption Action Plan'. G20 Agenda for Action on Combating Corruption, Promoting Market Integrity, and Supporting a Clean Business Environment, Seoul, November 12. http://www.g20.utoronto.ca/2010/g20seoul-anticorruption.html (December 2014).

G20 (2010). 'The G20 Seoul Summit Document'. Seoul, November 12. http://www.g20. utoronto.ca/2010/g20seoul-doc.html (December 2014).

G20 (2010). 'The G20 Seoul Summit Leaders' Declaration'. Seoul, November 12. http:// www.g20.utoronto.ca/2010/g20seoul.html (December 2014).

G20 (2010). 'The G20 Toronto Summit Declaration'. Toronto, June 27. http://www.g20. utoronto.ca/2010/to-communique.html (December 2014).

G20 (2010). 'Policy Commitments by G20 Members'. Seoul, November 12. http://www. g20.utoronto.ca/2010/g20seoul-commitments.pdf (December 2014).

G20 (2011). 'Annex to the Cannes Action Plan for Growth and Jobs'. Cannes, November 4. http://www.g20.utoronto.ca/2011/2011-cannes-action-annex-111104-en.pdf (December 2014).

G20 (2011). 'Cannes Action Plan for Growth and Jobs'. Cannes, November 4. http:// www.g20.utoronto.ca/2011/2011-cannes-action-111104-en.html (December 2014).

G20 (2011). 'Cannes Summit Final Declaration – Building Our Common Future: Renewed Collective Action for the Benefit of All'. Cannes, November 4. http://www.g20. utoronto.ca/2011/2011-cannes-declaration-111104-en.html (December 2014).

G20 (2011). 'Communiqué: G20 Leaders Summit'. Cannes, November 4. http://www.g20. utoronto.ca/2011/2011-cannes-communique-111104-en.html (December 2014).

G20 (2012). 'G20 Leaders Declaration'. Los Cabos, June 19. http://www.g20.utoronto. ca/2012/2012-0619-loscabos.html (December 2014).

G20 (2012). 'Los Cabos Growth and Jobs Action Plan'. Los Cabos, June 19. http://www. g20.utoronto.ca/2012/2012-0619-loscabos-actionplan.html (December 2014).

G20 (2012). 'Policy Commitments by G20 Members'. Los Cabos, June 19. http://www. g20.utoronto.ca/2012/2012-0619-loscabos-commitments.pdf (December 2014).

G20 (2013). 'Annex 1: St Petersburg Fiscal Templates – G20 Advanced Economies'. St Petersburg, September 6. http://www.g20.utoronto.ca/2013/Annex_1_-_St_ Petersburg_Fiscal_Strategies___AEs___FINAL.pdf (December 2014).

G20 (2013). 'Annex 2: St Petersburg Fiscal Templates – G20 Emerging Market Economies'. St Petersburg, September 6. http://www.g20.utoronto.ca/2013/Annex_2_-_St_ Petersburg_Fiscal_Strategies___EMEs_FINAL.pdf (December 2014).

BIBLIOGRAPHY

G20 (2013). 'Annex 3: MAP Policy Templates'. St Petersburg, September 6. http://www.g20.utoronto.ca/2013/Annex_3_MAP_Policy_Commitments_by_Members_September_5.pdf (December 2014).

G20 (2013). 'Annex 4: St Petersburg Accountability Assessment'. St Petersburg, September 6. http://www.g20.utoronto.ca/2013/Accountabilty_Assessment_FINAL.pdf (December 2014).

G20 (2013). 'G20 5th Anniversary Vision Statement'. St Petersburg, September 6. http://www.g20.utoronto.ca/2013/2013-0906-vision.html (December 2014).

G20 (2013). 'G20 Leaders Declaration'. St Petersburg, September 6. http://www.g20.utoronto.ca/2013/2013-0906-declaration.html (December 2014).

G20 (2013). 'St Petersburg Accountability Report on G20 Development Commitments'. August 28. http://www.g20.utoronto.ca/2013/Saint_Petersburg_Accountability_Report_on_G20_Development_Commitments.pdf (December 2014).

G20 (2013). 'St Petersburg Action Plan'. St Petersburg, September 6. http://www.g20.utoronto.ca/2013/2013-0906-plan.html (December 2014).

G20 Agriculture Ministers (2011). 'Action Plan on Food Price Volatility and Agriculture'. June 23, Paris. http://www.g20.utoronto.ca/2011/2011-agriculture-plan-en.pdf (December 2014).

G20 Anti-Corruption Working Group (2013). 'St Petersburg Strategic Framework for the G20 Anti-Corruption Working Group'. http://www.g20.utoronto.ca/2013/G20_ACWG_St_Petersburg_Strategic_Framework.pdf (December 2014).

G20 Counter-Summit (2013). 'Declaration of the G20 Counter-Summit'. St Petersburg, September 4. http://www.canadians.org/blog/declaration-g20-counter-summit (December 2014).

G20 Development Working Group (2011). '2011 Report of the Development Working Group'. October 28. http://www.g20.utoronto.ca/2011/2011-cannes-dwg-111028-en.pdf (December 2014).

G20 Development Working Group (2012). '2012 Report of the Development Working Group'. June 19, Los Cabos. http://www.g20.utoronto.ca/2012/2012-0619-dwg.html (December 2014).

G20 Finance Ministers and Central Bank Governors (2012). 'Communiqué of Meeting of G20 Finance Ministers and Central Bank Governors'. Mexico City, November 5. http://www.g20.utoronto.ca/2012/2012-121105-finance-en.html (December 2014).

G20 Finance Ministers and Central Bank Governors (2013). 'Communiqué'. Moscow, July 20. http://www.g20.utoronto.ca/2013/2013-0720-finance.html (December 2014).

G20 Framework Working Group (2012). 'Proposal: Framework Working Group's 2013 Work Plan'. November 1. http://en.g20.ria.ru/load/780982134 (December 2014).

G20 Research Group and International Organisations Research Institute (2012). '2011 Cannes G20 Summit Final Compliance Report'. June 16. http://www.g20.utoronto.ca/compliance/2011cannes-final/ (December 2014).

G20 Research Group and International Organisations Research Institute (2013). '2012 Los Cabos G20 Summit Final Compliance Report'. September 4. http://www.g20.utoronto.ca/compliance/2012loscabos-final (December 2014).

G20 Study Group on Financing for Investment (2013). 'G20 Workplan on Financing for Investment Study Group's Findings and Ways Forward'. July, G20 Russian presidency. http://en.g20russia.ru/load/782804292 (December 2014).

G20–B20 Dialogue Efficiency Task Force (2013). 'From Toronto to Saint Petersburg: Assessing G20-B20 Engagement Effectiveness'. June, International Organisations Research Institute and G20 Research Group. http://www.g20.utoronto.ca/g20-b20 (December 2014),

G(irls)20 Summit (2013). 'Communiqué'. June 19, Moscow. http://www.girls20summit. com/wp-content/uploads/2013-communique-english.pdf (December 2014).

Gates, Bill (2011). 'Innovation with Impact: Financing 21st Century Development'. Report to G20 leaders at the Cannes Summit, November. http://www.gatesfoundation.org/~/media/GFO/Documents/2011%20G20%20Report%20PDFs/Full%20Report/g20reportenglish.pdf (December 2014).

Gill, Indermit S. and Martin Raiser (2012). *Golden Growth: Restoring the Lustre of the European Economic Model*. Washington DC: World Bank. http://documents.worldbank.org/curated/en/2012/04/16234385/golden-growth-restoring-lustre-european-economic-model (December 2014).

Gilman, Martin (2010). 'What Comes after the G20?' *International Organisations Research Journal* (5): 121–22. http://iorj.hse.ru/data/2011/03/15/1211463629/13.pdf (December 2014).

Global Trade Alert (2013). 'Statistics: Worldwide'. http://www.globaltradealert.org/ (December 2014).

Global University Summit (2013). 'Universities and Economic Growth: Pre-summit Report'. May 28–30, London. http://gus2013.org/files/9513/6938/2184/Global_University_Summit_-_pre-Summit_report.pdf (December 2014).

Grant, Ruth W. and Robert O. Keohane (2005). 'Accountability and Abuses of Power in World Politics'. *American Political Science Review* 99(1): 29–43. doi: 10.1017. S0003055405051476.

Guebert, Jenilee and Caroline Bracht (2010). 'Assessing the Results and Impacts of G8 Accountability Reports to Help Pave the Way Forward'. Paper prepared for Partnership for Progress: From the 2010 Muskoka-Toronto Summits to the Seoul Summit, 27–28 October, Moscow.

Hajnal, Peter I. (1989). *The Seven-Power Summit: Documents from the Summits of Industrialized Countries, 1975–1989*. Millwood NY: Kraus International Publishers.

Hajnal, Peter I., ed. (2002). *Civil Society in the Information Age*. Aldershot: Ashgate.

Hajnal, Peter I. (2007). *The G8 System and the G20: Evolution, Role, and Documentation*. Aldershot: Ashgate.

Hajnal, Peter I. (2011). 'Civil Society and G8 Accountability'. In *Building Global Democracy? Civil Society and Accountable Global Governance*, Jan Aart Scholte, ed. Cambridge: Cambridge University Press, pp. 182–205.

Hajnal, Peter I. (2014). *The G20: Evolution, Interrelationships, Documentation*. Farnham: Ashgate.

Hamilton, Karen (2010). 'Inspired Leadership'. In *G8 & G20: The 2010 Canadian Summits*, John J. Kirton and Madeline Koch, eds. London: Newsdesk, p. 308. www.g8.utoronto. ca/newsdesk/g8g20 (December 2014).

BIBLIOGRAPHY

Hamilton, Karen and Charles Reed (2013). 'After 13 Years, The Millennium Development Goals Are Still Pertinent'. In *The UK Summit: The G8 at Lough Erne 2013*, John J. Kirton and Madeline Koch, eds. London: Newsdesk, pp. 234–35. http://www.g8.utoronto.ca/newsdesk/lougherne (December 2014).

Hampson, Fen Osler and Paul Heinbecker (2011). 'The "New" Multilateralism of the Twenty-First Century'. *Global Governance* 17(3): 299–310.

Harper, Stephen (2010). 'Statement by the Prime Minister at the Clsoing of the G20 Summit'. Toronto, June 27. http://www.g20.utoronto.ca/2010/to-harper-en.html (December 2014).

High-Level Panel of Eminent Persons on the Post-2015 Development Agenda (2013). 'A New Global Partnership: Eradicate Poverty and Transform Economies through Sustainable Development'. United Nations, New York. http://www.post2015hlp.org/wp-content/uploads/2013/05/UN-Report.pdf (March 2014).

Hodges, Michael R., John J. Kirton, and Joseph P. Daniels, eds (1999). *The G8's Role in the New Millennium*. Aldershot: Ashgate.

Ikenberry, G. John (2001). *After Victory: Institutions, Strategic Restraint, and the Rebuilding of Order after Major Wars*. Princeton: Princeton University Press.

Ikenberry, G. John (2011). *Liberal Leviathan: The Origins, Crisis, and Transformation of the American World Order*. Princeton: Princeton University Press.

Indigenous Peoples Summit (2008). 'Nibutani Declaration of the 2008 Indigenous Peoples Summit in Ainu Mosir'. July 4, Ainu Mosir (Hokkaido), Japan. http://www.galdu.org/govat/doc/nibutani_declaration_of_indigenous_peoples_final_copy3.pdf (December 2014).

InterAction (2012). '2013 G8 Summit Recommendations: Lough Erne, United Kingdom'. Washington DC, December. http://www.interaction.org/document/2013-g8-summit-recommendations-lough-erne-united-kingdom (December 2014).

Interfaith Leaders Summit (2010). 'A Time for Inspired Leadership and Action'. 23, June, Winnipeg. http://www.faithchallengeg8.com/pdfs/2010%20Interfaith%20Statement%20-%20English.pdf (December 2014).

Interfaith Leaders Summit (2011). 'The Bordeaux G8 Religious Leaders' Summit'. 23–24, May, Bordeaux. http://www.g8.utoronto.ca/interfaith/2011-interfaith-leaders-en.pdf (December 2014).

Interfaith Leaders Summit (2011). 'Statement of the Bordeaux Religious Leaders Summit'. May 23–24, Bordeaux. http://www.g8.utoronto.ca/interfaith/2011-interfaith-leaders-en.pdf (December 2014).

International Labour Organization, Organisation for Economic Co-operation and Development, International Monetary Fund, et al. (2012). 'Boosting Jobs and Living Standards in G20 Countries'. A joint report prepared for the G20, June. http://www.ilo.org/wcmsp5/groups/public/---dgreports/---dcomm/documents/publication/wcms_183705.pdf (December 2014).

International Monetary Fund (2010). 'G20 Mutual Assessment Process: Alternative Policy Scenarios'. June 26, Washington DC. http://www.imf.org/external/np/g20/pdf/062710a.pdf (December 2014).

International Monetary Fund (2010). 'Navigating the Fiscal Challenges Ahead'. Fiscal Monitor, May, Washington DC. http://www.imf.org/external/pubs/ft/fm/2010/fm1001.pdf (December 2014).

International Monetary Fund (2012). 'Toward Lasting Stability and Growth: Umbrella Report for G20 Mutual Assessment Progress'. Washington DC. http://www.imf.org/external/np/g20/pdf/062012.pdf (December 2014).

International Monetary Fund (2012). 'World Economic Outlook: Coping with High Debt and Sluggish Growth'. October, Washington DC. http://www.imf.org/external/pubs/ft/weo/2012/02/ (December 2014).

International Monetary Fund (2013). 'Imbalances and Growth: Update of Staff Sustainability Assessments for G20 Musual Assessment Process'. September, Washington DC. http://www.imf.org/external/np/g20/pdf/map2013/map2013.pdf (December 2014).

International Organisations Research Institute and G20 Research Group (2012). 'Mapping G20 Decisions Implementation: How G20 Is Delivering on the Decisions Made'. National Research University Higher School of Economics, Moscow. https://www.hse.ru/data/2012/12/13/1301054564/Mapping_G20_Decisions_Implementation_full_report.pdf (December 2014).

International Organisations Research Institute and G20 Research Group (2013). 'Tracking Progress on the G20 Development Commitments'. https://www.hse.ru/data/2013/02/26/1307405287/Development%20Report%20130226.pdf (December 2014).

International Organizations Research Institute (2009). 'G20 London Summit Commitments Compliance Report 2009'. September 18, Moscow. http://www.g20.utoronto.ca/analysis/hse/2009-london-compliance.pdf (December 2014).

International Organizations Research Institute and G20 Research Group (2010). '2009 Pittsburgh G20 Summit Compliance Report'. June 21. http://www.g20.utoronto.ca/analysis/Pittsburgh_G20_compliance_report.pdf (December 2014).

IO Working Group (2013). 'G20 Action Plan on the Development of Local Currency Bond Markets: Implementation Report to G20 Ministers and Central Bank Governors'. January. http://en.g20russia.ru/load/783432293 (December 2014).

Juricevic, Diana (2000). 'Controlling for Domestic-Level Commitments: An Analysis of the Authoritative National Commitments Made in Canada and the United States from 1995 to 2000'. G8 Research Group. http://www.g8.utoronto.ca/scholar/juricevic2000/juricevic.pdf (December 2014).

Keohane, Robert O. (2002). 'Global Governance and Democratic Accountability'. Chapter prepared for a volume to be edited by David Held and Mathias Koenig-Archibugi from the Miliband Lectures, London School of Economics, Durham NC. http://unpan1.un.org/intradoc/groups/public/documents/apcity/unpan034133.pdf (December 2014).

Keohane, Robert O. (2006). 'Accountability in World Politics'. *Scandinavian Political Studies* 29(2): 75–87.

Keohane, Robert O. and Joseph S. Nye (1977). *Power and Interdependence: World Politics in Transition*. Boston: Little, Brown.

BIBLIOGRAPHY

Kirsch, David (2013). Accountability in Children's Development Organizations, PhD thesis, Institute of Medical Science, University of Toronto, Toronto. Unpublished.

Kirton, John J. (1989). 'Introduction'. In *The Seven-Power Summit: Documents from the Summits of Industrialized Countries, 1975–1989*, Peter I. Hajnal, ed. Millwood NY: Kraus International Publishers.

Kirton, John J. (2006). 'Explaining Compliance with G8 Finance Commitments: Agency, Institutionalization, and Structure'. *Open Economies Review* 17(4): 459–75.

Kirton, John J. (2006). 'Implementing G8 Economic Commitments: How International Institutions Help'. *International Affairs* (6): 31–58. http://ecsocman.hse.ru/hsedata/2011/02/28/1211519513/Implementing_G8_economic_commitments.PDF (December 2014).

Kirton, John J., ed. (2009). *International Organization*. Farnham: Ashgate.

Kirton, John J. (2013). *G20 Governance for a Globalized World*. Farnham: Ashgate.

Kirton, John J. (2013). 'A Summit of Significant Success: Prospects for the G8 Leaders at Lough Erne'. June 12. http://www.g8.utoronto.ca/evaluations/2013lougherne/kirton-prospects-2013.html (December 2014).

Kirton, John J., Caroline Bracht and Leanne Rasmussen (2012). 'Implementing the G20 Seoul Development and Employment Commitments: An Assessment'. Paper produced with the financial support of the International Labour Office through the ILO–Korea Partnership Program, G20 Research Group, Toronto. http://www.g20.utoronto.ca/biblio/SDC_Assessment.pdf (December 2014).

Kirton, John J. and Jenilee Guebert (2010). 'North American Health Governance: Shocks, Summitry, and Societal Support'. *Revista Norteamericana* 5(1): 221–44. http://www.scielo.org.mx/scielo.php?script=sci_arttext&pid=S1870-35502010000100008 (July 2012).

Kirton, John J. and Jenilee Guebert (2011). 'Shaping a United Nations High-Level Meeting on Non-communicable Diseases that Delivers'. Paper commissioned by the Pan American Health Organization/World Health Organization, Global Health Diplomacy Program, Toronto. http://www.ghdp.utoronto.ca/pubs/shaping-un-hlm.pdf (December 2014).

Kirton, John J., Jenilee Guebert, and Julia Kulik (2014). 'G8 Health Governance for Africa'. In *Moving Health Sovereignty in Africa: Disease, Governance, Climate Change*, John Kirton, Andrew F. Cooper, Franklyn Lisk, et al., eds. Farnham: Ashgate, pp. 127–63.

Kirton, John J. and Madeline Koch, eds (2013). *Russia's G20 Summit: St. Petersburg 2013*. London: Newsdesk. http://www.g8.utoronto.ca/newsdesk/stpetersburg (March 2014).

Kirton, John J. and Madeline Koch, eds (2013). *The UK Summit: The G8 at Lough Erne 2013*. London: Newsdesk. http://www.g8.utoronto.ca/newsdesk/lougherne (March 2014).

Kirton, John J. and Julia Kulik (2012). 'The Shortcomings of the G20 Los Cabos Summit'. G20 Research Group, June 27. http://www.g20.utoronto.ca/analysis/120627-kirton-kulik-shortcomings.html (December 2014).

Kirton, John J. and Julia Kulik (2012). 'A Summit of Significant Success: G20 Los Cabos Leaders Deliver the Desired Double Dividend'. G20 Research Group, June 19. http://www.g20.utoronto.ca/analysis/120619-kirton-success.html (December 2014).

Kirton, John J., Julia Kulik, and Caroline Bracht (2014). 'The Political Process in Global Health and Nutrition Governance: The G8's 2010 Muskoka Initiative on Maternal,

Child, and Newborn Health'. *Annals of the New York Academy of Sciences* 40: 1–15. doi: 10.1111/nyas.12494.

Kirton, John J. and Marina V. Larionova, eds (2012). *BRICS: The 2012 New Delhi Summit*. London: Newsdesk. http://www.brics.utoronto.ca/newsdesk/delhi (March 2014).

Kirton, John J., Marina V. Larionova, and Paolo Savona, eds (2010). *Making Global Economic Governance Effective: Hard and Soft Law Institutions in a Crowded World*. Farnham: Ashgate.

Knaack, Peter and Saori N Katada (2013). 'Fault Lines and Issue Linkages at the G20: New Challenges for Global Economic Governance'. *Global Policy* 4(3): 236–46.

Kokotsis, Eleanore (1999). *Keeping International Commitments: Compliance, Credibility, and the G7, 1988–1995*. New York: Garland.

Kokotsis, Eleanore and John J. Kirton (1997). 'National Compliance with Environmental Regimes: The Case of the G7, 1988–1995'. Paper prepared for the annual convention of the International Studies Association, 18–22 March, Toronto.

Kokotsis, Ella (2010). 'The Muskoka Accountability Report: Assessing the Written Record'. Paper prepared for Partnership for Progress: From the 2010 Muskoka-Toronto Summits to the Seoul Summit, 27–28 October, Moscow.

Kokotsis, Ella and Joseph P. Daniels (1999). 'G8 Summits and Compliance'. In *The G8's Role in the New Millennium*, Michael R. Hodges, John J. Kirton, and Joseph P. Daniels, eds. Aldershot: Ashgate, pp. 75–91.

Krasner, Stephen (1983). 'Structural Causes and Regime Consequences: Regimes as Intervening Variables'. In *International Regimes*, Stephen Krasner, ed. Ithaca NY: Cornell University Press, pp. 1–21.

Kremlin (2008). 'BRIC Leaders Meet'. Moscow, July 9. http://www.brics.utoronto.ca/docs/080709-leaders.html (November 2014).

Larionova, Marina V. (2011). 'Assessing G8 and G20 Effectiveness in Global Governance So Far'. Paper prepared for Princeton Global Governance Conference on Rivalry and Partnership: The Struggle for a New Global Governance Leadership, 14–15 January, Princeton NJ.

Larionova, Marina V. and John J. Kirton (2013). 'Prospects for the BRICS Summit'. In *Invest in South Africa 2013*, Barry Davies, ed. London: Newsdesk, p. 113. http://www.brics.utoronto.ca/newsdesk/durban (March 2014).

Lewallen, Ann-Elise (2008). 'Indigenous at Last! Ainu Grassroots Organizing and the Indigenous Peoples Summit in Ainu Mosir'. *Asia-Pacific Journal: Japan Focus* 48 (November). http://www.japanfocus.org/-ann_elise-lewallen/2971 (December 2014).

Lowy Institute on International Policy (2014). 'Think20 2014: A Progress Report on Australia's g20 Presidency'. Sydney. http://www.lowyinstitute.org/files/think20-2014-a-progress-report.pdf (December 2014).

McKibbon, Warwick J., Andrew B. Stoeckel, and YingYing Lu (2012). 'Global Fiscal Adjustment and Trade Rebalancing'. Policy Research Working Paper 6044, World Bank, Washington DC. doi: 10.1596/1813-9450-6044.

Mexico. Secretaría de Relaciones Exteriores (2012). 'Think 20 Meeting Concludes Successfully'. Press release 64, Mexico City, February 29. http://saladeprensa.sre.gob.mx/index.php/es/comunicados/1208-064 (December 2014).

BIBLIOGRAPHY

Minsky, Hyman (1992). 'The Financial Instability Hypothesis'. Working Paper No. 74, May, Levy Economics Institute of Bard College, Annandale-on-Hudson NY. http://www.levyinstitute.org/pubs/wp74.pdf (December 2014).

Mobiliations G8 G20 (2011). 'Propositions clés portées au sein de la Coalition G8G20'. October 24. https://web.archive.org/web/20120227090340/http://www.mobilisationsg8g20.org/la-coalition/article/propositions-cles-portees-au-sein-de-la-coalition-g8g20.html (December 2014).

New Rules for Global Finance (2012). 'Revised FSB Charter: Shift Toward Improved Transparency and Inclusion'. Washington DC. http://www.new-rules.org/news/program-updates/411-revised-fsb-charter-shift-toward-improved-transparency-and-inclusion (December 2014).

New York Times (2012). 'The Troupble with Mrs. Merkel'. June 19. http://www.nytimes.com/2012/06/20/opinion/the-trouble-with-ms-merkel.html?_r=0 (December 2014).

Nye, Joseph S. (2011). *The Future of Power*. New York: PublicAffairs.

One (2012). 'The 2012 Data Report: Europe's African Promise'. July 6. http://one-org.s3.amazonaws.com/us/wp-content/uploads/2012/11/dr2012.pdf (December 2014).

Organisation for Economic Co-operation and Development (2012). 'Economic Policy Reforms: Going for Growth 2012'. Paris. http://www.oecd.org/eco/monetary/economicpolicyreformsgoingforgrowth2012.htm (December 2014).

Oxfam (2010). 'The Making of a Seoul Development Consensus: THe Essential Development Agenda for the G20'. October 7. http://www.oxfam.org/en/policy/making-seoul-development-consensus (December 2014).

Oxfam (2013). 'Fixing the Cracks in Tax: A Plan of Action'. September 3. http://www.oxfam.org/en/policy/fixing-cracks-tax-plan-action (December 2014).

Oxfam (2013). 'Oxfam Verdict on the G20 Russia Summit'. Press release, September 6. http://www.oxfam.org/en/pressroom/pressrelease/2013-09-06/oxfam-verdict-g20-summit-russia (December 2014).

Parker, George, Charles Clover, and Courtney Weaver (2013). 'G20 Leaders Split over Syria'. *Financial Times*, September 6. http://www.ft.com/intl/cms/s/0/5ba75aac-1619-11e3-a57d-00144feabdc0.html#axzz2zCeogh74 (December 2014).

People's Summit (2009). 'Vision Statement of the People's Summit: "Another World Is Possible"'. Pittsburgh. https://web.archive.org/web/20120227011442/http://www.peoplessummit.com/page/peoples-summit (December 2014).

People's Summit (2010). 'The 2010 People's Summit: Building a Movement for a Just World'. https://web.archive.org/web/20100612154338/http://peoplessummit2010.ca/section/2 (December 2014).

People's Summit (2010). 'The 2010 People's Summit: Program'. http://peoplessummit2010.ca/section/18 (June 2010).

Post Globalization Initiative (2013). 'St. Petersburg Counter Summit Opposes US Plans'. September 13. http://www.pglobal.org/news/548/ (December 2014).

Postel-Vinay, Karoline (2011). *Le G20, laboratoire d'un monde émergent*. Paris: Les Presses de Sciences Po.

Powell, Joseph (2012). 'G20 Is Getting a Reputation for Over-Promising and Under-Delivering'. (Blog). One. 21 June. http://www.one.org/international/blog/g20-is-getting-a-reputation-for-over-promising-and-under-delivering (December 2014).

Powell, Joseph (2012). 'Good Intentions Continue at G20, But Promises on Development Are Not Being Kept'. (Blog). One. 20 June. http://www.one.org/international/blog/good-intentions-continue-at-g20-but-promises-on-development-are-not-being-kept (December 2014).

Put People First (2009). 'Put People First G20 Counter Conference Report and Audio'. November 7–8. http://www.putpeoplefirst.org.uk/2009/12/put-people-first-g20-counter-conference-report-and-audio/ (December 2014).

Putnam, Robert and Nicholas Bayne (1984). *Hanging Together: Co-operation and Conflict in the Seven-Power Summit*. 1st ed. Cambridge MA: Harvard University Press.

Putnam, Robert and Nicholas Bayne (1987). *Hanging Together: Co-operation and Conflict in the Seven-Power Summit*. 2nd ed. London: Sage Publications.

Qureshi, Zia (2010). 'G20: Global Growth and Development Agenda'. *International Organisations Research Journal* (5): 25–30. http://iorj.hse.ru/data/2011/03/15/1211462180/6.pdf (December 2014).

Raustiala, Kal and Anne-Marie Slaughter (2002). 'International Law, International Relations, and Compliance'. In *Handbook of International Relations*, Walter Carlsnaes, Thomas Risse, and Beth A. Simmons, eds. London: Sage Publications, pp. 538–58.

Roubini, Nouriel (2011). 'That Stalling Feeling'. Project Syndicate (Blog). 21 June. http://www.project-syndicate.org/commentary/that-stalling-feeling (December 2014).

Rude, Christopher and Sara Burke (2009). 'Towards a Socially Responsible and Democratic Global Economic System: Transparency, Accountability, and Governance'. Briefing Paper 15, November, Friedrich Ebert Stiftung, New York. http://library.fes.de/pdf-files/bueros/usa/06778-20091105.pdf (December 2014).

Ruggie, John G. (1983). 'International Regimes, Transactions, and Change: Embedded Liberalism in the Postwar Economic Order'. In *International Regimes*, Stephen D. Krasner, ed. Ithaca: Cornell University Press, pp. 195–232.

Ruggie, John G. (1993). 'Territoriality and Beyond: Problematizing Modernity in International Relations'. *International Organization* 47(1): 139–74.

Sachs, Jeffrey and Steve Killelea (2011). 'Holding G8 Accountability to Account'. Institute for Economics and Peace and the Earth Institute, Columbia University. http://economicsandpeace.org/wp-content/uploads/2011/10/Holding-G8-Accountability-to-Account.pdf (December 2014).

Salutin, Rick (2010). 'What Happened at Jailapalooza?' *Globe and Mail*, August 27. http://www.theglobeandmail.com/globe-debate/what-happened-at-jailapalooza/article1378333/ (December 2014).

Savona, Paolo, John J. Kirton, and Chiara Oldani, eds (2011). *Global Financial Crisis: Global Impact and Solutions*. Farnham: Ashgate.

Scholte, Jan Aart, ed. (2011). *Building Global Democracy? Civil Society and Accountable Global Governance*. Cambridge: Cambridge University Press.

BIBLIOGRAPHY

Scholte, Jan Aart (2011). 'Global Governance, Accountability, and Civil Society'. In *Building Global Democracy? Civil Society and Accountable Global Governance*, Jan Aart Scholte, ed. Cambridge: Cambridge University Press, pp. 8–41.

Think 20 (2012). 'Report to G20 Sherpas'. March, Mexico City. http://think20. consejomexicano.org/?page_id=69 (December 2014).

Think 20 (2012). 'Think 20 Summary Report by Co-chairs'. Moscow, December 13. http:// en.g20russia.ru/docs/think_20/summary_report.html (December 2014).

Transparency International (2013). 'Corruption Perceptions Index'. http://www. transparency.org/cpi2013 (December 2014).

United States (2010). 'The National Security Strategy'. Washington DC, May. http:// www.whitehouse.gov/sites/default/files/rss_viewer/national_security_strategy.pdf (December 2014).

United States Federal Reserve System (2014). 'Press Release'. January 29, Washington DC. http://www.federalreserve.gov/newsevents/press/monetary/20140129a.htm (December 2014).

Université de Franche-Comté (2010). 'Welcome to University Summit 2011'. April 26, Dijon, France. https://web.archive.org/web/20140509011323/http://www.univ-fcomte.fr/download/partage/document/actualite/lettre-flash/10-ufc-lettre10.pdf (December 2014).

Vestergaard, Jakob and Robert H. Wade (2012). 'Establishing a New Global Economic Council: Governance Reform at the G20, the IMF and the World Bank'. *Global Policy* 3(3): 257–69.

von Furstenberg, George M. (2008). 'Performance Measurement under Rational International Overpromising Regimes'. *Journal of Public Policy* 28(3): 261–87.

von Furstenberg, George M. and Joseph P. Daniels (1992). *Economic Summit Declarations, 1975–1989: Examining the Written Record of International Cooperation* (Princeton Studies in International Finance No. 72). Princeton: Princeton University Press.

World Bank (2011). 'Rebalancing, Growth, and Development: An Interconnected Agenda'. Paper prepared for the G20, October, Washington DC. http://siteresources. worldbank.org/DEC/Resources/84797-1320153303397/Rebalancing_Growth_and_ Development-WB_paper_for_G20.pdf (December 2014).

World Bank (2012). 'Inclusive Green Growth: The Pathway to Sustainable Development'. May, Washington DC. http://siteresources.worldbank.org/EXTSDNET/Resources/ Inclusive_Green_Growth_May_2012.pdf (December 2014).

World Bank (2012). 'Restoring and Sustaining Growth'. Paper prepared for the G20 finance ministers and central bank governors, June 19, Washington DC. http://go.worldbank. org/Q3U4L7U9L0 (December 2014).

World Bank (2012). 'World Development Report 2013: Jobs'. Washington DC. http:// go.worldbank.org/TM7GTEB8U0 (December 2014).

World Bank (2013). 'China 2030: Building a Modern, Harmonious, and Creative Society'. Washington DC. http://documents.worldbank.org/curated/en/2013/03/17494829/ china-2030-building-modern-harmonious-creative-society (December 2014).

World Bank (2013). 'Doing Business'. Database, Washington DC. http://data.worldbank. org/data-catalog/doing business-database (December 2014).

World Bank (2013). 'Doing Business 2013: Smarter Regulations for Small and Medium-Size Enterprises'. Washington DC. http://www.doingbusiness.org/~/media/GIAWB/Doing%20Business/Documents/Annual-Reports/English/DB13-full-report.pdf (December 2014).

World Bank (2013). 'Global Economic Prospects January 2013: Assuring Growth over the Medium Term'. January 15, Washington DC. http://go.worldbank.org/YF5N2YO550 (December 2014).

World Bank (2013). 'Long-Term Investment Financing for Growth and Development: Umbrella Paper'. Prepared for the G20 finance ministers and central bank governors, February. http://en.g20russia.ru/load/781255094 (December 2014).

World Bank (2013). 'Temporary Trade Barriers Database Including the Global Antidumping Database'. Washington DC. http://data.worldbank.org/data-catalog/temporary-trade-barriers-database (December 2014).

World Bank (2014). 'Enterprise Surveys'. Database, Washington DC. http://www.enterprisesurveys.org (December 2014).

World Economic Forum (2011). 'Global Risks 2011, Sixth Edition'. Davos. http://reports.weforum.org/global-risks-2011/ (December 2014).

World Economic Forum (2012). 'Global Risks 2012, Seventh Edition'. Davos. http://reports.weforum.org/global-risks-2012/ (December 2014).

Index

Abbott, Tony 52
academia 16, 206, 208, 217, 221, 222, 223, 233, 234, 236, 238, 239, 249, 259, 261, 262, 263
accountability 82–3, 84, 86–8, 106, 114, 118, 120, 174, 175, 183–93, 201–24, 233–9, 241–50, 258–9, 261–3
  see also self-accountability; accountability assessments
  accountability, defined 202–3
accountability assessments, G8 219
accountability assessments, G20 220–22
Accountability Assessment Framework 84
Accountability Working Group 187, 192, 214, 244
Action Plan on Asset Recovery 105
Action Plan on Food Price Volatility and Agriculture 154
Action Plan on Nuclear Safety 96
ActionAid 205, 207
advanced economies 48, 49, 112, 118, 119, 123, 124–5, 129, 131, 132, 133, 135, 136, 152, 159
  see also developed countries; industrialized countries
Afghanistan 21, 99, 100
Africa 102, 186, 204, 236
Africa Partnership Forum 205
African Development Bank 222
African Union 100, 213, 222, 235, 236, 237
Agricultural Market Information System 84
agriculture 126, 153–4, 156
aid 47, 98, 185, 188, 189, 190, 191, 219, 223, 261
  see also ODA
Algeria 21
altermondialiste 210
alternative summits 210–14
Amnesty International 205, 207
Annan, Kofi 100, 119
Another World Is Possible 210

Antalya Summit (G20 2015) 52
Anti-Corruption Action Plan 220
Anti-Corruption Working Group 84, 220, 236
anticorruption see corruption
APEC (Asia-Pacific Economic Cooperation) Forum 16, 28, 243–4
Arab League 100
Argentina 18
Asia–European Union Meeting 28
Asian financial crisis, 1997–99 15, 36, 91, 22
  and G20 16, 22
Assad, Bashir 21
attendance see leaders, attendance
Australia 18, 43, 112, 117
  as G20 host 204, 208
  civil society 204, 208
Axworthy, Lloyd 212

B20 (Business 20) 143–75, 208, 258, 261
  Australia (2014) 204, 209
  Cannes Summit (2012) 204
  corruption 169–71
  creation 143, 145, 204
  employment 162–4
  financial regulation 148–50
  financing for development 171–3
  food security 153–5
  global governance 175
  international monetary system 150–51
  investment 157–60
  Los Cabos Summit (2012) 204
  macroeconomic issues 151–3
  Russia 145, 151
  St Petersburg (2013) 204
  trade 155–7
B20 Global Governance Task Force 173
B20 Task Force on Financing for Growth and Development 171–2
B20 Task Force on Global Economic Policy Imperatives 150

B20 Task Force on Impact and Accountability 174
B20 Task Force on Innovation and Development as a Global Priority 148, 167, 168
B20 Task Force on Investment and Infrastructure 145
B20 Task Force on Job Creation, Employment, and Investment in Human Capital 145, 163
B20 Task Force on the International Monetary System 150
B20 Task Force on Trade 155
B20 Transparency and Anti-Corruption Task Force 170–71
B20 Working Group on Funding and Nurturing the Small and Medium-Sized Enterprise Sector 166
B20 Working Group on Increasing Access to Healthcare in Developing Countries 172
B20 Working Group on Unleashing Technology-Enabling Productivity Growth 166
B20–L20 Joint Understanding of Key Elements on Quality Apprenticeships 163
Bail Out the People 215
Bali ministerial conference (WTO) 156
Ban Ki-moon 118–19
Bank for International Settlements 45, 85, 236
Basel Committee on Banking Supervision 104, 150
Basel III 23, 149, 156
BASIC (Brazil, Australia, South Africa, Indonesia, Canada) 18
Biological and Toxin Weapons Convention 100
Black Bloc 216
Blair, Tony 103
Bono 204
Brazil 38, 46, 112, 117, 133
Bretton Woods conference 49
Bretton Woods system 48, 50
BRICS 18, 24–5, 41, 50, 86, 118, 123, 242, 247, 255, 256, 257, 260, 261
    agenda 55, 63, 65–7

compliance 245
creation 24
expansion 25
and global financial crisis 65
membership 16, 65
performance 24–5, 33, 255
and risk 63–5
support for G7/8 25
support for G20 25
BRICS development bank 24, 65
BRICS Urbanization Forum 65
Brisbane Summit (G20 2014) 52, 208
    civil society 212
Brookings Institution 206, 219
Brown, Gordon 37
Brundtland, Gro Harlem 119
Brussels Summit (G7 2014) 26n, 218
Bush, George W. 37
business *see* B20; private sector

C20 (Civil 20) 171, 174, 207–8
    France (2011) 208
    Korea (2010) 207
    Moscow (2013) 208
    origin 207
    Russia (2013) 208
Cameron, David 21, 40, 173, 249
'Camp David Accountability Report: Actions, Approach, Results' 190, 219
Camp David Summit (G8 2012) 40, 61, 190–91
Canada 21, 36, 43, 110, 112–13, 116, 189, 212
    as G8 and G20 host 203
    as G8 host 92, 209
    as G20 host 118
Canadian Council of Chief Executives 143
Canadian Council of Churches 212
Cancun climate change conference 97, 110
Cannes Action Plan for Growth and Jobs 150, 220, 221, 235–6
Cannes Summit (G20 2011) 135–7, 150, 153, 158, 161, 172, 204–5
    B20 153, 158, 165, 166, 169, 172, 173
    C20 208, 209
    civil society 209, 211
    demonstrations 216

INDEX

capability 17, 18, 19, 22, 24, 25, 55, 56, 57, 65, 110, 116, 241, 256, 260

capital flows 46, 47, 49, 157–8, 160

causes of success 115–19

CCFD-Terre Solidaire 208, 209

celebrities 204–5

Center for Global Development 219

Centre for Global Studies, University of Victoria 205–6

Centre for International Governance Innovation 206

Chatham House 206

chemical weapons 15, 20, 21, 23

Cheonan 98, 113, 115, 118

China 18, 38, 41, 47, 50, 51, 116, 118, 123, 126, 131, 135, 150

CIVETS (Colombia, Indonesia, Vietnam, Egypt, Turkey, South Africa) 18

Civil 8 207

Civil 20 Task Force on Inequality 61

Civil G20 *see* C20

civil society 16, 116, 187, 192, 201–24, 239, 257, 258, 263, 264

    and accountability 217–23, 258–9

    and BRICS 25

    and Cannes Summit (G20 2011) 209, 211

    defined 201–2

    Korea 209

    Los Cabos Summit (G20 2012) 211

    private sector 202, 203–4

    see also nongovernmental organization

Climate Action Network 205

Climate and Clean Air Coalition 96

climate change 19, 20, 41, 57, 95, 96, 97, 110, 119, 137, 138, 189, 203, 205, 211, 261

climate finance 41, 97, 164, 205

club 16, 117, 256–7

    see also systemic club model

Coalición Mexicana frente al G-20 217

Commonwealth 28, 243

Community Mobilization Network 215

compliance 84–8, 94, 121, 183, 251, 242, 243, 244–9, 262, 263

    BRICS 25, 244

    G8 114, 183, 184, 189, 190–93, 217, 218, 238, 244 5, 258–9

G20 22, 47, 82, 106, 114, 149, 218, 233, 235, 236, 237, 244–6, 249, 258–9

Comprehensive Test Bank Treaty 190

concert equality model 39, 110, 115, 256

connectivity 18, 22, 25, 256

Consumers International 207

Convention on Nuclear Safety 102

Cooper, Andrew F. 207

Cooper, Helene 222

Coordination SUD 208, 209, 211

Copenhagen Accord 189

Copenhagen climate conference 96

corruption 59, 61, 67, 81, 120, 169–71, 174, 175, 184, 219, 220, 237

    B20 169–71

Council of Councils 206

Council on Foreign Relations 206

Counter-Terrorism Action Group 100

Courchene, David 213

Creditor Report System Database 219

crisis management 22, 37, 39, 109, 123, 139, 235, 256

currency war 39, 48

cyber security 19, 57, 63

Daniels, Joseph 183

DATA (Debt, AIDS, Trade, Africa) 204, 218–9

Davutoglu, Ahmet 52

'Deauville Accountability Report—G8 Commitments on Health and Food Security: State of Delivery and Results' 189, 219

Deauville Partnership 21, 100

Deauville Summit (G8 2011) 63, 188–90

debt 51, 48, 49, 50, 51, 119, 123, 125, 151, 152, 223

debt crisis 46–7

    see also sovereign debt crisis

debt relief 112, 114, 185

decision making 56, 57, 77, 78, 83, 238, 239, 259

    see also performance

    BRICS 25, 65

    G7/8 20, 40, 42, 61, 81–2, 83, 99–100, 114

    G20 22, 45, 59, 60, 79, 80, 83, 84, 89, 106, 143–5, 148, 149, 151, 153, 154,

156, 157, 159, 160–66, 168–71, 175, 209, 258
Delhi Summit (BRICS 2012) 65
deliberation 57
    see also performance
    BRICS 25
    G7/8 61, 78–80, 84, 106, 113, 256
    G20 20, 22, 78, 79–80, 113
delivery 242, 244, 246
    BRICS 25
    G7/8 20, 79, 81, 82–3, 86, 88, 106, 114, 187, 189–92, 238
    G20 22, 78, 79, 82–4, 88, 106, 175, 220, 221, 222, 238, 256, 262
    see also compliance
democracy 19, 24, 38, 113, 117, 210, 233, 239, 247
demonstrations 111, 211, 215–17, 224
developed countries 89, 152, 154
    see also advanced economies; industrialized countries
developing countries 38, 51, 59, 60, 65, 84, 98, 101, 119, 131, 132, 135, 154, 159, 165, 169, 172, 185, 190
    see also emerging economies; emerging powers
Development Assistance Committee 188, 218–19
development of global governance 246
    see also performance; direction setting; domestic political management
    G7/8 20, 25, 79, 83, 84, 115
    G20 25, 78, 79, 83, 84, 106
Development Working Group 98, 159, 193, 222, 236, 237
direction setting 57, 246, 248, 262
    G7/8 78, 80, 113, 185, 193, 236
    G20 78, 79, 81, 84, 106, 113, 175, 256, 258
    see also performance
dispute resolution 243, 246
division of labour 35, 40–43, 55–6, 59, 63, 67, 88, 90–91, 102, 106, 109, 110, 113, 114, 115, 203, 250, 257, 258, 262
Doha Round 21, 93–4, 135–7, 155, 156, 157, 249

domestic political management 17, 244, 246
    BRICS 112–13
    domestic political management, G7/8 112
    domestic political management, G20 112–13
    see also performance
Durban climate conference 97
Durban Summit (BRICS 2013) 25

Ease of Doing Business Index 128–30
economic recovery 61, 110, 125, 132, 139
education 163, 169, 166–7, 171, 173
Education for All 81
Edwards, Leonard 117
effectiveness 47, 51, 55, 56, 65, 77–106, 119, 139, 174, 185, 191, 193, 235, 238, 239, 241–50, 258, 259, 260, 262
emerging economies 16, 23, 41, 45, 46, 47, 48, 50, 52, 59, 60, 65, 84, 89, 116, 117, 119, 123, 124, 125, 126, 132, 133, 135, 137, 148, 247, 152, 261
emerging markets and developing economies 50, 84
emerging powers 15, 19, 22, 24, 38, 40, 41, 117
employment 132, 138, 162–4, 166, 166, 172, 174, 175
    B20 162–4
    see also job creation, labour market
energy 40–41, 164–5, 166, 167–9, 261
Enhanced Heavily Indebted Poor Countries Initiative 81
Enterprise Surveys 130
entrepreneurship 152, 163–4, 223
environment 96–7, 118, 132, 137–8, 165, 190, 211, 213
euro crisis 22, 23, 110, 113, 115–16, 118, 120, 123, 125, 222
Euro-Mediterranean Union 28
Europe 20, 35, 36, 37, 47, 48, 49, 51, 110, 116, 124, 125, 133, 223
European Commission 84
European Union 39
    free trade with Canada 21
    free trade with United States 21
exchange rates 46, 47, 48, 150, 151

INDEX

faith leaders 212–13
  see also religious leaders' summits
FATF (Financial Action Task Force) 104
FIM-Forum for Democratic Global
    Governance 206, 207, 209
financial crisis 19, 35
  and United States 36
  as risk 57
  see also Asian financial crisis; euro crisis;
    global financial crisis
financial regulation *see* regulation,
    financial
financial stability 113, 116
financial transaction tax 173, 211, 216
  see also tax
fiscal consolidation 23, 61, 110, 112, 115,
    116, 125, 131, 152, 256
fiscal sustainability 92, 124–5
Flaherty, Jim 204
Fletcher, Stephen 213
food security 57, 61, 65, 67, 98, 153–5,
    189, 190, 219
Ford, Gerald 37
foreign direct investment 158, 160
Forum for the Peoples (Forum des
    Peuples) 211, 216
fossil fuel subsidies 96, 165, 166, 168, 223,
    261
foundations 187, 192
Framework for Strong, Sustainable, and
    Balanced Growth 23, 84, 79, 220,
    221–2, 237, 256
France 21, 255
  as G8 host 110, 189, 208
  as G20 host 60, 110, 154
Francophonie 28
Friedrich-Ebert-Stiftung 206, 214
Friends of the Earth 207
FSB (Financial Stability Board) 45, 50,
    59–60, 83–4, 104, 105, 156, 220,
    222, 235, 236
  G20 45
FSF (Financial Stability Forum) *see* FSB
Fukushima 63, 95

G(irls) 20 Summit 213
G5 (Group of Five) 24, 28, 41
  see also outreach

G7/8
  agenda 55, 61 65–7
  achievements 20–21
  as club 16
  creation 19, 35–6, 45, 255
  and Libya 21
  and Russia 19, 20, 21, 36, 38–9, 116
  chemical weapons 20
  decline 18
  differences from G20 37–40
  as hegemon 41
  expansion 20
  global financial crisis 20
  membership 16–17, 20
  outreach 20, 38, 41
  performance 29–31
  similarity to G20 35–7
  support for BRICS 21–2
  support for G20 21–2
  and risk 61–3
G7 finance ministers and central bank
    governors 36–7
G8 *see* G7/8
G8 Accountability Senior Level Working
    Group 219
G8 Declaration on Preventing Sexual
    Violence in Conflict 204
G8 development ministers 205
G8 foreign ministers 204
G8 Muskoka Declaration: Recovery and
    New Beginnings 219
G8 Parliamentarians' Group 205
G8 Preliminary Accountability Report 185
G8 Research Group 183, 185, 189, 190,
    191, 193, 217–18, 236
G8 Statement on Counter-Terrorism 237
G8/G20 Global Working Group 205
G20 Action Plan to Support the
    Development of Local Currency
    Bond Markets 84
G20
  agenda 37, 55, 59, 65–7
  Asian financial crisis 16
  attendance 51–2
  civil society outreach 204
  as club 16
  compliance 22
  creation 16, 22, 45, 256

differences from G7/8 37–40
euro crisis 23
expansion 23
global financial crisis 16, 77
leaders' level 38, 39
membership 16–17
performance 22–3, 32
as premier forum for economic
    cooperation 23, 36, 65, 77, 84, 104,
    109, 139
and risk 59–61
similarity to G7/8 35–7
as steering committee 22, 38, 77, 109,
    139, 175, 210
and United Nations 104, 118–19
G20 agriculture ministers 37
G20 Anti-Corruption Working Group 81,
    105, 170–71, 174
G20 Basic Set of Financial Inclusion
    Indicators 61
G20 Business Scorecard 236–7
G20 Civil Society Vision for the Russian
    Presidency 208
G20 Climate Finance Study Group 164
G20 Development Action Plan 214
G20 development ministers 37
G20 Energy Sustainability Working Group
    164, 168
G20 finance ministers and central bank
    governors 16, 22, 36–7, 84, 117,
    151, 205, 221, 235, 236, 255, 257
    2013 52
    civil society 210
    creation 16
G20 foreign ministers 23, 37
G20 labour ministers 37
G20 Meltdown 215
G20 Project Preparation Fund 160
G20 Research Group 47, 206, 217–18,
    236, 244
G20 Seoul Summit Document 220
G20 Seoul Summit Leaders Declaration
    220
G20 Study Group on Financing for
    Investment Work Plan 153, 160
G20 Task Force on Employment 237
G20 tourism ministers 37n
G20 Working Group on Employment 148

G20–B20 Dialogue Efficiency Task Force
    204
Gates, Bill 204–5
GCAP (Global Call to Action against
    Poverty) 205, 207, 217
GDP (gross domestic product) 45–6, 126,
    131
Geldof, Bob 204
Geneva Communiqué 100
Geneva peace process 21
Genoa, demonstrations (2001) 111
Germany 49, 138, 189, 209
Giscard d'Estaing, Valéry 36
Gleneagles Plan of Action: Climate
    Change, Clean Energy, and
    Sustainable Development 95
Gleneagles Summit (G8 2005) 98, 103,
    112, 186, 204, 207, 212, 218, 236
Global Agricultural Geo-monitoring
    Initiative 84
global financial crisis 15, 36, 45, 46–7, 48,
    96, 120, 123, 124, 128, 132, 139,
    256
    and BRICS 24
    effects 46–7
    and G7/8 20, 85, 106
    and G20 22, 85
    and trade 134
    United States 15
Global Fund on HIV/AIDS, Tuberculosis
    and Malaria 119
global governance 38, 41, 42, 65, 67, 77,
    88, 119, 120, 173–4, 193
    and B20 175, 204
global governance failure 56, 57, 59, 61,
    63, 67, 260
    see also development of global
    governance; global governance
    functions
global governance functions 17, 77–88,
    106, 236, 244, 247, 256, 257
    see also decision making; deliberation;
    delivery; performance
Global Partnership against the Spread of
    Weapons and Materials of Mass
    Destruction 81, 99, 102, 236, 256
Global Partnership for Financial Inclusion
    61

INDEX

Global Strategy for Women's and Children's Health 189
Global Trade Alert 235, 236, 237, 249
Global University Summit 214
Global Week of Action 216
globalization 16, 22, 18–19, 36, 38, 43, 46, 49, 113
  as risk 61
  negative effects 61
Greece 23, 110, 115, 116
Green Climate Fund 97–8
green growth 80, 98, 118, 137–8, 145, 164–6, 167, 168, 169, 175, 222
greenhouse gases 57, 86, 168
Greenpeace 205, 207
Griffith University 212
Group of Five *see* G5
Guidelines for Public Debt Management 151
Guiding Principles to Combat Solicitation 171

Hague, William 204
Haiti 99, 114, 120
Halifax Initiative 205, 206, 207
Hamilton, Karen 212
Hampson, Fen Osler 222
Harper, Stephen 112, 117, 118, 119, 193, 204, 219
health 18, 41, 119, 138, 172, 189, 190, 258, 261
  see also maternal, newborn and child health; noncommunicable diseases
hegemony 41, 49, 116, 241
Heinbecker, Paul 222
Heinrich Böll Foundation 206, 214
High-Level Anti-Corruption Conference for G20 Governments and Business 171
High-Level Panel for Infrastructure Investment 158, 172
HIPCs (heavily indebted poor countries) 81
HSE (National Research University Higher School of Economics) 184, 185, 190, 191, 193, 217–18, 236, 244
human capital 162–4
Human Rights Watch 205, 207

Hurricane Katrina 19

IBSA (India-Brazil-South Africa) Dialogue Forum 28, 41
ICT (information and communications technology) 18, 24, 145, 148, 154, 156, 166–7, 171, 175, 204
  and agriculture 154
IFIs *see* international financial institutions
ILO (International Labour Organization) 166, 220, 237
imbalance 47, 49, 59, 61, 91, 218, 220, 221, 223, 256
  current account 152
  external 92, 123, 124, 126, 131
  fiscal 57, 59, 61, 65, 93
  labour market 57, 59, 67
  payment 48
  trade 46, 49
'Imbalances and Growth: Update of Staff Sustainability Assessments for G20 Mutual Assessment Process' 221
IMF 15, 23, 45, 47, 50, 51, 84, 116, 151, 220, 237, 242, 248, 260
  and euro crisis 23
  financial crisis 47, 116
  and G20 45
  reform 23, 24, 51, 84, 110, 150
  Seoul Summit 49
  and United States 50
income disparity 59–60
  as risk 56, 57, 59, 60, 61, 63, 65, 67, 261
India 46, 65, 118, 130, 132, 133
indigenous peoples 215
Indigenous Peoples' Summit 213–14
Indonesia 18, 46, 130
industrialized countries 16, 41, 118
  see also advanced economies; developed countries
inequality 56, 61, 126
infrastructure 23, 41, 56, 65, 67, 106, 130, 138, 145, 160–62
  investment in 124, 126, 131–2, 158, 159, 161, 223
Infrastructure Crisis Facility 98
Infrastructure Productivity Institute 161
InterAction 208, 209
Interfaith Partnership 212

International Atomic Energy Agency 63, 96, 102
International Chamber of Commerce 204, 236–7
International Civil Aviation Organization 96
International Energy Agency 169
International Energy Forum 169
international financial institutions 150, 172, 221, 256
   reform of 83, 89, 114, 261
International Maritime Organization 96
International Model Investment Treaty 158
International Monetary and Finance Committee 248
international monetary system 49, 150–51, 175
International Organisations Research Institute *see* HSE
International Seminar on Alternatives to G20 211
International Trade Union Confederation 205
internet 63, 166
investment 45–6, 51, 94, 113, 120, 124, 126, 128–30, 133, 137, 138, 184, 175, 237, 260
   financing for 23, 60, 84, 161
   B20 145, 152, 156, 157–60, 164–6, 169
   see also infrastructure, investment in
IOSCO (International Organization of Securities Commissions) 104
Iran 110, 115, 116, 117, 118, 119
Israel 15, 99
Italy 43, 129, 184, 188, 189

Japan 21, 35, 43, 49, 51, 52, 113, 116, 118, 125, 189, 218
job creation 90, 132–4, 139, 172
   see also employment; labour; unemployment
Joint Action Week 211
Joint Oil Data Initiative 168
Jolie, Angelina 204
Jubilee Debt Campaign 207
Jubilee Movement 205
Junior 8 207, 214

Kan, Naoto 112

Kananaskis Summit (G8 2002) 81, 209, 236
Kenya 21
Keohane, Robert 239
Kirton, John J. 222
Kokotsis, Ella 183, 217
Korea 43, 50, 89, 98–9, 110, 116, 118, 138, 203
   Cheonan 98, 113
   civil society 207, 209, 211, 217
   as G20 host 118, 203
Kulik, Julia 222
Kyrgyz Republic 99

L'Aquila Food Security Initiative 115, 189
L'Aquila Summit (G8 2009) 20, 109, 185, 219
L20 (Labour 20) 148, 164, 174, 175, 208, 209
   Cannes 2011 209
La Paz, Mexico 211, 216
labour *see* employment; job creation; unemployment
labour market 90, 124, 125, 153, 163, 222
Larionova, Marina 244
Latin America 126
Leaders 20 37
leaders, attendance 22, 24–5, 112, 117–18
Lee Chang-yong 207
Lee Myung-bak 113, 118
Lee Seong-hun 207
legitimacy 36, 40, 51, 77, 86, 88, 106, 173, 175, 184, 201, 206, 211–12, 235, 242, 243, 258, 259, 261, 262
Library Group 35, 36–7, 45
Libya 21
like-mindedness 19, 38, 39–40, 41, 43, 116
Live 8 204
London Summit (G20 2009) 23, 39, 47, 78, 79, 82, 83, 91, 93, 96, 98, 153, 158, 209, 235, 237, 245–6
   demonstrations 111, 215, 216, 217
Los Cabos Growth and Jobs Action Plan 220
Los Cabos Summit (G20 2012) 59, 61, 80, 83, 153, 154, 157, 204, 220–22, 223, 235
   accountability 220
   civil society 211, 214, 217
   demonstrations 216

'Lough Erne Accountability Report: Keeping Our Promises' 191, 219, 236
Lough Erne Summit (G8 2013) 21, 24, 42, 61–2, 100, 191, 204, 214, 218
demonstrations 217
Louvre Accord 46
Lowy Institute for International Policy 206, 208
Lula da Silva, Luiz Inácio 117, 118

macroeconomic issues 109, 124, 151–3, 174
B20 151–3
Major Economies Forum on Energy Security and Climate Change 28, 96, 241
Major Economies Meeting on Energy Security and Climate Change 241
Make Poverty History 205, 207, 217
Mali 21, 102
'Mapping G20 Decisions Implementation: How G20 Is Delivering on the Decisions Made' 218
Martin, Paul 37, 255
maternal, newborn and child health 116–17, 119, 120, 139, 186, 208–9, 219, 258
see also Muskoka Initiative on Maternal, Newborn, and Child Health
MDG review summit 114
MDGs (Millennium Development Goals) 40, 89, 98, 116, 119, 120, 159, 186, 213, 258
Merkel, Angela 222
Mexican Council on Foreign Relations 208
Mexico 18, 113
as G20 host 60–61, 130, 172, 206, 208, 214
demonstrations 216
Middle East 21, 99, 119, 132
middle powers 43
middle-income countries 89, 128, 132
middle-income trap 125–6
Minsky, Hyman 48
mission creep 42, 83, 91
monitoring 217–23, 235, 259, 263
see also accountability
Montebello Summit (G7 1981) 210, 215

Montreal Consensus 113
Moscow Nuclear Safety and Security Summit 95
Multi-Year Action Plan on Development 80, 84, 158, 222
multilateral development banks 84, 97, 158, 164, 172
Multilateral Framework for Investment 158
Multilateral Investment Guarantee Agency 160
multipolarity 35, 36, 37, 43, 255
'Muskoka Accountability Report' 40, 82, 109, 112, 114, 183–93, 245, 259
Muskoka Initiative on Maternal, Newborn, and Child Health 20, 40, 209, 112, 113, 114, 115, 116, 119, 120, 186, 189, 256
Muskoka Summit (G8 2010) 39–40, 118, 192, 203, 208, 184, 188, 256, 257, 258
accountability 219, 247
civil society 212
cost 109, 111
Mutual Assessment Process (MAP) 23, 84, 92, 201, 220, 259

NATO (North Atlantic Treaty Organization) 21, 28, 40, 248
NEPAD (New Partnership for Africa's Development) 81, 235, 236, 237
Netherlands 116
New Alliance for Food Security and Nutrition 21
New Development Bank *see* BRICS development bank
New Rules for Global Finance 217, 222
newly industrializing economies 16
NGOs (nongovernmental organizations) 16, 120, 187, 188, 192, 202, 207, 208–9, 233, 258, 259, 263, 238, 239
accountability 234
see also civil society
Nibutani Declaration 213
non-state threats 19, 20, 25, 115, 116, 256
noncommunicable diseases 119, 172
North Africa 21, 99, 132
North American Commission for Environmental Cooperation 243

North American Leaders Summit 241
North Korea 110, 98–9, 113, 116, 118, 119
NPT (Nuclear Non-Proliferation Treaty)
    190, 191
nuclear non-proliferation 115
nuclear safety 95, 96, 99, 102, 169
nuclear security 63, 98, 109, 261
Nuclear Security Summit 242

Obama, Barack 40, 117
ODA (official development assistance) 89,
    98, 120, 172, 189, 190–91, 218
OECD (Organisation for Economic
    Co-operation and Development) 84,
    151, 158, 159, 166, 188, 219, 220,
    236, 237
OECD Anti-Bribery Convention 170
Okinawa Summit (G8, 2000) 111, 119
One 204, 208, 209, 217, 218, 222, 236
Organisation for Islamic Cooperation 28
Organization of American States 248
Oxfam 205, 207, 208, 209, 213, 214, 216, 222

Pakistan 99
Palestine 99
parliamentarians 111, 202, 205, 224
participation 20, 23, 117–18
People's G20 Response Preparation
    Committee 211
People's Summits 210–11
    2010 215
    2012 216
performance 16, 112
    see also BRICS; decision making;
    deliberation; development of global
    governance; direction setting;
    domestic political management;
    G7/8; G20; global governance
    functions
Permanent Five 16, 116
    see also UNSC
Peter G. Peterson Institute for
    International Economics 206
Pittsburgh G20 Resistance Project 215
Pittsburgh Summit (G20 2009) 23, 36, 40,
    84, 118, 139
    civil society 210
    demonstrations 215

Plan of Action for Global Energy Security
    95
Plaza Accord 46
plurilateral summit institution 25, 26, 55,
    117, 243–4, 256, 258
population growth as risk 57, 59, 65, 67
PPPs (public-private partnerships) 132,
    158, 161–2, 165, 191
Preliminary Accountability Report 219
price volatility 7, 56, 57, 59, 61, 65, 67, 92,
    95, 153, 154, 261
'Principles for Innovation Financial
    Inclusion' 113
private sector 48, 126, 127, 131, 143–75,
    186, 187, 191, 192
    civil society 202, 203–4
    see also B20
productivity 123, 126, 130, 133
protectionism 123, 134–7, 155–6, 158, 175,
    235, 237, 245
protests see demonstrations
Put People First 215
Putin, Vladimir 51, 52

Quality of Official Development
    Assistance Database 219

Rambouillet Summit (G7 1975) 35–6, 45
Rapid Social Response Fund 98
regulation 80, 133, 156, 158
    energy markets 169
    financial 18, 59, 90, 93, 145, 145–50,
    173, 175, 237
    negative consequences 56, 57, 59, 61,
    63, 67, 261
religious leaders' summits 212–13
Report on the G8 Global Partnership
    against the Spread of Weapons and
    Materials of Mass Destruction 237
risk 55–74
Roma/Lyon Group 100, 237
Roubini, Nouriel 47
Ruggie, John 247
Russia 38–9, 50, 115, 116, 118, 119, 130,
    184, 188
    and BRICS 25–6, 55
    and G7/8 19, 20, 21, 25–6, 26n, 36,
    38–9, 55, 119, 189

INDEX

and G20 25–6, 61
as B20 host 145, 148, 151, 152, 155, 157, 159, 164, 16, 171, 175, 204, 258
as G8 host 55, 207
as G20 host 15, 51, 55, 151, 159–60, 166, 171, 175, 204, 208, 258

Sarkozy, Nicolas 37, 204, 209
SARS (severe acute respiratory syndrome) 19, 20
Saudi Arabia 18, 118
Save the Children 205
Schmidt, Helmut 36
Scholte, Jan Aarte 10, 238
SDRs (special drawing rights) 23, 24, 150, 151
Sea Island Summit (G8 2004) 112
secretariat 243, 260, 261
self-accountability 237, 238, 219–22
  see also accountability; accountability assessments
Seoul Action Plan 98
Seoul Development Consensus for Shared Growth 39, 80, 81, 84, 98, 193
Seoul Summit (G20 2010) 39, 40, 47, 49, 84, 110, 118, 158, 193, 203, 209, 220
  B20 148, 153, 157, 163, 164, 166, 167, 172
  civil society 209, 211, 217
September 11, 2001 19, 15
Shanghai Cooperation Organisation 28
SME Innovative Technology Development Funds 166
SMEs (small and medium-sized enterprises) 130, 148, 149, 153, 163, 170, 175
  finance 173
Snowdon, Edward 18
social protection 61, 153, 163
Somalia 21, 102
South Africa 38, 46, 130, 133
  and BRICS 24, 25, 65, 242
sovereign debt crisis 22, 118, 151
Spain 84, 116
St Petersburg Accountability Assessment 221
'St Petersburg Accountability Report on G20 Development Commitments' 221, 22

St Petersburg Summit (G8 2006) 95, 119, 207
St Petersburg Summit (G20 2013) 15, 23, 42, 51–2, 60–61, 90, 119, 150, 193, 204, 208, 218, 238, 212, 222
St Petersburg Action Plan 153, 163, 221
St Petersburg Development Outlook 98
St Petersburg International Economic Forum 204
St Petersburg Leaders Declaration 153
St Petersburg Strategic Framework for the G20 Anti-Corruption Working Group 81, 171
Stop G8 Movement 217
structural reform 61, 123, 124, 126, 132, 139, 152–3, 218, 260
sub-Saharan Africa 98, 132
Sub-Saharan African Public-Private Sector Dialogue 102
Sudan 99
Summers, Lawrence 37
summit cost 109, 111, 120
Summit of the Americas 28, 248
Superstorm Sandy 19
Switzerland 49
Syria 15, 18, 21, 23, 42, 51, 100
systemic club model 110, 115, 116
  see also club
systems failure as risk 57, 59, 61, 63, 67

T20 (Think 20) 206, 208
  Australia 2014 208
  Mexico 2012 208
  origin 208
  Russia 2013 208
tax 21, 23, 24, 42, 124–5, 130, 138, 148, 149, 150, 152, 164, 223
  see also financial transaction tax
Tearfund 207
technology transfer 154, 165, 261
technology 145, 148, 166–7, 171, 175, 213
  agricultural 153
  clean energy/green 97, 165, 166, 175
  see also ICT
terrorism 21, 102, 120, 191
terrorist finance 22, 113
Themed Days of Resistance 215

291

think tanks 201, 203, 205, 206, 208, 209, 217, 242
  see also T20
Tomlinson, Ian 215
Toronto commitments on deficit and debt 119
Toronto Summit (G7 1988) 15–16, 112
Toronto Summit (G20 2010) 118, 143, 193, 203, 209, 256, 257
  civil society 207, 210, 212
  cost 109, 111
  demonstrations 109, 111, 215–16
'Toward Lasting Stability and Growth: Umbrella Report for G20 Mutual Assessment Process' 221, 235
trade 21, 119, 134–7, 171, 175, 190
  B20 155–7
  G20 45–6
trade finance 150, 156, 173
Trade Finance Experts Group 236
trade negotiations 42, 137
  European Union and Canada 21
  European Union and United States 21
Trade Policy Review Mechanism 248
Trans-Pacific Partnership 21
transparency 21, 63, 78, 84, 96, 100, 106, 135, 154, 168, 169, 170–71, 173–4, 175, 184, 187, 189, 192, 193, 202, 204, 208, 209, 212, 213, 214, 220, 221, 224, 234, 235, 236, 238–9, 242, 259, 261, 262
Transparency International 206, 207, 217, 219
Turkey 43, 46, 52, 113, 138

Ukraine 26n, 36, 38–9
UNCAC (United Nations Convention against Corruption) 104, 170, 171
UNCTAD (United Nations Conference on Trade and Development 158, 159, 220, 235, 237
unemployment 123, 132–4
  youth 132, 133, 163
  see also job creation, employment
UNESCO (United Nations Educational, Scientific, and Cultural Organization) 166

UNFCCC (United Nations Framework Convention on Climate Change) 96, 104, 189
UNICEF (United Nations Children's Emergency Fund) 116, 207
unions 203, 205, 209, 210
United Kingdom 138
  as G8 host 21, 50, 42, 103, 191
  as G20 host 82
United Nations 15, 38, 41, 100, 102, 103, 248, 257, 261
  and G20 104, 118–19
United Nations High-Level Meeting on Non-communicable Diseases 119
United Nations Rio+20 Conference 214
United Nations secretary general 120
United Nations Summit on the Millennium Development Goals 116, 119, 186
United States 15, 19, 20, 21, 36, 39, 47, 48, 50, 51, 113, 116, 118, 123, 124, 125, 126, 131, 188, 189, 191, 218, 241, 242, 255
  as G8 host 117
  and G20 39
  as hegemon/superpower 18, 49
United States Federal Reserve 51, 46
University of Winnipeg 212
UNSC (United Nations Security Council) 16, 21, 38, 98, 110, 116, 119, 261
  reform 40
  Resolution 1540 99

von Furstenberg, George 183
vulnerability 17, 19, 20, 22, 43, 115, 241, 256, 257
Vulnerability Framework 98

Washington Summit (G20 2008) 36, 46–7, 78, 79, 89, 109, 116, 151, 156, 158, 235
  demonstrations 215
WikiLeaks 18
Working Group on the Framework for Strong, Sustainable, and Balanced Growth 123
World Bank 23, 45, 51, 84, 126, 151, 156, 171, 220, 222, 236, 237, 259
World Development Movement 207

INDEX

'World Development Report 2013: Jobs' 132–3
World Economic Forum 56, 204
World Health Organization (WHO) 116, 119
World Religions Summit 213
World Social Summit 210
World Trade Organization (WTO) 21, 42, 45, 93–4, 105, 135, 155, 156, 159, 169, 220, 235, 237, 243, 248, 249
    Trade Facilitation Agreement 156

World Vision 205, 206, 208, 209
WWF (World Wildlife Fund) 205, 207, 208, 209

Yekaterinburg Summit (BRIC 2009) 24, 65
Yeonpyeong 99
Youth 20 208
youth groups 203, 207

Zarco, Carlos 222